Silke Ruth Laskowski [Ed.]

Environmental Justice in Türkiye and Germany

Concept, Issues at Law and Developments in Legal Policy

Nomos

The Deutsche Nationalbibliothek lists this publication in the Deutsche Nationalbibliografie; detailed bibliographic data are available on the Internet at http://dnb.d-nb.de

ISBN 978-3-8487-4008-6 (Print)
978-3-8452-8293-0 (ePDF)

Online Version
Nomos eLibrary

1st Edition 2025

Table of Contents

Preface

This anthology is the result of a three-year legal research project on 'Environmental Justice' at the University of Kassel and the renowned University of Istanbul (Fatih, 1453), which was completed in 2018. The participants were German and Turkish law students, young academics and professors. The project was a constructive and productive collaboration between Prof. Dr. Ayşe Nur Tütüncü and Prof. Dr. Silke Ruth Laskowski, financed by the DAAD (German Academic Exchange Service). It took place alternately in Istanbul and Kassel.

Although time has passed since then (also due to unforeseeable complications such as the corona epidemic), the articles in the anthology are still relevant. The ongoing global environmental crisis, which today is primarily characterised by the continuing climate crisis, is endangering the natural foundations of life for people living today and for future generations. Today, there is a real risk of exceeding the climatic tipping points and the ecological planetary boundaries. A sustainable and fair transformation law is needed.

Against this background, government measures are required in Germany and Türkiye to safeguard the ecological and climatic impact limits, in accordance with international and European environmental and climate protection law. Germany is a member state of the EU and therefore bound by EU law; Türkiye is an accession state of the EU, i.e. a future EU member state, and must therefore comply with the 'acquis communautaire'. Even if the accession negotiations have been 'frozen' for various reasons, there is now much to be said in favour of a strong European environmental and climate alliance that takes effective action against climate change and includes Türkiye as an equal and equally committed member. This is because binding EU law, which is monitored by the European Court of Justice, up to date offers the highest level of environmental and climate protection Europe-wide.

The articles in this anthology provide an instructive overview of the state of environmental law in Türkiye and Germany. The project has shown that the comparative view at German, Turkish and European law and accompanying legal discourses are of great value to jurisprudence. Cross-border legal projects that promote German-Turkish-European dialogue should therefore receive much more support!

Kassel/Berlin, December 2024 *Silke Ruth Laskowski*

Accompanying notes

Moritz Banzhaf

Dear guests from Istanbul, dear ladies and gentlemen,

On behalf of the International Office, I would like to warmly welcome you here in Kassel! Well, Kassel is not Istanbul. But it still has some very special things to offer:

- In Kassel you can find the first theater building which was ever built in Germany. It was built in 1888 and is called the Ottoneum. Nowadays it is a museum for natural history.
- You can also find the oldest public museum ever built on the european continent. This museum, which is called the Friedericianum is the centre of the biggest fair of modern art in the world. It is called Documenta and it takes place here in Kassel every 5 years. The next one will take place in 2017. Kassel is a different city during that time. Last time nearly a million people visited it and even Brad Pitt came ☺ Kassel really transforms to a cosmopolitan city during that time.
- Kassel is the capital city of the famous Brothers Grimm. The Brothers Grimm spent a large part of their life in here. And they once said, that they had their most hard working and fruitful time here in Kassel. This is why Kassel became a centre of research of their work and life. Indeed the University of Kassel holds the only Grimm research professorship nationwide. In addition in September this year the Grimm World will open its doors. The Grimm World is sort of a huge museum presenting all the aspects of the life of and work of the Brothers Grimm.
- Another very special thing to mention is Kassels beautiful hillside park. The so called Bergpark Wilhelmshöhe is the second biggest of it's kind in the World and the biggest in Europe. It is famous for its baroque watergames, which take place every Wednesday and Saturday (during the summer months). Since 2013 it is listed as a UNESCO World heritage. As I have seen in the programme, you will visit the park on Wednesday. I am sure you will enjoy it.

- What I personally like a lot about Kassel is, that it perfectly combines urban life with the beautiful countryside around it. You have the benefits of a pretty big city - you can find cinemas, libraries, vibrant nightlife and a big University - but don't have to go without the nature. Within about 15 min. you can reach it the outskirts from nearly everywhere in the city. There you find endless forests, mountain ranges and beautiful small villages like Melsungen and Hann Münden. I am quite sure, that the beautiful countryside around Kassel also inspired the Brothers Grimm.

Well, Kassel is not Istanbul. But there is also lot of people with Turkish roots living here. And like in other german cities, they enrich the urban life with their culture and religion and their excellent food – what would we do without the turkish food ☺.

There is about 12500 Turks living here in Kassel, what makes them the biggest minority. Please note, that this number does not include in Germany born children of former turks who now hold a german passport. Unfortunately there were no statistics available telling this number.

Many of the turks living in Kassel do study or have studied here at this University. Indeed turks are the biggest group of students with a foreign passport at the University of Kassel. Last spring term 450 students with a Turkish passport were matriculated. Second biggest group is the Chinese with 311 matriculated students. Unfortunately no exact numbers exist of how many german passport holders with Turkish roots are matriculated. But I am quite sure, that this is a pretty big number.

Having so many students with a Turkish passport or Turkish roots is surely not the only reason, why the University of Kassel has excellent relations to Turkish Universities all over Turkey.

As the Erasmus-Coordinator of the University of Kassel I do of course have insight into the Erasmus-Statistics.

So, looking at our bilateral Erasmus agreements it can be seen, that we signed 48 agreements with Turkish Universities. In fact this is the biggest number of bilateral agreements we do have with a single country. This is followed by Spain with 42 agreements and France with 38 agreements.

In total we currently have 327 bilateral agreements with partners all over Europe. These agreements are the basis for student and staff exchange in the frame of the Erasmus programme – without agreement no mobility is possible. The two Institutions involved agree on a certain number of students and staff members to be exchanged as well as on the duration of each mobility. The participants of the programme receive an Erasmus Grant for their mobility as well as other benefits like organizational support.

Now, looking at the number of realized student mobilities between the years 2013 and 2015. It can be seen, that Turkey is second most popular destinations among our students . In the last 3 years 104 students from Kassel spent their semester abroad at one of our turkish partner Institutions.

And surely not only students with Turkish roots choose Turkey as destination for their semester abroad.

The only country, which is currently more popular among our students is spain. In the last three years 130 students chose a Spanish University to realize their semester abroad.

Looking at the statistics of students coming to the University of Kassel it is striking, that the country which sends most students to Kassel in the frame of the Erasmus-Programme is Turkey. In the last 3 years we received 151 students from partner Universties all over Turkey. Followed by Italy with 107 mobilities and France with 102.

As I already mentioned, the Erasmus-Programme does not only support student mobility, but also mobility of University staff. It supports mobilities for teaching purposes as well as mobilities for training purposes – a training purpose can be a seminar (like this for example – probably some of you received an Erasmus grant for their participation), job shadowing, language courses or workshops.

A staff mobility has to have a minimum duration of 2 days and a maximum duration of 2 months.

Now, having a look at those figures it can be highlighted, that Turkey is among the 4th popular destination for staff mobilities for training and number 1 destination for staff mobilities for teaching among the staff of the University of Kassel. Again, also in this approach Turkey appears to be a very valuable partner of our University.

I am very happy about those great relations between Turkey and our University. And I am very looking forward to contribute my part to even foster and strengthen those relations in the future. I wish you a great seminar and wonderful stay here in Kassel!

I. Environmental Justice

Environmental Justice in Times of Climate Change and Sustainable Transformation

Prof. Dr. Silke Ruth Laskowski, Kassel University Germany

I. Introduction

The discussion about "environmental justice" and the normative concept behind it is currently experiencing a renaissance in the context of the climate crisis as part of the global triple environmental crisis – for Germany and most member states of the European Union (EU) it is a rather new discussion. Unlike in the USA, where environmental justice from the point of view of discrimination has been debated since the 1980s, the "spillover" to Europe was long-delayed and focused on possible discriminatory effects of environmental law on ethnic minorities in the population.[1] Today, in view of the consequences of climate change, the term "climate justice" comes to the fore. Against this background, the article examines the normative base of the "concept of climate and environmental justice", the importance of international climate law, the principle of sustainability and human rights in this respect. It also draws conclusions for sustainable just transformation law. A special focus is placed on the EU, Germany as a member state and Türkiye as an accession state.

1 Cf. *Ludwig Krämer*, Environmental Justice and European Union Law, 2020, 16 Croatian Yearbook of European Law and Policy (CYELP), p. 1 ff.; with regard to social distribution of environmental pollution, "environmental justice" is rather part of the European and German "public health" discussion in the context of environmental sociology and epidemiology, see *WHO* (Regional Office for Europe), Environmental health inequalities in Europe, Assessment report, 2012, p. xv, xvi: income, education, employment, age, gender, "race"/ethnicity, specific locations; *Horst-Dietrich Elvers*, Umweltgerechtigkeit (Environmental Justice): Integratives Paradigma der Gesundheits- und Sozialwissenschaften?, UFZ Discussion Paper, No. 14/2005, Umweltforschungszentrum Leipzig-Halle, Leipzig 2005; *Gabriele Bolte/Andreas Mielck* (eds.), Umweltgerechtigkeit. Die soziale Verteilung von Umweltbelastungen, Weinheim 2004.

II. Environmental Justice

The idea and movement of "environmental justice" emerged in the USA in the 1980s. People realized that infrastructural projects with negative environmental effects (pollution, noise) like waste disposal plants, incinerator plants or highways, airports etc. were predominantly built in areas where many socially disadvantaged people lived, especially people of colour, mainly black Americans. The focus was on *environmental discrimination* based on "race"[2] or social class – in line with the civil rights movement in the USA which dates back to the 1960s.[3] It became clear that socially disadvantaged groups bore a higher burden of environmental exposure from air, water, and soil pollution than other people in the USA – now proven by many studies.[4]

Today, the definition of environmental justice developed by the *US Environmental Protection Agency* (*EPA*) is often used as a basis for political and legal discussions worldwide. It still focuses on the aspect of *discrimination.* According to EPA (2023) "*environmental justice is the fair treatment and meaningful involvement of all people regardless of race, color, national origin, or income, with respect to the development, implementation, and enforcement of environmental laws, regulations, and policies.*"[5] Amazingly, the *gender impact*, i.e. the *effects on women*, is still missing – although today it is known that *women,* half of the population, are the most disadvantaged "group" among

2 The term "race" is problematic. It is recognized today, that there are no different human races, but only one, and that is the human being - in all its diversity.

3 See the overview of the movement in the *Internet Encyclopedia of Philosophy* (IEP), The American Environmental Justice Movement, https://iep.utm.edu/enviro-j/. The black environmental sociologist *Robert D. Bullard* is regarded as "father" of environmental justice, his work *Dumping in Dixie*, 1990, is considered to be the first book addressing environmental injustice in real life, with a focus on African Americans. See also *Robert D. Bullard*, Environmental Justice in the 21st Century, Environmental Justice Resource Center at Clark Atlanta University, Atlanta 2008, http://www.ejrc.cau.edu/ejinthe21century.htm. For the civil rights movement see *Maurice Isserman/Michael Kazin*, America divided. The civil war of the 1960s, Oxford University Press 2000; *Belinda Robnet*, African-American Women in the Civil Rights Movement, 1954-1965: Gender, Leadership, and Micromobilization, American Journal of Sociology (AJS) Vol. 101 No. 6, May 1996, p. 166 ff.

4 See *Paul Mohai/David Pellow/J. Timmons Roberts*, Environmental Justice, Annual Review of Environment and Resources 2009, 34, p. 405, 406 ff.; in view of Europe see *Krämer* (footnote 1), p. 1 ff; *Elvers* (footnote 1), p. 3 ff.

5 *EPA*, Environmental justice, https://www.epa.gov/environmentaljustice (accessed January 2024).

all socially deprived groups.[6] Therefore, gender equality must be a core element of the definition of environmental justice to prevent and remove discrimination against women ("environmental gender justice"); there is a broad consensus on this in the international context today.[7]

The rare European discourse about environmental justice is currently focusing on unequal exposure and impacts in European countries. New findings show that environmental inequalities usually result from various forms of social or demographic disadvantage. Socio-economic deprivation (especially due to poverty and low income) is associated with higher exposure to various environmental pressures.[8] Across Europe, for example, inequalities in access to safely managed drinking water and sanitation services exist – both services affect natural water resources: water abstraction, wastewater discharge –, characterized by geographical, economic and social disparities. Vulnerable groups in this context are especially women and girls, people with special physical needs and homeless people.[9] The *European Environmental Agency (EEA)* is now addressing the "social vulnerability" of certain population groups in Europe – the elderly, children, people with low socio-economic status or health problems – in relation to air pollution, noise and climate-related extreme temperatures.[10] In Germany, "environmental justice" has become a topic as well. Due to the *German Environment Agency/Umweltbundesamt (UBA)* 2022, people from lower social classes are more affected by environmental pollution than members of higher social classes.[11] Recognizable

---

6 *Fabiano de Andrade Correa/UN Development Programme (UNDP),* Gender equality: A cornerstone for environmental and climate justice, March 29, 2022, p. 2, https://www.undp.org/blog/gender-equality-cornerstone-environmental-and-climate-justice; *UN WomenWatch,* Fact Sheet: Women, Gender Equality and Climate Change, 2009, p. 1, http://www.un.org/womenwatch/feature/climate_change/.

7 *Fabiano de Andrade Correa/UNDP* (footnote 6), 2022, p. 2, 4; *UN WomenWatch* (footnote 6), p. 1 ff.; regarding urban planning in Germany, see *Nina Dieckmann*, Umweltgerechtigkeit in der Stadtplanung, Neue Zeitschrift für Verwaltungsrecht (NVwZ) 2013, p. 1575.

8 *WHO Regional Office for Europe*, Environmental health inequalities in Europe, 2. assessment report, 2019, p. 128.

9 *WHO* (footnote 8), p. 40, 45.

10 *EEA*, Environmental justice, environmental hazards and the vulnerable in European society, 2019; *EEA*, Briefing no. 09/2022, Towards just resilience: leaving no one behind when adapting to climate change, p. 3; focus on minorities *Krämer* (footnote 1), p. 1 ff.

11 See *UBA*, Environmental justice – Environment, health and social conditions, 2022, www.umweltbundesamt.de/en/topics/health/environmental-impact-on-people/environmental-justice-environment-health-social#outlook.

are environment- and health-related social inequalities.[12] Climate change exacerbates these differences.

At the international level, the discussion about "environmental justice" is now being stepped up by the UN. The *UN Development Programme (UNDP)* highlights the following aspects in the "Environmental Justice Report" 2022:[13] "***Intra and intergenerational equity*** *in the environmental context, including the realization that degradation of environmental conditions has been mostly led by industrialized countries, and its impacts more acutely experienced by developing countries which contributed the least to such degradation.* ***Distributive environmental justice****: (...) environmental benefits and burdens should be distributed fairly and in a way that does not contribute toward further marginalization of vulnerable groups, from both intra and intergenerational perspectives, within and among nations.* ***Corrective justice for environmental harm****, including compensation mechanisms, access to justice and effective remedy, and legal empowerment.* ***Procedural fairness in environmental issues****, requiring open, transparent and inclusive decision making, and access to information at national and international levels. The idea of justice for the environment, as something to be protected in its own right. Finally, the consideration of sustainability as a condition for justice: although justice is primarily a human-centric concept, it must be viewed in a context of ecological sustainability given the interdependence between man and nature.*"

1. Climate Change and Climate Justice

Currently, the debate about "environmental justice" is combined with climate change and linked to the new term "climate justice" which concretizes and completes the idea of environmental justice.[14] Both terms are associated with the global environmental crisis (see below 2). A movement for climate

12 See *Christa Böhme/Thomas Franke/Daniela Michalski/Thomas Preuß/Bettina Reimann/Wolf-Christian Strauss/Deutsches Institut für Urbanistik,* Umweltgerechtigkeit in Deutschland: Praxisbeispiele und strategische Perspektiven, edited by UBA, Berlin 2022, p. 6; *Gabriele Bolte/Christiane Bunge/Claudia Hornberg/Heike Köckler,* Umweltgerechtigkeit als Ansatz zur Verringerung sozialer Ungleichheiten bei Umwelt und Gesundheit, Bundesgesundheitsblatt 2018, Vol. 61, p. 674, 675 ff.; see also references in footnote 1.

13 *UNDP*, Environmental Justice: securing our right to a clean, healthy and sustainable environment, 2022, p. 12, 13.; see also *WHO/Regional Office for Europe*, (footnote 8) p. 145; *Robert D. Bullard*, Environmental Justice in the 21st Century, Atlanta 2008, p. 6.

14 *Mohai/Pellow/Roberts*, (footnote 4), p. 405, 418, 420.

and environmental justice has emerged,[15] which includes a young global civil society movement ("Fridays for Future"), international and national non-governmental organizations (e.g. "Greenpeace"), civil society groups such as older women in Switzerland ("Klimaseniorinnen/Schweiz"), parents in Germany ("parents 4 future Germany") or individuals protesting against ineffective climate change measures, filing climate lawsuits against states and companies ("climate litigation").[16] They can be seen as part of a global civil society movement calling for effective action on climate change and emphasizing the responsibility of states in view of different social groups in an intergenerational perspective.[17]

This development is understandable. As numerous studies have shown, climate change is affecting the natural resources and ecosystems on which people depend for their livelyhoods beings. Consequences are climate-related diseases of individuals, premature loss of individual life and significant health costs that ultimately must be borne by the respective national society.[18] Different countries ("North-South divide")[19] and different population groups within these societies are affected and "vulnerable" in different ways. Certain areas like *small islands*, e.g. *Vanuatu* or other Pacific Islands, are among the earliest and most severely affected areas in the world. Rising sea levels combined with more frequent and extreme weather events, such as tropical storms, have a direct impact on food security, livelihoods, health and well-being of

15 See *Joan Martinez-Alier/Leah Temper/Daniela Del Bene/Arnim Scheidel*, Is there a global environmental justice movement?, The Journal of Peasant Studies 2016, 43:3, p. 731.

16 The number of climate court cases has more than doubled between 2017 and 2022 and is growing worldwide, see *Michael Burger/Maria Antonia Tigre*, Global Climate Litigation Report: 2023 Status Review, Sabin Center for Climate Change Law, Columbia Law School & UNEP, 2023, https://scholarship.law.columbia.edu/sabin_climate_change/202; the Sabin Center/New York provides two current databases of climate change caselaw: for cases in the U.S. and for global cases.

17 See *Alexandra Endres/Roda Verheyen*, Wir alle haben ein Recht auf Zukunft, 2023.

18 A recent *WHO* assessment (2023) shows that "environmental health inequalities occur in all countries, irrespective of the level of development and the environmental or economic status", https://www.who.int/europe/news-room/fact-sheets/item/environmental-health-inequalities#; see also *Matthias Braubach/Friederike Reichel/Marco Martuzzi*, in: *WHO Regional Office for Europe* (footnote 8), p. 1 ff., 4 ff.

19 Almost all rich industrialised countries are found in the northern hemisphere in Europe and North America, while poorer developing and emerging countries are mainly located in the southern part of the earth on the continents of Africa, Asia and South America.

the citizens in the region.[20] People in these states, most of the world's poorest countries, feel the climate crisis most strongly though they contribute the least to this crisis: The average per capita emissions in the world's poorest countries, such as the African states of Niger and Somalia, are more than 110 times smaller than the average per capita emissions in Germany or other states in the Global North[21] that bear a special historical climate responsibility. Due to industrialization in the past, they have caused most of the emissions that have accumulated in the atmosphere since then. A glance at the shares of total global emissions in the period 1751-2017 makes that clear: North America 29%, of which USA 25%; Europe 33%, of which the EU-28 22%, Russia 6%, Ukraine 1.2%, Türkiye 0.6%; Asia 29%, of which China 12.7%, India 3%; Africa 3%; South America 3%, of which Brazil 0.9%; Oceania 1.2%, of which Australia 1.1%.[22]

In 2021, global CO_2 emissions reached a level of 38 billion tonnes. The G20 countries (not only industrialized countries)[23] accounted for around 81% of these emissions.[24] In 2022, the G20-states China, USA, India, the EU-27, Russia and Brazil were the six world largest greenhouse gas (GHG) emitters. Together they accounted for 50% of global population, 63% of global fossil fuel consumption and around 62% of global GHG emissions. Among the largest emitters, China, the USA and India increased their emissions in 2022

20 See *IPCC,* Special Report on the Ocean and Cryosphere in a Changing Climate, 2019, Chapter 4: Sea Level Rise and Implications for Low-Lying Islands, Coasts and Communities, 4.3 Exposure, Vulnerability, Impacts and Risk Related to Sea Level Rise, https://www.ipcc.ch/srocc/.

21 See *Hannah Ritchie*, Who has contributed most to global CO2 emissions?, 2019, https://ourworldindata.org/contributed-most-global-co2.

22 See *Hanna Wang-Helmreich/Bundeszentrale für politische Bildung (BPB)*, Klimaziele: Wohin soll es gehen? Und wer soll was beitragen?, 2022, https://www.bpb.de/themen/klimawandel/dossier-klimawandel/509859/klimaziele-wohin-soll-es-gehen-und-wer-soll-was-beitragen/, referring to *Hannah Ritchie*, Who has contributed most to global CO_2 emissions?, 2019.

23 G20 comprises 19 countries (2023): Argentina, Australia, Brazil, Canada, China, France, Germany, India, Indonesia, Italy, Japan, Republic of Korea, Mexico, Russia, Saudi Arabia, South Africa, Türkiye, United Kingdom and United States and two regional bodies: the EU and the African Union.

24 *Statistisches Bundesamt*, International statistics, G20 responsible for approximately 81% of global CO2 emissions, 2022, https://www.destatis.de/EN/Themes/Countries-Regions/International-Statistics/Data-Topic/Environment-Energy/Environment/G20_CO2.html.

compared to 2021 - the other three top emitters reduced their emissions in 2022.[25]

In 2022, several EU-27 countries experienced a decrease in their emission levels compared to the year 2021. The largest relative decreases were recorded in Luxembourg (-11.1%), Belgium (-6.4%), Lithuania (-6.3%), Estonia (-6.3%) and the Netherlands (-6.1%). On the other hand, the largest increase in 2022 was noticed in Bulgaria (+8.0%), followed by Spain (+7.4%), Portugal (+3.7%), Greece (+3.4%), Ireland (+2.2%), and Malta (+2.0%). In terms of EU27 GHG emissions, Germany remained the largest emitter (21.9%) in 2022, followed by France (12.0%), Poland (11.2%), Italy (11.0%), and Spain (9.2%). Moreover, in the EU-27, all other sectors except transport and energy showed a decrease in their GHG emissions in 2022.[26] In addition: A new study (2020), analysing the distribution of the CO_2 footprint of households in 26 EU countries shows that the top 10% of the EU population have a higher emission share than the bottom 50 %.[27]

Different people and regions can adapt to climate change in different ways, for better or worse. People's adaptability depends on their residence in the poor global South or the rich global North, additionally on criteria such as gender, the economic status, age, disability, or membership of a particular social or ethnic group. The climate crisis is exacerbating pre-existing social inequalities and related environmental injustices.[28] Remarkable: Studies show that in natural disasters such as floods, *more women than men* usually die - the different life situations of men and women play an important role.[29]

---

25 *EU Commission*, GHG emissions of all world countries, Science for Policy report, 2023, p. 10, https://edgar.jrc.ec.europa.eu/report_2023.

26 *EU Commission* (footnote 25), p. 10; see also *European Parliament*, Greenhouse gas emissions by country and sector, 28 March 2023, https://www.europarl.europa.eu/topics/en/article/20180301STO98928/greenhouse-gas-emissions-by-country-and-sector-infographic.

27 See *Diana Ivanova/Richard Wood*, The unequal distribution of household carbon footprints in Europe and its link to sustainability, Global Sustainability 2020/3, p. 1, 3, https://doi.org/10.1017/sus.2020.12; referring to this article also *Jenny Kurwan, Klimagerechtigkeit, in: BPB*, Klimagerechtigkeit, 17 March 2023, https://www.bpb.de/themen/klimawandel/dossier-klimawandel/515255/klimagerechtigkeit/.

28 *Jenny Kurwan/BPB*, (footnote 27).

29 Women are less able to swim due to gender-specific education and social norms of behaviour as well as gender-specific unequal distribution of resources; women have less access to information and transport etc., making it harder for them to escape, see *Fabiano de Andrade Correa /UNDP* (footnote 6); see also *Gotelind Alber/Diana Hummel/Ulrike Röhr/Meike Spitzner/Immanuel Stieß*, Geschlechtergerechtigkeit und Klimapolitik, Aus Politik und Zeitgeschichte (APuZ) 21-23/2018, p. 40, 43, 47.

Moreover, it becomes evident that younger generations and generations yet unborn will be more affected by the effects of the climate crisis than today's generations.

Overall, the climate crisis appears *unfair* in two ways: industrialized and developed countries which have contributed or are contributing the most to this crisis tend to suffer the least from the negative consequences. They usually have sufficient financial and technological resources to adapt to climate change and protect against its harmful effects. In addition, their financial resources were or are often generated by CO_2-intensive, fossil fuel-based, climate-damaging economic activities.[30] On the other hand, countries that have hardly contributed anything to climate change, are most affected by its negative consequences. It is mostly economically weak states of the global South – "developing states" – which rely on financial and technical support from the main contributors to climate change.

2. Triple Planetary Crisis in the Anthropocene

The discussion about environmental and climate justice is embedded in the international debate on the "triple planetary crisis of climate change, pollution, and nature loss".[31] The *UNDP* (2022) speaks of a "triple planetary crisis of climate change, biodiversity and ecosystem loss, and pollution".[32] It increases conflicts and *structural inequalities;* people are forced into increasingly vulnerable situations. The crisis has direct and indirect impacts on a wide range of *human rights*, which are derived from the *International Covenant on Civil and Political Rights* (ICCPR) and the *International Covenant on Economic, Social and Cultural Rights* (ICESCR)[33] – the planetary crisis endangers in particular the *human right to adequate food*, the *right to water and sanitation*,[34] *education, housing, health development* and even the *right to*

30 *Jenny Kurwan/BPB* (footnote 27).

31 *UN High Commissioner for Human Rights, Michelle Bachelet,* statement at the 48th session of the Human Rights Council, 13 September 2021, https://www.ohchr.org/en/2021/09/environmental-crisis-high-commissioner-calls-leadership-human-rights-council-member-states?LangID=E&NewsID=27443; in this session the Resolution on the Human Right to a Clean, Healthy and Sustainable Environment, A/HRC/RES/48/13, was adopted by the Human Rights Council on 8 October 2021.

32 *UNDP* (footnote 13), p. 4.

33 *UNDP* (footnote 13), p. 4.

34 More on this, *Silke Ruth Laskowski*, Das Menschenrecht auf Wasser, Tübingen 2010.

life itself.[35] *Environmental threats* are becoming one of the greatest challenges to human rights and environmental justice.[36]

Many scientists see the *crisis* as expression of "*the arrival of a new geological epoch, the Anthropocene*", in which "*humankind is exerting such a strong influence on the Earth system that we are in the process of leaving the safe environmental conditions of the Holocene behind.*"[37] Humans have become a dominant force shaping the planet that rivals the forces of nature in the balance of the environment.[38] The term "Anthropocene" goes back to the atmospheric chemist *Paul Crutzen*.[39] It is dated to the middle of the 20th century and leaves behind permanent geologically relevant deposits of artificial substances in the earth system, disturbances in the carbon, nitrogen and phosphorus cycles, changes in the climate and sea level rise.[40] But according to the *International Union of Geological Sciences* (IUGS) in 2024, the Anthropocene will not be added to the chronostratigraphic chart featured in textbooks to record the major changes in Earth history.[41] Nevertheless this the term is already globally established in environmental and social science, politics, economics and public discussion.[42] Therefore, the term is also used here.

---

35 *UN High Commissioner for Human Rights, Michelle Bachelet* (footnote 31).

36 *UNDP* (footnote 13), p. 4.

37 *German Advisory Council on the Environment* (SRU), Special Report: Democratic government within environmental limits – on the legitimation of environmental policy (Summery), June 2019, p. 6; full report/German, https://www.umweltrat.de/SharedDocs/Downloads/DE/02_Sondergutachten/2016_2020/2019_06_SG_Legitimation_von_Umweltpolitik.html; see also *Reinhold Leifelder*, Das Zeitalter des Anthropozäns und die Notwendigkeit der großen Transformation, Zeitschrift für Umweltrecht (ZUR) 2017, p. 259 ff.

38 Pioneering *German Advisory Council on Global Change* (WBGU), World in Transition. A Social Contract for Sustainability, 2011, https://www.wbgu.de/fileadmin/user_upload/wbgu/publikationen/hauptgutachten/hg2011/pdf/wbgu_jg2011_en.pdf; see also *Gerd Winter*, Rechtsprobleme im Anthropozän: Vom Umweltschutz zur Selbstbegrenzung, ZUR 2017, p. 267 ff.; *Andreas Fisahn*, Earth4All und Green New Deal – Überlegungen zu einem Literaturbericht, ZUR 2023, p. 656 ff.

39 See *IUGS*, The Anthropocene, 20 March 2024, https://www.iugs.org/_files/ugd/f1fc07_40d1a7ed58de458c9f8f24de5e739663.pdf?index=true.

40 See *Gerd Winter*, ZUR 2017, p. 267 ff.

41 See *IUGS*, The Anthropocene, 20 March 2024, p. 1.

42 See *Gino Grandoni*, The Washington Post June 10, 2024, https://www.washingtonpost.com/climate-environment/2024/06/10/anthropocene-epoch-human-climate-impacts/.

The *climate crisis* is part of the *Anthropocene* with all its negative impacts.[43] Mankind is in danger to overstep all *planetary boundaries* that are a prerequisite for human survival. Today, the Earth is considered a complex system that provides the basis for a decent life, a life in dignity, respecting nature and human rights.[44] This means far more than just the lack of 'apocalyptic conditions' that the *German Federal Constitutional* Court (Bundesverfassungsgericht, BVerfG) refers to in its 2021 climate decision.[45] The decisive factor is the *non-negotiable planetary preconditions* that humanity must comply with in order to avoid the risk of catastrophic environmental changes worldwide.[46] Therefore, so-called *guard rails* for natural resources must be observed. These guard rails include, in particular, the still acceptable increase in global warming – according to the *Paris Agreement* 1.5° to 2° Celsius above the level of the non-industrial age, but according to the current state of science max. 1.5° Celsius. That´s why, in 2018, the *Intergovernmental Panel on Climate Change (IPCC)*, in its special report on global warming, called for a 45 % reduction in greenhouse gas emissions by 2030 compared to 2010 levels in order to limit global warming to 1.5 °Celsius. If the 1.5-degree target were to be exceeded, this would have serious consequences, namely an increase in climate-related risks for health, livelihoods, food security, water supply and economic growth. The Report is also about the progressive loss of flora and fauna, i.e. biodiversity.[47]

The situation becomes particularly difficult and dangerous when certain critical values of so-called *tipping elements* or *tipping points* are exceeded. *Tipping elements* are critical threshold values above which strong and in some cases unstoppable and irreversible changes occur.[48] The result is a rapid and

43 *UNDP*, Human Development Report 2020. The Next Frontier: Human Development and the Anthropocene, New York 2020, p. 8 ff, https://hdr.undp.org/system/files/documents/hdr2020overviewenglish.pdf.

44 *UNDP* (footnote 13), p. 7 ff.

45 BVerfG, Order of the First Senate, 24 March 2021 - 1 BvR 2656/18 -, para. 114 = BVerfGE 157, p. 30, 96 = ECLI:DE:BVerfG:2021:rs20210324.1bvr265618, https://www.bverfg.de/e/rs20210324_1bvr265618en.html; see also BVerfG, Order of the Second Chamber of the Second Senate, 18 February 2010 - 2 BvR 2502/08 -, para. 13.

46 *UNDP* (footnote 13), p. 7 ff.

47 *IPCC*, Special Report Global Warming of 1.5 °C, Summary for Policymakers, 2018, p. 5, 7 ff., 12, https://www.ipcc.ch/sr15/.

48 See *Potsdam Institute for Climate Impact Research*, Tipping Elements – big risks in the Earth System, https://www.pik-potsdam.de/en/output/infodesk/tipping-elements/tipping-elements.

ultimately unstoppable deterioration in living conditions.[49] A well-known example of a tipping element is when temperatures exceed 0° Celsius, which leads to the thawing of ice masses or permafrost soils. Permafrost is one of the most important carbon sinks on earth. The rapid environmental changes in the Arctic and in Sibiria have an impact on the entire Earth system. Thawing permafrost ecosystems are releasing greenhouse gases into the atmosphere. The large-scale thawing of permafrost in connection with global warming is considered one of the most important *tipping elements* of *climate change*.[50] The current major changes caused by climate change threaten to reach the *tipping points* – and thus accelerate the destruction of the natural foundations. According to the *Global Tipping Point Report 2023* that was launched at the 28th Conference of the Parties (COP 28) to the UN Framework Convention on Climate Change (UNFCCC) in Dubai on 6 December 2023, it is very urgent: "*Harmful tipping points in the natural world pose some of the gravest threats faced by humanity. (...) Five major tipping points are already at risk of being crossed due to warming right now and three more are threatened in the 2030s as the world exceeds 1.5°C global warming.*"[51] In addition, the *European Environment Agency* (EEA) 2024 warned of "*failing to protect key ecosystems from climate risks*". This "*would lead to large-scale disruption of biodiversity and ecosystem services that may involve biological or climatic tipping points*" and "*critically impact the existing water cycle, food production and infrastructure – with repercussions on carbon sinks, human health and economic activities.*"[52]

49 *Gerd Winter*, ZUR 2017, p. 267.

50 See *Richard Edward Fewster/Paul J. Morris/Ruza F. Ivanovic et al.*, Imminent loss of climate space for permafrost peatlands in Europe and Western Siberia, Nature Climate Change 2022, Vol. 12 (4), p. 373 ff.; *Edward A. G. Schuur/Benjamin W. Abbott/Roisin Commane/Jessica Ernakovich et al.*, Permafrost and Climate Change: Carbon Cycle Feedbacks From the Warming Arctic, Annual Review of Environment and Resources 2022, Vol. 47(1), p. 343 ff.; *Gustaf Hugelius/Julie Loisel/Sarah Chadburn/Zicheng Yu*, Large stocks of peatland carbon and nitrogen are vulnerable to permafrost thaw', Proceedings of the National Academy of Sciences 2020, Vol. 117 (34), p. 20438 ff.

51 *Timothy M. Lenton, D.I. Armstrong McKay, S. Loriani, J.F. Abrams et al.* (eds), The Global Tipping Points Report 2023. University of Exeter, Exeter, UK, 2023, https://global-tipping-points.org/ .

52 *EEA*, European Climate Risk Assessment, Report 01/2024, 2024, p. 269, https://www.eea.europa.eu. It is the first European Climate Risk Assessment as announced in the 2021 EU strategy on adaptation to climate change and also a contribution to the European Green Deal: All 27 EU Member States committed to turning the EU into the first climate neutral continent by 2050. They must reduce emissions by at least 55% by 2030, compared to 1990 levels, see *EU Commission*, https://commission.europa.eu/str

Regarding this critical situation, there is global consensus on the need for a fundamental and *just and sustainable transformation.*[53]

III. Sustainable Development

The *concept of the principle of sustainability* forms the basis for a *just and sustainable transformation* in line with environmental and climate justice. A historical look back at the "Brundtland conception" of 1987, which was concretized by the UN Agenda 2030 in 2015, already shows this.

1. Brundtland Report (1987), UNCED in Rio de Janeiro (1992) and the "Three Pillars"

The *idea of sustainability* traces back to the *Brundtland Report* which presented the term "sustainable development" at the UN General Assembly in 1987[54] and essentially defines it as *meeting the needs of the present without compromising the ability of future generations to meet their own needs.*[55] Five years later, sustainable development was postulated as a global goal at the *UN Conference on Environment and Development in Rio de Janeiro 1992* (UNCED), concretized by the *Rio Declaration*[56] and *Agenda*

---

ategy-and-policy/priorities-2019-2024/european-green-deal/delivering-european-green-deal_en.

53 *UNDP* (footnote 13), p. 7; *UNDP* (footnote 43), p. 9; *EEA* (footnote 52), p. 95 ff., 136, 233, 280, 281 ff.; *Patrick Huntjens,* Towards a Natural Social Contract. Transformative Social-Ecological Innovation for a Sustainable, Healthy and Just Society, Berlin, 2021; *J. D. Sachs/G. Schmidt-Traub/M. Mazzucato/D. Messner/N. Nakicenovic/J. Rockström*, Six Transformations to achieve the Sustainable Development Goals, Nature Sustainability 2019 Vol. 2, p. 805 ff.; *Winter*, ZUR 2017, p. 267 ff.; *Wolfgang Köck,* Erfordernisse des Umweltrechts im Anthropozän – Rechtskonzepte für eine „Große Transformation", ZUR 2017, p. 257 ff.; *Rainer Wolf,* Biodiversität im Anthropozän, Natur und Recht (NuR) 2023, p. 6 ff.; *Jens Kersten,* Das Anthropozän-Konzept, Baden-Baden 2014.

54 *UN*, Report of the World Commission on Environment and Development, Our Common Future, 1987, Part I. Common Concerns, Chapter 2 Towards Sustainable Development, p. 37 ff. para. 1 ff., 4 ff. It was transmitted to the UN General Assembly as an Annex to document A/42/427 - Development and International Cooperation: Environment.

55 *UN*, Our Common Future (footnote 54), p. 16 para. 27.

56 Report of the UN Conference on Environment and Development, Rio de Janeiro, 3–14 June 1992, vol. I, Resolutions Adopted by the Conference (UN publication, Sales No. E.93.I.8 and corrigendum), resolution 1, annex I.

21.[57] Since then, *sustainable development* has been primarily discussed in terms of the "three-pillar model", according to which the three elements of *ecology, social affairs and economy* are to be balanced on an equal footing. It has become the key term to characterise international development and environmental policy, accompanied by various "Post Rio conferences". The last conference took place in New York in 2015 and led to the UN Agenda 2030 (see below). However, the basic idea can still be found in the Brundtland report´s definition, which reads in full: "*Humanity has the ability to make development sustainable to ensure that it meets the needs of the present without compromising the ability of future generations to meet their own needs. The concept of sustainable development does imply limits - not absolute limits but limitations imposed by the present state of technology and social organization on environmental resources and by the ability of the biosphere to absorb the effects of human activities.*"[58]

The definition initially expresses that sustainability relates not only to the generations currently living, but also to those living in the future. This approach follows the realisation that today's generations "*borrow environmental capital from future generations with no intention or prospect of repaying*".[59] The concept of sustainability therefore places children, young people and unborn future generations at the centre and insofar demands *intergenerational justice.*[60] In addition, the definition includes the needs of *today's generations* in global terms and regarding individual states. In this respect, sustainability requires not only a balance between different social groups and their specific needs within a single country but also a balance between the countries of the Global South and the Global North. As for natural resources, they must be shared equally among the present generation. It is a question of fair and just access and distribution. In this regard, the concept of sustainability demands comprehensive *intragenerational justice.* Summing up, *intra- and intergenerational justice* are the *two core elements* of sustainability, anchored in the Brundtland Report and in the Rio documents.

---

57 Report of the UN Conference on Environment and Development, Rio de Janeiro, 3–14 June 1992, vol. I, Resolutions Adopted by the Conference (UN publication, Sales No. E.93.I.8 and corrigendum), resolution 1, annex II.

58 *UN*, Our Common Future (footnote 54), p. 16 para. 27.

59 *UN*, Our Common Future (footnote 54), Overview (p. 10-24), p. 14 para. 25.

60 *UN*, Our Common Future (footnote 54), Overview (p. 10-24), p. 15, para. 25, 26; see also *Till Markus/Roda Verheyen*, in: Hans-Joachim Koch/Ekkehard Hofmann/Moritz Reese (eds.), Handbuch Umweltrecht, 6th edition Munich 2024, Chapter § 1, p. 30 para. 66.

According to the Brundtland report, sustainable development requires an *integrated approach* that shall take into consideration environmental concerns along with economic and social concerns and development.[61] In this context, the report emphasizes that *environmental protection* is the fundamental basis of sustainable development: "*At a minimum, sustainable development must not endanger the natural systems that support life on Earth: the atmosphere, the waters, the soils, and the living beings.*"[62] This necessarily has consequences for the understanding of the "balance" between economic growth and the protection of natural resources respectively between economy and ecology. A balanced economy respects the limits of environment, it is "*a new era of economic growth - growth that is forceful and at the same time socially and environmentally sustainable.*"[63] From this follows a *clear ecological orientation* of the three-pillar model. This must be remembered.

Since the UN conference in Rio de Janeiro in 1992, followed by the "post-Rio process",[64] the *sustainability concept of the "three pillars"* has become widely accepted in political and legal discourse.[65] Sustainability is seen as an *integrative concept* that aims to harmonize social, ecological and economic concerns. The three components should be balanced. But the crucial question is how. It is criticised that the three-pillar concept could lead to a softening of sustainability.[66] This danger certainly exists, if the "equal" three-pillar concept does not consider the clear ecological orientation since 1987 and the decades-long favouring of the economy over ecology in reality. The existing imbalance by favouring economy would first have to be eliminated to create an "equal" starting position between all pillars. Otherwise, the three-pillar model will in fact continue to favour the economy. Given the decades of exploitation of nature, the "three pillar model" must primarily be understood as *ecological integrity*.[67] The Brundtland Report 1987 already emphasises this

61 *UN*, Our Common Future (footnote 54), Overview, p. 16 para. 27.

62 *UN*, Our Common Future (footnote 54), Part I. Common Concerns, Chapter 2 Towards Sustainable Development, p. 36 f. no. 9.

63 *UN*, Our Common Future (footnote 54), p. 7.

64 For more details, see *Philippe Sands/Jaqueline Peel*, Principles of International Environmental Law, 4th edition, Cambridge 2018, p. 45, 46 ff.

65 *Klaus Mathis*, Nachhaltige Entwicklung und Generationengerechtigkeit, Tübingen 2017, p. 135.

66 To this end, in detail, see *Mathis* (footnote 65), p. 131 ff.

67 *Cf. Laskowski* (footnote 34), p. 107; *Mathis* (footnote 65), p. 131 ff.

– sustainability is clearly focussed on an economy that respects the limits of environment, the *"ecosystem ́s overall integrity"*.[68]

It is obvious and seems widely accepted today, that the "**ecological pillar**" has a special status.[69] The other two pillars cannot exist without an intact natural basis for life. The carrying capacity of nature sets a limit for economic and social development - for example, nature as a supplier of raw materials and as a sink for greenhouse gases.[70] This capacity of nature is weakened by over-exploitation of the environment, with harmful global consequences for all natural resources, ecosystems and the climate. Sustainability must therefore first and foremost be a question of *protecting environmental and climate integrity*. This inevitably leads to a *prioritisation of the environmental and climate dimension* within the sustainability concept.[71] Consequently, the weight of "environmental and climate sustainability" is immense, also in the context of balancing the three pillars.[72] It is always "living within ecological limits".[73] Finally, this leeds to an environmentally compatible, resource-saving, climate-friendly and ecosystem-based economic approach of the "**economic pillar**" – and requires a "greening" of the conventional economy, which is necessary to achieve international climate goals as well.

2. UN Agenda 2030 (2015)

The current state of the understanding of sustainability is reflected in the UN Agenda 2030 *"Transforming our world: the 2030 Agenda for Sustainable Development"*. It was unanimously adopted as a resolution by the UN General Assembly in 2015 and "entered into force" on 1 January 2016.[74] It contains 17 global "Sustainable Development Goals" (SDGs) and 169 sub-goals that are interlinked. The SDGs concretize and further develop the concept of

68 *UN*, Our Common Future (footnote 54), Part I. Common Concerns, Chapter 2 Towards Sustainable Development, p. 38 no. 14; also *Anna Vanhellemont*, Towards sustainable EU Environmetal Law, in: Marlin Boeve/Sanne Akerboom/Chris Backes/Marleen van Rijswick (eds.), Envirnonmetal Law for Transition to Sustainabilty, European Environmetal Law Forum Series, Volume 7, Cambridge 2021, p. 11.

69 *Mathis* (footnote 65), p. 131 ff., 135.

70 *Mathis* (footnote 65), p. 135.

71 Also *Mathis* (footnote 65), p. 133; *Gerd Winter*, Umweltrechtliche Prinzipien des Gemeinschaftsrechts, ZUR 2003, p. 137, 144 f.

72 *Markus/Verheyen* (footnote 60), Chapter § 1, p. 31 para. 68.

73 *Boeve/Akerboom/Backes/van Rijswick*, Introduction, (footnote 68), p. 1.

74 UN Doc. A/RES/70/1, adopted by the General Assembly on 25 September 2015.

sustainability as result of an international negotiation process involving more than 70 states and numerous NGOs.[75] The SDGs provide a comprehensive universal framework that must be "translated" into the policies of states and into their legal and financial systems.

a. Eco-social approach

The SDGs were built on the Millennium Development Goals (MDGs) from 2000, which were in place until 2015.[76] What is new about the 2030 Agenda, however, is that the *ecological goals*, which concretize the weighty ecological approach of sustainability, are now much more visible.[77] Numerous SDGs are clearly focused on environmental and climate protection - namely SDG 13 "climate change", SDG 14 "oceans, seas and marine resources", SDG 15 "terrestrial ecosystems, forests, desertification, land degradation and biodiversity loss", SDG 6 "water and sanitation for all", SDG 7 "energy for all". The special status of "environmental sustainability" or the "ecological pillar" is very clear in the sustainability concept of the 2030 Agenda.[78]

In particular, the ongoing climate change is identified as *unsustainable*.[79] it follows that **sustainable development** necessarily is **climate-friendly, i.e. climate-neutral**. In other words: **Climate change mitigation** (and adaptation) play a **key role** for **sustainable development**. This consideration finds a scientific basis in the *IPCC´s Special Report on Global Warming*, 2018.[80] This leads to the conclusion that "sustainable development" at the expense of planet Earth or the living conditions of other people and other

75 See *Frank Biermann/Thomas Hickmann*, Globale Ziele ohne Wirkung oder normative Leitplanken?, Vereinte Nationen (German Review on the UN) 5/2020, p. 195, 197. In detail *Macharia Kamau/Pamela Chasek/David O´Connor*, Transforming Multilateral Diplomacy: The Inside Story of Sustainble Development Goals, New York 2018.

76 UN Doc. A/RES/55/2 of 18 September 2000. The MDGs aimed primarily at combating global poverty in developing and emerging countries. They can still be found in the SDGs.

77 See *Frank Biermann/Thomas Hickmann* (footnote 75), p. 195, 196 f.

78 UN Doc. A/RES/70/1, p. 12, para. 51, see also *Laskowski*, Nachhaltige Wasserwirtschaft zwischen UN-Agenda 2030 und CETA, ZUR 2017, p. 65.

79 UN Doc. A/RES/70/1, p. 3, 5 para. 14.

80 *IPCC*, Special report on Global Warming, 2018, Chapter 5 "Sustainable Development, Poverty Eradication and Reducing Inequalities", 5.2.2, 5.2.3, https://www.ipcc.ch/sr15/chapter/chapter-5/.

societies is inconceivable.[81] That also means not at the expense of women any more. Therefore SGD 5 calls for the "achievement of **gender equality**" as a *cross-cutting task* and a *cross-cutting obligation of the states* – women and girls should benefit from all SDGs in the same way as men worldwide.

The UN Agenda 2030 aims to transform the world fundamentally. The basic idea is that sustainable development and well-being is only possible if the environment and climate are protected and preserved. All people have equal rights in real life, without any exploitation of nature and people. This concept of sustainability includes a strong *social content* that does not compete with the ecological one, both go hand in hand. It is an **eco-social approach** of sustainability that corresponds with the idea of **environmental and climate justice**.

b. State Responsibility

The 2030 Agenda has replaced the classic division between developing countries and developed or industrialized countries – regarding sustainability, all states are viewed as "developing countries" with a lot of catching up to do. The Agenda considers all states to be responsible and holds all states accountable. Nevertheless, industrialised countries such as Germany and other EU Member States have a special responsibility for reaching the 2030 Agenda goals in view of people and ecosystems in their own countries and abroad, as their economic growth has led to environmental and climate damage in the pasts. But the states worldwide must hurry if they want to reach the goals by 2030.[82] This becomes clear in the *UN´s last* "SDG progress report 2023".[83] It shows that the triple ecological and climate crisis is going on – also because of effects of other crises such as Russia's war of aggression against the Ukraine.[84] The report criticises the implementation

---

81 In this sense, *Deutsche Gesellschaft für die Vereinten Nationen* (DGVN), Agenda 2030 für nachhaltige Entwicklung, https://nachhaltig-entwickeln.dgvn.de/agenda-2030/agenda-2030-fuer-nachhaltige-entwicklung.

82 Approving *German Federal Ministry for Economic Cooperation and Development*, Agenda 2030, Ernüchternde Halbzeitbilanz, 2023, https://www.bmz.de/de/agenda-2030/halbzeitbilanz.

83 *UN*, The Sustainable Development Goals Report 2023: Special edition, Towards a Rescue Plan for People and Planet, 2023, https://unstats.un.org/sdgs/report/2023/.

84 For details, see *Silke R. Laskowski*, Sanktionen gegen den Angriffskrieg, Zeitschrift für das Gesamte Sicherheitsrecht (GSZ), Special edition 1/2022, p. 5 ff.

deficits which mainly affect "*developing countries and the world's poorest and most vulnerable people*", seen as "*a direct result of global injustices.*".[85]

c. Legal significance?

Against this background the question arises as to whether the UN Agenda 2030 and the SDGs have only political significance or also legal significance – as "normative guardrails".[86] Most authors limit their focus to the fact that the 2030 Agenda, as a UN resolution, does not constitute formal international law, but merely "soft law". This view falls short of the mark: It is true, as a resolution of the UN General Assembly, the Agenda 2030 does not constitute formal international law and is therefore not legally binding.[87] But the Agenda differs from other resolutions, not only because of the previous two-year negotiation process. The content is similar to an international treaty, as the states commit to the SDGs and pledge to achieve them between 1 January 2016 and 2030 at the latest with the help of their national measures. But in fact, these are only state obligations in a contract-like framework without any formal legal binding effect. Nevertheless, a certain legal obligation of states to the resolution arises from general principles of international law pursuant to Art. 38 (1) ICJ Statute, namely" bona fides", "good faith", "venire contra factum proprium" and "estoppel", from which trust in the previous state´s behaviour is derived, i.e. a guarantee for the protection of legitimate expectations.[88] A state that has publicly agreed to the Agenda 2030 and its implementation by 2030 in the UN General Assembly may not subsequently contradict its own behaviour and subsequently disregard the 2030 Agenda.[89] Moreover, the resolution expresses the legal conviction of 193 states that the 2030 Agenda has a *binding legal basis* in *binding international law*, i.e. in various international

85 *UN* Sustainable Development Goals Report 2023 (footnote 83), p. 4; see also *Phoebe Koundouri/Angelos Alamanos/Angelos Plataniotis et al.*, Assessing the sustainability of the European Green Deal and its interlinkages with the SDGs, npj Climate Action 2024 Vol. 3, p. 1, 2 ff.

86 *Biermann/Hickmann* (footnote 75), p. 195, 199.

87 Likewise *Alexander Proelß*, in: the same (ed.), Völkerrecht, 9th edition Berlin/Boston 2024, Chapter 5, p. 643 para. 112. For "soft law" in general, see *Jörn A. Kämmerer*, Chapter 1, p. 102 para. 148.

88 Cf. *Matthias Herdegen*, Völkerrecht, 22nd edition Munich 2023, § 17 p. 171 ff. para. 3.

89 It is also conceivable that the Agenda will become legally binding through a long-term consensus and implementation process (2015-2024) of the 193 UN states, but this is not decisive here. On the dispute over "consensus as a source of law", see in detail *Knut Ipsen*, Völkerrecht, 7th edition Munich 2019, § 20 p. 499 f.

agreements which the Agenda refers to.[90] Full respect for international law explicitly guides the Agenda and the interconnected 17 SDGs.[91] A closer look shows, the Agenda´s sustainability concept finds a legal base in *binding international law to protect the environment, climate and the human rights* – especially in Art. 2, Art. 3, Art. 4 (1) d), (2) a) of the UNFCCC,[92] in the expired Kyoto Protocol to the UNFCCC[93] and the current Paris Agreement to the UNFCCC,[94] in Art. 1 and Art. 2 of the Convention on Biological Diversity (CBD)[95], in Art. 1 (4) and Art. 192 ff. of the UN Convention on the Law of the Sea (UNCLOS),[96] furthermore in the International Covenant on Civil and Political Rights (ICCPR)[97] and the International Covenant on Economic, Social and Cultural Rights (ICESCR)[98], in view of Europe also in the Euro-

---

90 *Proelß* also points out that the SDGs are overwhelmingly based on existing obligations under international and multinational treaties, cf. *Proelß* (footnote 87), Chapter 5, p. 643 para. 112.

91 UN Agenda 2030, Resolution A/RES/70/1, Declaration, p. 4 para. 10.

92 UNFCCC, May 9, 1992, Treaty Doc No. 102–38 (1992), 1771 U.N.T.S. 107; German Federal Law Gazette (Bundesgesetzblatt, BGBl.) 2016 II p. 1082, 1083. The UNFCCC entered into force on 21 March 1994, there are 198 parties (197 states and the EU), see UN Treaty Collection, https://treaties.un.org/.

93 Kyoto Protocol to the UNFCCC, UN Doc FCCC/CP/1997/7/Add.1, 10 December 1997; 37 ILM 22 (1998); Dec. 11, 1997, 2303 U.N.T.S. 162. Doha Amendment to the Kyoto Protocol, Doha, 8 December 2012, C.N.718.2012.TREATIES-XXVII.7.c (Depositary Notification). The Kyoto Protocol was adopted on 11 December 1997, it entered into force on 16 February 2005 – 192 parties (191 states and the EU), see UN treaties, https://treaties.un.org/. It operationalized the UNFCCC by committing industrialized countries to reduce greenhouse gas emissions in line with agreed individual targets. An important element was the establishment of flexible market mechanisms, i.e. the trade of emissions permit. The Protocol expired with the 2nd commitment period of the Protocol (2013-2020) in 2020. The successor agreement is the Paris Agreement of 2015. For more information see UN Climate Change, https://unfccc.int/kyoto_protocol.

94 Paris Agreement to the UNFCCC, 12 December 2015, Dec. 1/CP.21, Annex, UN Doc. FCCC/CP/2015/10/Add.1.

95 CBD of 5 June 1992, 1760 U.N.T.S. 69; BGBl. 1993 II, p. 1742 ff. The convention introduced novel legal concepts such as biodiversity, ecosystems, genetic resources etc., see *Elisa Morgera/Elsa Tsioumani*, Yesterday, Today, and Tomorrow: Looking Afresh at the Convention on Biological Diversity, Yearbook of International Environmental Law, Vol. 21, Issue 1, 2010, p. 3 ff., https://doi.org/10.1093/yiel/yvr003.

96 UNCLOS, 10 December 1982, entered into force 16 November 1994, 1833 U.N.T.S. 396; BGBl. 1994 II p. 1798.

97 ICCPR, adopted by General Assembly resolution 2200A (XXI) of 16 December 1966, entry into force 23 March 1976, 999 U.N.T.S. 171; BGBl. 1973 II, p. 1533.

98 ICESCR, adopted by the General Assembly on 16 December 1966, entered into force on 3 January 1976, 993 UNTS 3, [1976] ATS 5, 6 ILM 360 (1967), UN Doc. A/RES/21/2200A, UN Doc. A/6316; BGBl. 1973 II p. 1569.

pean Convention on Human Rights and Fundamental Freedoms (ECHR).[99] The 17 SDGs explicitly aim "*to realize the human rights of all and to achieve gender equality*".[100]

3. Legal Principle of Sustainability

Today, the concept of sustainability is seen as a *legal principle* that has become established in international, European and national law and practice.[101] It is being discussed whether the *principle of sustainability* already constitutes *customary international law*[102] or at least *customary international law "in progress"*.[103] Already the Rio Declaration and Agenda 21 of 1992 concretized the principle of sustainability. Even though they are "soft law" and therfore not binding under international law, they were important.[104] They already expressed the global consensus of the international community of states at the highest level to implement the goals of the "Sustainable Development Agenda 21" through international cooperation and national measures. In 2015, the international community substantiated and updated the principle of sustainability with the help of 17 sustainability goals through the UN Agenda 2030. Here, the *relevant concretizing criteria* for the three dimensions of sustainability can be found.[105] This shows the "core content" of the principle

---

99 ECHR of 4 November 1950, entered into force on 3 September 1953, Europe Treaty Series 005; BGBl. 1952 II p. 685, corr. p. 953, new announcement BGBl. 2002 II p. 1054, 1055. Since 1950 the ECHR has been amended by further Protocols.

100 UN Agenda 2030, Resolution A/RES/70/1, Preamble, p. 1.

101 *Sands/Peel* (footnote 64), p. 206; also *Mathis* (footnote 71), p. 61, 63, with reference to *Hans Kelsen*, General Theory of Law and State, Cambridge 1945, reprint New York 2005, p. 161, *Mathis* emphasises the transformation into a legal concept via case law and the inclusion in the legal discourse; see as well *Astrid Epiney/Martin Scheyli* (eds.), Das Konzept der nachhaltigen Entwicklung. Völker- und europarechtliche Aspekte. Swiss papers on European integration, Zürich 1999; *the same*, Strukturprinzipien des Umweltrechts, Baden-Baden 1998.

102 *Sands/Peel* (footnote 64), p. 217, 219 f.; *Alexander Proelß*, Internationales Umweltrecht, 2022, Section 3, para. 56; Peter M. Huber/Andreas Voßkuhle/*Astrid Epiney*, Grundgesetz. Kommentar, 8th edition Munich 2024, Art. 20a no. 51; Günther Dürig/Roman Herzog/Rupert Scholz/*Christian Calliess*, Grundgesetz-Kommentar, 104th supplement Munich April 2024, Art. 20a para. 100; *Laskowski* (footnote 34), p. 99, 100 ff.

103 *Markus/Verheyen* (footnote 60), Chapter § 1, p. 30 para. 66.

104 See Dürig/Herzog/Scholz/*Calliess* (footnote 102), Art. 20a para. 99, 10.

105 Cf. *Proelß* (footnote 87), Chapter 5, p. 657 f. para. 128. Previously, criteria are already found in UN Doc. A/RES/66/288, "The future we want", Resolution adopted by the General Assembly on 27 July 2012, para. 56 ff. "green economy", para. 119 ff. "water is

of sustainability, even if the implementation process is not yet complete.[106] Because of a continuous process of juridification through legislation and jurisprudence worldwide and recognizable great acceptance of the States in the UN General Assembly since 1987 – as was most recently evident in 2015 with the unanimous adoption of the 2030 Agenda – the Agenda can be seen as a "resolution of principle on questions of international law",[107] as element in the development of customary law - there is every reason to believe that the principle of sustainability now also applies in *customary international law*.[108] In detail:

a. Normative implementation

Firstly, the principle of sustainability has found its way into numerous *international agreements*, especially the UNFCCC, e.g. Preamble, Art. 2, Art. 3 Nos. 1, 4 and 5, Art. 4 (1) d), (2) a) UNFCCC, the Paris Agreement to the UNFCCC and the CBD. There, the concept of sustainability is legally concretised and thus balanced by *legal standards* to protect the climate and environment. These UN conventions can be regarded as *key agreements for sustainable development under international law* – in view of the impending *tipping points*, the main focus is on the protection of the *climate and biodiversity*.

The principle of sustainable development was also implemented into primary and secondary law of the European Union and into national law of the Member States. It became one of the EU's fundamental goals under Art. 3(3) of the Treaty on European Union (TEU). It is also anchored in Art. 11 of the Treaty on the Functioning of the European Union (TFEU) and in Art. 37 (environmental protection) of the Charter of Fundamental Rights of the EU (EUCFR). The "integration clause" in Art. 11 TFEU explicitly promotes sustainable development and amounts to a kind of "strategic environmental impact assessment" in all policy areas of the EU (energy, agriculture,[109] transport, public procurement law[110] etc.).[111] Art. 11 TFEU contains a legal obligation to

at the core of sustainable development", para. 190 ff. "climate change", para. 236 ff. "gender equality", para. 245 ff. "sustainable development goals".

106 Cf. *UN* Sustainable Development Goals Report 2023 (footnote 83).

107 Cf. *Herdegen,* (footnote 88) § 22, p. 176 ff. para. 2.

108 *Proelß* (footnote 87), p. 658 para. 129. See also the references in footnotes 140, 142.

109 EuGH C-428/07, ECLI:EU:C:2009 : 458, Slg. 2009, I-6355 Rn. 29 – Horvath.

110 EuGH C-513/99, ECLI:EU:C:2002 : 495, Slg. 2002, I-7251 – Concordia.

111 Matthias Pechstein/Carsten Nowak/Ulrich Häde/*Sebastian Heselhaus,* Frankfurter Kommentar EUV/GRC/AEUV, 2nd edition Tübingen 2023, AEUV Art. 11 para. 10, 21;

greening the sustainable sector policy that can be reviewed by the ECJ.[112] In view of the "three-pillar model" Art. 11 TFEU supports that the aspects of environmental and climate protection must be recognised and given (relative) priority in the consideration process.[113] The "integration clause" is reflected today above all in the European Green Deal[114] and associated EU legislation. Of great importance is the "European Climate Law" of 2021, Regulation (EU) 2021/1119,[115] which states the legally binding targets of reducing emissions 55% by 2030 and achieving *climate neutrality* in the EU by 2050 – it is one of the core legal instruments to reach the binding goals of the Paris Agreement. To reach the 2030 target, the EU approved a package of new and revised legislation known as "Fit for 55" in 2023, comprising 13 interlinked revised laws (e.g. the EU's Emissions Trading Scheme, to include more polluting sectors: buildings, road transport as of 2027 and maritime transport) and six laws on climate and energy. Already in 2018, Regulation (EU) 2018/842 was established which fixes the binding annual national targets for limiting greenhouse gas emissions from 2021 to 2030.[116]

Moreover, Art. 11 TFEU supports an environmentally - and climate - friendly interpretation of EU primary and secondary legislation; it has also an impact on the interpretation of Member States´ law which has to be interpreted in conformity with EU law, Art. 4 (3) TEU.[117] Furthermore, Art. 3 TEU, Art. 11 TFEU and Art. 37 EUCFR are flanked by the fundamental rights obligations of the EU and Member States to protect human life and health: Art. 2 (right to life), Art. 3 (right to physical and mental integrity), Art. 7 (right to respect for his or her private and family life) EUCFR; Art. 2 (right to life), Art. 8 (right to private and family life) ECHR; Art. 2 (2) (right to life and

Christian Calliess/Matthias Ruffert/*Calliess*, EUV/AEUV, 6th edition Munich 2022, Art. 11 AEUV para. 10.

112 Rudolf Geiger /Daniel-Erasmus Khan/Markus Kotzur/Lando Kirchmair/*Kotzur*, EUV/AEUV, 7th edition Munich 2023, TFEU Art. 11 para. 6.

113 See Pechstein/Nowak/Häde/*Heselhaus* (footnote 111), Art. 11 AEUV para. 20.

114 COM(2019) 640 final; see Geiger/Khan/Kotzur/Kirchmair/*Kotzur* (footnote 112), Art. 11 AEUV para. 1.

115 Regulation (EU) 2021/1119 of the European Parliament and of the Council of 30 June 2021 establishing the framework for achieving climate neutrality and amending Regulations (EC) No 401/2009 and (EU) 2018/1999 ("European Climate Law"), OJ L 243, 9.7.2021, p. 1.

116 Regulation (EU) 2018/842 of the European Parliament and of the Council of 30 May 2018 on binding annual greenhouse gas emission reductions by Member States from 2021 to 2030 contributing to climate action to meet commitments under the Paris Agreement and amending Regulation (EU) No 525/2013, OJ L 156, 19.6.2018, p. 26.

117 Pechstein/Nowak/Häde/*Heselhaus* (footnote 111), Art. 11 AEUV para. 3.

physical integrity) German Basic Law. Finally, the principle of sustainability has been incorporated into secondary EU law as well, e.g. legislative acts concerning greenhouse gas emissions or water protection.

All EU *Member States* have implemented the *principle of sustainability* in their national legislation, e.g. **Germany** in Article 20a Basic Law (BL) – "protection of the natural foundations of life" – as well as in Federal environmental, energy or planning law:[118] e.g. §§ 1, 6 (1) Federal Water Protection Act,[119] § 1 (1) Federal Renewable Energy Sources Act,[120] § 1 (5) Federal Building Code[121] and - regarding climate protection (mitigation) - § 1 Federal Climate Change Act (Bundes-Klimaschutzgesetz, KSG).[122] § 1 KSG refers directly to the binding goals of the Paris Agreement. All these laws also implement EU secondary legislation. Regarding climate adaptation, a new Federal Climate Adaptation Act (Bundes-Klimaanpassungsgesetz, KAnG)[123] entered into force on 24 July 2024, § 14 KAnG.[124] It overlaps with natural climate protection and the protection of biodiversity, § 3 (3) KAnG, and helps to achieve SDG 13 and further sustainability goals – namely SDG 2, 3, 5, 6, 8, 9, 10, 11, 14 and SDG 15.[125] Especially the KSG and the KAnG serve not only to implement the UN Agenda 2030 but to implement the obligations arising from Article 20a

118 See the overview by *Eckardt Rehbinder*, Das deutsche Umweltrecht auf dem Weg zur Nachhaltigkeit, Neue Zeitschrift für Verwaltungsrecht (NVwZ) 2002, p. 657 ff.; see also Landmann/Rohmer/*Wolfgang Durner*, Umweltrecht, Umweltvölkerrecht – Vol. I, 105nd supplement Munich September 2024, para. 59.

119 Law on the organisation of the water balance/Federal Water Act (Wasserhaushaltsgesetz, WHG) of 31 July 2009 (BGBl. 2023 I p. 2585), last amended by Art. 7 of the Act of 22 December 2023 (BGBl. 2023 I No. 409).

120 Renewable Energy Sources Act (Erneuerbare-Energien-Gesetz/EEG 2023) of 21 July 2014 (BGBl. 2024 I p. 1066), last amended by Art. 1 of the Act of 21 February 2025 (BGBl. 2025 I No. 52).

121 Building Code (Baugesetzbuch, BauGB) in the version published on 3 November 2017 (BGBl. 2017 I p. 3634), last amended by Art. 3 of the Act of 20 December 2023 (BGBl. 2023 I No. 394).

122 Federal Climate Change Act of 12 December 2019 (BGBl. 2019 I, p. 2513), as last amended by Art. 1 of the Act of 15 July 2024 (BGBl. 2024 I, No. 235).

123 BGBl. 2023 I No. 393 of 20. December 2023. See also the legislative materials: Bundestag Doc. 20/8764 (Federal Government, Draft of a Federal Climate Adaptation Act [KAnG]) and Doc. 20/9342 (Recommended resolution and report of the Committee on the Environment, Nature Conservation, Nuclear Safety and Consumer Protection [16th Committee] on the draft bill - Document 20/8764).

124 BGBl. 2023 I No. 393 of 22. December 2023, p. 1, 7.

125 See the assessment of the Parliamentary Advisory Council on Sustainable Development, expert opinion to the KAnG-Draft, Bundestag Doc. 20/9342, p. 20.

BL, EU law and the international Paris Agreement to the UNFCCC.[126] The goals of climate protection and adaptation are complementary to each other.[127] The principle of sustainability in German law and European law implies that the environment should only be utilised to the extent that the needs of future generations are met from the remaining resources.[128]

Many other states have implemented the principle of sustainability into national law as well, especially into their constitutional law - like Belgium in Art. 7bis, 23 Constitution; Bulgaria in Art. 15, 55 Constitution; Estonia in §§ 5, 53 Constitution; Finland in § 20 Constitution; France in the Preamble to the Constitution and Art. 1, 2, 6 Environmental Charter; Greece in Art. 24 Constitution; Ireland in Art. 10 Constitution; Italy in Art. 9 Constitution; Switzerland in Art. 2 (4), Art. 73, 74, 78 and Brazil in Art. 225 Constitution.[129]

b. International Jurisdiction

Secondly, the International Court of Justice (ICJ) and international tribunals have referred to the principle of sustainable development. Above all, the case law of the ICJ should be emphasized. The ICJ has taken up the concept of sustainability as principle of international law in its legal reasoning – and: the court´s focus is on the environment. In the "Gabcikovo-Nagymaros" case (1997), which concerned a dam project at the river Danube and a dispute between Hungary and Slovakia, the ICJ referred to the concept and principle of sustainable development for the first time.[130] Against the background "*that in the field of environmental protection, vigilance and prevention are required on account of the often irreversible character of damage to the environment and of the limitations inherent in the very mechanism of reparation of this type of damage*", the ICJ pointed out, the "*need to reconcile economic development with protection of the environment is aptly expressed in the concept of sustainable development*".[131] Moreover, the ICJ defined "*mankind*" as "*present and future generations*".[132] This judgement already speaks in favour

126 Explanatory memorandum to the law, Bundestag Doc. 20/8764, p. 14.

127 Bundestag Doc. 20/8764, p. 14.

128 Landmann/Rohmer/*Durner* (footnote 118), para. 58.

129 See the overview in Huber/Voßkuhle/*Epiney* (footnote 102), Art. 20a para 51 ff.

130 ICJ, Judgement of 25 September 1997, No. 97/10, Gabcikovo-Nagymaros Project (Hungary v. Slovakia), I.C.J. Reports 1997, p. 7, 75 para. 140, https://www.icj-cij.org/case/92.

131 ICJ, Judgement of 25 September 1997, I.C.J. Reports 1997, p. 7, 75 para. 140.

132 ICJ, 25 September 1997, I.C.J. Reports 1997, p. 7, 75 para. 140.

of recognising the concept of sustainability as a legal principle of international law. Further decisions by the ICJ and the WTO followed which confirmed this – namely the "Shrimps-Turtle" case (WTO 1998)[133] and the "Pulp Mills" case (ICJ 2010)[134]. In the latter case, which concerned pulp mills at the river Uruguay and a dispute between the riparian states Argentina and Uruguay, the ICJ emphasized, "*the interconnectedness between equitable and reasonable utilization of a shared resource and the balance between economic development and environmental protection that is the essence of sustainable development*".[135] Both states were responsible for a "*sustainable management and environmental protection of the river*".[136]

c. Normative core

Against this background, the discussion about the "legal character" and the "normative core" of the principle of sustainability[137] should now be over. In the view expressed here, the *normative core* of sustainability can already be found in the Brundtland Report 1987. The focus has always been on safeguarding ecological performance so that future generations are not worse off in terms of quality and quantity of natural resources and the supply of resources.[138] The *normative core* of sustainability has become clearer through normative implementation and jurisdiction, most recently by the 2030 Agenda. The relevant sustainability criteria can be found there.[139] The *normative core* of sustainable development, as derived from the 2030 Agenda and international

133 WTO case Nos. 58, 61, Ruling adopted on 6 November 1998, USA — Import Prohibition of Certain Shrimp and Shrimp Products (India, Malaysia, Pakistan, Thailand v. USA). The appellate and panel reports were adopted in 1998, see WTO, Environment: Disputes, www.wto.org/english/tratop_e/envir_e/edis08_e.htm.

134 ICJ, 20 April 2010, No. 135, Pulp Mills on the River Uruguay (Argentina v. Uruguay), I.C.J. Reports 2010, p. 10, 38 f. para. 76, p. 64 para. 177.

135 ICJ, 20 April 2010, I.C.J. Reports 2010, p. 64, 65 para. 177.

136 ICJ, 20 April 2010, I.C.J. Reports 2010, p. 76 para. 178.

137 Cf. *Peter Sieben*, Was bedeutet Nachhaltigkeit als Rechtsbegriff? Neue Zeitschrift für Verwaltungsrecht (NVwZ) 2003, p. 1173, 1174 f.; *Markus/Verheyen* (footnote 60), § 1, p. 30 para. 66.

138 Similar *Markus/Verheyen* (footnote 60), § 1, p. 30 para. 66: "clear normative core".

139 Cf. *Proelß* (footnote 87), Chapter V., p. 657 f. para. 128. The SDG-criteria are already found in UN Doc. A/RES/66/288, "The future we want", Resolution adopted by the General Assembly on 27 July 2012, see para. 56 ff. "green economy", para. 119 ff. "water is at the core of sustainable development", para. 190 ff. "climate change", para. 236 ff. "gender equality", para. 245 ff. "sustainable development goals".

law associated with the Agenda, in particular the *international climate and environmental protection law and the human rights,*[140] can be seen in a *climate- and environment oriented approach to intra- and intergenerational justice.* The overarching goal is to *safeguard the natural foundations of life in the long term* as base for *social and economic development in line with ecological load limits and tipping points in the climate system.* This means achieving climate-neutral, environmentally sound economic and social development from an intra- and intergenerational perspective. The natural foundation of life is especially safeguarding freedoms for future generations, as the BVerfG rightly points out in the 2021 Climate Order.[141] It is the *natural foundation of life* that gives individuals the opportunity to make full use of their human and fundamental rights and freedoms.[142] Therefore, the stock of natural capital must be kept at least constant ("strong sustainability").[143] In other words: The *core content* is *intra- and intergenerational environmental- und climate justice.*

IV. Climate protection and human rights

Ineffective climate protection measures lead to damage to livelihoods and violate human rights. This has now become clear through landmark decisions and expert opinions by European and international courts.

1. Climate Protection Law

The relevant climate law is currently the Paris Agreement (PA) to the UNFCCC. It is the legally binding international treaty on climate change and protection. It was adopted by 196 Parties including the EU at the UN Climate Change Conference (COP21) in Paris on 12 December 2015 and entered into force on 4 November 2016 - after it was ratified by 55 countries that emitted at least 55 % of global greenhouse gases. Today, nearly all parties have ratified

140 Cf. Dürig/Herzog/Scholz/*Calliess* (footnote 102), Art. 20a GG Rn. 267 ff.

141 BVerfG, 24 March 2021 – 1 BvR 2656/18 -, para. 197 f.

142 BVerfG, 24 March 2021 – 1 BvR 2656/18 -, para. 182 ff.; *Johannes Rux*, in: Epping/Hillgruber (eds.), BeckOK Grundgesetz. Kommentar, 57th edition, 2024, Art. 20a GG, para. 17.

143 Dürig/Herzog/Scholz/*Calliess* (footnote 102), para. 98; Calliess/Ruffert/*Calliess* (footnote 111), Art. 11 AEUV para. 13.

the agreement,[144] including the **EU**, **Germany**, all other EU Member States and the **Republic of Türkiye** which is an important EU Accession State.

As is well known, the ultimate objective of all agreements under the UNFCCC is to stabilize greenhouse gas concentrations in the atmosphere at a level that will prevent dangerous human interference with the climate system, in a time frame which allows ecosystems to adapt naturally and enables sustainable development. The *overarching binding goal of the Paris Agreement* is to hold "the increase in the global average temperature to well below 2 degree Celsius above pre-industrial levels" and pursue efforts "to limit the temperature increase to 1.5° Celsius above pre-industrial levels", Art. 2 (1) (a) PA. This aim is explicitly embedded in the "context of sustainable development", Art 2 (1) PA. But today there is broad agreement that the 1.5° Celsius limit is the decisive goal - following the findings of the *Intergovernmental Panel on Climate Change* (IPCC) 2018[145] that clearly show, when warming exceeds 1.5° Celsius, the climate risks increase rapidly. Therefore, the climate decision of the ECtHR 2024 and the Advisory Opinion No. 31 (2024) of the ITLOS also based on the 1.5° C-target (see below).

In addition, according to Article 4 (1) all signatory states have to "achieve a balance between anthropogenic emissions by sources and removals by sinks of greenhouse gases in the second half of this century". This means nothing other than the *obligation of states* to achieve *climate neutrality from 2050*, in line with Art. 2 and Art. 4 PA. For the sake of completeness, it should be noted that Art. 4 (1) obliges States to achieve this objective "*on the basis of equity, and in the context of sustainable development*".

Unlike the Kyoto Protocol, which expired in 2020 and only obliged industrialized countries to reduce their greenhouse gas emissions, the PA obliges all signatory states, including developing countries. The states are obliged to make effective national climate contributions, so called Nationally Determined Contributions (NDC), to reach the goals of the PA. They must take concrete steps to implement the NDCs and report regularly on the progress of their efforts. It is therefore irrelevant if a state declares itself a "developing country" in an additional declaration to the PA as in the case

144 Still missing: Iran, Yemen, Libya, see UN Treaty Collection, Status of Treaties, TREATIES-XXVII.7.d Paris Agreement, Paris, 12 December 2015, https://treaties.un.org/.

145 *IPCC* (footnote 80), p. 5, 7 ff., 12; also *UN* (footnote 92), p. 4: "*to limit the rise in global temperatures to 1.5 degrees Celsius, prevent the worst impacts of the climate crisis*".

of the **Republic of Türkiye.**[146] This declaration does not exempt from the obligations of the PA.

However – according to Art. 4 (4) PA developing countries may report NDCs with lower climate protection efforts than industrialised countries. According to Art. 7 (13) PA developing countries are entitled to climate protection support ("ongoing and increased international support"). These provisions are in line with Art. 2 (2) PA which expressly refers to the principle of "common but different responsibilities". This legal principle[147] shows considerations of fairness regarding the distribution of costs arising from climate protection in the countries affected differently and differently responsible for climate change. It is a question of *climate justice* – as the preamble to the PA makes clear, referring explicitly to "climate justice" and Art. 3 (1) UNFCCC, demanding climate protection "on the basis of justice".[148]

In this respect, the responsibility of **Türkiye** for climate change will have to be assessed differently from the responsibility of industrial states such as **Germany**. In addition, Türkiye is considered to be particularly vulnerable to the consequences of climate change, which can inhibit the country´s social and economic development.[149] The PA affirms that developed countries – industrialised countries – should take the lead in providing financial assistance to countries that are financially poorly equipped and more vulnerable, Art. 4 (4) and (5) PA. Insofar Art. 2 (2) PA in conjunction with Art. 4 (4) and (5) PA can be seen as the basis for special support, including financial

---

146 Declaration of Türkiye made upon ratification of the PA on 11 Oct 2021: "The Republic of Türkiye (...) declares that Türkiye will implement the PA as a developing country", UN Treaty Collection, Status of Treaties, TREATIES-XXVII.7.d Paris Agreement, Paris, 12 December 2015, https://treaties.un.org/.

147 Mainly regarded as legal principle, so *Ulrich Beyerlin/Thilo Marauhn*, International Environmental Law, 2011, p. 70; *Christian Glass*, Die gemeinsame, aber unterschiedliche Verantwortlichkeit als Bestandteil eines umweltvölkerrechtlichen Prinzipiengefüges: Konkretisierungsvorschläge für künftige Übereinkommen zum Schutz globaler Umweltgüter, Berlin 2008, p. 25 ff., 40 „Basic principle of modern international environmental law"; *Jessica Schröter*, Strukturprinzipien des Umweltvölkerrechts und ihr Beitrag zur Eindämmung des Klimawandels, 2015, p. 248, 249.

148 See *Till Markus,* Die Problemwirksamkeit des internationalen Klimaschutzrechts – Ein Beitrag zur Diskussion um die Effektuierung völkerrechtlicher Verträge, Zeitschrift für ausländisches öffentliches Recht und Völkerrecht (ZaöRV)/ Heidelberg Journal of International Law (HJIL) 76 (2016), p. 715, 739. See as well *Cecilia Albin,* Justice and Fairness in International Negotiations, 2001, 54 ff.; *Astrid Epiney, Gerechtigkeit im Umweltvölkerrecht,* Aus Politik und Zeitgeschichte 24 (2007), p. 31 ff.

149 See *The Federal Government of Germany*, International Climate Initiative, Türkiye, November 2023, https://www.international-climate-initiative.com/en/Türkiye/.

support, in favour of vulnerable, weaker states by developed, richer states. In this respect, Art. 2 (2) in conjunction with Art. 4 PA could work in favour of Türkiye though today it is no longer seen as developing state but as emerging economy ("Schwellenland").[150]

At the 28th UNFCCC Climate Conference (COP28) in Dubai in 2023[151] it became clear, that more government action is needed to reach the PA's goals. In Dubai the results of the *first global stocktaking*[152] were presented. The stocktaking is a process for countries and stakeholders to see whether and where they are collectively making progress towards meeting the goals of the PA – and where they are not. The results were disturbing because the "*historical cumulative net carbon dioxide emissions already account for about four fifths of the total carbon budget, for a 50 % probability of limiting global warming to 1.5° C*". Therefore, it was called for "*transitioning away from fossil fuels in energy systems, in a just, orderly and equitable manner (...) to achieve net zero by 2050 in keeping with the science*".[153]

2. ICJ Advisory Opinion Request 2023 – States´ obligations on climate change

This process could become more progressive by the ICJ´s advisory opinion on "obligations of states in respect of climate change". On 29 March 2023 the UN General Assembly adopted unanimously Resolution 77/276. Pursuant to Art. 65 of the Statute of the ICJ[154] the Court was requested to render an advisory opinion on which obligations states must fulfil to contain the climate crisis with "*particular regard to the Charter of the UN, the International Covenant on Civil and Political Rights, the International Covenant on Economic, Social and Cultural Rights, the UNFCCC, the Paris Agreement, the UNCLOS,*

150 Deutsche Vertretungen in der Türkei, Wirtschaftliche Zusammenarbeit und Entwicklung, 2024, https://tuerkei.diplo.de/tr-de/03-Themen/001-DeutschlandunddieTuerkei/wirtschaft/-/2606418.

151 It is also the fifth session of the Conference of the Parties to the Paris Agreement (CMA 5).

152 FCCC/PA/CMA/2023/L.17, 13 December 2023.

153 ECtHR (Grand Chamber), 9 April 2024, 53600/20, (Verein KlimaSeniorinnen Schweiz and others/Switzerland), para. 140 p. 60 – climate change.

154 The ICJ has a twofold role: first, to settle, in accordance with international law, through judgments which have binding force and are without appeal for the parties concerned, legal disputes submitted to it by States; second, to give advisory opinions on legal questions referred to it by duly authorized UN organs and agencies.

the duty of due diligence, the rights recognized in the Universal Declaration of Human Rights, the principle of prevention of significant harm to the environment and the duty to protect and preserve the marine environment". In addition, the ICJ was asked about the legal consequences of breaches of these obligations.[155] It is recognizably about environmental and climate protection in conjunction with universal human rights. The initiative for this UN Resolution came from *Vanuatu*, a small island state in the South Pacific. In view of the consequences of climate change – sea level rise – it is particularly at risk to disappear soon. The ICJ´s advisory opinion is expected in 2025.[156] Parallel requests were made for expert opinions from the *Inter-American Court of Human Rights* (IACtHR) and the *International Tribunal for the Law of the Sea* (ITLOS) on state obligations in the context of the climate crisis.

3. ITLOS Advisory Opinion 2024 – States´ obligations on climate change

On 21 May 2024, the ITLOS has published its Advisory Opinion No. 31[157] and affirmed state climate protection obligations under the UNCLOS. UNCLOS, often referred to as the "Constitution of the Sea", defines the rights and duties of states regarding the use of the seas. The Tribunal delivered its unanimous Advisory Opinion on the Request submitted by the *Commission of Small Islands States on Climate Change and International Law* on 12 December 2022.[158] According to the Advisory Opinion, UNCLOS serves climate protection and adaptation and calls for effective measures in line with the Paris Agreement to the UNFCC in relation to the 1.5 ° Celsius target, to protect the marine environment from the effects of greenhouse gases (GHG), i.e.to reduce GHG.

First, the Tribunal clarified that "*anthropogenic GHG emissions into the atmosphere constitute pollution of the marine environment*" within the mea-

155 UN General Assembly, resolution A/RES/77/276 adopted on 29 March 2023.

156 Latest developments see ICJ, https://www.icj-cij.org/case/187. For climate lawsuits before the ICJ, see *Paul Vitter Thiessen*, Zukunftsmusik? – Der Klimawandel vor dem Internationalen Gerichtshof, ZUR 2023, p. 338 ff.

157 ITLOS, Advisory Opinion No. 31, 21 May 2024, https://www.itlos.org/fileadmin/itlos/documents/cases/31/Advisory_Opinion/C31_Adv_Op_21.05.2024_orig.pdf; ITLOS, Press Release 350, 21 May 2024, p. 1-5: requests of the commission and answers by the Tribunal, https://www.itlos.org/fileadmin/itlos/documents/press_releases_english/PR_350_EN.pdf.

158 ITLOS, Advisory Opinion Case No. 31, 21 May 2024, para. 3.

ning of Art. 1 (1), subpara. 4 UNCLOS.[159] Secondly, in view of the general obligation of State Parties under Art. 192 UNCLOS it clarified, this duty includes "*the specific obligation to protect and preserve the marine environment from climate change impacts and ocean acidification. Where the marine environment has been degraded, this obligation may call for measures to restore marine habitats and ecosystems.*" Moreover, the *precautionary principle* (Art. 3 (3) UNFCCC) is emphasised which calls for protective measures even under uncertainty. Art. 192 UNCLOS obliges the states to "*anticipate risks relating to climate change impacts and ocean acidification.*"[160] Thirdly, the ITLOS specified the obligations under Art. 194 (1) UNCLOS in the context of the Paris Agreement. According to this, states "*have the specific obligations to take all necessary measures to prevent, reduce and control marine pollution from anthropogenic GHG emissions.*"[161] They have to comply with "*the best available science and relevant international rules and standards contained in climate change treaties such as the UNFCCC and the Paris Agreement, in particular the global temperature goal of limiting the temperature increase to 1.5°C above pre-industrial levels and the timeline for emission pathways to achieve that goal*". [162] Important: "*The necessary measures include (...) those to reduce GHG emissions.*"[163] Moreover, under Art. 194 (1) UNCLOS "*the obligation to take all necessary measures to prevent, reduce and control marine pollution from anthropogenic GHG emissions is one of due diligence.*" And – "*the standard of due diligence (...) is stringent*".[164] The due diligence standard under article 194 (2) UNCLOS in relation to transboundary pollution "*can be even more stringent*".[165] Regarding specific sources of marine pollution from anthropogenic GHG emissions, the Tribunal identifies "*pollution from land-based sources, pollution from vessels, or pollution from or through the atmosphere.*"[166]

Under Art. 207 and Art. 212 UNCLOS, States Parties have the specific obligation "*to adopt laws and regulations to prevent, reduce and control marine pollution from GHG (...) taking into account internationally agreed rules, inter*

159 ITLOS, Advisory Opinion Case No. 31, 21 May 2024, para. 179.
160 ITLOS, Advisory Opinion Case No. 31, 21 May 2024, para. 441.
161 ITLOS, Advisory Opinion Case No. 31, 21 May 2024, para. 243.
162 ITLOS, Advisory Opinion Case No. 31, 21 May 2024, para. 243.
163 ITLOS, Advisory Opinion Case No. 31, 21 May 2024, para. 243.
164 ITLOS, Advisory Opinion Case No. 31, 21 May 2024, para. 243.
165 ITLOS, Advisory Opinion Case No. 31, 21 May 2024, para. 258.
166 ITLOS, Advisory Opinion Case No. 31, 21 May 2024, para. 441.

alia, in climate change treaties such as the UNFCCC and the Paris Agreement."[167]

To sum up, the ITLOS derived numerous specific state obligations from the UNCLOS to take effective measures to protect the climate, the marine environment and to adapt to climate change in line with the PA to the UNFCCC.[168] In addition, the Advisory Opinion No. 31 supports UN Agenda 2030, SDG 13 (climate action) and SDG 14, which is about conservation and sustainable use of the oceans, seas and marine resources. Here, support is urgently needed: according to the *UN Sustainable Development Report 2023*, "*the ocean is in a state of emergency.*"[169]

The Advisory Opinion No. 31 is not only important for the 169 State Parties. Given the broad ratification by 169 Parties, UNCLOS is the most important source of international law of the sea and maritime protection law.[170] Moreover today, UNCLOS, even with its innovations (with the exception of the regulation of deep-sea mining) is largely considered *customary international law*.[171] As customary international law, it also legally binds states that have not signed UNCLOS, such as the USA, Israel and Türkiye.

4. UNGA Resolution 2022 – Human right to a good and healthy environment

Environmental protection in conjunction with human rights has been discussed at the international level for several years. The focus is on a

167 ITLOS, Advisory Opinion Case No. 31, 21 May 2024, para. 441, 273, 276, 277.

168 ITLOS, Advisory Opinion Case No. 31, 21 May 2024, para. 441; see the commentary by *Korey Silverman-Roati/Maxim Bönnemann*, The ITLOS Advisory Opinion on Climate Change: An introduction into the joint blog symposium, VerfBlog, 2024/5/22, https://verfassungsblog.de/the-itlos-advisory-opinion-on-climate-change/, DOI: 10.59704/8034cca584b1594b; on due diligence see *Kate McKenzie*, Sorgfaltspflichten – Der Stand der Dinge aus der Perspektive des Meeresklimas, Klima und Recht (KlimR) 2024, p. 7, 10 f.

169 *UN* (footnote 92) The Sustainable Development Goals Report, Special edition 2023, p. 40.

170 *Markus Krajewski*, Völkerrecht, 2nd edition Baden-Baden 2020, § 14 p. 346 para. 9.

171 *Herdegen* (footnote 87), § 31 p. 247 para. 5 with reference to ICJ, Territorial and Maritime Dispute (Nicaragua v. Colombia), ICJ Reports 2012, p. 624, p. 673 ff. para. 137 ff. - customary character of UNCLOS in relation to the exclusive economic zone, the continental shelf and the status of islands; *Krajewski* (footnote 170), § 14 p. 346 para. 9; *Tullio Treves (Judge of the ITLOS from 1996-2011)*, UN Convention on the Law of the Sea, United Nations Audiovisual Library of International Law, 2008, p. 1, 4, https://legal.un.org/avl/pdf/ha/uncls/uncls_e.pdf.

universal human right to a good and healthy environment.[172] This is based on the insight that ecological framework conditions are crucial for a dignified life. The current environmental and climate crisis lead to existential threats to present and future societies and their individual members. It is therefore obvious that ecological and climate framework conditions can be part of human rights guarantees.[173] This became clear as early as 1997 in the dissenting opinion of the Vice-President of the ICJ *Weeramantry* on the ICJ's Gabčíkovo-Nagymaros judgement: "*The protection of the environment is likewise a vital part of contemporary human rights doctrine, for it is a sine qua non for numerous human rights such as the right to health and the right to life itself.*"[174]

On 28 July 2022, the UN General Assembly confirmed the "*human right to a clean, healthy and sustainable environment*" by adopting a resolution of the same name[175] - 161 votes in favour (of 169 states present), 8 abstentions[176] and no votes against.[177] This result shows a clear legal conviction of almost all states worldwide. According to the resolution, which explicitly refers to the 2030 Agenda, the universal human right to a clean, healthy and sustainable environment is derived from other human rights enshrined in legally binding international agreements. This is decisive. The legal base can

172 On the associated controversial concept of" third generation human rights" (rights to development, environmental protection, democracy, peace, etc.) cf. *Christian Tomuschat*, Human rights: between idealism and realism, Oxford/New York, 2003, p. 24 ff.; see also *Ulrich Beyerlin*, Umweltschutz und Menschenrechte, ZaöRV 2005, p. 525 ff.; in view of climate protection, Report of the Special Rapporteur on the issue of human rights obligations relating to the enjoyment of a safe, clean, healthy and sustainable environment, *David R. Boyd*, UN Doc. A/74/161, 15 July 2019, p. 10 ff.

173 *Beyerlin*, ZaöRV 2005, p. 525 f.; *Rüdiger Breuer/Klaus F. Gärditz*, Öffentliches und privates Wasserrecht, 4th edition, Munich 2017, "Ökologische Menschenrechte", p. 122 f. para. 223; with a special focus on the existential natural resource of water and the human right to water, derived from Art. 11 and Art. 12 ICESCR, see *Laskowski* (footnote 34), p. 163 ff.; *Mark Williams/Sharmila Murthy*, Reconciling the carbon market and the human right to water: the role of suppressed demand under clean development mechanism and the gold standard, Environmental Law, Vol. 43, no. 3, 2013, p. 517, 545 ff.; *Gärditz*, in: Wolfgang Kahl (ed.), Nachhaltigkeit als Verbundbegriff, 2008, p. 137, 161.

174 ICJ, Gabcikovo-Nagymaros Project (Hungary/Slovakia), 25 September 1997, No. 92, I.C.J. Reports 1997, p. 7, separate opinion of Vice-President *Weeramantry*, p. 88, 91, https://www.icj-cij.org/sites/default/files/case-related/92/092-19970925-JUD-01-03-EN.pdf.

175 UN Doc. A/RES/76/300.

176 China, Russian Federation, Belarus, Cambodia, Iran, Syria, Kyrgyzstan and Ethiopia.

177 Official Records: A/76/PV.97.

be found there, regardless of the mere "soft law" quality of the UN General Assembly resolution itself. The right can be derived from the guarantees under the ICCPR and the ICESCR. As partial element, the right to a non-toxic environment can be identified.[178]

a. UN Human Right Covenants

The legal base for a *human right to a good, healthy and sustainable environment* can be found in the *International Covenant on Civil and Political Rights (ICCPR / UN Civil Covenant)* that was adopted by the UN General Assembly on 16 December 1966,[179] together with the *International Covenant on Economic, Social and Cultural Rights (ICESCR / UN Social Covenant).*[180] Both came into force under international law in 1976. Germany and Türkiye are states party to the Covenants.[181] Upon entry into force, the conventions have a comprehensive binding effect on the parties ("pacta sunt servanda"), Art. 26 Vienna Convention on the Law of Treaties.[182] Today, both covenants are seen as core instruments of universal human rights.[183] Though the covenants do not explicitly regulate the human right to a healthy environment, both covenants include certain human rights which can be seen as basis for the derivation of this human right:

Regarding the *ICCPR* that primarily contains rights to freedom, such as the right to self-determination of all peoples under Art. 1. The base for the human right to a healthy environment can be found in the right to life under Art. 6 and the protection of private life and the family under Art. 17 ICCPR.

---

178 UN Doc. A/RES/76/300, p. 1-3, para. 3, 6, p. 15 ff. para. 67 ff. referring to human rights institutions and courts.

179 UN General Assembly resolution 2200A (XXI) of 16 December 1966, entry into force 23 March 1976, UN, Treaty Series, vol. 999, p. 171 and vol. 1057, p. 40; 174 parties, see UN Treaty Collection, https://treaties.un.org/.

180 UN General Assembly resolution 2200A (XXI) of 16 December 1966, entry into force 3 January 1976, UN, Treaty Series, vol. 993, p. 3; 172 parties, see UN Treaty Collection, https://treaties.un.org/.

181 Both German states (German Federal Republic and German Democratic Republic, reunified since 3 October 1990) have ratified the conventions in 1973, Türkiye in 2003; for the status of ratification see UN Treaty Collection, https://treaties.un.org/.

182 Cf. *Kämmerer*, in Proelß (footnote 87), section 1, p. 75 para. 105.

183 *Herdegen*, (footnote 88) § 48 para. 3, 8 ff., 13 ff.; *Marcel Kau*, in Proelß (footnote 87), section 3, p. 331 ff. para. 255 ff. In addition, there are other international human rights treaties, see UN Treaty Collection, CHAPTER IV: Human Rights, https://treaties.un.org/.

In view of the First Optional Protocol, which came into force in 1976 and regulates the right to individual complaints,[184] the ICCPR is considered justiciable.

Regarding the *ICESCR,* states are obliged to realize economic, social and cultural rights, including the right to self-determination under Art. 1, to an adequate standard of living for individuals and their families under Art. 11 and to health under Art. 12. The base for the human right to a clean, healthy and sustainable environment can be found especially in Art. 11 and Art. 12 – like the human right to water and sanitation which is derived from Art. 11 and Art. 12 ICESCR[185] in connection with the General Comment No. 15 (2002).[186] The ICESCR-rights contain the material framework conditions for individual existence in appropriate living conditions.[187] According to Art. 2 (1) ICESCR, states are obliged to "achieve the full realisation of the rights (...) gradually by all appropriate means". Art. 2 aims at a progressive approximation to the specified level of guarantees.[188] Against the background of the Optional Protocol to the ICESCR from 2008[189] which entered into force on 5 May 2013 and provides for individuals and groups of individuals to submit individual complaints to the *Committee on Economic, Social and Cultural Rights* (Art. 2 ff.), the previously held view that the human rights of the ICESCR - in

184 Optional Protocol to the International Covenant on Civil and Political Rights of 16 December 1966, entry into force on 23 March 1976, UN, Treaty Series , vol. 999, p. 171; Germany ratified it in 1993, Türkiye in 2006. The Second Optional Protocol on the Abolition of the Death Penalty of 15 December 1989 entered into force on 11 July 1991, UN, Treaty Series, vol. 1642, p.414; Germany ratified it in 1993, Türkiye in 2006, see UN Treaty Collection, https://treaties.un.org/.

185 Cf. UN Doc. A/HRC/49/53, 12 January 2022, The right to a clean, healthy and sustainable environment: non-toxic environment - Report of the Special Rapporteur on the issue of human rights obligations relating to the enjoyment of a safe, clean, healthy and sustainable environment, *David R. Boyd* - with the collaboration of the Special Rapporteur on the implications for human rights of the environmentally sound management and disposal of hazardous substances and wastes, *Marcos Orellana* -, p. 11 para. 47: "a wide range of human rights, including the rights to life, health, water, food, housing (...), adequate standard of living".

186 UN Doc/E/C.12/2002; see also *Laskowski,* Time for Implementation of the Right to Water and Sanitation—e.g. The Missing Implementation in Germany, Journal for European Environmental & Planning Law (JEEPL) 2012 Vol. 9(2), p. 164ff; *Laskowski,* Zugang zu Wasser für den menschlichen Gebrauch für alle auch in Deutschland, ZUR 2022, p. 641; *Laskowski,* Weltwassertag 2025, ZUR 2025, p. 193.

187 *Herdegen,* (footnote 88) § 48 para. 13.

188 *Herdegen,* (footnote 88) § 48 para. 13.

189 ILM 48 (2009), p. 256 ff.

contrast to the human rights of the ICCPR - are too vague and not justiciable, can now be considered outdated.[190]

Today, civil and political rights (ICCPR), together with economic, social and cultural rights (ICESCR), are seen as an inseparable unit, as a global human rights system. Together with the *Universal Declaration of Human Rights* (1948),[191] the covenants form the *International Bill of Human Rights.*[192] Although there is no consensus on the legally binding effect of the Universal Declaration of Human Rights[193] - the spectrum of opinion ranges from non-binding to ius cogens[194] -, today there is widespread opinion that nearly all human rights enshrined therein are to be regarded as "fundamental human rights" that apply under customary international law.[195] Overall, human

190 As here *Krajewski* (footnote 170), § 12 p. 310, no. 112; *German Federal Administrative Court* (BVerwG), 29. April 2009 - 6 C 16/08 -, para. 46 ff., https://www.bverwg.de/290409U6C16.08.0; *Nico Schrijver*, Fifty years international human rights covenants improving the global protection of human rights by bridging the gap between the two covenants, NTM|NJCM-Bull. 41 (2016), no. 4, p. 457, 459, 460 f., 463; *Christian Courtis*, The Right to Food as a Justiciable Right: Challenges and Strategies, Max Planck UNYB 11 (2007), S. 317 ff.; *Laskowski* (footnote 34), 2010, p. 174 ff., 193; probably also *Kau* (footnote 183), section 3, p. 332, 333, para. 258 ff.

191 Universal Declaration of Human Rights, G.A. res. 217A (III), U.N. Doc A/810 at 71 (1948). The Declaration was proclaimed by the UN General Assembly in Paris on 10 December 1948 "as a common standard of achievement for all peoples and all nations" (Preamble) and explicitly named as "International Bill of Human Rights".

192 The International Bill of Rights is understood as overview of those standards that are expressed in the Universal Declaration of Human Rights, the ICCPR and the ICESCR which have been given the status of customary international law, cf. *Moritz Renner/Johan Horst* in: Jörg P. Terhechte, Verwaltungsrecht der EU (ed.), 2nd edition, Baden-Baden 2022, § 42 para. 29.

193 See the overview by *Kau* (footnote 183) section 3, p. 329, 330, para 253 ff.

194 Against legally binding effect: *Volker Epping*, in Ipsen, Völkerrecht, 7th edition 2018, § 7 para. 11; different view *Hector Gros Espiell*, The Evolving Concept of Human Rights: Western, Socialist and Third World Approaches, in B. Ramcharan (ed.), Human Rights: Thirty Years After the Universal Declaration, The Hague 1979, p. 41, 46 ff.; for customary law validity of most of the rights contained in the UDHR *Stephan Hobe*, Einführung in das Völkerrecht, 11th edition 2020, p. 424 ff.

195 So *Hobe* (footnote 194), p. 424 ff.; see also *Jerome J. Shestack*, Globalization of Human Rights Law, Fordham International Law Journal 1997, Vol.21, Issue 2, p. 558, 568: "fundamental human rights principles have become universal by virtue of their entry into international law as jus cogens, customary law, or by convention"; *Javaid Rehmann*, International Human Rights law. A practical approach, Harlow 2003, p. 23 referring to *Ian Brownlie*, Principles of Public International law, 4th edition Oxford 1990, p. 513.; *Renner/Horst* (footnote 192), § 42 para. 29.

rights today are universal, indivisible, interdependent and interrelated.[196] According to today´s understanding, there are three different dimensions of state obligations arising from international human rights: the state duty to respect, to protect and to fulfil.[197] Hence, states have the obligation to respect, protect and promote the human right to a clean, healthy, sustainable and non-toxic environment.[198]

b. African Charter on Human and Peoples' Rights

So far, the human right to a healthy environment has only been explicitly regulated in two regional human rights treaties. One is the *African Charter on Human and Peoples' Rights.*[199] According to Art. 24 of the Charter, "*all peoples shall have the right to a general satisfactory environment favourable to their development.*"

c. American Convention on Human Rights and San Salvador Additional Protocol

Furthermore, Art. 11 of the *San Salvador Additional Protocol to the American Convention on Human Rights in the Fields of Economic, Social and Cultural Rights*[200] includes the right to a healthy environment: "*Everyone shall have the right to live in a healthy environment and to have access to basic public services.*"[201] In its legal opinion of 15 November 2017 on "*Environment and Human Rights*", the *Inter-American Court of Human Rights* (IACtHR) clarified the environmental guarantees of the *American Convention on Human Rights,* referring to the right to life in Art. 4:[202] "*In order to respect and ensure*

196 See World Conference on Human Rights (25 June 1993), 'Vienna Declaration and Programme of Action', UN Doc A/CONF. 157/23, adopted by consensus.

197 Cf. *Krajewski* (footnote 170), § 12 p. 295, no. 42 ff.

198 UNGA Doc. A/RES/76/300, p. 3, 6 f. para 21 ff., p. 19, para. 86.

199 African (Banjul) Charter on human and peoples´ rights, adopted on 27 June 1981, entered into force on 21 October 1986, OAU Doc. CAB/LEG/67/3 rev. 5, 21 I.L.M. 58 (1982).

200 OAS Treaty Series No. 69, OEA/Ser.A/44, the Protocol was adopted on 17 November 1988, entry into force: 16 November 1999. American Convention on Human Rights "Pact of San Jose, Costa Rica" (B-32), OAS, Treaty Series, No. 36, adopted on 22 November 1969, entry into force: 18 July 1978.

201 More on this see *Ulrich Beyerlin*, ZaöRV 2005, p. 525 f.

202 Corte Interamericana de Derechos Humanos, OpiniónConsultiva OC-23/17, 15 Novembre 2017,

the rights to life and integrity of persons under their jurisdiction, States are obliged to prevent significant environmental damage within or outside their territory".[203] The responsibility of the states with regard to cross-border environmental damage – which already follows from the *prohibition of (significant) transboundary environmental damage* under customary international law (No-Harm-Rule, Trial Smelter)[204] – is noticeably expanded, with reference to the *human right to life* which is a universal human right, also enshrined in Art. 6 ICCPR and Art. 3 of the Universal Declaration of Human Rights, as well as in Art. 2 ECHR.

On 9 January 2023, a new advisory opinion of the IACtHR on the climate crisis and human rights was requested by the Republic of Colombia and the Republic of Chile. The states asked the court "*to clarify the scope of State obligations, in their individual and collective dimension, in order to respond to the climate emergency within the framework of international human rights law, paying special attention to the differentiated impacts of this emergency on individuals from diverse regions and population groups, as well as on nature and on human survival on our planet.*"[205] The advisory opinion will contribute to the understanding of the universal right to a good, healthy and sustainable environment; it is not available yet.[206]

d. European Convention on Human Rights

The *European Convention for the Protection of Human Rights and Fundamental Freedoms (ECHR)*[207] expressly does not regulate a human right to a

Solicitada por la Republica de Colombia, Medio Ambiente y Derechos Humanos, https://corteidh.or.cr/docs/opiniones/seriea_23_esp.pdf.

203 Corte Interamericana de Derechos Humanos (footnote 229), p. 97 para. 5. For details, see *Till Markus/Pedro Pablo Silva-Sánchez*, Zum Schutz der Umwelt durch die Amerikanische Menschenrechtskonvention: Das Gutachten des IAGMR OC-23/2017, ZUR 2019, p. 150, 152 ff.

204 Cf. *Till Markus/Roda Verheyen* (footnote 60), Chapter § 1 p. 27 no. 59.

205 Request for an advisory opinion on the Climate Emergency and Human Rights submitted to the Inter-American Court of Human Rights, p. 1, https://www.corteidh.or.cr/docs/opiniones/soc_1_2023_en.pdf.

206 See IACtHR, https://www.corteidh.or.cr/observaciones_oc_new.cfm?nId_oc=2634.

207 The ECHR is legally binding the 46 member states of the Council of Europe, including Türkiye and Germany and all other Members States of the EU. Due to the war of aggression against Ukraine starting 24 February 2022, the 47th member, the Russian Federation, was excluded, see the decision of the Committee of Ministers of 16 March 2022, CM/Del/Dec(2022)1428ter/2.3.

healthy environment. Therefore, so far, the ECtHR denied an explicit right to a clean and healthy environment. At the same time, however, the ECtHR emphasised that the right to respect for private and family life under Art. 8 ECHR may be applicable if a person is directly and seriously affected by noise or other environmental pollution.[208] The Court derived an *environment-related human right* from Art. 8 ECHR which protects against environmental hazards and imposes a corresponding state responsibility to protect.[209] Furthermore, the ECtHR has clarified that the right to life under Art. 2 ECHR can also be affected if there is a 'real and immediate' danger to life, e.g. in cases of dangerous activities that lead to industrial or environmental disasters.[210]

5. ECtHR judgment 2024 – Human right to effective climate protection

On 9 April 2024, the ECtHR has set a new course with the historic "climate decision".[211] The Court derived a new "human right to effective climate protection" from Art. 8 EHCR and Art. 2 ECHR. The lawsuit was brought by Swiss women, all of whom were on average 73 years old, and an association that

208 See ECtHR (Fifth Section), 12 May 2009, 18215/06 (Greenpeace e.V. and others/Germany), p. 4; ECtHR, 8 July 2003, 36022/97 (Hatton and others/United Kingdom), para. 96, ECHR 2003-VIII; ECtHR, 9 December 1994, 16798/90 (López Ostra/Spain), para. 51, Series A no. 303-C.; see also *Birgit Peters,* Zur Anwendbarkeit der europäischen Menschenrechtskonvention in Umwelt- und Klimaschutzfragen, Archiv des Völkerrechts (AVR) 2021 (59), p. 164 ff.

209 See ECtHR (Grand Chamber), 8 July 2003, 36022/97 (Hatton and others/United Kingdom), para. 96, ECHR 2003-VIII; ECtHR (Forth Section), 20 September 2011, 25002/09 (Frankowski and others/Polen), ECLI:CE:ECHR:2011:0920DEC002500209; ECtHR (Second Section), 10 January 2012, 30765/08 (di Sarno and Others v. Italy), ECLI:CE:ECHR:2012:0110JUD003076508; ECtHR (Fith Section), 4 September 2014, 42488/02 (Dzemyuk/Ukraine), ECLI:CE:ECHR:2014:0904JUD004248802.

210 See ECtHR, 17 November 2015 (final 2 May 2016), 14350/05, 15245/05 and 16051/05 (M. Özel and others/Türkiye), para. 171 – earthquake, magnitude of 7.4 on the Richter scale; ECtHR (Grand Chamber), 30 April 2004, Nr. 48939/99 (Öneryıldı z /Türkiye), ECHR 2004 XII – risks of waste-collection sites, methane explosion; see also ECtHR, 9 April 2024, 53600/20, (Verein KlimaSeniorinnen Schweiz), para. 507 f., 513.

211 ECtHR, 9 April 2024, 53600/20 (Verein KlimaSeniorinnen Schweiz). The ECtHR held, by a majority of 16 votes to one, that there had been a violation of Art. 8 of the ECHR and, unanimously, that there had been a violation of Art. 6 (1) (access to court). Two other appeals were dismissed by the Court as inadmissible: ECtHR (Grand Chamber), 9 April 2024, 7189/21 (Carême/France); ECtHR (Grand Chamber), 9 April 2024, 39371/20 (Duarte Agostinho ua/Portugal and 32 other States).

campaigns for climate protection and to which the elderly Swiss women belonged. The women saw their health particularly endangered by increasingly severe and longer-lasting heat waves because of climate change. The aim was to force the Swiss legislator and government to introduce stricter climate laws and measures. The decision is remarkable and convincing.[212]

First of all, it should be emphasized that the decision is explicitly based on the current scientific findings on climate change. The ECtHR stated that climate change is a **science-based fact,** endangering the realisation of human rights - and that the risks are lower if global warming is limited to 1.5° Celsius.[213] The Court included the results of the first global stocktaking of the COP28 (2023)[214] and made clear, that limiting the global warming to 1.5° Celsius is decisive with regard to UNFCCC and PA. On this basis the ECtHR concluded: The serious risk of damage to human rights through the omission of necessary climate protection measures is sufficient to justify a violation of the human right under Art. 8 ECHR – because Art. 8 ECHR encompasses "*a right for individuals to effective protection by the State authorities from serious adverse effects of climate change on their life, health, well-being and quality of life*",[215] in short: the **human right to effective climate protection.**

In the end, the Court affirmed violations of Art. 8 ECHR by Swiss authorities for failing to implement sufficient measures to combat climate change. However, the ECtHR also referred to Art. 2 ECHR, which was not examined

212 Approving *Philipp Eschenhagen,* Anmerkung zum EGMR-Urteil „Verein KlimaSeniorinnen
Schweiz and Others v. Switzerland", Klima und Recht (KlimR) 2024, p. 147; *Uwe M. Erling,* „KlimaSeniorinnen": Das Urteil des EGMR, Zeitschrift für nachhaltige Unternehmensführung (ESGZ) 2024, 31 f.; *Ludger Giesberts/Dario Westarp,* Reichweite und Auswirkungen des EGMR-Urteils für Menschenrechte zum Klimaschutz - Besprechung des Urteils vom 09.04.2024 (Antrag Nr. 53600/20), Zeitschrift für materielles und prozessuales Klimarecht (KlimaRZ) 2024, p. 73 ff.; *Julia Hänni,* Essentialia und Leitlinien zum Klimaschutz für die Mitgliedstaaten des Europarats/Verein KlimaSeniorinnen gegen die Schweiz (EGMR-Urteil, 9. April 2024), Europäische Grundrechte Zeitschrift (EuGRZ) 2024, p. 25 ff.;
critical of climate lawsuits *Bernhard W. Wegener,* Menschenrecht auf Klimaschutz?, NJW 2022, p. 425 ff.

213 See ECtHR, 9 April 2024, 53600/20, (Verein KlimaSeniorinnen Schweiz), para. 436, 456.

214 ECtHR, 9 April 2024, 53600/20, (Verein KlimaSeniorinnen Schweiz), para. 140, 417.

215 ECtHR, 9 April 2024, 53600/20, (Verein KlimaSeniorinnen Schweiz), para. 435, 440, 519.

separately only because the Court proceeded on the basis of largely the same principles in Art. 2 and Art. 8 ECHR.[216]

a. Admissibility of the action

The ECtHR surprisingly denied the applicant elderly women's right to bring an action. From the ECtHR´s point of view, they had not proven that their health was particularly endangered by climate change and its effects. Therefore, the **individual applicants** lacked the necessary "victim status", Art. 34 ECHR.[217] On the other hand – and this is of great importance – the plaintiff association, which campaigned for climate protection and represented the rights of the female climate seniors, was recognised as having standing to appeal. This was the first time that an association has been recognised by the ECtHR as having standing in an environmental case. The Court derived this **right of action for associations** from the ECHR. It also considered the Aarhus Convention,[218] which has been signed and ratified by most of the European Council states - including all EU Member States and the EU, Switzerland, not Türkiye.[219] But ultimately, the Aarhus Convention was not decisive. The ECHR was.[220] It is true that the Court has been guided by the requirements of the Aarhus Convention in order to exclude an *actio popularis* - without adopting them, because the Convention has a different objective.[221] According to the ECtHR, an association with legal standing must fulfil certain require-

216 ECtHR, 9 April 2024, 53600/20, (Verein KlimaSeniorinnen Schweiz), para. 538.

217 ECtHR, 9 April 2024, 53600/20, (Verein KlimaSeniorinnen Schweiz), para. 527. Similar European General Court (Second chamber), Order of 8 May 2019, T-330/18 (Carvalho et. al. v. European Parliament and Council of the EU, lack of individual concern, inadmissibility), ECLI:EU:T:2019:324 and CJEU (Sixth Chamber), 25 March 2021, C-565/19 P, (Armando Carvalho, lack of individual concern), ECLI:EU:C:2021:252 – climate litigation. Rightly critical *Claudio Franzius*, Klimaklagen – warum tut sich der EuGH so schwer?, ZUR 2023, p. 650 ff.; *Gerd Winter*, Armando Carvalho et alii versus Europäische Union: Rechtsdogmatische und staatstheoretische Probleme einer Klimaklage vor dem Europäischen Gericht, ZUR 2019, p. 259 ff.; see also *Verheyen*, Klagen für Klimaschutz, Zeitschrift für Rechtspolitik (ZRP) 2021, p. 133 ff.

218 UNECE Convention on Access to Information, Public Participation in Decision-making and Access to Justice in Environmental Matters – with annexes – Aarhus/Denmark, 25 June 1998, entry into force: 30 October 2001, (Aarhus Convention), UN Treaty Series, vol. 2161, p. 447.

219 47 parties, see UN Treaty Collection, https://treaties.un.org/.

220 ECtHR, 9 April 2024, 53600/20, para. 492 ff., 499.

221 ECtHR, 9 April 2024, 53600/20, para. 501-503.

ments: It must be "*lawfully established in the jurisdiction concerned or have standing to act there*", furthermore "*able to demonstrate that it pursues a dedicated purpose in accordance with its statutory objectives in the defence of the human rights of its members or other affected individuals within the jurisdiction concerned, whether limited to or including collective action for the protection of those rights against the threats arising from climate change*" and "*demonstrate that it can be regarded as genuinely qualified and representative to act on behalf of members or other affected individuals (…) who are subject to specific threats or adverse effects of climate change on their lives, health or well-being as protected under the Convention.*"[222] Furthermore, it can be relevant "*whether, and to what extent, its individual members or other affected individuals may have enjoyed access to a court in the same or related domestic proceedings.*"[223]

b. Merits of the action

The Court interprets the ECtHR in accordance with international law, in particular the climate protection agreements to which all signatory states to the ECHR have committed themselves – the UNFCCC, PA and related documents. In addition, the ECtHR refers to the principle of sustainability and calls for an "*intergenerational burden-sharing, both in regard to different generations of those currently living and in regard to future generations*".[224] Moreover, the "principle of common but differentiated responsibilities and respective capabilities of states", Art. 3 (1) UNFCCC and Art. 2 (2) PA, is emphasised.[225] In this regard the Court made clear, a state´s responsibility is determined "*on the basis of its own conduct and by reference to its own international obligations.*"[226]

The ECtHR also includes UN *soft law* documents in its argumentation, in particular the above-mentioned UN Resolution on the **human right to a clean, healthy and sustainable environment**" of 2022 - 45 out of 46 member States of the Council of Europe (ECHR parties) voted in favour of that UN

222 ECtHR, 9 April 2024, 53600/20, para. 502.
223 ECtHR, 9 April 2024, 53600/20, para. 503.
224 ECtHR, 9 April 2024, 53600/20, para. 419.
225 ECtHR, 9 April 2024, 53600/20, para. 442.
226 ECtHR, 9 April 2024, 53600/20, para. 443.

resolution, one was absent.[227] The resolution clearly shows the legal recognition of the human right by the EHCR parties. Moreover, looking closer to the derivation of the **human right to climate protection** pursuant to Art. 8 and Art. 2 ECHR, it shows an overlap with Art. 6 ICCPR (right to life) and Art. 17 ICCPR (right to private and family life).[228] For the ECtHR, it is not decisive whether UN resolutions themselves – "soft law"– lead to specific legal obligations. Regarding UN resolution 76/300 and also Council of Europe Recommendation CM/Rec(2022)20, the ECtHR recognizes "*a development as part of the international-law context in which the Court assesses Convention issues before it (...), notably as regards the recognition by the Contracting Parties of a close link between the protection of the environment and human rights*".[229]

Moreover, the ECtHR defines **a new role for courts** in the climate context. Because "*climate change is a common concern of humankind*",[230] the Court stressed **courts today** have a **special role** in connection with **climate lawsuits,** – in line with the *UN High Commissioner for Human Rights.*[231] Courts should address the impacts of environmental harms on the enjoyment of human rights[232] and help to enforce effective climate protection contributions by states in accordance with the obligations of the Paris Agreement to which all ECHR-States are bound.[233] Apparently, the ECtHR sees a collective dimension of human rights, a "common global concern".[234]

Furthermore, the ECtHR **concretises** the **state's obligation to protect the climate**, which arises from the ECHR. Not every climate protection measure is sufficient. Rather, **effective** government measures are needed in line with the Paris Agreement and the 1.5 ° C target. It is about the state protection of the lives of citizens from the dangers of environmental and climate change in a timely and effective manner.[235] The ECHR protects actual rights, not theoretical or illusory ones.[236]

227 UN Doc. A/RES/76/300; Türkiye is missing, it does not appear in the Official records as a voting country. In addition the ECtHR refers to resolution 48/13 of October 2021 by the UN Human Rights Council, recognising the human right to a healthy environment, see ECtHR, 9 April 2024, 53600/20, para. 144 f., 173.
228 See ECtHR, 9 April 2024, 53600/20, para. 171.
229 See ECtHR , 9 April 2024, 53600/20, para. 448.
230 ECtHR, 9 April 2024, 53600/20, para. 420, 436, 451.
231 ECtHR, 9 April 2024, 53600/20, para. 376.
232 ECtHR, 9 April 2024, 53600/20, para. 451.
233 ECtHR, 9 April 2024, 53600/20, para. 445-451, 456.
234 Cf. *Julia Hänni*, EuGRZ 2024, p. 25 ff.
235 ECtHR, 9 April 2024, 53600/20, para. 538.
236 ECtHR, 9 April 2024, 53600/20, para. 538.

In addition, the **importance of sustainable climate protection** in the context of **weighing up decisions** becomes clear. Climate protection should be given considerable weight in the weighing-up *"of any competing considerations"* because of the "*urgency of combating the adverse effects of climate change (...), including the grave risk of their reaching the point of irreversibility*".[237] The measures must consider the "generations of those currently living" - who fall under the jurisdiction of a particular ECHR-Contracting Party - and "future generations". They are "*likely to bear an increasingly severe burden of the consequences of present failures and omissions to combat climate change*" and "*have no possibility of participating in the relevant current decision-making processes*".[238] In short: State measures must be (ecologically) sustainable.

In conclusion, the human right to effective climate protection is enshrined in Art. 8 and Art. 2 ECHR - in consistent further development of its case-law on environment-related human rights. All ECHR states are bound by this. Since climate protection is part of environmental protection, it stands to reason that a **human right to effective and sustainable environmental protection** can also be derived from Articles 8 and 2 ECHR – in line with the human right to a clean, healthy and sustainable environment. Lawsuits before the ECtHR by environmental associations that meet the criteria laid down by the Court seem quite likely.

6. Other European Courts – Climate lawsuits on effective climate protection

As part of its argumentation, the ECtHR comparatively looked at the climate case law of other European courts, in particular the following:

Supreme Court of the Netherlands 2019: In the decision of 20 December 2019 of the "*Hoge Raad*" – *State of the Netherlands v. Stichting Urgenda* – the Supreme Court upheld the lower courts' order directing the State of the Netherlands to reduce greenhouse gas emissions by the end of 2020 by at least 25% compared to 1990.[239] The Supreme Court referred explicitly to Art. 2 and Art. 8 ECHR and stated that courts "*can and may conclude that the State is obliged to achieve that reduction, due to the risk of dangerous climate change*

237 ECtHR, 9 April 2024, 53600/20, para. 436, 542.

238 ECtHR, 9 April 2024, 53600/20, para. 119, 410, 420.

239 Hoge Rad, 20 December 2019, NL:HR:2019:2007, cited from ECtHR, 9 April 2024, 53600/20, para. 256.

that could have a severe impact on the lives and welfare of the residents of the Netherlands."[240]

German Federal Constitutional Court 2021: In the Climate Order of the BVerfG of 24 March 2021,[241] the Court examined four constitutional complaints directed against certain provisions of the Federal Climate Change Act (KSG) of 12 December 2019 and against a State's failure to take effective measures to reduce greenhouse gas emissions.[242] The Court found that the provisions of the KSG/2019 were incompatible with fundamental rights in so far as they did not contain sufficient requirements for further emission reductions from 2031 onwards. Because emissions will have an impact on practically every kind of freedom, all aspects of human life are linked to greenhouse gas emissions and therefore were potentially at risk of drastic restrictions after 2030. Therefore, the challenged provisions of the KSG violated the freedoms of the partly very young complainants, as the provisions irreversibly shifted major emission reduction burdens to periods after 2030.[243] Surprisingly, the BVerfG did not find that the legislature had violated its constitutional duty to reduce greenhouse gas emissions and to protect the complainants from the risks of climate change, followed from the fundamental rights and the state´s duty to reach the climate goals in line with the Paris Agreement – unlike the ECtHR and ITLOS 2024 without focusing on the 1.5 ° Celsius target – , derived from Art. 20a BL.[244] However, the BVerfG left open the question of whether the BL contains a "*fundamental right to an ecological minimum subsistence level*" or a comparable "*right to a humane future*".[245] Anyway, the BVerfG affirmed the state obligation to protect against environmental degradation "*of catastrophic or even apocalyptic proportions*".[246]

French Conseil d'État 2021/2023: In the "Grande-Synthe case" (municipalty of Grande-Synthe)[247] the Conseil has decided on 1 July 2021 that the measures taken by the French authorities to combat climate change had not been sufficient and ordered the Government to take all necessary measures

240 See ECtHR, 9 April 2024, 53600/20, para. 261.
241 BVerfG, 24 March 2021, 1 BvR 2656/18, BVerfGE 157, p. 30 – see footnote 45.
242 See ECtHR, 9 April 2024, 53600/20, para. 254, 255.
243 ECtHR, 9 April 2024, 53600/20, para. 256.
244 BVerfG, 24 March 2021, 1 BvR 2656/18, BVerfGE 157, p. 30 headnote no. 2. – see footnote 45.
245 BVerfG, 24 March 2021, 1 BvR 2656/18, BVerfGE 157, p. 30 para. 113.
246 BVerfG, 24 March 2021, 1 BvR 2656/18, BVerfGE 157, p. 30 para. 114 f.
247 Conseil d'État, 1 July 2021, No. 427301; see also ECtHR, 9 April 2024, 7189/21 (Carême v. France), ct. ECtHR, 9 April 2024, 53600/20, para. 236 ff.

by 31 March 2022 to reduce greenhouse gas emissions by 40% below 1990 levels by 2030 in order to comply with the UNFCCC, the Paris Agreement and the European commitments (Annex I Regulation (EU) 2018/842). On 10 May 2023[248] the Conseil decided that there was still no credible evidence that the greenhouse gas emission reduction trajectory could be effectively respected. Consequently, it ordered the Government to take new measures by 30 June 2024 and to provide a progress report with details on the measures and their effectiveness before.

7. Conclusion

The legal opinions and court decisions show that states are obliged to take effective and sustainable measures for climate protection under international law. This safeguards the natural foundations of life and protects universal and European human rights. Of particular importance for Germany, Türkiye and the EU Member States is the ECtHR's 2024 climate decision, in which it derived a new human right to effective climate protection from Art. 8 and Art. 2 ECHR. Although the ECtHR decisions are only directly binding on the contracting states that are parties to the court proceedings - in this case Switzerland - the decisions have a legal "guiding effect". The ECtHR's rulings become decisive for concretizing the human rights guarantees of the ECHR.[249] If states deviate from this interpretation, there is a strong risk of a violation of the ECHR. Germany and Türkiye as contracting parties to the EHCR[250] are comprehensively bound by the Convention (legislation, government, administration and judiciary).[251]

Federal Republic of Germany: In Germany, the ECHR ranks below the Basic Law (BL) in domestic law, Art. 59 (2) BL ("dualism"[252]). However, ac-

248 Conseil d'État, 10 May 2023, No. 467982, Commune de Grande-Synthe and others, https://www.conseil-etat.fr/en/news/greenhouse-gas-emissions-the-government-must-take-new-measures-and-submit-an-initial-report-by-the-end-of-the-year.

249 *Christoph Grabenwarter*, EMRK, 4th edition 2009, p. 98 para. 9.

250 The Federal Republic of Germany has ratified the ECHR on 7 August 1952; for the territory of the former GDR, the ECHR entered into force upon accession on 3 October 1990. The Republic of Türkiye has ratified the ECHR on 18 Mai 1954.

251 Cf. Meyer-Ladewig/Nettesheim/von Raumer, EMRK, 5th edition 2023, Art. 1 EMRK, para. 5, 6.

252 Dualism and monism as theoretical models in international law, cf. *Krajewski* (footnote 170), p. 102 para. 4-6; *Christine Amrhein-Hofmann*, Monismus und Dualismus in den Völkerrechtslehren, Berlin 2003, p. 300 ff.

cording to the BVerfG, the provisions of the BL must be interpreted in a manner that is "friendly" to international law. Consequently, in cases of doubt, German law must be interpreted in accordance with international law. The requirement of interpretation in conformity with international law is widely recognized in case law and in literature and applies to German constitutional law as well.[253] In this regard, international human rights treaties are primarily considered for interpretation in accordance with international law, as their guarantees often correspond to the fundamental rights of the Basic Law. This applies to the ECHR, but also to the ICCPR, the ICESCR or UN treaties on protection against discrimination.[254] The case law of international courts, in particular the ICJ and the ECtHR, must be taken into particular consideration.[255] At the level of constitutional law, especially the guarantees of the ECHR and the case law of the ECtHR serve as interpretative aids for determining the content and scope of fundamental rights and constitutional principles of the BL[256] – in the context of a methodically justifiable interpretation of the law.[257]

A comparable right to Art. 2 ECHR can be found in Art. 2 (2) BL (right to life and physical integrity).[258] With regard to Art. 8 ECHR, there is no explicit corresponding fundamental right in the BL; here, various fundamental rights are affected in sub-areas: Art. 1 BL - protection of human dignity; Art. 6 BL - marriage and family; Art. 10 BL - secrecy of correspondence; Art. 13 BL - home. There the Basic Law provides guarantees that encompass those of Art. 8 ECHR.[259] According to the ECtHR judgment 2024, Art. 2 and Art. 8 ECHR impose positive obligations on the state to effectively protect individuals against climate change that endangers life and health, intergenerational and future oriented, in short sustainable. Linked to this is the (new) "human right to effective climate protection", derived from Art. 8, Art. 2 EHCR. With regard to the case law of the BVerfG, it is to be expected that the climate decision by

253 Cf. *Mehrdad Payandeh* in: Uwe Kischel/Hanno Kube, Handbuch des Staatsrechts, Heidelberg 2024, 2. Gebot der völkerrechtskonformen Auslegung, para. 87 with further evidence.

254 *Niels Petersen* in: Kischel/Kube (footnote 253), C. Völkerrechtsfreundliche Auslegung, para. 22.

255 *Krajewski* (footnote 170), p. 106 para. 23.

256 Cf. BVerfGE 74, 358, 370; BVerfGE 111, p. 307, 317 f.; BVerfGE 149, p. 293, 328 - established case law.

257 Cf. BVerfGE 128, 326, 367 ff.; BVerfGE 148, 296, 354, 379.

258 Jarass/Pieroth/*Jarass*, Grundgesetz. Kommentar, 18th edition Munich 2024, Art. 2 Rn. 96.

259 Meyer-Ladewig et. al. (footnote 251), Art. 8 EMRK, para. 1.

the ECtHR will lead to an ECHR-compliant interpretation of Art. 2 (2) BL in conjunction with Art. 1 (human dignity) and Art. 20a BL (state mandate to environmental and climate protection; not a fundamental right) - and consequently to a new *fundamental right to effective climate protection*, derived from the BL. In addition, as climate protection is regarded as a sub-area of environmental protection, there is much to suggest that in future decisions of the ECtHR, the *human right to effective climate protection* will be further developed into the *human right to effective environmental protection*. It is therefore to be expected that *a fundamental right to effective environmental protection* will soon become visible in the Basic Law through the case law of the BVerfG as well.

This would be an ECHR-consistent further development of the previous environmental and climate case law of the BVerfG. According to this, the state is obliged to protect human life and physical integrity from unlawful interference by others[260] and from the dangers of environmental damages and climate change.[261] The fundamental rights in connection with Art. 20a BL protect across generations, "intertemporal".[262] Due to the Climate Order of 2021, protecting future freedom also requires the transition to climate neutrality, initiated by the state "in good time".[263] The protection by the state must be "appropriate and effective".[264] Violations of the state´s duty can be asserted by the holders of the fundamental rights.[265]

This sounds like the criteria of the decision of the ECtHR 2024, but it is not. Why? In fulfilling the duty to protect, the German legislator has so far had considerable "leeway in assessment, evaluation and design".[266] This means: state protection measures must not be "completely unsuitable or completely inadequate" or "fall significantly short of the protection goal".[267] Therefore, a breach of the state's duty to protect can hardly ever be considered. The BVerfG even denied a breach of the legislator's duty to protect life and physical integrity, Art. 2 (2) sentence 1 BL, with regard to the (partially) unconstitutional Climate Protection Act/KSG of 2019.[268] This ´legislator fri-

260 BVerfGE 157, p. 30, 111 para. 145 – Climate 2021; BVerfGE 115, p. 320, 346.
261 BVerfGE 157, p. 30, 111.
262 BVerfGE 157, p. 30, 111.
263 BVerfGE 157, p. 30, 168 f. para. 253.
264 BVerfGE 88, p. 203, 254.
265 BVerfGE 157, p. 30, 111 para. 145.
266 BVerfGE 157, p. 30, 114, 118, 124 para. 152, 162, 172; BVerfGE 159, p. 223 para. 171.
267 BVerfGE 142, p. 313 para. 152.
268 BVerfGE 157, p. 30, 116 para. 157.

endly´ view is now being changed by the ECtHR's 2024 climate decision. The appropriateness of "climate protection legislation" is now specified by the standard of "effectiveness" as defined by the ECtHR. The ECtHR demands demonstrably effective protective measures in connection with the binding climate targets of the PA, above all, compliance with the 1.5° C target. The actual effectiveness of climate (and environmental) protection measures will therefore be subject to stricter judicial review by the ECtHR in the future and probably also by the BVerfG.

Republic of Türkiye: Regarding the Turkish Constitution (TC), the fundamental rights can be found in Articles 12 – 74 TC. These fundamental rights are not only defensive rights against the state, but also against anyone who wants to expand their freedom at the expense of others (third-party effect). According to Art. 12 TC, the principle of social obligation applies to all fundamental rights.[269] The protection of fundamental rights in the TC is structurally and formally based on the constitutional norms of Western European countries and the ECHR.[270]

Regarding the decision of the ECtHR 2024, Art. 17, Art. 20, Art. 56 and Art. 90 TC come to the fore. In view of Art. 8 ECHR, the corresponding fundamental right can be found in Art. 20 TC. According to this, everyone has the right to demand respect for their private and family life.

In view of Art. 2 EMRK, the corresponding right can be found in Art. 17 TC which states that everyone has the right to the protection and development of their life and their material and non-material existence. Furthermore - different from Art. 20a BL (state objective, no fundamental right) -, Art. 56 TC regulates the *right to live in a healthy and balanced environment.* Art. 56 (1) TL stipulates: "*developing the environment, ensuring a healthy environment and preventing pollution are the duty of the state and citizens*". The wording of Art. 56 TC alone demands a strong climate and environmental commitment and strong climate and environmental action from the Turkish state and already speaks for a "right to effective climate and environmental protection". But in any case, an ECHR-compliant interpretation of Art. 56 TC in connection with Art. 17 and Art. 20 TC in the sense of the ECtHR decision 2024 is very much in favour of this. According to Art. 90 (5) TC, international treaties such as the ECHR carry great weight in the Turkish legal system. This

---

269 *Christian Rumpf*, Die Verfassung der Türkei, in: Bernd Rill/Hanns-Seidel-Stiftung (ed.), Türkische Innenpolitik, Argumente und Materialien zum Zeitgeschehen 86, Munich 2013, p. 29, 30.

270 *Christian Rumpf* (footnote 269), p. 29, 30.

is because, according to Art. 90 TC, if international treaties by which Türkiye is bound include fundamental rights and freedoms which do not correspond to statutory provisions with the same regulatory content in Turkish law, the provisions of the international treaties take precedence. This shows a monistic approach with the primacy of international law.[271] Since the ECtHR had repeatedly taken the view in the past that the ECHR does not contain a right to a healthy environment, this could be seen as the reason for the rather cautious interpretation of Art. 56 TC by the Turkish Constitutional Court so far – even though Art. 53 ECHR allows for more favourable provisions in national constitutions. But in view of the climate judgment of the ECtHR 2024, it is now to be expected that, in conjunction with Art. 90 TC, a "synchronization" with Art. 2 and Art. 8 ECHR will take place and a *fundamental right to effective climate protection* and a *fundamental right to effective environmental protection* will be derived from the Turkish Constitution soon.

European Union: In addition, the ECtHR's 2024 climate ruling will have an impact on EU law. In this context the Charter of Fundamental Rights of the European Union (EUCFR)[272] and Art. 2 TEU are important. According to Art. 52 (3) EUCFR, rights of the Charter must have "the same meaning and scope" as corresponding rights and guarantees of the ECHR. Art. 52 (3) EUCFR rules out any divergence between the Charter´s rights and human rights in the ECHR.[273] Under no circumstances should the protection afforded by the Charter be less than that afforded by the ECHR.[274] But according to Art. 52 (3) sentence 2 EUCFR, the EU is free to go beyond the ECHR´s guarantees by granting a higher level of protection for the rights enshrined in the Charter. In addition, Art. 53 EUCFR aims to avoid contradictions between the Charter and other fundamental rights under international law.[275] In view of the new human right to effective climate protection Art. 2, 7 and 37 EUCFR become relevant: Art. 2 EUCFR corresponds to Art. 2 ECHR, Art. 7 EUGRC corresponds to Art. 8 ECHR, in addition Art. 37 EUCFR (environmental protection) is significant – in short: the *minimum* granted by the Charter is a *fundamental right to effective climate protection in accordance with the EHCR/*

271 Monism and dualism cf. *Amrhein-Hofmann* and *Krajewski* (footnote 253).

272 Official Journal of the EU C 202, 7.6.2016, p. 389 ff. The EUCFR has the same legal value as the EU treaties.

273 Hans von der Groeben/Jürgen Schwarze/Armin Hatje/Jörg P. *Terhechte*, Europäisches Unionsrecht, 7th edition 2015, Art. 52 EUCFR para. 15.

274 *Terhechte* (footnote 278), Art. 52 EUCFR para. 15.

275 Cf. Jürgen Meyer/Sven Hölscheidt/Tilman *Hoppe*, Charta der Grundrechte der EU, 6th edition 2024, Art. 53 EUCFR para 13.

ECtHR 2024. Furthermore, there is every indication that the Charter also provides a basis for the *fundamental right to effective environmental protection.*

This has consequences for the EU member states and accession states. As EU member states implement EU law within the meaning of Art. 51 (1) sentence 1 alt. 2 EUCFR, the obligation to comply with the Charter applies in addition to the obligation to comply with the ECHR.[276] This results in a double commitment to the ECHR for the EU states – as signatory states of the ECHR and – stricter – as EU member states according to Art. 51 (1), Art. 52 (3) EUCFR. Accession states such as the Republic of Türkiye, which must adopt the EU acquis, must also comply with the EUCFR and the minimum protection of guarantees resulting from the ECHR and the ECtHR judgment.

Moreover - the obligation of all EU Member States to comply with human rights also arises from Art. 2 TEU. It contains the *fundamental values* of the EU, among others, the protection of human rights. The landmark ruling by the ECJ in 2023 ("Poland, rule of law")[277] made it clear that EU member states are bound by these fundamental values, even if they do not implement or apply EU law, but purely national law. It follows that the guarantees of the ECHR and universal human rights must be respected by all member states as fundamental values of the EU; this can be reviewed by the ECJ. Accession states such as Türkiye must adopt the EU acquis and thus also comply with the fundamental values under Art. 2 TEU.

V. Sustainable and Just Transformation Law

The legal elements of the concept of environmental and climate justice outlined above form the legal basis for a *new sustainable and just transformation law.* In view of the current environmental and climate crisis, the need for a far-reaching transformation of society and economy to climate neutrality in line with international law is evident. A coherent multi-level legal system is needed "*as a global response to the growing concern that development is out of balance*".[278] This implies necessarily "*the fast lane towards a low-carbon future*

276 Meyer/Hölscheidt/*Schwerdtfeger*, (footnote 275), Art. 52 EUCFR para. 52.

277 ECJ (Grand Chamber), 5 June 2023 - C-204/21 - European Comm. v. Republic of Polen, ECLI:EU:C:2023:442.

278 *Winfried Huck*, Die EU und die Globale Agenda 2030 der VN: Reflexion, Strategie und rechtliche Umsetzung, Europäische Zeitschrift für Wirtschaftsrecht (EuZW) 2019, p.

without nuclear energy" and an end of the "*the carbon-based economic model (…) as it endangers the climate system's stability, and therefore the natural life support system for future generations.*"[279] The *UNDP´s* "Environmental Justice Report 2022" concludes: "*The challenges related to addressing environmental justice, including climate justice, require equitable solutions and the respect, protection and fulfilment of human rights in the context of climate change mitigation and adaptation, biodiversity conservation and pollution control efforts.*"[280]

To strengthen the democratic legitimacy of the transformation process, the aspects of transparency and participation should be emphasized to enable an accompanying civil society process; access to court is of great importance.[281]

VI. Summery and Outlook

There is no way around the climate neutral, environmentally friendly, sustainable and just transformation in Germany, Türkiye, the EU and worldwide. National transformation as part of European and international transformation must be compatible with the requirements of European and international law.[282] This applies to EU member states and accession states (acquis communautaire). Here the binding provisions of the PA and the human right to effective climate (and environmental) protection, the human right to a good and healthy environment and the principle of sustainability, concretized by the UN Agenda 2030, are highly relevant - in accordance with climate and environmental justice.

581, 582; see also *Susan Ann Samuel*, 'Greening' International Law en route to Agenda 2030: The Role of Youth in Enhancing the Soft Power of Climate Justice, Yearbook of International Environmental Law, 2022, 33, p. 3 ff.; *Franke/Verheyen* (footnote 60), § 11, p. 738 para. 8.

279 *WBGU* 2011 (footnote 42), p. 1. Similar *UNEP*, Emissions Gap Report 2023: Broken Record – Temperatures hit new highs, yet world fails to cut emissions (again), 11/2023, https://www.unep.org/resources/emissions-gap-report-2023. The report is launched annually in advance of the Climate negotiations (COP).

280 *UNDP* (footnote 13), p. 13.

281 Cf. ECtHR, 9 April 2024, 53600/20, para. 420, 436, 451, 503; *UNDP* (footnote 13), p. 4 f., 18, 21 ff.

282 *Winter*, ZUR 2017, p. 267, 268.

Environmental Justice – The European Perspective

*Adviye Damla Ünlü**

Abstract

This study aims to consider the concept of environmental justice within the framework of its origins and development and evaluate the European perspective on environmental justice. The first section of the study outlines the evolution of the environmental justice concept and underlines the difference between the American and European perspectives. The following sections examine the European approach to environmental justice and discuss the tools of the EU to combat environmental injustices.

Keywords: Aarhus Convention, Court of Justice of the European Union, Environmental Justice, European Union

I. Introduction

The concept of environmental justice was first discussed around the issues of polluting factories and waste sites and appeared as grassroots activism, especially in African American neighborhoods in the USA in the 1980s. Since then, environmental injustices have continued to unfold both in the USA and in other parts of the world by including "new forms of injustices associated with climate change, energy use, natural disasters, urban green spaces, and public policies that adversely affect minority, indigenous, and low-income communities, as well as other socially disadvantaged groups and future generations".[1]

In Europe, the debate on environmental justice began in a different context from the American approach. From the European perspective, environmental justice discussions include policy areas such as health, transport, housing, employment, waste, and the subject of injustices is defined in a broader term. The American "environmental justice paradigm"[2] instead reflects a narrow

---

* Research Assistant, Dr. Istanbul University, Faculty of Political Science, Department of Politi-cal Science and International Relations. damla.unlu@istanbul.edu.tr

1 *J. Chakraborty*, Focus on Environmental Justice: New Directions in International Research, Environmental Research Letters, 2007, 12. p.1.

2 According to Taylor, the civil rights movement in the USA led to the development of the environmental justice paradigm, and it "is the first paradigm to link environment and race, class, gender, and social justice concerns in an explicit framework". *D. E.*

approach to environmental justice since framed by a certain group of people. Therefore, the American "environmental justice frame is too limited to be meaningfully applied to most European societies".[3]

Robert Bullard defines environmental justice as a principle "that all people and communities are entitled to equal protection of environmental and public health laws and regulations".[4] Cole and Foster highlight the importance of protection by law and participation in decision-making and state that "current environmental decision-making processes have not been effective in providing meaningful participation opportunities for those most burdened by environmental decisions".[5] The United States Environmental Protection Agency (EPA) definition of environmental justice points out the importance of access to decision-making processes and the protection from environmental bads.[6] Definitions and discussions highlight two dimensions of environmental justice which are the distribution of environmental goods and bads and access and participation in decision-making processes. In Europe, first of all in the UK, especially in Scotland, and then in other countries, environmental justice has been discussed by focusing on the distribution of goods and bads. Therefore, discussions took place within the EU by focusing on access and participation in the decision-making processes and legal tools to achieve environmental justice has begun to be effective. The following sections of the study review the origins of environmental justice and discuss the European and EU approaches.

A. Evolution of the Environmental Justice Concept

Scholars and activists generally trace back the environmental justice movement to the Warren County protests in 1982. Four years before the protests, it was decided to construct a waste disposal dump for toxic chemicals including

---

Taylor, The Rise of the Environmental Justice Paradigm: Injustice Framing and the Social Construction of Environmental Discourses, American Behavioral Scientist, 2000, 43(4), pp. 537- 542.

3 *H. D. Elvers, M. Gross & H. Heinrichs*, The Diversity of Environmental Justice: Towards a European Approach, 2008, 10(5), p. 838.

4 *R. D. Bullard*, Dumping in Dixie: Race, Class and Environmental Quality, 3rd ed., 2000.

5 *L. W. Cole & S. R. Foster*, From the Ground Up: Environmental Racism and the Rise of the Environmental Justice Movement, 2001, p. 16.

6 *United States Environmental Protection Agency*, https://www.epa.gov/environmentaljus tice,
(Access date: 20.01.2022).

polychlorinated biphenyls (PCBs) in Shocco Township in Warren County, North Carolina where 75% of the residents were African Americans and ranked 97th of 100 for GDP by county state-wide. EPA "allowed state officials to place the toxic waste 7% above the water table instead of the normal 50% feet required for PCBs".[7] Residents made public appeals and protests with the support and collaboration of civil rights and environmental groups. During protests, 523 protestors were arrested, and waste disposal could not be stopped. However, it was the first time in history that African Americans with low income raised an environmental problem, and it was the beginning of the environmental justice movement. This movement made a significant contribution to the popularisation of the concept of environmental justice and served as an impetus for further movements and new research by raising the issue. In 1983 the U.S. General Accounting Office shared the results of its study (1983) and stated that "Blacks make up the majority of the population in three of the four communities where the landfills are located. At least 26 percent of the population in all four communities have income below the poverty level".[8] In 1987 United Church of Christ Commission for Racial Justice released the first national study "to comprehensively document the presence of hazardous wastes in racial and ethnic communities throughout the United States".[9]Protests and these studies led to the coining of the term "environmental racism".[10] After years, the term "environmental equity movement was used to describe the growing movement to address racial, gender and social class environmental equalities".[11] The "environmental justice" term emerged during the preparations of the 1991 "First National People of Colour Environmental Leadership Summit" in Washington, D.C.

7 *K. Shrader-Frechette*, Environmental Justice: Creating Equality, Reclaiming Democracy, 2002, p. 8.

8 *United States General Accounting Office*, Siting of Hazardous Waste Landfills and Their Correlation with Racial and Economic Status of Surrounding Communities, 1983, http://archive.gao.gov/d48t13/121648.pdf, (Access date: 20.01.2022).

9 *Commission for Racial Justice United Church of Christ*, Toxic Wastes and Race in the United States, A National Report on the Racial and Socio-Economic Characteristics of Communities with Hazardous Waste Sites, 1987, https://www.nrc.gov/docs/ML1310/ML13109A339.pdf, (Access date: 20.01.2022).

10 Environmental racism is a term coined by Benjamin Chavis during the protests in 1982.

11 *D. E. Taylor*, The Rise of the Environmental Justice Paradigm: Injustice Framing and the Social Construction of Environmental Discourses, American Behavioral Scientist, 2000, 43(4), p. 532.

In this Summit, 17 principles of environmental justice were developed.[12] These principles highlighted that "the goals of the movement include broader social justice issues, such as economic and cultural liberation for all people of color" and stressed "the importance of increased participation of people of color as equals at all levels of decision-making".[13]

Warren County protests became effective on the political and legal developments. In 1990, a group of academics from the University of Michigan advocated for EPA's creation of a Work Group on Environmental Equity. The "Office of Environmental Equity" became the first official institution addressing environmental justice in 1992 and was renamed the "Office of Environmental Justice" in 1993 by the newly appointed EPA Administrator Carol Browner.[14] In 1994, USA president Bill Clinton "issued an executive order requiring all federal agencies to make environmental justice an integral part of their missions".[15] President Clinton's Executive Order 12898 (Federal Actions to Address Environmental Justice in Minority Populations and Low-Income Populations) on environmental justice reinforced the 1964 Civil Rights Act Title (VI) "prohibiting discriminatory practices in programs receiving federal funds and directed all federal agencies to begin to develop policies to reduce environmental inequity".[16]

B. European Approach to the Environmental Justice

After the development of environmental justice in the USA, debates also emerged in other countries. The environmental justice approach of European counties and institutions gained momentum because "Europe, as much as the USA, is confronted with the challenge of environmental justice".[17] In Europe,

12 *R. D. Bullard & G. S. Johnson*, Environmental Justice: Grassroots Activism and Its Impacts on Public Policy Decision Making, Journal of Social Issues, 2000, 56(3), pp. 556-557.

13 *J. T. Roberts*, Globalizing Environmental Justice, in: R. Sandler & P. C. Pezzulo (eds.), Environmental Justice and Environmentalism: The Social Justice Challenge to the Environmental Movement, 2007, p. 288.

14 *L. W. Cole & S. R. Foster*, From the Ground Up: Environmental Racism and the Rise of the Environmental Justice Movement, 2001, p. 24.

15 *D. E. Newton*, Environmental Justice, 2nd ed., 2009, p. xviii.

16 *J. Agyeman*, Constructing Environmental (in)Justice: Transatlantic Tales, Environmental Politics, 2002, 11(3), 36.

17 *É. Laurent*, Issues in Environmental Justice within the European Union, Ecological Economics, 2011, 70, p. 1849.

the UK was among the first countries where the discussion took place. The Environment Agency was established in 1995, and it has been the driving force of the environmental agenda within the government. Outside the government, campaigning groups such as Friends of Earth (FoE) in England, Wales, and Scotland raised the issue.[18]In 1999, FoE published a detailed study that revealed the relationship between socio-economic conditions and exposure to environmental hazards. The same year, Friend of Earth Scotland (FoES) launched a campaign for environmental justice on its 21st anniversary to promote environmental justice.

Within the government, the first official recognition of environmental justice was in the 2002 speech of Scotland First Minister Jack McConnell. McConnell addressed an environmental conference in Edinburgh and stated that "the gap between the haves and have nots is not just an economic issue - improving quality of life demands environmental justice too".[19]Following McConnell, in 2003, the UK Prime Minister Tony Blair stated that "by raising the standards of our local environments overall, we have the greatest impact on the poorest areas". These political expressions were followed by various reports and strategies. In 2004, "Environment and Social Injustice: Rapid Research and Evidence Review" pointed out that "environmental justice is a real and substantive problem within the UK" and highlighted its effect on "deprived communities and socially excluded groups".[20] The UK government launched a national sustainable development strategy in 2005 that underlined the importance of ensuring a decent environment for everyone, and "researching environmental limits and environmental inequalities" was stated as one of the key commitments of the strategy.[21]

In Germany, environmental justice was discussed within the framework of environmental health at first. In the late 1990s, Bundestag published the first report and revealed the relationship between exposition to air pollution, diseases based on air pollution, and the situation of socially excluded disad-

18 *H. Bulkeley & G. Walker*, Environmental Justice: A New Agenda for the UK, Local Environment: The International Journal of Justice and Sustainability, 2005, 10 (4), p. 330.

19 McConnell Delivers Green Pledge, *BBC News,* February 18, 2002, http://news.bbc.co.uk/2/hi/uk_news/scotland/1824752.stm, (Access date: 20.01.2022).

20 *K. Lucas, et al*, Environment and Social Justice: Rapid Research and Evidence Review, 2004.

21 The UK Government Sustainable Development Strategy, https://assets.publishing.service.gov.uk/government/uploads/system/uploads/attachment_data/file/69412/pb10589-securing-the-future-050307.pdf, 2005, p. 8-9, (Access date: 20.01.2022).

vantaged people. The common points between the UK and Germany have been their socio-economic focus and the introduction of environmental justice by governmental actors instead of grassroots movements.[22] Generally, environmental justice issues are not discussed in terms of racial and ethnic characteristics in Europe. Instead, the focus of discussions is socio-economic characteristics. According to Laurent, there is a historical and institutional explanation for this difference. "Environmental justice was born in the context of the broader civil rights movement", and it was racialized and became a basis for legal action in courts while income could not be.[23]The common point between these approaches is the concern of community recognition and public participation.

Environmental justice has a different meaning in different parts of the world. What is crucial as Cole and Foster have argued, "environmental justice requires democratic decision-making, community empowerment, and the incorporation of social structure in environmental decision-making processes."[24] There are different views and approaches for the subjects of the environmental injustices, their origins, and their relation with other social problems. However the "justice" dimension is common in all approaches. The distributional justice approach refers to the equal distribution of environmental benefits and burdens among peoples and communities regardless of income, race, or education. On the other hand, combatting injustices requires the principle of participative justice to ensure that "there are institutional and procedural norms that guarantee all people the equal opportunity for consideration in decision-making".[25]Distributive justice is not enough because purely "distributive paradigms tend to ignore the institutional contexts that influence or determine the distributions".[26]Participative justice and distributive justice are essential parts of the search for environmental justice together.

22 *H. D. Elvers, M. Gross & H. Heinrichs*, The Diversity of Environmental Justice, The Diversity of Environmental Justice, European Societies, 2008, 10(5), p. 841.

23 *É. Laurent*, Issues in Environmental Justice within the European Union, Ecological Economics, 2011, 70, p. 1849.

24 *L. W. Cole & S. R. Foster*, From the Ground up: Environmental Racism and the Rise of the Environmental Justice Movement, 2001, p. 15-16.

25 *K. Shrader-Frechette*, Environmental Justice: Creating Equality, Reclaiming Democracy, 2002, p. 28.

26 *I. M. Young*, Justice and the Politics of Difference, 1990, p.15.

C. European Union and Environmental Justice

The EU environmental policy has been developing since the 1970s conspicuously and around comprehensive legislation. However, the environmental justice issue is a recent subject of discussion in the EU. The environmental justice approach of the EU has its roots back in 1998, the Convention on Access to Information, Public Participation in Decision-making, and Access to Justice in Environmental Matters (Aarhus Convention). Aarhus Convention is the international instrument to protect the environmental rights of people and communities by empowering their participation in the decision-making process. Article 19 of the Consolidated Version of the Treaty on European Union that recognizes the right of access to justice in the EU legal order states that "the Member States shall provide remedies sufficient to ensure effective legal protection in the fields covered by Union law".[27] Article 263(4) of Consolidated Version of the Treaty on the Functioning of the European Union (TFEU) regulates the access to the Court of Justice of the European Union (CJEU) in environmental matters states that

> "any natural or legal person may, under the conditions laid down in the first and second paragraphs, institute proceedings against an act addressed to that person or which is of direct and individual concern to them, and against a regulatory act which is of direct concern to them and does not entail implementing measures."[28]

However, the CJEU "has given a restrictive interpretation of this provision on direct/individual concern that individuals and NGOs rarely have given Access to the Court for environmental matters".[29] This has begun to change with the Aarhus Convention. The Convention, adopted within the framework of the UN Economic Commission for Europe (UNECE), draws on Principle 10 of the 1992 Rio Declaration on Environment and Development.[30] The aim

27 Consolidated version of the Treaty on European Union, https://eur-lex.europa.eu/legal-content/EN/TXT/HTML/?uri=CELEX:12012M/TXT&from=EN, (Access date: 20.01.2022).

28 Consolidated Version of the Treaty on the Functioning of the European Union (TFEU), https://eur-lex.europa.eu/legal-content/EN/TXT/PDF/?uri=CELEX:12012E/TXT&from=LV, (Access date: 20.01.2022).

29 *L. Krämer*, The EU Courts and Access to Environmental Justice, in: B. Boer (eds.), Environmental Law Dimension of Human Rights, 2015, p. 107.

30 United Nations Declaration on Environment and Development, 1992, https://www.un.org/en/development/desa/population/migration/generalassembly/docs/globalcompact/A_CONF.151_26_Vol.I_Declaration.pdf (Access date: 20.01.2022).

of the Aarhus Convention is "to contribute to the protection of the right of every person of present and future generations to live in an environment adequate to his or her health and well-being".[31] To achieve this aim, Convention guarantees the right to know-rights to environmental information, the right to participate in the decision-making process, and the right to access to justice - a guaranteed right to the enforcement of the above rights via access to courts or other independent bodies. The Convention was signed by the EU on 25 June 1998, and it was approved through Council Decision 2005/370/EC of 17 February 2005. Under the terms of Article 216 (2) of the TFEU to comply with international obligations, Aarhus Convention is an integral part of the EU legal order and binding on the Member States. Therefore, some provisions of the Aarhus Convention can be found in different directives and regulations that are the EU's secondary legislation. For instance; Directive 2003/4/EC on Public Access to Environmental Information[32], Directive 2003/35/EC Providing for Public Participation in Respect of the Drawing up of Certain Plans and Programmes[33] and EC Regulation 1367/2006 on the Application of the Provisions of the Aarhus Convention to Community Relating to the Environment[34] which applies the Aarhus Convention to the EU institutions and bodies.

Despite harmonized EU secondary legislation, the current legislative provisions in the Member States on access to justice in environmental matters differ considerably. At the same time, the CJEU has issued significant rulings clarifying EU requirements on access to justice in environmental matters, both within and outside the context of the harmonized secondary legislation. The result is a sizeable and valuable body of the CJEU case law touching on all aspects of the subject.[35] The CJEU case law contributed to the achievement of environmental justice with some of its rulings. *In the Judgement of the Court of Justice in case of Dieter Janecek vs. Freistaat Bayern*[36], the Court recognised

31 Convention on Access to Information, Public Participation in Decision-making and Access to Justice in Environmental Matters, 1998, https://www.unece.org/fileadmin/DAM/env/pp/documents/cep43e.pdf, (Access date: 20.01.2022).

32 Directive: European Parliament and of the Council 2003/4/EC on Public Access to Environmental Information, OJ 2003 L41/26.

33 Directive: European Parliament and of the Council 2003/35/EC on Providing for Public Participation in Respect of the Drawing up of Certain Plans and Programmes Relating to the Environment, OJ 2003 L156/17.

34 Regulation: European Parliament and of the Council Regulation No. 1367/2006 on the Application of the Provisions of the Aarhus Convention to Community, *OJ 2006 L 264.*

35 Commission Notice on Access to Justice in Environmental Matters (2017), C 275/01.

36 ECJ Judgement: Case C-237/07, Dieter Janecek v Freistaat Bayern (2008) ECR I-06221.

a citizen's entitlement to challenge the absence of an air quality management plan despite German law considering that the citizen had no standing to bring such a case. In *the Judgement of the Court of Justice in case of Slovak Brown Bears*[37], the Court found that Article 9(3) of the Aarhus Convention had no direct effect but that Member State courts must nevertheless facilitate the access by the general public. And in *the Judgement of the Court of Justice in case of Trianel*[38], the Court found the German legislation to be too restrictive and thereby hinder the objective of giving environmental NGOs wide access to justice.

There have been some developments by the case law and the EU legislation about the internalization of the Aarhus Convention. However, in March 2017, the Aarhus Convention Compliance Committee, in case ACCC/C/2008/32, concluded that the EU regarding access to justice at the Union level failed to comply with the Convention because neither the Aarhus Regulation nor the jurisprudence of the CJEU implemented or complied with the obligations arising those Article 9, paragraphs 3 and 4. Therefore, the Committee recommended that all relevant EU institutions take steps to overcome these shortcomings to ensure full compliance by the EU with its obligations under the Convention. Based on the findings, the Bureau of the Aarhus Convention prepared draft decision VI/8f concerning compliance by the EU with its obligations under the Convention.[39]

In June 2017, European Commission prepared a proposal for a Council Decision on the position to be adopted. Council Decision (EU) 2017/1346 of 17 July 2017 on the position to be adopted, on behalf of the EU, at the sixth session of the Meeting of the Parties to the Aarhus Convention as regards compliance case ACCC/C/2008/32.[40] Commission's proposal has widely criticized by the NGOs as European Environmental Bureau that they recommended the

37 ECJ Judgement: Case C-240/09, Lesoochranárske zoskupenie VLK v Ministerstvo životného prostredia Slovenskej republiky (2011) ECR I-1255.

38 ECJ Judgement: Case C-115-09, Bund für Umwelt und Naturschutz Deutschland, Landesverband Nordrhein-Westfalen eV v Bezirksregierung Arnsberg (2011) ECR I-3673.

39 United Nations, Economic Commission for Europe, Findings and recommendations of the Compliance committee with regard to communication ACC/C/2008/32 (Part II) concerning compliance by the European Union, 17th March 2017, https://www.unece.org/fileadmin/DAM/env/pp/compliance/C2008-32/Findings/C32_EU_Findings_as_adopted_advance_unedited_version.pdf, (Access date: 20.01.2022).

40 Council Decision on the position to be adopted, on behalf of the European Union, at the sixth session of the Meeting of the Parties to the Aarhus Convention as regards compliance case ACCC/C/2008/32, 2017/1346.

EU should block those findings when they are presented for adoption by the Convention's governing body, the Meeting of the Parties (MoP), in Montenegro in September.[41] On 11 September 2017, at the sixth session of the MoP held in Budva, Montenegro, the MoP discussed the draft decision VI/8f but did not agree with the Union proposals to amend it in line with Decision (EU) 2017/1346. In the absence of agreement, the MoP decided to postpone the discussion on this draft decision until its next ordinary session in 2021. By that time, on 11 June 2018, the Council requested the European Commission to submit "a study on the Union's options for addressing the findings of the Aarhus Convention Compliance Committee and, if appropriate in view of the outcomes of the study, a proposal for a Regulation of the European Parliament and of the Council amending Regulation (EC)".[42] The Council asked the European Commission to complete the study by 30 September 2019. Furthermore, if changes to Regulation (EC) No 1367/2006 were considered appropriate based on the study's outcomes, the European Commission was required to prepare a proposal for an amendment of the Regulation by 30 September 2020. In October 2020, the European Commission adopted a proposal, and in June 2021, a provisional political agreement was reached between the European Parliament and the Council. The EU adopted the amendment in October 2021. Thus, a positive step has been taken, strengthening the EU's commitment to fully comply with the Aarhus Convention, reinforcing the rights of the public, and improving their access to information, justice, and participation in decision-making processes.

D. Conclusions

Originally, the concept of environmental justice emerged in response to the environmental problems faced by African American and indigenous communities living near polluting factories and waste sites, with a focus on addressing racial inequality in environmental matters. Over time, the environmental justice agenda has broadened, encompassing issues of distri-

41 European Environmental Bureau, https://eeb.org/european-commission-seeks-to-block-access-to-justice-for-eu-citizens/, 30 June 2017, (Access date: 20.01.2022).

42 Council Decision requesting the Commission to submit a study on the Union's options for addressing the findings of the Aarhus Convention Compliance Committee in case ACCC/C/2008/32 and, if appropriate in view of the outcomes of the study, a proposal for a Regulation of the European Parliament and of the Council amending Regulation (EC) No 1367/2006.

bution and equity both within and among nation-states. The discussion has extended to encompass transnational and global environmental inequalities. Presently, environmental justice is recognized as a global issue linked to challenges such as climate change, global warming, and species extinction. Contemporary discussions on environmental justice include concerns about the over-exploitation of global commons, ecological footprints, and the ecological debts incurred by countries. The concept has evolved from its localized origins to a broader framework addressing global environmental challenges and disparities.

The EU acknowledges the global significance of environmental justice and the importance of addressing injustices at both Member States and EU levels. Within the European perspective, procedural justice takes center stage, shaping the development of environmental justice through legal frameworks. However, the effectiveness of these legal steps in fostering a robust mechanism involving citizens and civil society remains to be determined.

To effectively address environmental injustices, it is essential not only to strengthen the existing legal steps but also to establish an approach that specifically targets structural injustices. This comprehensive strategy goes beyond legal measures, aiming to tackle the root causes of environmental inequalities. By combining strengthened legal frameworks and a focus on addressing structural injustices, the fight against environmental injustices can be advanced more effectively.

Bibliography

Commission for Racial Justice United Church of Christ, Toxic Wastes and Race in the United States, A National Report on the Racial and Socio-Economic Characteristics of Communities with Hazardous Waste Sites, 1987, https://www.nrc.gov/docs/ML1310/ML13109A339.pdf, (Access date: 20.01.2022).

Commission Notice on Access to Justice in Environmental Matters (2017), C 275/01.

Consolidated version of the Treaty on European Union, https://eur-lex.europa.eu/legal-content/EN/TXT/HTML/?uri=CELEX:12012M/TXT&from=EN, (Access date: 20.01.2022).

Consolidated Version of the Treaty on the Functioning of the European Union (TFEU), https://eur-lex.europa.eu/legal-content/EN/TXT/PDF/?uri=CELEX:12012E/TXT&from=LV, (Access date: 20.01.2022).

Convention on Access to Information, Public Participation in Decision-making and Access to Justice in Environmental Matters, 1998, https://www.unece.org/fileadmin/DAM/env/pp/documents/cep43e.pdf, (Access date: 20.01.2022).

Council Decision on the position to be adopted, on behalf of the European Union, at the sixth session of the Meeting of the Parties to the Aarhus Convention as regards compliance case ACCC/C/2008/32, 2017/1346.

Council Decision requesting the Commission to submit a study on the Union's options for addressing the findings of the Aarhus Convention Compliance Committee in case ACCC/C/2008/32 and, if appropriate in view of the outcomes of the study, a proposal for a Regulation of the European Parliament and of the Council amending Regulation (EC) No 1367/2006.

D. E. Newton, Environmental Justice, 2nd ed., 2009, ABC-CLIO, California.

D. E. Taylor, The Rise of the Environmental Justice Paradigm: Injustice Framing and the Social Construction of Environmental Discourses, American Behavioral Scientist, 2000, 43(4), pp. 508-580.

Directive: European Parliament and of the Council 2003/35/EC on Providing for Public Participation in Respect of the Drawing up of Certain Plans and Programmes Relating to the Environment, OJ 2003 L156/17.

Directive: European Parliament and of the Council 2003/4/EC on Public Access to Environmental Information, OJ 2003 L41/26.

É. Laurent, Issues in Environmental Justice within the European Union, Ecological Economics, 2011, 70, pp. 1846-1853.

ECJ Judgement: Case C-115-09, Bund für Umwelt und Naturschutz Deutschland, Landesverband Nordrhein-Westfalen eV v Bezirksregierung Arnsberg (2011) ECR I-3673.

ECJ Judgement: Case C-237/07, Dieter Janecek v Freistaat Bayern (2008) ECR I-06221.

ECJ Judgement: Case C-240/09, Lesoochranárske zoskupenie VLK v Ministerstvo životného prostredia Slovenskej republiky (2011) ECR I-1255.

European Environmental Bureau, https://eeb.org/european-commission-seeks-to-block-access-to-justice-for-eu-citizens/, 30 June 2017, (Access date: 20.01.2022).

H. Bulkeley & G. Walker, Environmental Justice: A New Agenda for the UK, Local Environment: The International Journal of Justice and Sustainability, 2005, 10 (4), pp. 329-332.

H. D. Elvers, M. Gross & H. Heinrichs, The Diversity of Environmental Justice, The Diversity of Environmental Justice, European Societies, 2008, 10(5), pp. 835-856.

I. M. Young, Justice and the Politics of Difference, 1990, Princeton University Press, Princeton.

J. Agyeman, Constructing Environmental (in)Justice: Transatlantic Tales, Environmental Politics, 2002, 11(3), 31-53.

J. Chakraborty, Focus on Environmental Justice: New Directions in International Research, Environmental Research Letters, 2007, 12. p.1-4.

J. T. Roberts, Globalizing Environmental Justice, in: R. Sandler & P. C. Pezzulo (eds.), Environmental Justice and Environmentalism: The Social Justice Challenge to the Environmental Movement, 2007, The MIT Press, Cambridge, pp. 285-309.

K. Lucas, et al, Environment and Social Justice: Rapid Research and Evidence Review, 2004, Policy Studies Institute, London.

K. Shrader-Frechette, Environmental Justice: Creating Equality, Reclaiming Democracy, 2002, Oxford University Press, Oxford.

L. Krämer, The EU Courts and Access to Environmental Justice, in: B. Boer (eds.), Environmental Law Dimension of Human Rights, 2015, Oxford University Press, Oxford, pp. 107-135.

L. W. Cole & S. R. Foster, From the Ground up: Environmental Racism and the Rise of the Environmental Justice Movement, 2001, New York University Press, New York.

McConnell Delivers Green Pledge, BBC News, February 18, 2002, http://news.bbc.co.uk /2/hi/uk_news/scotland/1824752.stm, (Access date: 20.01.2022).

R. D. Bullard & G. S. Johnson, Environmental Justice: Grassroots Activism and Its Impacts on Public Policy Decision Making, Journal of Social Issues, 2000, 56(3), pp. 555-578.

R. D. Bullard, Dumping in Dixie: Race, Class and Environmental Quality, 3rd ed., 2000, Westview Press, Colorado.

Regulation: European Parliament and of the Council Regulation No. 1367/2006 on the Application of the Provisions of the Aarhus Convention to Community, OJ 2006 L 264.

The UK Government Sustainable Development Strategy,

https://assets.publishing.service.gov.uk/government/uploads/system/uploads/attachment_data/file/69412/pb10589-securing-the-future-050307.pdf, 2005, p. 8-9, (Access date: 20.01.2022).

United Nations Declaration on Environment and Development, 1992, http://www.unesco.org/education/pdf/RIO_E.PDF, (Access date: 20.01.2022).

United Nations, Economic Commission for Europe, Findings and recommendations of the Compliance committee with regard to communication ACC/C/2008/32 (Part II) concerning compliance by the European Union, 17th March 2017, https://www.unece.org/fileadmin/DAM/env/pp/compliance/C2008-32/Findings/C32_EU_Findings_as_adopted_advance_unedited_version.pdf, (Access date: 20.01.2022).

United States Environmental Protection Agency, https://www.epa.gov/environmentaljustice, (Access date: 20.01.2022).

United States General Accounting Office, Siting of Hazardous Waste Landfills and their Correlation with Racial and Economic Status of Surrounding Communities, 1983, http://archive.gao.gov/d48t13/121648.pdf, (Access date: 20.01.2022).

II. Challenge Water

Protection of Coastal Waters in Turkish Law

*Dr. Verda Neslihan Akün**

Abstract

Water Framework Directive, the key document, establishing a framework for Community action in the field of water policy, is a set of rules, and a result of European water legislation. It includes the protection of the coastal waters. Turkey, as a candidate country to EU have paved the road for harmonisation its legislation with EU, but according to progress reports has still to do. For this reason, on this paper we examined the Turkish legislation in the light of EU *acquis communautaire* and international law. Union's marine policy is not disregarded.

Keywords: Marine Environment, Marine pollution, Coastal Waters, Turkey, Turkish Straits, Black Sea, Mediterranean Sea.

I. Introduction

In this paper, presented at Kassel University, in October 2017, main aim is to set the framework of water protection under Turkish Law, with the special focus on coastal waters of Turkish Peninsula. The subject "coastal waters" gives a higher impression of saline water, in other words, marine water than freshwater. For this respect, the author shall deal with the term from both aspects. European legal rules and standards designated for freshwater shall be prior, in the absence of a world-wide multilateral convention about freshwaters. The international law of the sea shall be following by a comparative view with EU Directive on Water Framework, lastly, Turkish legislation shall be held for both aspects. Turkey, as a candidate country to the EU since 1999, has obligations to fulfil under the negotiations about the environmental chapter. 27th chapter, titled as "The Environment", opened in 2009, is still on the table. The EU is not only encouraging but also supporting Turkey's efforts to bring its institutions and policies harmonized with the EU *acquis* through the pre-accession programme.[1] A high amount of financial assistance is covered for the 2014-2020 environment and climate change programme. This new

* Research Assistant, Department of Public International Law, Istanbul University Faculty of Law.

1 https://www.avrupa.info.tr/en/environment-and-climate-change-most-important-and-challenging-eu-policy-areas-259. (last visited on 10.8.2017)

programme aims to improve environmental protection by addressing main issues including capacity building for the *management of water.*[2]

Turkey's water policy has undergone continuous reforms that can be identified in three phases; decentralization, privatization and Europeanization.[3] The Europeanization phase has been started by the EU Accession Partnership Document's Environmental Chapter. For the very first step, the adjustment of Turkish legislation with the European legal legislation on environment, in particular, directives on the protection of water from pollution and Water Framework Directive (WFD)[4] were the essential documents to be achieved.

A. European Legislation on Water

Water Framework Directive (2000), the key document, establishing a framework for Community action in the field of water policy, is a set of rules, and a result of European water legislation had begun in early 1970's, by the intention to establish the rules and standards for the drinking water derived from rivers and lakes. Meanwhile, groundwaters were also introduced. Under this process, the quality objectives were the primary concern. Protection of water and prevention from the pollutants, i.e., contamination of waste substances were targeted by some concurrent EU directives; Urban Waste Water Treatment Directive, Integrated Pollution and Prevention Control Directive, Nitrates Directive, and others adopted in 1990's. The resent WFD, is a result of series of negotiations, and may be characterized as a "water constitution" for EU. It aims to maintain and improve the aquatic environment in the Community.[5] The ambition of the Drafters was to harmonize and unify the existing EU legislation about water management and protection, to achieve the good water status. This purpose is primarily concerned with the quality of the waters concerned.[6]

The Directive, has expanded the scope of the protection of water to all waters, the surface waters and the groundwater, not only chemical protection

---

2 *Id.*

3 *A. Kibaroğlu, V.Sümer &W. Scheumann*, "Fundamental Shifts in Turkey's Water Policy", Journal of Mediterranean Geography, 119, 2012,p.27, https://journals.openedition.org/mediterranee/6453, (last visited 21.8.2017)

4 Directive 2000/60/EC of the European Parliament And of the Council of 23 October 2000 establishing a framework for Community action in the field of water policy, OJ, L.327, 22.12.2000, p.1. (Hereinafter Water Framework Directive or WFD)

5 Preamble, para.19.

6 *Id.*

but also ecological protection, by coordinated measures and public participation with a combined approach. For the topic of this paper, the core is on coastal waters, which considered as surface water in the art. 2 of the Directive; groundwater, shall only briefly mentioned. Special emphasis shall be given to the former.

1. What to Protect?

a. Groundwater

Groundwater is defined to be the water below the surface of the ground in the saturation zone and in direct contact with the ground or subsoil.[7]

In order to protect the waters, different standards are considered for the surface waters and the groundwater. Unlike from surface water protection standards, for groundwater, qualitative status does not play significant role, instead, quantitative status takes the major role. Groundwaters are assumed to be not polluted at all. Instead of setting chemical quality standards, the good management and sustainability of this source have been preferred as a better approach to the issue, not to give rise to an acceptable minimum level of pollution.

b. Surface Water

In respect of the Directive, "surface water" means inland waters, except groundwater; transitional waters and coastal waters, except in respect of chemical status for which it shall also include territorial waters. "Transitional waters" are bodies of surface water in the vicinity of river mouths which are partly saline in character as a result of their proximity to coastal waters but which are substantially influenced by freshwater flows.

c. Coastal water

"Coastal water" means the surface water on the landward side of a line, every point of which is at a distance of one nautical mile on the seaward side from the nearest point of the baseline from which the breadth of territorial

7 *Id.* at Art. 2/2.

waters is measured, extending where appropriate up to the outer limit of transitional waters.

d. Basic Standards of The Surface Water

For all surface waters, both on the "good ecological status" and the "good chemical status" are agreed to be followed as general minimum standards. Good ecological status, is described in Annex V of the WFD, on both biological and hydromorphological elements, including chemical and physico-chemical elements supporting the biological elements. This definition contains, flora and fauna of the water, dynamic of flow and connection to other waters, depth, salinity, temperature, transparency, and oxygenation and acidification as physico-chemical elements.

The WFD classification scheme for surface water ecological status includes five categories: high, good, moderate, poor and bad. In general, for rivers, lakes, transitional and coastal waters; 'high status' means no or very minor evidence of distortion; 'good status' means a 'slight' deviation from this condition, low levels of distortion from human activity; and, 'moderate status' means 'moderate' deviation, moderate signs of distortion from human activity and significantly more disturbed from the good status.[8]

On the other hand, to define good chemical status, environmental quality standards have been established for 33 new and eight previously regulated chemical pollutants of high concern across the EU. The WFD is backed up by other EU legislation such as the regulation on chemicals and the Directive for Integrated Pollution and Prevention Control (IPPC) for industrial installations.[9]

B. International Law of The Sea and Protection of Marine Environment

From the LOS perspective, "coastal water" at first sight, makes a sense of internal waters literally. However, the definition in WFD art.2, gives an impression of the inclusion of territorial waters. In the light of LOS, internal waters are formed by the waters on the landside of the baseline of the

8 Annex V.

9 http://ec.europa.eu/environment/pubs/pdf/factsheets/water-framework-directive.pdf, (last visited on 7.9.2017)

territorial sea.[10] And the normal baseline is the low-water line along the coast. As aforementioned, according to EU Directive, "coastal water", is a part of surface water on the landward side of a line, every point of which is at a distance of one nautical mile on the seaward side from the nearest point of the baseline from which the breadth of territorial waters is measured, extending where appropriate up to the outer limit of transitional waters. In the meaning of Directive, coastal water consists of both internal waters and the very first nautical mile of the territorial waters. And the aforementioned "surface water" definition, the chapeau of coastal waters, without any distinction chemical status of the water, includes territorial waters explicitly. In this regard, a view expanding up to high seas- that the Directive requires the achievement of good surface water chemical status for all surface water up to 12 nautical miles seaward from the baseline from which territorial waters are measured- is asserted.[11] Without debating the breadth of the protection wholly territorial waters, by protecting these part of waters, the Directive contributes to the protection of territorial and marine waters.[12] However, Member States are only required to identify water bodies in coastal waters, not in territorial waters. Therefore, for the protection of coastal water, besides the WFD rules, the LOS rules, in general, the rules of marine protection of UNCLOS, should be applied to the coastal waters.

In respect of UNCLOS, "pollution of the marine environment" means the introduction by man, directly or indirectly, of substances or energy into the marine environment, including estuaries, which results or is likely to result in such deleterious effects as harm to living resources and marine life, hazards to human health, hindrance to marine activities, including fishing and other legitimate uses of the sea, impairment of quality for use of sea water and reduction of amenities.[13] Two elements are met under this provision: The pollution is a result of human activity and this activity causes unnecessary negative impacts on the marine environment. Though, the marine environment has not been defined under the UNCLOS apparently, - under the Part XII, about the protection and preservation of the marine environment, while addressing the duties of the coastal states, port states

10 UNCLOS art.8

11 https://circabc.europa.eu/sd/a/85912f96-4dca-432e-84d6-a4dded785da5/GuIdance%20No%205%20-%20characterisation%20of%20coastal%20waters%20-%20COAST%20(WG%202.4).pdf, p.24. (last visited on 10.9.2017)

12 WFD, art.1/(e)

13 Art. 1/4.

and flag states- is stated in an indirect way. Under that provision, marine environment, consists of "rare or fragile ecosystems as well as the habitat of depleted, threatened or endangered species and other forms of marine life."[14]

On the other hand, WFD, does not exclude international agreements containing important obligations on the protection of marine waters from pollution, besides these agreements, particular attention made to regional agreements.[15] Moreover, the WFD, referred to make a contribution towards enabling the Community and Member States to meet those obligations.[16]

WFD, also, states that its ultimate aim is to achieve the elimination of priority hazardous substances and contribute to achieving concentrations in the marine environment.[17] For this intention, relevant international agreements, including those which aim to prevent and eliminate pollution of the marine environment, under Article 16(3) to cease or phase out discharges, emissions and losses is targeted. Under implementing measures pursuant to paragraph 3 of article 11, Member States shall also take all appropriate steps not to increase pollution of marine waters.[18]

WFD defines pollution, as the direct or indirect introduction, as a result of human activity, of substances or heat into the air, water or land which may be harmful to human health or the quality of aquatic ecosystems or terrestrial ecosystems directly depending on aquatic ecosystems, which result in damage to material property, or which impair or interfere with amenities and other legitimate uses of the environment.[19] WFD, defines pollution in plain and precise terms, and distinctly, inserts harmful human activity to "terrestrial ecosystems directly depending on aquatic ecosystems" to the definition. This purposeful addition makes sense to the subject to inland waters, in other words, surface waters.

A well-known principle of international environmental law, the "polluter pays principle", which is a fruit of 1992 Rio Declaration, takes its place in WFD. Even if the precautionary approach fails, and any damage occurs on aquatic environment, member states shall ensure the costs of recovery.[20]

Nearly two decades earlier than WFD, UNCLOS, attempted to provide a global framework for the convenient exploitation and conservation of

14 UNCLOS art. 194/(5).
15 Preamble, para. 21.
16 *Id.*
17 Preamble, para. 27.
18 Art. 11/6.
19 art 2/33.
20 Preamble, para.38, 40,45; Art. 9/1

marine resources and the protection of its environment.[21] For this reason, it focuses on the prevention mostly, so, due diligence is required. It emphasizes the need to take all appropriate measures necessary to prevent, reduce and control pollution. The state parties are given regulatory powers and enforcement powers. Coastal states and flag states are under the duty and has the power to adopt laws and regulations for the prevention, reduction and control pollution on the marine environment from land-based resources, seabed activities, by dumping, from vessels and atmosphere.[22] UNCLOS made a special contribution to international environmental law in the field of marine pollution caused by vessels, by building the existing law, borrowing, citing, clarifying, and expanding the law created after major oil tanker accidents, i.e. *Torrey Canyon*, *Amoco Cadiz* incidents.[23] And the Convention determined- International Maritime Organisation (IMO) and IMO mandated legal instruments- "generally accepted rules and standards established through competent international organisations or diplomatic conference" as a minimum criteria for these anticipated laws and regulations. On the other hand, state parties are furnished with the enforcement powers to ensure the aforementioned laws and regulations; these states are coastal states, flag states, *inter alia* the port state this time.[24] Pre-existing rules did not meet the environmental needs of the coastal states.[25] Port state jurisdiction was an important challenge in order to set and to enforce pollution standards to vessels entering voluntarily into its ports. [26]

In this context, protection of coastal waters from pollution, is intersected on the duties and obligations of coastal states expectedly. Under the Convention, the coastal state's enforcement power is unlimited in its territorial waters, but, imprisonment is an exception to it within certain punishment limitations.[27] Only, in the case of "a wilful and a serious act of pollution in the territorial

21 *P. Birnie, A.Boyle & C.Redgewell*, International Law & Environment, 3rd ed., Oxford University Press, 2009, p.383.
22 Art. 202-212
23 *V. Nanda, G. Pring*, International Environmental Law and Policy for 21st Century, 2nd revised ed., Martinus Nijhoff Publishers, p.433-434.
24 Port states and flag states duties and obligations serve as a basis for the pollution occurred on high seas, and related cites to it.
25 *Nanda*, *supra* note 23, p.434.
26 *Id*, at. p.436.
27 *Id*, at. p.437.

sea" punishment shall be acceptable because the passage is no more innocent according to the clear provision of UNCLOS art.19.[28]

C. Protection of Turkish Coastal Waters: Turkish Legislation

The author would like to address related national institutions and legislation respectively. As a starting point, the geographical location of Turkey, lies in the middle of three regional seas, as a transcontinental county, holding a coastline of more than 8300 kilometres: By Aegean Sea, Turkish Straits connecting the Black Sea and the Mediterranean Sea, on a main route of international maritime traffic. Both on Mediterranean Sea and Aegean Sea shores, marine and coastal protected areas and special environmental protection areas are existing. Some are protected maritime archaeological heritage cites, some of them are breeding cites of special species, i.e., *caretta* turtles at Köyceğiz-Dalyan. The existence of these areas, bring up the importance of coastal protection and preservation of Turkish coastal waters not only on national level, but also both on European and global level. A table of Marine and Coastal Protected Areas, and a second table for Special Environmental Protection Areas on Turkish coastline are given in Country Report on Turkey of European Commission about Maritime Spatial Planning in the Mediterranean Sea, based on Turkish Former Ministry of Environment and Forestry data.[29]

1. Related Institutions

a. The Main National Authorities and Institutions Related With The Protection of Coastal Waters of Turkey

The Ministry of Agriculture and Forestry
The Ministry of Transport and Infrastructure
The Ministry of Environment, Urbanisation and Climate Change
The Ministry of Energy and Natural Sources

28 *Id.*

29 Further information available on https://ec.europa.eu/maritimeaffairs/sites/maritimeaffairs/files/docs/body/turkey_01_en.pdf. (last visited on 11.9.2017)

2. Related Legislation

a. Turkish Legislation Related to Turkish Coastal Waters

The author takes into consideration the legislation, but only some of them, which, includes legal provisions directly about marine environment and marine pollution shall be held in detail.

LAWS: The Turkish Code on Territorial Waters (1982) The Turkish Code on Harbours (1800's) The Turkish Code on Environment (1983) The Turkish Code on the Protection of Life and Property at Sea (1946) The Turkish Code on Coastal Safety Commandership (1982) The Turkish Code on Navigation and Hydrography Services (1973) The Turkish Code on Cabotage (1926) The Code Pertaining to Principles of Emergency Response and Compensation for Damages in Pollution of Marine Environment by Oil and Other Harmful Substances (Emergency Response Code) (2005)
By-LAWS: The by-law on Turkish Straits Vessel Traffic Regulation (1998)
REGULATIONS: The Regulation on the Control over the Water Pollution (2004) The Regulation on the Control over the Pollution caused by Hazardous Substances on Waters and Periphery of Waters (2005) The Implementation Regulation of the Code Pertaining to Principles of Emergency Response and Compensation for Damages in Pollution of Marine Environment by Oil and Other Harmful Substances (Emergency Response Code's Implementation Regulation)(2006) The Regulation on the Notifications according to SOLAS& MARPOL Conventions (2006) The Regulation on the Procedures of the Determination and Collection of the Administrative Fines rising from breach of The Code on Environment (2007) The Regulation of Turkish Harbours (2012)

b. Marine Protection under The Turkish Code on Environment (1983)

According to The Turkish Code on Environment,[30] marine environment or marine pollution has not been defined. Only pollution is defined in a brief manner without any distinction to marine environment. It is any negative impact, may impair health of living beings, environmental worths, and ecological equilibrium, occurred in the environment.[31] The code, includes the protection of marine waters besides ground and underground waters.[32] In this manner, protected areas and special protected areas are precluded from aquacultural production.[33] For the sustainability of biodiversity and ecosystem, endangered species at the water covered areas are prohibited from trade.[34] It is very interesting that, under art.2, "water covered areas", defined very widely, that can cover some streams, canals, lakes, wetlands or coastal waters. Coastal waters, without explicitly addressing, included within the protected areas. These waters, are prohibited from pollution in the wider context of the prohibition of pollution under article 8. All institutional activities, likely to cause environmental issues, are under the obligation to file an environmental impact assessment report, at the end a need of an affirmative result, otherwise never get any licence for their project.[35] According to the Code, oil, mineral and geothermal exploration are not subject to EIA process. From my opinion, this provision is the most incompatible rule with international environmental protection standards and WFD Annex V provisions.

Coastal installations as ports, docks should be responsible for the receipt, storage, transport and disposal of the waste substances regarding oil, limber and ballast water and other solid wastes.[36] This Code shall be enforced by the The Ministry of Urbanisation, Environment and Climate Change. It may also be enforced by Coastal Guard Command, if delegated.[37] Any discharge to marine waters shall be punished by administrative fines.[38] This enforcement power, expanded to, marine waters under the jurisdiction of Turkey and

30 Official Gazette of Turkey, date 09/08/1983, No: 18132.
31 Art. 2.
32 Art. 9/(h)
33 *Id.*
34 Art. 9/(e)
35 Art. 10/1.
36 Art. 11.
37 Art. 12/1
38 Art. 20.

related areas; marine pollution caused by the release and discharge of oil and like products.[39] If the discharged material was hazardous, the fine shall be augmented ten times.[40] Vacuuming of sand from marine areas, in the light of our topic, at the coastal waters, is also subject to permission, if violated it is punished.[41] This code is in connection with The Turkish Ports Code, and Aquacultural Products Code.

The "polluter pays" principle features itself, as a legal rule in the heart of article 28. Polluters and damage causers in the environment are directly liable under this provision. The polluter shall be required to pay compensation for the resulting damage according to the general provisions.

c. The Code Pertaining to Principles of Emergency Response and Compensation for Damages in Pollution of Marine Enviroment by Oil and Other Harmful Substances (2005)[42]

The purpose of this Law, in view of rights and obligations stemming from international and national law in matters of assuring marine safety and preventing marine pollution.[43] It aims to reduce, control and eliminate the marine pollution by oil and harmful substances. The most important provisions of the Code, are about "Compulsory Liability Insurances"[44] This code is highly debatable in Turkey, because of some provisions of it, whether they are compatible with innocent passage rights of foreign vessels, and Montreux Convention on Turkish Straits. The Code, against well-established rules of LOS and the Montreux Convention, asks about a notification about the navigation and cargo of the ship, 48 hours before of the passage. And also, a very well-known right of innocent passage within the territorial waters of a coastal state, lies on the code in English version as "harmless passage" which is an improper translation.

---

39 *Id.*

40 *Id.*

41 Additional Provision 1/(d)

42 Official Gazette of Turkey, date 11/3/2005, No.25752. (Hereinafter Emergency Response Code).

43 Art. 1.

44 Art. 6-9.

Turkey, as a costal state, shall apply the Code to vessels greater than 500 grostones carrying oil and other hazardous substances or other vessels may cause pollution because of their operations by oil and hazardous substances.[45]

According to the Code, pollution, means, mixing of petroleum or other noxious substances with marine environment, as a result of an incident, in a way that might cause harm to *living resources* and marine life, constitute a hazard to human health, hinder maritime activities including fishing and other legal utilization of the seas, change the quality of sea water, and disturb ecological balance. This definition is in conformity with UNCLOS rules which Turkey is not a party.

For the purposes of enforcement of this Code; Turkish maritime jurisdiction expands from inland waters, territorial waters, continental shelf, exclusive economic zone and, also, to open sea areas beyond territorial waters, this latter, however, only in case of emergency situations as envisaged under this Law and as confined to purposes of emergency response to such incidences and compensation for damages thereof, and furthermore depending on the decision to be made by the Undersecretariat by obtaining opinion of the Ministry, Ministry of Foreign Affairs, and other relevant public institutions.[46] Coastal waters in the meaning of WFD, surely, is included by this Code, moreover, in special cases, Turkey, has the power to respond in emergency situations beyond its territorial waters, even on high seas as a coastal state, if it causes high risk to its waters.

According to the Code, powers, duties, and responsibilities for preparing emergency response plans, implementing emergency response plans in coastal areas, determining kind and impact of pollution, assessment of damage to environment and rehabilitation of the areas affected by post-incident pollution shall belong to the The Ministry of Environment, Urbanisation and Climate Change. Finally, the powers, duties, and responsibilities pertaining to public order and law enforcement shall belong to Coastal Guard Command.[47]

For the identification of the pollution, The Ministry executes or ensures the execution of the necessary studies on the type, extend, amount, direction and speed of dissemination, possible outcomes and methods of disposal of the pollution resulting from an incident, and conveys this information to the relevant emergency intervention unit.[48]

45 Art. 2.
46 Art. 3/(p)
47 Art. 4/2.
48 Art. 14.

The power of intervention of Turkish authorities, may be examined in two distinct cases: In case pollution or risk of pollution. For both it should be understood directly as The Ministry of Transport and Infrastructure. [49]

National emergency response plan, comprising the principles that pertain to activities and international cooperation in emergency response to pollution of marine environment by oil and (or) other harmful substances, shall be prepared by the Ministry of Transport and Infrastructure, in coordination with General Directorate of Emergency Management of Turkey and other relevant institutions.[50]

Under article 22, in case, serious concerns that a vessel might cause an incident or pollution or constitute such a risk under this Code, then, The Ministry of Transport and Infrastructure officials, probably from Directorate General of Coastal Safety, may inspect the ship for a definite determination. This authority may be delegated to other institutions concerned, where it deems necessary to do so. Coast Guard Command shall carry out all public order and law enforcement services as they pertain to application of this Code.

As a final analysis for the Code, we may easily say that strict liability has arisen and polluter pays principle applies strictly.

d. The Regulation on the Control over the Water Pollution (2004)[51]

Under this regulation, coastal waters and marine waters are explicitly mentioned. The aim of the regulation is the prevention of waters in quality. For this reason, disposal of waste waters is forbidden or subject to permission if it is eligible for refining. Article 23 of the Regulation, designed only for the prohibition of the pollution of the marine environment of any kind. Any usage and discharge having risk of pollution is forbidden. Any waste material, ballast or bilge water contaminated with oil or petroleum products, are strictly forbidden to be discharged. In addition to these, excavation and building remains, refinery wastes are wholly forbidden to be discharged into coastal or marine waters. For the operations carried on the seabed, the wastes of it, are subject to permission on EIA. The regulation includes strict rules especially about the deep discharge of wastes on permission after refinery process.

---

49 Art. 15.

50 Art. 18.

51 Official Gazette of Turkey, date 31/12/2004, No: 25687.

II. Further Remarks about the Protection Marine Environment of EU and Turkey at Regional Level and European Policies

Heretofore, on this paper, the topic has been approached in the light of WFD, International Law of The Sea and Turkish Legislation. As a last point, the author deals with the topic from a connected policy aspect. EU, in 2005, established a coherent path to maritime issues, with increased coordination between different policy areas, named as Integrated Maritime Policy.[52] As a part of this policy, The Water Framework Directive sets a goal of achieving good ecological and chemical status for all EU surface and groundwaters, tying it with the EU Marine Strategy Framework Directive[53] (2008) planning the actions to reduce marine pollution from land- based sources and will protect ecosystems in coastal and transitional waters.[54] Marine Directive, considers marine environment is a precious heritage that must be protected, preserved and, where practicable, restored with the ultimate aim of maintaining biodiversity and providing diverse and dynamic oceans and seas which are clean, healthy and productive.[55] It also supports regional cooperation among Member States and with neighbouring coastal states.

It is closely linked to WFD, and referring WFD definition, determines coastal waters, including their seabed and suboil, integral part of the marine environment; covers particular aspects environmental status of the marine environment are not addressed through WFD.[56] Similar to WFD, good environmental status of coastal waters, in general, marine waters, determined on the basis of qualitative descriptors at the level of marine region or subregion.[57] This region refers to marine waters under the sovereignty and jurisdiction of Member States of the European Union include waters in the Mediterranean Sea, the Baltic Sea, the Black Sea and the North-east Atlantic Ocean.[58]

52 https://ec.europa.eu/maritimeaffairs/policy_en (last visited 9.9.2017)

53 Directive 2008/56/EC of The European Parliament and of The Council of 17 June 2008, establishing a framework for community action in the field of marine environmental policy, OJ, L.164, 25.6.2008, p.19. (hereinafter Marine Directive)

54 European Commission, Sea for Life: Protected- Sustainable- Shared European Seas by 2020, Publications Office of EU, Luxemburg, 2011, p.28. https://publications.europa.eu/en/publication-detail/-/publication/ff3c7a4d-7ce5-4427-b9c3-8ed90d58a4a0. (last visited 9.9.2017)

55 Marine Directive, Preamble, para.3.

56 Marine Directive, Preamble, para.12, art.3/1(b).

57 Art. 3/5(b).

58 Preamble, para.1.

In great interest of Turkey, as a coastal state to Mediterranean Sea, and the Black Sea, is a state party to revised version the Convention on the Protection of the Mediterranean Sea Against Pollution (Barcelona Convention), renamed as "The Convention for the Protection of the Marine Environment and the Coastal Region of the Mediterranean" and its Protocols; and also Convention on the Protection of the Black Sea Against Pollution (Bucharest Convention), its Protocols. As a consequence of the latter, Turkey is participant to the Strategic Action Plan for the Environmental Protection and Rehabilitation of the Black Sea.[59] Turkey, has also been a member of MED-POL Project of Mediterranean Action Plan (MAP) of UNEP from the initiation from in 1970's.[60]

EU, since 1970's, simultaneous to these coastal protection initiatives mentioned and The UN Earth Summit (Rio Declaration and Agenda 21 arises from), was in effort of an integrated coastal zone management, for the risks of climate change, fruited by a recommendation of European Parliament and Council in 2002,[61] and with a EC directive proposal dating 2013.[62] Certainly, they were the outcomes of *Erika* Incident, what had highlighted the benefits of a joint EU approach on marine safety, in the early 2000's.

III. Final Remarks

Rapid urbanization in Turkey, particularly along the coastal zone, has resulted in several impacts on marine environment indirectly by lacking in adequate infrastructure and sanitation facilities, disposal of wastes into the sea. Uncontrolled development of tourism affects coastal ecology, disruption of ecological balance caused by land based pollution of coastal

---

59 http://www.mfa.gov.tr/convention-on-the-protection-of-the-black-sea-against-pollution-_bucharest-convention_.en.mfa. (last visited 8.9.2017)

60 PAP/RAC: Coastal Area Management in Turkey, Priority Actions Programme Regional Activity Centre, Split, 2005, p.29, https://www.medcoast.net/uploads/documents/Coastal_Area_Management_in_Turkey.pdf, (last visited 8.9.2017)

61 Recommendation of the European Parliament and of the Council of 30 May 2002 concerning the implementation of Integrated Coastal Zone Management in Europe, *Official Journal L 148, 06/06/2002, pp.24-27.*

62 Proposal for a Directive of The European Parliament and of The Council establishing a framework for maritime spatial planning and integrated coastal management, http://ec.europa.eu/environment/iczm/pdf/Proposal_en.pdf. (last visited 7.9.2017)

waters generates local eutrophication.[63] Construction in coastal regions, have destructive effects on fauna and flora and, in particular, on endemic species (e.g. monk seal and *caretta* turtles).[64]An interesting effect has noticed by Turkish marine ecologists, according to hydro-geological analysis, the over pumping and abstraction of groundwater illegally drilled out of the sole authority in charge (State Hydraulic Affairs-DSI) causes the intrusion of saline water into aquifers, in particular seasonal periods.[65]Agriculture in the coastal regions with productive fields irrigated by various rivers within the deltas, products with high market values, subsidised for chemical fertilizers, is another issue affects marine environment from land- based sources and activities.[66] Industralization surrounding Sea of Marmara is an another huge problem. The need of cooling water for power plants at coastal regions is an another important issue not to be dismissed. Especially, the projects of nuclear power plants in Sinop and Kırklareli on Black Sea coast, in Mersin on the Mediterranean Coast needs high concern on the protection of marine environment of Turkey. Aside of pollution generated by oil tankers, pollution in bays by cruising and yachting is another point to consider.

In brief, marine pollution along the Turkish coastline, is due to various reasons. Firstly from land-based sources such as untreated wastewater from domestic and industrial facilities, pollutants brought from inland areas by rivers containing toxic substances, agricultural practices, energy plants and finally tourism activities; secondly, pollution generated from vessels, maritime transportation with a heavy traffic of oil tankers across Mediterranean to Black Sea and backwards, including Turkish Straits.[67] Lastly, aquacultural production activities and transboundary pollution from neighbouring countries, the remains of carried by the Danube River.[68] A special risk of marine pollution from vessels to Turkish coasts, cited by Turkish marine ecologists, gives a high risk of introducing exotic species into native marine fauna and flora of Turkish marine waters by ballast waters, in particular, Sea of Marmara,

63 *S.Burak, E.Doğan, C.Gazioğlu*, "Impact of Urbanization and Tourism on Coastal Environment", Ocean and Coastal Management, 47 (2004), p. 520.

64 *Id.*

65 *Id.*

66 *Id.*, at p.21

67 *Id.*, at p.29-30

68 *Id.*

effecting supplies of fresh water reservoir and pipes of Istanbul.[69] Most of these marine pollutant factors are common for Turkey and EU.

Since the initiation of negotiations of Environmental Chapter with EU, a comparison on Turkey's Progress Reports may be clarifying the progress. When we review the reports for ten years period from 2009-2019, the common and main fields examined under Environmental Chapter, includes water quality.

Water quality, in 2009 and 2010 reports were in infancy. The institutional framework for water management assessed as unorganised on a river basin basis, and, transboundary consultations on water issues premature.[70] A joint declaration providing for increased cooperation on the management of the Meric/Evros river basin signed with Greece was welcomed. In 2016, progress on water quality field, rated to be moderate. Regarding the directives on marine strategy, quality control and bathing water alignment is pending.[71] Partial alignment was achieved in recent changes in secondary legislation on water quality standards, nitrates pollution and flood management plans; generally transboundary issues are note aligned.[72] The very last report, announced in the preparation period of this paper, despite of the moderate progress in 2016, a pause in reporting period examined.[73] It states such: " *Turkey has begun transboundary consultations on water issues with neighbouring countries on the Maritsa (Meriç) river but these are generally still at an early stage. Wastewater treatment capacity has slightly increased.* ***Alignment has not yet begun with regard to directives on marine strategy and bathing water. Alignment with the Water Framework Directive is not yet completed.***"

In our view, sadly, measures to prevent environment in general terms, are taken after a damage occurs or the polluting conditions deteriorates. This attitude is not compatible with the precautionary principle governing the international environmental law. Therefore, the management of coastal zones, should be planned at macro level, in the light of sustainability and

---

69 *Bayram Öztürk, Ayaka Öztürk & Nesrin Algan*, "Ship Originated Pollution in The Turkish Straits System", Proceedings of the International Symposium on the Problems of Regional Seas, ed.by. Bayram Öztürk, Turkish Marine Research Foundation, 2001, p.90-91.

70 Progress Report of 2009, p.81. https://www.ab.gov.tr/files/AB_Iliskileri/Tur_En_Realitons/Progress/turkey_progress_report_2009.pdf , (last visited 8.9.2017)

71 Progress Report of 2016, p.87. https://www.ab.gov.tr/files/pub/2016_progress_report_en.pdf , (last visited 8.9.2017)

72 *Id.*

73 Progress Report of 2018, p.91 https://ec.europa.eu/neighbourhood-enlargement/sites/near/files/20180417-turkey-report.pdf, (last visited 18.5.2018)

precautionary principle; and implemented at micro level local authorities. Coastal zone management is uncoordinated, and institutions in charge are overlapping or poorly tied to each other.

From the point of view of the author, in order to ensure the protection of coastal waters, Turkey should direct and implement waste management from land based activities strictly, then, work very hard with its institutions and civil society on Marine Directive to assure conformity of its legal legislation and implementation.

Again, from the Author's view, administrative challenges in the composition of Ministries related with the issue, regretfully, shall likely to cause loss of time. But, news about a plan of establishment of Turkish Environmental Institution, a comprehensive frame for a more coordinated administrative structure is pleasing, if not any bureaucratic delay occurs.

Bibliography

Books

European Commission, Sea for Life: Protected- Sustainable- Shared European Seas by 2020, Publications Office of EU, Luxemburg, 2011, p.28. https://publications.europa.eu/en/publication-detail/-/publication/ff3c7a4d-7ce5-4427-b9c3-8ed90d58a4a0

P. Birnie, A.Boyle & C.Redgewell, International Law & Environment, 3rd ed., Oxford University Press, 2009

Ved P. Nanda, George Pring, International environmental Law and Policy for 21st Century, 2nd revised ed., Martinus Nijhoff Publishers

Articles

Ayşegül Kibaroğlu, Vakur Sümer & Waltina Scheumann, "Fundamental Shifts in Turkey's Water Policy", Journal of Mediterranean Geography, 119, 2012, pp. 27-34, https://journals.openedition.org/mediterranee/6453.

S.Burak, E.Doğan, C.Gazioğlu, "Impact of Urbanization and Tourism on Coastal Environment", Ocean and Coastal Management, 47 (2004), pp.515-527.

Bayram Öztürk, Ayaka Öztürk & Nesrin Algan, "Ship Originated Pollution in The Turkish Straits System", Proceedings of the International Symposium on the Problems of Regional Seas, ed.by. Bayram Öztürk, Turkish Marine Research Foundation, 2001, pp.86-98.

EU Legislation

Directive 2000/60/EC of the European Parliament And of the Council of 23 October 2000 establishing a framework for Community action in the field of water policy, OJ, L.327, 22.12.2000, p.1.

Directive 2008/56/EC of The European Parliament and of The Council of 17 June 2008, establishing a framework for community action in the field of marine environmental policy, OJ, L.164, 25.6.2008, p.19.

Proposal for a Directive of The European Parliament and of The Council establishing a framework for maritime spatial planning and integrated coastal management, http://ec.europa.eu/environment/iczm/pdf/Proposal_en.pdf

Recommendation of the European Parliament and of the Council of 30 May 2002 concerning the implementation of Integrated Coastal Zone Management in Europe, *Official Journal L 148, 06/06/2002, pp.24 – 27.*

EU Reports

Common Implementation Strategy for the Water Framework Directive (2000/60/EC), Guidance document n.o 5, Transitional and Coastal Waters, Typology, Reference Conditions and Classification Systems, 2003, https://circabc.europa.eu/sd/a/85912f96-4dca-432e-84d6-a4dded785da5/GuIdance%20No%205%20-%20characterisation%20of%20coastal%20waters%20-%20COAST%20(WG%202.4).pdf

Country Report on Turkey of European Commission about Maritime Spatial Planning in the Mediterranean Sea, https://ec.europa.eu/maritimeaffairs/sites/maritimeaffairs/files/docs/body/turkey_01_en.pdf

Progress Report of Turkey, 2009, https://www.ab.gov.tr/files/AB_Iliskileri/Tur_En_Realitons/Progress/turkey_progress_report_2009.pdf

Progress Report of Turkey, 2010, https://www.ab.gov.tr/files/AB_Iliskileri/Tur_En_Realitons/Progress/turkey_progress_report_2010.pdf

Progress Report of Turkey, 2016, https://www.ab.gov.tr/files/pub/2016_progress_report_en.pdf

Progress Report of Turkey, 2018, https://ec.europa.eu/neighbourhood-enlargement/sites/near/files/20180417-turkey- report.pdf

Other International Documents

PAP/RAC: Coastal Area Management in Turkey, Priority Actions Programme Regional Activity Centre, Split, 2005, p.29, https://www.medcoast.net/uploads/documents/Coastal_Area_Management_in_Turkey.pdf

United Nations Convention of The Law of The Sea (UNCLOS), https://www.un.org/depts/los/convention_agreements/texts/unclos/unclos_e.pdf

Turkish Legislation

Turkish Constitution as amended on April 16, 2017; Act No. 6771, Official Gazette of Turkey, date 27/4/2017, No: 30050.

The Turkish Code on Environment, Official Gazette of Turkey, date 09/08/1983, No: 18132.

The Code Pertaining to Principles of Emergency Response and Compensation for Damages in Pollution of Marine Environment by Oil and Other Harmful Substances, Official Gazette of Turkey, date 11/3/2005, No.25752.

The Regulation on the Control over the Water Pollution, Official Gazette of Turkey, date 31/12/2004, No: 25687.

Websites

https://ec.europa.eu/maritimeaffairs/policy_en

https://www.avrupa.info.tr/en/environment-and-climate-change-most-important-and-challenging-eu-policy-areas-259.

http://ec.europa.eu/environment/pubs/pdf/factsheets/water-framework-directive.pdf

http://www.mfa.gov.tr/convention-on-the-protection-of-the-black-sea-against-pollution-_bucharest-convention_.en.mfa.

Focus on Water Protection in Turkey: Implementation Status of the EU Water Framework Directive and Upcoming Legal Challanges in Turkey

*Elif Başkaracaoğlu**

Abstract

In the accession negotiations process between Turkey and the European Union (EU), under the environment chapter, it is stated that Turkey should harmonize its legislation with the EU Water Framework Directive. The main aim of this paper is to present the implementation status of the EU Water Framework Directive and upcoming legal challenges in Turkey in this regard. For this purpose, Turkey's organisational structure and Turkish legislation are outlined to discuss the forms of efficient applicability of the Directive. The organisational structure makes the holistic protection of the environment difficult. In this respect, Turkey has already adopted a considerable part of secondary legislation, but has not yet adopted a single Water Law. The most challenging issue for Turkey will obviously be transboundary waters.

Keywords: European Union Water Framework Directive, water protection in Turkey, water management in Turkey, Turkish legislation on water protection.

I. Introduction

According to the classification based on water wealth and the annual volume of water available per capita, which is 1,346 m^3 in 2020[1], Turkey is a water stress country. It is projected that factors such as population increase, economic growth rate and change of water consumption patterns will increase the need for water in the future.[2] Day by day, climate change pressure over the water resources increases.[3] Therefore, they should be protected and well managed.

---

* Research Assistant Dr., Department of International Law, Istanbul University Faculty of Law.
The author wishes to express her thanks to Assoc. Prof. Dr. Gökçe Çataloluk Asal and Assoc. Prof. Dr. Galip Engin Şimşek for the correction of this paper.

1 For the statistics see Toprak Su Kaynakları, official website of General Directorate of State Hydraulic Works retrieved from https://www.dsi.gov.tr/Sayfa/Detay/754# (last visited 24.03.2022).

2 Land&Water Resources, retrieved from http://en.dsi.gov.tr/land-water-resources (last visited 27.02.2017, actually this page is not found).

3 See Republic of Turkey (RT) Ministry of Development, Eleventh Development Plan (2019-2023), Special Commission Report on the Management and Security of Water Resources Management, 2018, pp. 49-54, available at https://www.sbb.gov.tr/wp-conten

Transboundary and boundary waters constitute approximately 39% Turkey water potential.[4] However, water sharing constitutes an important problem for the neighbouring countries of Turkey in the Middle East.

In the accession negotiations process with the EU, under the environment chapter, it is stated that Turkey should harmonize its legislation with the EU water legislation and enforce them effectively. The basis of the EU legislation concerning water protection is the Directive 2000/60/EC of the European Parliament and of the Council of 23 October 2000 establishing a framework for Community action in the field of water policy (Water Framework Directive - WFD)[5]. One of the six closing benchmarks for the Chapter on Environment is to adopt legislation aiming "*at transposing the acquis in the field of water quality*", its own Framework Water Protection Law and to establish River Basin Protection Action Plans.[6] In the National Programme of Turkey for the Adoption of the EU Acquis[7], it is stated that harmonization with this directive "*will be ensured within the framework of full membership [ ] perspective*".[8] In this respect, in the 2021 Turkey's Report, it is pointed out that the legislative alignment on water quality "*is advanced but implementation and enforcement should be improved*".[9]

---

t/uploads/2020/04/SuKaynaklariYonetimi_ve_GuvenligiOzelIhtisasKomisyonuRaporu.pdf (last visited 22.03.2022).

4 RT Ministry of Agriculture and Forestry, 1st Water Council, Document of Working Group (Doc. WG) on the Management of Waters in Basin Scale, p. 71, available at: https://cdniys.tarimorman.gov.tr/api/File/GetFile/467/Sayfa/1497/1861/DosyaGaleri/suyun_havza_olceginde_yonetimi_grubu_calisma_belgesi.pdf (last visited 29.03.2022).

5 OJ 2000 L 327/1.

6 Chapter 27 – Environment, official website of Republic of Turkey Ministry of Foreign Affairs Directorate EU Affairs, retrieved from https://www.ab.gov.tr/chapter-27-environment_92_en.html (last visited 23.02.2022).

7 Decision of the Council of Ministers no: 2008/1448: National Programme of Turkey for the Adoption of the EU Acquis and Decision on its implementation, coordination and monitoring, Official Gazette (OG) 31 December 2008 No. 27097, bis 5. For the English translation, see https://www.ab.gov.tr/42260_en.html (last visited 23.02.2022).

8 *Id.* at. p. 330, footnote 2. Regarding to this Directive, in the Turkey's Programme for Alignment with the Acquis (2007-2013), that "*fulfillment of gradual harmonization with the EU and consideration of full harmonization at the time of membership*" is mentioned [Turkey's Programme for Alignment with the Acquis (2007-2013), p. 336, retrieved from https://www.ab.gov.tr/files/Muktesebat_Uyum_Programi/En/Chapter_27.pdf (last visited 23.02.2022)].

9 European Commission (EC), Commission Staff Working Document, Turkey 2021 Report SWD (2021) 290 Final/2, 19 October 2021, p. 107, available at https://ec.europa.eu/neighbourhood-enlargement/turkey-report-2021_en (last visited 21.02.2022).

This paper concentrates on the implementation process of the EU Water Framework Directive in Turkey and draws attention to the challenges it is faced. To comment on this process, firstly, organisational structure of Turkey and the dilemmas in this respect are examined. After that, current and prospective Turkish legislation are examined to point out at the necessary changes that still need to be implemented to complete the harmonization process. In the same perspective, finally river basin management is treated.

II. Organisational Structure

At the beginning of the negotiations for the chapter on environment, the competent authority for the implementation of the WFD was the Ministry of Environment and Forestry. But firstly in 2011, while some ministries were reorganized, the environment administration was separated from the forestry[10], and two distinct ministries were established: Ministry of Environment and Urbanisation (MEU)[11] and Ministry of Forestry and Water Affairs (MFWA)[12]. Thereafter in 2018[13], the latter was united with the Ministry of Food, Agriculture and Livestock under the name of the Ministry of Agriculture and Forestry (MAF)[14]. Finally, in 2021, the name of MEU was changed to the Ministry of Environment, Urbanisation and Climate Change (MEUCC)[15] and MAF's duties related to combating desertification and erosion were transferred to it.

Water sector is now under the authority of the MAF. This reorganisation, which puts one of the most important environmental elements such as water under the authority of a separate ministry, causes difficulties in context of an integrated approach to the issues under the title of environment.

10 Whereas a short time ago before this reorganisation, Decree Law No. 636 on Organisation and Duties of Ministry of Environment, Forestry and Urbanisation had been adopted (OG 8 June 2011 No. 27958 bis).

11 Decree Law No. 644 on Organisation and Duties of the Ministry of Environment and Urbanisation, OG 4 July 2011 No. 27984 bis.

12 Decree Law No. 645 on Organisation and Duties of Ministry of Forestry and Water Affairs, OG 4 July 2011 No. 27984 bis.

13 Constitution of the Republic of Turkey was amended as a result of the referendum held on 16 April 2017 and presidential system of government was adopted. After the elections held on 24 June 2018, the governmental structure was adapted to this new system.

14 Presidential Decree No. 1 on Organisation of Presidency, Fourteenth Section, OG 10 July 2018 No. 30474.

15 Presidential Decree No. 85 on Amendment of Certain Presidential Decrees, Articles 1-7, OG 29 October 2021 No. 31643.

After combating desertification and erosion[16] came under MEUCC, this time implementation of an integrated approach to the water issues might become more difficult. This reorganisation might lead to institutional coordination problems.

There are many institutions directly and indirectly related to water management within the administrative structure at the national, regional and provincial level.[17] In the documents of different working groups at the 1st Water Council, which was convened recently in 2021, it was indicated that sometimes their powers and responsibilities overlap and conflict as well as an effective coordination between them is still lacking.[18]

Under the MAF, General Directorate of Water Management and General Directorate of State Hydraulic Works are responsible for WFD. In 2011, Water Institute was established[19], to serve as a scientific advisory board on water management issues.

In 2012, Water Management Coordination Committee (WMCC) was established.[20] It is in charge of determining the necessary measures to protect water resources within the framework of integrated river basin management perspective; providing cross-sectoral coordination, cooperation and acceleration of water investments for an effective water management; developing a strategy, plan and policy to achieve the targets in the national and international documents; assessing the implementation of the matters that

---

16 Among the duties of MEUCC, these have been added: "*to make planning at the national and regional level aiming at developing water basins, for the purpose of combating desertification and erosion, to carry out studies for determination of policies and strategies.*" (*id* at Article 2).

17 For these institutions see RT MAF, National Water Plan (2019-2023), pp. 19-20, 60-65, available at: https://www.tarimorman.gov.tr/SYGM/Belgeler/NHYP%20DEN%C4%B0Z/ULUSAL%20SU%20PLANI.pdf (last visited 22.03.2022), RT MAF, 1st Water Council, Doc. WG on Water Law and Politics, p. 24, available at: https://cdniys.tarimorman.gov.tr/api/File/GetFile/467/Sayfa/1497/1861/DosyaGaleri/su_hukuku_ve_politikasi_grubu_calisma_belgesi.pdf, (last visited 28.02.2022); Doc. WG on the protection and monitoring of water resources as quality and quantity, pp. 21-22. available at: https://cdniys.tarimorman.gov.tr/api/File/GetFile/467/Sayfa/1497/1861/DosyaGaleri/su_kaynaklarinin_kalite_miktar_olarak_korunmasi_ve_izlenmesi_grubu_calisma_belgesi.pdf (last visited 28.02.2022).

18 Doc. WG on Water Law and Politics, *supra* note 17 at p. 24; Doc. WG on the Management of Waters in Basin Scale, *supra* note 4 at pp. 116 – 118, 163-164; Doc. WG on the protection and monitoring of water resources as quality and quantity, *supra* note 17, pp. 143, 148. Apart from these, see National Water Plan (2019-2023), *supra* note 17 at p. 20.

19 Decree Law No. 658 on Establishment and Duties of Turkish Water Institute, OG 2 November 2011 No. 28103.

20 Prime Ministry Circular No. 2012/7 on WMCC, OG 20 March 2012 No. 28239.

should be realized in river basin plans by state institutions and organisations; ensuring high-level coordination and cooperation.

In 2021, its composition was changed in accordance with the reorganisation of the Ministries and enlarged.[21] The head of which is the Minister of MAF or delegated deputy minister in their absence. Other members of the Committee are: relevant deputy ministers of MEU (now MEUCC), Ministry of Foreign Affairs, Ministry of Energy and Natural Resources, Ministry of Internal Affairs, Ministry of Culture and Tourism, Ministry of Health, Ministry of Industry and Technology, Ministry of Transport and Infrastructure, President of Strategy and Budget (or general director of relevant units to be appointed), President of Disaster and Emergency Management. It also includes the general directors of Water Management, Nature Conversation and Natural Parks, Agriculture Reform, Agricultural Research and Policies, Fisheries and Aquaculture, Plant Production, Combating Desertification and Erosion, European Union and Foreign Relations, State Hydraulic Works, Forestry, Meteorology and head of Turkish Water Institute, General Director of The Bank of Provinces (İlbank) and Secretary General of Municipalities of Turkey. Its new composition might contribute to solve the institutional coordination problem in some degree.

The representatives of the relevant state institutions and organisations, universities, NGOs, professional associations and private sector would be invited to the meetings of this committee. In this way, a necessary step was partly taken concerning the implementation of the participation principle.

III. WFD and Turkish Legislation

In general terms, WFD's purpose "*is to establish a framework for protection of inland surface waters, transnational waters, coastal waters and groundwaters*".[22] It also aims at protecting and qualitatively and quantitatively improving the surface and groundwaters and sustainable utilisation of water resources with an integrated approach. The main target obviously is to raise the quality of all waters to a "*good status*".[23] To realize this, the Directive adopts a combination of two approaches: One focusing on water quality

21 Presidential Circular No. 2021/17 on WMCC, OG 6 August 2021 No. 31560.

22 Art. 1.

23 For the surface water "*good ecological status*" and "*good chemical status*", for groundwater "*good chemical status*" and "*good quantitative status*". (Introduction to the new EU

objectives and the determination of minimum water quality standards, and the other focusing on emission limit on pollutants, based on maximum quantity of pollutants to be discharged from a specific source.[24]

Turkey has no single legal framework to regulate all these areas. The relevant water legislation[25] corresponding to the scope of the Directive is rather dispersed. Law on Water dated 1926[26], Law on Groundwater dated 1960[27], Law on Drinking Water for Village dated 1960[28], Environment Law dated 1983[29], Law on Geothermal Resources and Natural Mineral Waters dated 2007[30], By - law on Water Pollution Control dated 2004[31] are examples of this fragmentation. The fragmentation in primary and secondary legislation complicates the implementation of holistic policies.

A new Water Law was drafted "*to ensure the protection, use, remediation and improvement of water resources in a sustainable way; to collect information related to water and monitor; to analyse and plan on the basis of river basin level; to determine usage priorities and ensure water allocation by a single authority; to improve effectiveness and participation in water management*".[32] The Draft Law has not yet submitted to the Turkish Grand National Assembly.[33]

Water Framework Directive, pp. 3-4; retrieved from http://ec.europa.eu/environment/water/water-framework/info/intro_en.htm (last visited 24.03.2022).

24 Avrupa Birliği Çevre Mevzuatı Yayınları, Bölgesel Çevre Merkezi, REC Türkiye, 2010, Ankara, pp. 147-148. Available at: https://rec.org.tr/wp-content/uploads/2017/08/ab-cevre-mevzuati.pdf (last visited 24.03.2022).

25 After the constitutional amendment in 2018, a Decree Law was enacted in order to harmonize the legislation. It is excluded when indicating the date of amendments to the legislation in this paper.

26 OG 10 May 1926 No. 368. It was amended in 1934 and in 1956.

27 OG 23 December 1960 No. 10688 (last amend. in 2018).

28 OG 16 May 1960 No. 10506 (last amend. in 2008).

29 OG 11 August 1983 No. 18132. In 2006, several articles were amended. It set forth administrative fine for discharge of waste within all waters (Art. 20). Last amend. in 2023.

30 OG 13 June 2007 No. 26551 (last amend. in 2021).

31 OG 31 December 2004 No. 25687 (last amend. in 2023).

32 Draft Water Law (version 2012), Art. 1. For draft Water Law see official website of General Directorate of Water Management, http://suyonetimi.ormansu.gov.tr/AnaSayfa/su_kanunu_taslagi.aspx?sflang=tr (last visited 23.06.2017, actually this page is not found). The final version was not accessible. Therefore, all the observations and comments are based on the 2012 version and information obtained via secondary sources.

33 Draft Water Law has been working for a long time. In 2012, Draft Water Law was submitted to the public. In 2014, it was presented to Prime Ministry. After meetings were held at Prime Ministry between 2016-2017, it was returned to the relevant Ministry in 2018 to adjust to the new system. At the 1st Water Council, studies were carried out on its re-evaluation, improvement and revise. (Doc. WG on Water Law and Politics, *supra* note 17 at p. 3.)

In Turkey's National Action Plan (NAP) for the EU Accession[34], covering the period between January 2021 – December 2023, Water Law was announced to be published in 2023.[35] The Draft Law excludes geothermal waters and seas. It includes all issues related to surface and ground waters resources including coastal waters, and allocation of natural mineral waters and control of this allocation. It does not cover territorial waters with regard to their chemical status, which is however regulated by the WFD within the definition of surface waters.[36] By virtue of this Law, the fragmented and dispersed structure in the legislation and the confusion on the allocation of authority between institutions will be eliminated.[37] It will be an important part of the harmonisation with the WFD.

For the implementation of the WFD, Turkey also promulgated some by-laws concerning water quality. These are:

- By-law on Surface Water Quality Management[38],
- By-law on the Quality of Surface Water, which is Used or Intended to be Used for Drinking Water[39],
- By-law on the Protection of Groundwater against Pollution and Deterioration[40],
- By-law on protection of drinking-utility water basins[41],
- By-law on the identification of sensitive water bodies and of areas affecting those bodies and on improvement of water quality[42].

Additionally in NAP between 2021-2023, it has been foreseen that By-law on the Quality of Irrigation Water and Reuse of Waste Water will be enacted.[43]

34 Available at: https://www.ab.gov.tr/siteimages/birimler/kpb/uep/21_23_UEP_EN.pdf (last visited 23.02.2022).

35 *Id* at p. 243, no. 8.

36 "*Surface water means inland waters, except groundwater; transitional waters and coastal waters, except in respect of chemical status for which it shall also include territorial waters.*" (WFD Art. 2/1).

37 Doc. WG on Water Law and Politics, *supra* note 17 at p. 25.

38 OG 30 November 2012 No. 28483 (last amend. in 2023).

39 OG 29 June 2012 No. 28338. It was abrogated and By-law on quality and treatment of water, which is used for drinking water came into force in 2019 (OG 6 July 2019 No. 30823). Amend. in 2021.

40 OG 7 April 2012 No. 28257 (last amend. in 2023).

41 OG 28 October 2017 No. 30224. Amend. in 2020.

42 OG 23 December 2016 No. 29927 bis. Amend. in 2021.

43 NAP (2021-2023), *supra* note 34 at p. 249. no. 21.

WFD envisions programs to be arranged in order to monitor the quality and quantity of surface and ground waters in a systematic way.[44] To this purpose, Turkey has put into force By-law on Monitoring Surface Water and Groundwater[45]. In Turkey's NAP between 2016-2019[46], the amendment of this by-law was envisaged but it has not yet been enacted. In accordance with this by-law, Communiqué on biological monitoring[47] and Communiqué on hydromorphological monitoring of River and Lake[48] were published.

IV. River Basin Management

WFD adopts a model of water management, which is based on river basin as a natural geographical and hydrological unit. According to this, first of all, the individual river basins lying within the national territory shall be identified and assigned into individual river basin districts.[49] Following this regulation, 25 river basins were determined in Turkey and was concluded that for each river basin district, a river basin management plan (RBMP) should be prepared.

In order to realize this model of water management, Turkey also published:

- By-law on the Protection of Water Basins and Preparation of Basin Management Plans in 2012[50],
- Communiqué on the Organisation, Duties, Working Principles and Procedures of Basin Management Committees in 2013[51].

44 WFD Art. 8.

45 OG 11 February 2014 No. 28910.

46 Turkey's National Action Plan for the EU Accession: January 2016 – December 2019, p. 204, no. 11, available at: http://www.ab.gov.tr/files/5%20Ekim/uepkitapcik2016-2019-EN.pdf (last visited 23.03.2022).

47 OG 21 June 2019 No. 30808.

48 OG 28 January 2021 No. 31378. It was abrogated and Communiqué on hydromorphological monitoring came into force in 2023 (OG 25 April 2023 No. 32171).

49 WFD Art. 3/1.

50 OG 17 October 2012 No. 28444. It was amended in 2017. Its new name is "By-law on Preparation, Implementation and Monitoring of Basin Management Plans", (OG 28 October 2017 No. 30224). This was amended in 2019.

51 OG 18 June 2013 No. 28681. It was abrogated and "Communiqué on Organisation, Duties, Working Principles and Procedures of Basin Management Central Committee, Basin Management Committees and Provincial Water Management Coordination Committees" came into force in 2019 (OG 18 January 2019 No. 30659).

In 2014, a National Basin Management Strategy (2014-2023)[52] was adopted. Between 2009-2013, the river basin protection action plans, which constitute the groundwork of RBMPs for 25 river basins, were prepared. By the end of 2021, the RBMPs prepared for 11 basins were approved by WMCC and began to be implemented.[53]

In a case of a river basin covering the territory of more than one country, there are different provisions in the Directive depending on whether all riparian states are EU members. If the river basin covers the territory of more than one Member State, Member States shall ensure that it is assigned to an international river basin district and shall ensure coordination with the aim of producing a single international RBMP.[54] If a river basin district extends beyond the territory of the Community, then the Member State or Member States concerned shall endeavour to establish appropriate coordination with relevant non-member states with the aim of achieving this Directive's objectives and shall endeavour to produce a single RBMP.[55]

There are five river basins of Turkey shared with the EU or non-EU member states. These are:

- Meric River basin shared with EU members of Greece and Bulgaria;
- Kura-Aras River basin shared with the non EU members of Iran, Georgia, Azerbaijan and Armenia;
- Orontes River basin shared with the non-EU members of Syria and Lebanon;
- Tigris - Euphrates River basin shared with the non-EU members of Iraq and Syria;
- Coruh River basin shared with the non-EU member of Georgia.

In the 2021 Turkey report, it is indicated that Turkey's transboundary consultations on water issues with neighbouring countries are still at an early stage.[56] In 2010, "*Turkey signed with Greece a joint declaration providing for increased cooperation on the management of the Meric/Evros river basin*"[57]

52 OG 4 July 2014 No. 29050.

53 Doc. WG on the Management of Waters in Basin Scale, *supra* note 4 at p. 68, 70.

54 WFD Art. 3/3.

55 WFD Art. 3/5.

56 Turkey 2021 Report, *supra* note 9 at p. 107.

57 EC, Commission Staff Working Document Turkey 2010 Progress Report, SEC(2010) 1327, 9 November 2010, p. 90, available at: http://www.ab.gov.tr/files/AB_Iliskileri/Tur_En_Realitons/Progress/turkey_progress_report_2010.pdf (last visited 22.02.2022). For more information about the cooperation between Turkey and Greece on the

and a joint declaration on cooperation in the field of water resources with Bulgaria in 2012.[58] Transboundary consultations have begun on water issues on the Meric River.[59] It should be noted that the conduct and success of these negotiations does not depend solely to Turkey's will.

Tigris - Euphrates River Basin and Orontes River Basin are problematic fields in terms of water sharing. Therefore, the completion of the negotiations regarding these river basins could take place in a long term as political conjuncture repeatedly influences negotiations. In a period of close relations with Syria in 2009, a series of agreements were signed between Turkey and Syria. Among them, there are: Cooperation Agreement in the Field of Environment Protection, which also includes articles regarding protection of water resources and rationalization of water use; Memorandum of Understanding (MoU) in the Field of Remediation of Water Quality and MoU in the Field of Efficient Utilization of Water Resources and Combating of Drought.[60] It is observed that the approach and principles adopted by WFD were reflected in these agreements.[61] In 2014, Turkey and Iraq signed MoU in the Field of Water[62]. The implementation of these agreements depends on the political developments in this region. As a result, it could easily be stated that implementation of the Directive in terms of transboundary waters is one of the challenging issues for Turkey.

Participation is an important principle, which required involving all stakeholders and the public in decision-making process. In the By-law on Preparation, Implementation and Monitoring of Basin Management Plans,

---

Meric/Evros river basin see *S. Sağlam*, Meriç Nehir Havzası'nın Avrupa Birliği Su Çerçeve Direktifi Açısından Değerlendirilmesi, Uzmanlık Tezi, T.C. Orman ve Su İşleri Bakanlığı, Ankara 2014, pp. 138-147.

58 *Sağlam*, p. 153. For more information about this declaration, see pp. 153-154.

59 EC, Commission Staff Working Document, Turkey 2018 Report SWD(2018) 153 Final, 17 April 2018, p. 91, available at: https://www.ab.gov.tr/siteimages/kapbtablolar/20180417-turkey-report.pdf (last visited 30.03.2022).

60 All of these agreements were done on 23 December 2009. Their ratifications have been decided respectively by the Council of Ministers Decrees No: 2011/1735, 2011/1734, 2011/1739. For their texts, see OG 28 May 2011 No. 27947 bis.

61 *A. Kibaroğlu & A. D. Öztürk*, Su Diplomasisinin Başlıca İlke ve Kurumları: Türkiye Örneği, in Z. Savaşan & H. Ünay (eds.), Türk Çevre Hukuku ve Politikaları: Dünden Bugüne ve Geleceğe, 2021, p. 213, 231.

62 Done on 25 December 2014. The ratification of this agreement has been decided by the Presidential Decision No: 4499. For its text see OG 11 September 2021 No. 31595.

a participatory approach is adopted.[63] In this regard, it mentions "*the active participation of relevant institutions and organisations*" and "*stakeholders'*[64] *access to information of*" in the process of preparation, review and update of RBMPs. This is ensured through WMCC, Basin Management Central Committee, Basin Management Committees and Provincial Water Management Coordination Committees.[65] In the By-law, there is a provision[66] similar to the relevant provision of WFD[67] related to public access to information and receiving their opinion. However, it is applicable only in the updating process of river basin management. In this regard, for example, there is not any regulation on the process to be carried out together with the stakeholders while preparing water management plans.[68] This is clearly not sufficient in terms of the participation principle.

In the 2021 Turkey Report, it is observed that there are problems generally in ensuring "*actual implementation on public participation and the right to access to environmental information.*"[69]

V. Conclusions

Turkey has gone through substantial organisational changes and has amended its legislation since the opening of the chapter on environment to negotiations on the 21 December 2009. The current organisational structure at the ministry level is inconvenient for implementing a holistic approach due to the separation of the environment, climate change and water issues. In addition, there is no effective coordination between the institutions related to water management.

For the purpose of implementation of the WFD, Turkey adopted mostly secondary form of legislation and its works on the Draft Water Law has reached the final stage. In my opinion, while drafting legislation, a balance should be struck among the needs of Turkey, neighbouring countries and

63 Art. 5 (1) (a) and 9. The participatory approach is defined as "*ensuring the participation of relevant public institutions and organisations, professional chambers, non-governmental organisations and local people in the planning process*" [Art. 4 (1) z].

64 Art. 4 (1) ff) Stakeholder means "*natural and legal persons that are probably affected by and may affect the management plans at the basin scale*".

65 Art. 9.

66 Art. 11 (2), (3), (4).

67 WFD Art. 14/1 (a), (b), (c).

68 Doc. WG on the Management of Waters in Basin Scale, *supra* note 4 at p. 165.

69 Turkey 2021 Report, *supra* note 9 at p. 106.

different segments of public; which is as important as the harmonization of EU Acquis. With the adoption of the Water Law some of the confusion for the allocation of authority will be eliminated and deficiencies in the legislation will be corrected.

However, for the implementation of the WFD, there are two problematic issues, namely transboundary waters and public participation, especially participation of people affected directly from water management activities. Considering the current political atmosphere in the region, it is rather hard to deal with the issue of cooperation with the neighbouring countries in the Middle East. Nevertheless, with the adoption of By-law on the Protection of Water Basins and Preparation of Basin Management Plans and its amendments, a huge step was taken for the participatory rights of the public. Yet detailed legal regulations are still required to use the participation right effectively.

Bibliography

Book

Kibaroğlu, A. & Öztürk, A. D. Su Diplomasisinin Başlıca İlke ve Kurumları: Türkiye Örneği, in Z. Savaşan & H. Ünay (eds.), Türk Çevre Hukuku ve Politikaları: Dünden Bugüne ve Geleceğe, 2021, pp. 213-238.

Thesis

Sağlam, S.: Meriç Nehir Havzası'nın Avrupa Birliği Su Çerçeve Direktifi Açısından Değerlendirilmesi, Uzmanlık Tezi, T.C. Orman ve Su İşleri Bakanlığı, Ankara 2014.

Turkey's Documents

Draft Water Law (version 2012), http://suyonetimi.ormansu.gov.tr/AnaSayfa/su_kanunu_taslagi.aspx?sflang=tr (last visited 23.06.2017).

National Basin Management Strategy (2014-2023); OG 4 July 2014 No. 29050.

National Programme of Turkey for the Adoption of the EU Acquis retrieved from https://www.ab.gov.tr/42260_en.html (last visited 23.02.2022).

Turkey's National Action Plan for the EU Accession: January 2016 – December 2019 available at: http://www.ab.gov.tr/files/5%20Ekim/uepkitapcik2016-2019-EN.pdf (last visited 23.03.2022).

Turkey's National Action Plan for the EU Accession: January 2021 – December 2023 available at: https://www.ab.gov.tr/siteimages/birimler/kpb/uep/21_23_UEP_EN.pdf (last visited 23.02.2022.

Turkey's Programme for Alignment with the Acquis (2007-2013) available at: https://www.ab.gov.tr/files/Muktesebat_Uyum_Programi/En/Chapter_27.pdf (last visited 23.02.2022).

RT MAF, 1st Water Council, Doc. WG on the Management of Waters in Basin Scale, available at: https://cdniys.tarimorman.gov.tr/api/File/GetFile/467/Sayfa/1497/1861/DosyaGaleri/suyun_havza_olceginde_yonetimi_grubu_calisma_belgesi.pdf (last visited 29.03.2022).

RT MAF, 1st Water Council, Doc. WG on the protection and monitoring of water resources as quality and quantity, available at: https://cdniys.tarimorman.gov.tr/api/File/GetFile/467/Sayfa/1497/1861/DosyaGaleri/su_kaynaklarinin_kalite_miktar_olarak_korunmasi_ve_izlenmesi_grubu_calisma_belgesi.pdf (last visited 28.02.2022).

RT MAF, 1st Water Council, Doc. WG on Water Law and Politics, available at: https://cdniys.tarimorman.gov.tr/api/File/GetFile/467/Sayfa/1497/1861/DosyaGaleri/su_hukuku_ve_politikasi_grubu_calisma_belgesi.pdf (last visited 28.02.2022).

RT MAF, National Water Plan (2019-2023) available at: https://www.tarimorman.gov.tr/SYGM/Belgeler/NHYP%20DEN%C4%B0Z/ULUSAL%20SU%20PLANI.pdf (last visited 22.03.2022).

RT Ministry of Development, Eleventh Development Plan (2019-2023), Special Commission Report on the Management and Security of Water Resources Management, 2018, available at https://www.sbb.gov.tr/wp-content/uploads/2020/04/SuKaynaklariYonetimi_ve_GuvenligiOzelIhtisasKomisyonuRaporu.pdf (last visited 22.03.2022).

EU Documents

EC, Commission Staff Working Document Turkey 2010 Progress Report, SEC(2010) 1327, 9 November 2010, available at: http://www.ab.gov.tr/files/AB_Iliskileri/Tur_En_Realitons/Progress/turkey_progress_report_2010.pdf (last visited 22.02.2022).

EC, Commission Staff Working Document, Turkey 2018 Report SWD(2018) 153 Final, 17 April 2018, available at: https://www.ab.gov.tr/siteimages/kapbtablolar/20180417-turkey-report.pdf (last visited 30.03.2022).

EC, Commission Staff Working Document, Turkey 2021 Report SWD (2021) 290 Final/2, 19 October 2021, available at https://ec.europa.eu/neighbourhood-enlargement/turkey-report-2021_en (last visited 21.02.2022).

Legislation

EU Legislation

Directive 2000/60/EC of the European Parliament and of the Council on 23th October 2000 establishing a framework for Community action in the field of water policy, OJ 2000 L 327/1.

Turkish Legislation

By-law on Monitoring Surface Water and Groundwater, OG 11 February 2014 No. 28910.

By-law on Preparation, Implementation and Monitoring of Basin Management Plans, OG 28 October 2017 No. 30224.

By-law on protection of drinking-utility water basins, OG 28 October 2017 No. 30224.

By-law on quality and treatment of water, which is used for drinking water OG 6 July 2019 No. 30823.

By-law on Quality of Surface Water, which is Used or Intended to be Used of Drinking Water, OG 29 June 2012 No. 28338.

By-law on Surface Water Quality Management, OG 30 November 2012 No. 28483.

By-law on the identification of sensitive water bodies and of areas affecting those bodies and on improvement of water quality, OG 23 December 2016 No. 29927 bis.

By-law on the Protection of Groundwater against Pollution and Deterioration, OG 7 April 2012 No. 28257.

By-law on the Protection of Water Basins and Preparation of Basin Management Plans, OG 17 October 2012 No. 28444.

By - law on Water Pollution Control, OG 31 December 2004 No. 25687.

Communiqué on biological monitoring OG 21 June 2019 No. 30808.

Communiqué on hydromorphological monitoring OG 25 April 2023 No. 32171.

Communiqué on hydromorphological monitoring of River and Lake OG 28 January 2021 No. 31378.

Communiqué on Organisation, Duties, Working Principles and Procedures of Basin Management Central Committee, Basin Management Committees and Provincial Water Management Coordination Committees OG 18 January 2019 No. 30659.

Communiqué on the organisation, duties, working principle and procedures of basin management committees; OG 18 June 2013 No. 28681.

Decision of the Council of Ministers no: 2008/1448: National Programme of Turkey for the Adoption of the EU Acquis and Decision on its implementation, coordination and monitoring, OG 31 December 2008 No. 27097, bis 5.

Decree Law No. 636 on Organisation and Duties of Ministry of Environment, Forestry and Urbanisation; OG 8 June 2011 No. 27958 bis.

Decree Law No. 644 on Organisation and Duties of the Ministry of Environment and Urbanisation, OG 4 July 2011 No. 27984 bis.

Decree Law No. 645 on Organisation and Duties of Ministry of Forestry and Water Affairs, OG 4 July 2011 No. 27984.

Decree Law No. 658 on Establishment and Duties of Turkish Water Institute, OG 20 March 2012 No. 28239.

Environment Law, OG 11 August 1983 No. 18132.

Law on Drinking Water for Village, OG 16 May 1960 No. 10506.

Law on Geothermal Resources and Natural Mineral Waters, OG 13 June 2007 No. 26551.

Law on Groundwater, OG 23 December 1960 No. 10688.

Law on Water, OG 10 May 1926 No. 368.

Presidential Circular No. 2021/17 on Water Management Coordination Committee, OG 6 August 2021 No. 31560.

Presidential Decree No. 1 on Organisation of Presidency, OG 10 July 2018 No. 30474.

Presidential Decree No. 85 on Amendment of Certain Presidential Decrees, Articles 1-7, OG 29 October 2021 No. 31643.

Prime Ministry Circular No. 2012 on Water Management Coordination Committee, OG 20 March 2012 No. 28239.

Internet Sources

Avrupa Birliği Çevre Mevzuatı Yayınları, Bölgesel Çevre Merkezi, REC Türkiye, 2010, Ankara; available at http://www.temizuretim.gov.tr/Files/referansbelgeler/ABcevremevzuat.pdf (last visited 24.03.2022).

Chapter 27 – Environment retrieved from http://www.ab.gov.tr/?p=92&l=2 (last visited 23.02.2022).

Introduction to the new EU Water Framework Directive; retrieved from http://ec.europa.eu/environment/water/water-framework/info/intro_en.htm (last visited 24.03.2022).

Land&Water Resources, retrieved from http://en.dsi.gov.tr/land-water-resources (last visited 27.02.2017).

Toprak Su Kaynakları, official website of General Directorate of State Hydraulic Works retrieved from https://www.dsi.gov.tr/Sayfa/Detay/754# (last visited 24.03.2022).

Agreements

Cooperation Agreement in the Field of Environment Protection, OG 28 May 2011 No. 27947 bis.

MoU in the Field of Remediation of Water Quality, OG 28 May 2011 No. 27947 bis.

MoU in the Field of Efficient Utilization of Water Resources and Combating of Drought, OG 28 May 2011 No. 27947 bis.

MoU in the Field of Water Between the Ministry of Forestry and Water Affairs of the Republic of Turkey and the Ministry of Water Resources of the Republic of Iraq, OG 11 September 2021 No. 31595.

Specially Protected Marine Areas in the Mediterranean and Protection of Marine Biodiversity

Nebile Pelin Mantı[*]

Abstract

The Mediterranean is home to 6% of all known marine species with its rich biodiversity. Turkey, as a part of the Mediterranean Basin is also remarkable for its rich marine biodiversity. But this wealth is under threat for many human-induced reasons, such as pollution, extreme and illegal fishing, and some of these problems are triggered by increasing effects of the climate change.

Establishing marine protected areas is one of the mechanisms to manage human activities and ultimately reduce the associated pressures on the environment. Turkey as of 1990s, became party to Conventions and started to adopt new policies to protect coastal and marine biodiversity, one of which is establishment of Protected Areas on the coasts and Specially Protected Marine Areas along Mediterranean. In this article, we will focus on the Specially Protected Marine Areas in the Mediterranean and Turkey's efforts to protect its marine biodiversity.

Keywords: Specially Protected Areas, Marine Biodiversity, Climate Change, Mediterranean, Turkey

I. Introduction

Biological resources are vital to economic and social development of States, as well as for the preservation of healthy ecosystems. Since the beginning of the industrial era in 1800s, climate change, has growing impacts on biodiversity and wildlife habitats across the planet that are already being known by international community. Rising temperatures, warming sea waters, along with human-driven actions such as land or vessel sourced pollution, and overfishing, threatens the rich biodiversity in marine ecosystems all over the world.

The Mediterranean is a huge inner sea, having 21 bordering States and Mediterranean ecosystem is characterized by its exceptional biological richness, on land and in the sea, and has been internationally recognized as a biodiversity hotspot, about 29 percent of the species are endemic[1].

---

* Research Assistant, Public International Law Deparment, Istanbul University Faculty of Law.

1 UNEP-MAP RAC/SPA 2010. The Mediterranean Sea Biodiversity: state of the ecosystems, pressures, impacts and future priorities. By Bazairi, H., Ben Haj, S., Boero, F., Cebrian,

Mediterranean Sea biodiversity is under threat, as surveys, funded by the Regional Activity Centre for Specially Protected Areas (UNEP RAC/SPA), established by the Contracting Parties to the Barcelona Convention, revealed that marine protected areas in the eastern Mediterranean have been inundated by these non-indigenous species, and may in fact function as hubs for their secondary dispersal[2].

A. Developing Legal Framework for Biodiversity Protection

Marine ecosystems are providing countless services which are essential for the survival of the mankind, including food security, feed for livestock, raw materials for medicines, building materials from coral rock and sand, and they also provide natural defences against hazards such as coastal erosion, and inundation as underlined by various NGOs.

The early efforts started in 1975, 16 Mediterranean countries and the European Community adopted the Mediterranean Action Plan (MAP), the first-ever Regional Seas Programme under UNEP's umbrella. The first international convention in this regard was "The Barcelona Convention for the Protection of the Marine Environment and the Coastal Region of the Mediterranean"[3], adopted on 16 February 1976 in Barcelona and entered into force in 1978. However, the failure of this early environmental policies left the entire Mediterranean Sea prone to colonization by highly impacting non-indigenous species, including poisonous and venomous ones. Scientific research has been documenting this bio-invasion for over a century, yet beyond the ambit of marine scientists there is a lack of awareness of the scale of Mediterranean-wide consequences and scant appetite to enact the necessary environmental policies.

D., De Juan, S., Limam, A., Lleonart, J., Torchia, G., and Rais, C., Ed. RAC/SPA, Tunis; September 2010, p.16.

2 Bella Galil, Ferdinando Boero, Simona Fraschetti, et al., "The Enlargement of the Suez Canal and Introduction of Non-Indigenous Species to the Mediterranean Sea", in

3 Turkey signed the Barcelona Convention on 16.02.76, and ratified the first version on 06.04.81. Turkey also signed the amended Convention on 18.09.02 and ratified the document on 09.07.04. The status can be followed from:https://wedocs.unep.org/bitstream/handle/20.500.11822/7096/StatusOfSignaturesAndRatifications_20201029.pdf

In 1995, The Barcelona Convention was amended[4] and renamed as "The Convention for the Protection of the Marine Environment and the Coastal Region of the Mediterranean", and the amendments to the Barcelona Convention entered into force in 2004.

The Barcelona Convention and its seven Protocols adopted in the framework of the Mediterranean Action Plan (MAP) and this document constitutes the principal regional legally binding Multilateral Environmental Agreement (MEA) in the Mediterranean.

The United Nations General Assembly, by its 2010 Resolution on "Oceans and the Law of the Sea"[5], reaffirmed the need for States to continue and intensify their efforts, directly or through competent international organizations, to develop and facilitate the use of diverse approaches and tools for conserving and managing vulnerable marine ecosystems, including the establishment of marine protected areas, consistent with international law, as reflected in UNCLOS, and based on the best scientific information available, and the development of representative networks of any such marine protected areas by 2012.

Climate change added some new environmental threats, such as the potential consequences of rising sea-levels, global warming, acid deposition, ozone depletion and marine pollution create territorial problems and impinge on traditional military-territorial concepts of security[6], and at the beginning of 1990s added the idea of "environmental security" to UN agenda[7].

Among other issues, environmental security regime is initiated firstly, because of the rise of the environmental agenda, which is generated because of the global warming, acid deposition, ozone depletion and marine pollution issues, which created differential costs to the states of the world. According to a study published in the Science journal, the speed and direction of climate change, as well as the timing of seasonal shifts, are moving just as fast in large bodies of water as inland, and these will lead to serious problems regarding

---

4 Annex, Amendments to the Convention For the (Available at: https://wedocs.unep.org/bitstream/handle/20.500.11822/3002/95ig6_7_bcamendments_eng.pdf)

5 A/RES/63/111, Resolution adopted by the General Assembly on 5 December 2008, 12 February 2009. (Available at: https://www.un.org/en/development/desa/population/migration/generalassembly/docs/globalcompact/A_RES_63_111.pdf)

6 M. Imber, Environmental security: A task for the UN system.*Review of International Studies, 17*(2), (1991), pp.201-212. (doi:10.1017/S0260210500112252)

7 Ibid.

conservation for regions having rich marine biodiversity[8]. Accordingly, defining a management model will not only contribute to the maintenance or increased resilience of ecosystems but also will promote the sustainable use of ecosystem services[9].

B. Specially Protected Areas and the Development of the Legal Framework for An Effective Protection Regime

The establishment of Specially Protected Areas and adoption of protected area regimes in the Mediterranean has started in 1990s, following major incidents and these triggered the attention of the United Nations to interfere.

UN environmental security regime is an apparent contribution to the 1990s diplomacy. As of 1989, the renewed opportunities for peacekeeping, and the credibility of economic sanctions created by the end of the Cold War and the beginning of the Gulf Crisis. Adam Roberts, entails the total amount of oil spilled into the Gulf almost certainly constituted the largest oil spill ever, as the size of the spill was probably between seven and nine million barrels in Gulf[10], and caused by the slicks was considerable, which resulted over 400 kilometres of the Saudi coast, as well as the southern Kuwaiti coast, affected coastal marshlands, to wildlife (over 15,000 birds killed), to coastal flora, to fishing, and to offshore oil operations[11].

8 Scott C. Doney, Mary Ruckelshaus, J. Emmett Duffy, James P. Barry, Francis Chan, Chad A. English, Heather M. Galindo, Jacqueline M. Grebmeier, Anne B. Hollowed, Nancy Knowlton, Jeffrey Polovina, Nancy N. Rabalais, William J. Sydeman, and Lynne D. Talley, Climate Change Impacts on Marine Ecosystems, Annual Review of Marine Science, 2012, 4:1, (pp. 11-37), p. 11.

9 Secretariat of the Convention on Biological Diversity, Netherlands Commission for Environmental Assessment (2006). Biodiversity in Impact Assessment, Background Document to CBD Decision VIII/28: Voluntary Guidelines on Biodiversity-Inclusive Impact Assessment, Montreal, Canada, x _ y pages.

10 Pentagon, *Final Report to Congress,* pp. 0-26. The Greenpeace paper by William M. Arkin, "Gulf War Damage to the Natural Environment", pp. 2-3, gave the same figure, but mentioned additionally that smaller quantities of oil continued to leak into the Gulf from a number of sources until May or early June 1991.

11 Adam Roberts, Environmental Destruction in the 1991 Gulf War, in *International Review of the Red Cross, 32*(291), (1992), pp. 538-553. doi:10.1017/S0020860400071151

The United Nation's (UN) recognized biological diversity as an asset of tremendous value to present and future generations[12]. The United Nations Environment Programme (UNEP) tasked experts to prepare an international legal instrument for the conservation and sustainable use of biological diversity. They were to take into account "the need to share costs and benefits between developed and developing countries" as well as "ways and means to support innovation by local people".

The text of the Convention was adopted on 22 May 1992 in Nairobi and was opened to signature on 5 June 1992, during the Rio "Earth Summit". Within a year, it had received 168 signatures. It entered into force on 29 December 1993[13]. The text of the Convention is signed by 150 government leaders at the 1992 Rio Earth Summit, the Convention on Biological Diversity is dedicated to promoting sustainable development. The text is conceived as a practical tool for translating the principles of Agenda 21[14] into reality, the Convention recognizes that biological diversity is about more than plants, animals and microorganisms and their ecosystems – it is about people and our need for food security, medicines, fresh air and water, shelter, and a clean and healthy environment in which to live.

The Protocol envisages three main elements to ensure the safeguard of biological diversity in the Mediterranean[15]:

1. The creation, protection and management of Specially Protected Areas (SPAs)
2. The establishment of a list of Specially Protected Areas of Mediterranean Importance (SPAMIs)
3. The protection and conservation of species

In order to meet this objective, the following aspects are developed:

- Conservation of types of marine and coastal ecosystem that are typical of the Mediterranean.

12 International Day for Biological Diversity, 22 May 2020; the achievement and delivery of the CBD's; 22 May 2020; (Available at: https://www.un.org/en/observances/biological-diversity-day)

13 History of the Convention on Biodiversity. (Available at: https://www.cbd.int/history/)

14 Agenda 21 is a comprehensive plan of action to be taken globally, nationally, and locally by organizations of the United Nations System, Governments, and Major Groups in every area in which human impacts on the environment. (Available at: https://sustainabledevelopment.un.org/outcomedocuments/agenda21).

15 SPA/BD Protocol, Official webcite. (Available at: https://www.rac-spa.org/protocol)

- Protecting habitats that are in danger of disappearance or are necessary for the survival, reproduction, and restoration of threatened or endemic species.
- Protecting sites of scientific, aesthetic, cultural or educational interest.
- Development and implementation of management plans.
- Setting up and promoting Specially Protected Areas.
- Conservation of species that are threatened of extinction, endangered, or to be managed.
- Sustainable use of biological resources[16]

1. Turkey`s Efforts for SPAs

Turkey signed the UN Convention on Biological Diversity, on June 11,1992, and following the ratification of the Treaty within parliament on February 14,1997; became party on May 15, 1997[17]. Turkey became party to the Cartagena Protocol[18] as well.

The Specially Protected Areas of Mediterranean Importance (SPAMIs) are marine and coastal sites of the Mediterranean, created under the Barcelona Convention Protocol for Specially Protected Areas and Biological Diversity in the Mediterranean (SPA/BD Protocol).

As a part of the Mediterranean, Turkey declared marine protected areas and specially protected areas firstly in the Aegean Sea to protect its rich habitat diversity. At the beginning of the 1990s, Turkey's efforts focused on the establishment of Specially Protected Areas in the Mediterranean Region, both for land and maritime areas for the protection of the endemic species. Turkey has started biodiversity protection efforts, along with other Mediterranean states in 1990s. The perception of pressures and threats on biodiversity as an environmental problem was accepted in 1992 with the signing of the Convention on Biological Diversity in Rio de Janeiro's Sustainable Development Conference. Thus, the Convention on Biological Diversity was raised in the international arena, countries have become parties to this agreement and the existence of an international concern on this issue has been formally put forward. The Convention on Biological Diversity

16 Ibid.

17 Turkey is not party to Nagoya Protocol on Access and Benefit-sharing and to Nagoya – Kuala Lumpur Supplementary Protocol on Liability and Redress of the present Convention.

18 Cartagena Protocol, signed by Turkey on May 24,2000; ratified on October 24,2003 and became party on January 24,2004.

(CBD) was adopted by Turkey in 2002, and the CBD defines biological diversity as "the variability among living organisms from all sources including inter alia terrestrial, marine and other aquatic ecosystems and the ecological complexes of which they are part; this includes diversity of species, between species and of ecosystems."

Other than the Convention for the Protection of the Marine Environment and the Coastal Region of the Mediterranean (Barcelona Convention) and the Protocol concerning Specially Protected Areas and Biological Diversity in the Mediterranean[19], Turkey enforced its efforts by conducting comprehensive research at the coastal and marine areas in the south and in the north, which resulted with the establishment of protected areas and marine specially protected areas at the beginning of 2000s. Turkey adopted several documents, including National Biodiversity Strategy and Action Plan (NBSAP) (2007) and National Biodiversity Action Plan (NBAP) (2018-2028)[20].

2. Gökçeada

The Aegean Sea forms part of the Mediterranean and is home to many islands and islets. This area is an ecologically sensitive area for many reasons, as the islands are isolated from each other, endemism, their relationship with the Black Sea, the gene pool of the Mediterranean monk seal, etc. At the same time, this sea contains many micro-habitats necessary for many species, and these species are of great importance in the balance of the ecosystem.

19 Turkey'a accession to SPA Protocol dates 06/11/1986 and ratification dates 06/12/1986. Turkey also accessed other protocols and adopted the amendments.(More detail available at: https://www.unep.org/unepmap/who-we-are/contracting-parties/turkey)

20 Ulusal Biyolojik Çeşitlilik Eylem Planı ve Ulusal Biyolojik Çeşitlilik Stratejisi ve Eylem Planı; adopted in accordance with Article 6 of the UN Convention on Biological Diversity, to which Turkey is a party, and accordingly is obliged to prepare or update the National Biological Diversity Strategy and Action Plan. NBSEP sets the limits of the international commitments of the States Parties under the Convention in terms of reflecting country priorities in the implementation of the decisions taken within the scope of the Convention on Biological Diversity. Our country's NBSEP was lastly revised in 2006-2007 as a result of a study carried out with the participation of the relevant groups and published in 2008 with the Approval of the Ministry of Environment in Turkey. Turkey also enacted the Law No. 2872 of 09.08.1983 on Environment and Law No. 1380 of 22.03.1971 on Aquaculture Products.

Turkey's largest island in the Aegean Sea, Gökçeada was declared as a Marine Protected Area in 1999, as its coasts are rich in biodiversity[21]. Before the area was declared as a protected area. However due to many bureaucratic reasons, it was not accomplished to provide an effective protection; as declaring protected areas was not among the government's priorities, and therefore, ongoing unsustainable fishing and uncontrolled tourism, illegal diving and night fishing put the biodiversity in the area in danger. Due to the lack of a coast guard boats on the islands, an effective control was not possible, and fishermen are unaware of the methods required and do not know the importance of biodiversity conservation.

On February 21, 1999, the area between Yıldız Bay and Yelken Rocks, the small area of 1nm along the coast and has a width of 200 meters, the total of which is 37 hectares, has been declared as a marine protected area. And accordingly, all fishing activities, diving and marine traffic are prohibited[22].

In May 2009 until October 2013, Turkish Government within Ministry of Environment and Urbanisation and with support of General Directorate for Protection of Natural Assets has initiated The Strengthening the System of Marine and Coastal Protected Areas of Turkey project[23].

3. Datça-Bozburun Specially Protected Area

Datca-Bozburun Specially Protected Area established as the largest SPA of Mediterranean basin, in 2002-2004. The Institute of Marine Sciences and Management of Istanbul University conducted an extended research in order to determine the marine biodiversity, its distribution and the condition of

21 An endemic seagrass, Posidona oceanica, 34 species of sponges, 17 species of cephalopods, 144 species of fish, 8 species of cetaceans, the critically endangered Mediterranean Monk Seal and the endangered Caretta caretta are found in Gökçeada. Öztürk, B., Öztürk, A. A., Environmental Problems of the Aegean Sea, in The Stockholm Declaration and Law of the Marine Environment, M. H. Nordquist, J.N. Moore, S. Mahmudi. (Eds), Kluwer Law Int. Netherlands, pp. 359-366.

22 Özel Koruma Alanları, TÜDAV (Available at: https://tudav.org/calismalar/koruma-alanlari/gokceada-deniz-parki/ozel-koruma-alanlari/)

23 Strengthening Protected Area Network of Turkey - Catalyzing Sustainability of Marine and Coastal Protected Areas, Project website. (Available at: https://www.thegef.org/project/strengthening-protected-area-network-turkey-catalyzing-sustainability-marine-and-coastal)

endangered or protected species and to make suggestions on management of coastal areas, and these studies revealed 536 species of fauna and flora[24].

Protection of marine ecosystems in this large area require more effective methods. Within the rich, industrialized countries the primary focus is always economic interests and environmental protection is considered as a secondary concern.

Within the last decade area management tools are becoming less effective in the Mediterranean Sea as a result of the augmentation of the activities, as mine extraction, fishery interests spatial mapping developed by other countries.

Turkey proposed a more effective protection regime to be implemented and called for cooperation[25]. In terms of continental shelve rights, Mediterranean is an open-ended area of dispute and Turkish Government considers the implementation of true, planned, timely, logical of marine ecosystem policies, which is partly difficult, as the SPAs are unequally distributed over the Mediterranean basin. An analysis of the country reports for the 2000 – 2007 period shows a strengthening of the legal instruments aimed directly or indirectly at the creation of SPAs and/or the protection of habitats. In the 1995 assessment, 122 SPAs were identified representing a surface area of over 17 670 km^2. Today there are over 750 SPAs which have been placed under the auspices of the Barcelona Convention by the Mediterranean States, i.e. a total surface area of over 144 000 km^2, nearly 2/3 of which are marine areas[26].

The big ecosystem of the Mediterranean Sea has been ignored by the coastal states and the European Union (EU), and not until recently the reduced marine protected areas and biodiversity conservation has started to be discussed, due to mining activities, and this initiated more reporting, mapping, setting targets for the next 10 years.

---

24 Okuş, E. & Yüksek, Ahsen & Yilmaz, I. Noyan & Aslan, Asli & Karhan, Selahattin & Öz, Melike & Demirel, Nazli & Tas, Seyfettin & Demir, Volkan & Zeki, Sibel & Koç, E.M. & Tural, U. & Yokes, Mehmet Baki & Kalkan, Evrim & Deniz, N. & Çaylarbaşi, Z & Savut, E. & Murat Dalkara, Elif. (2007). Marine biodiversity of Datça–Bozburun specially protected area (Southeastern Aegean Sea, Turkey). Journal of the Black Sea/ Mediterranean Environment. 13. 39-49.

25 A formed rear admiral Cihat YAYCI proposed, and issued the Blue Homeland Doctrine, by The Eastern Mediterranean Issue and Turkey's Blue Homeland Doctrine; (Available at: https://www.ifri.org/sites/default/files/atoms/files/denizeau_mavi_vatan_turkey_2021.pdf)

26 Specially Protected Areas in the Mediterranean Assessment and Perspectives, United Nations Environment Programme Mediterranean Action Plan Regional Activity Centre for Specially Protected Areas, RAC/SPA - Tunis, 2010, (Available at: https://www.rac-spa.org/sites/default/files/doc_cop/asp_2010_en.pdf+&cd=1&hl=tr&ct=clnk&gl=tr)

Unfortunately, the discussed failure of marine protection in the Mediterranean could not grasp attention, but economy does. As the climate change today less of a hypothetical threat, pollution, growing pressure of human activities and non-sustainable development reduce the resistance and adaptability of the ecosystems, habitats and species on the coastal fringe and the sea.

The configuration of the Mediterranean basin, the quality of the natural heritage thriving in the coastal and marine ecosystems and the considerable pressure on its natural resources is augmenting and the Mediterranean is becoming vulnerable, less resistant to biologic and ecologic threats. Although the SPA/BD Protocol provides tools, the conventions require effective implementation as regards the in situ sustainable management of coastal and marine biodiversity.

C. Conclusion

Mediterranean Sea comprises some of the most diversified and rich animal and plant species in the world, thus it is one of the richest biodiversity cradles in the world. The conservation and sustainable use of marine biodiversity and using biological resources sustainably have become issues of major international concern and one of the greatest challenges of the States today.

Protected area regimes constitute precious tools for the management and governance of biodiversity in the Mediterranean. are flexible instruments and protection measures are limited to the prescribed objectives, without unnecessarily burdening activities that can be carried out in an environmentally sustainable way.

The key role of the Barcelona Convention in achieving protection goals and bringing nations together and uniting coastal states around the management of a shared ecosystem in the Mediterranean is particularly important, and it symbolizes an attempt to not only create instruments along a trajectory of issues.

Turkey conducted the Presidency of the Bureau of the Barcelona Convention between 2014-2016, and improvement of the status of compliance of countries is still the most important problem for the protection.

For an effective implementation of conventional SPA protection, stronger partnerships, and collaborations as to integrated monitoring and quantitative environment reporting can be adopted, so the effectiveness of the measures adopted, regional level policies, strategies and plans can be assessed in the Mediterranean in a systematic way.

III. Challenge Climate

A Legal Analysis and Evaluation of Climate Change and Global Warming in Turkey

*Kutluhan Bozkurt**

Abstract

Global warming and climate change have reached a level that threatens both humankind and other living organisms. Although significant progress has been made in recent years to reduce and to stop global warming and prevent climate change, these efforts are still far from reaching the ideal level. At this point, it is clear that there is a need for a collective and global awareness both to combat global warming and climate change and to bind legal policies and regulations for the international community. Existing regulations and policies are inadequate to provide sufficient support for the positive transformation of the world and self-protection. At this stage, the recognition of the planet's right to self-protection by all nations and the international communities as well as drafting a declaration of planetary rights should be perceived as an urgent and crucial step.

Unfortunately, the rate of carbon emissions in Turkey has been increasing rapidly in recent years. The discourses, policies and actions of Turkey do not show any coherence, which would make this country among the most affected ones by global warming and climate change. It has become necessary for Turkey to introduce/integrate environmentally friendly energy resources to the production economy and to initiate a fundamental transformation by applying proper climate protection policies and zeroing of carbon emissions. In this study, the current situation, policies and legal determinations regarding climate change and global warming in Turkey are critically analysed.

Key words: global warming, climate change, protection mechanisms, climate policies, Turkey's climate change and global warming policies, legal perspectives

I. Introduction

Global warming and climate change are on their rapid way towards becoming one of the crucial problems of the 21st century. This situation does not have a partial area of impact, on the contrary, it does have a substantial global influence.

There are indeed various factors affecting global warming, however one of them should be taken into consideration in particular: The carbon-based economy and its system of production have emerged as a phenomenon that increases global warming directly. In other words, the support of consumption by the carbon economy and the shaping of economic growth targets by the carbon economy in this process have greatly affected global warming. Although growth and industrialisation based on carbon economy is

* *Prof. Dr., LL. M. Eur. (Munich), Istanbul Gedik University*

seen as one of the major factors in global warming, it is of necessity that faulty agricultural, forestry and water policies and practices, unsustainable and not eco-friendly urbanizing are taken into consideration as determinants as well. In order to combat this problem, the goals that need to be achieved initially can be named as having the accurate and consistent universal policies, a green economy aiming to protect the environment and the planet, and an efficient and high-level legal discipline.

Turkey, among many other countries, is clearly subject to global warming and climate change and the severity of this impact will be much greater in the long term. It is necessary for Turkey to perceive the emergency of this problem seriously, in order to reduce and eliminate carbon-based production radically and to have both an effective climate law and an uncompromising legal system.

According to the recent statistics Turkey's greenhouse gas emissions continue to increase dramatically: Turkish Statistical Institute (TurkStat) states that Turkey's greenhouse gas emissions have increased by 157.1 per cent between 1990 and 2021.[1] Solely between 2020-2021, with an increase of 7.7 percent, Turkey's greenhouse gas emissions reached 564.4 million tons of carbon dioxide equivalent (CO2e).[2] In the light of this situation, experts claim that the increase in the years proves that Turkey fails to separate the link between economic growth and greenhouse gas emissions.[3]

It is necessary to emphasize that according to the recent research, Turkey ranks 35th among 89 countries in total carbon emissions and 11th in carbon production in the world.[4] The data shows additionally that Turkey's greenhouse gas emissions from coal production were 87 tons in 2016 and 134 tons in 2019 which draws attention to the necessity for Turkey to reduce coal

1 'İklim krizi: Türkiye'nin sera gazı salımları neden artıyor, tehlikeli F-gazları niçin kullanılıyor?' (*BBC News Türkçe*, 3 April 2023) <https://www.bbc.com/turkce/articles/cjkyzkvxvglo> accessed 4 April 2023. Please see also data and statistics of the Turkish Statistical Institute: 'TÜİK Kurumsal' <https://data.tuik.gov.tr/Bulten/Index?p=Sera-Gazi-Emisyon-Istatistikleri-1990-2021-49672> accessed 4 April 2023.

2 'İklim krizi: Türkiye'nin sera gazı salımları neden artıyor, tehlikeli F-gazları niçin kullanılıyor?' (n 1).

3 ibid.

4 'Küresel Fosil Yakıtlar Veri Tabanı: Türkiye'nin 2040'a kadar kömür üretimini yüzde 73 oranında azaltması gerekiyor' (*BBC News Türkçe*, 22 September 2022) <https://www.bbc.com/turkce/articles/cn0ve1veq4yo> accessed 4 April 2023.

production by 73 percent by 2040[5] because of the carbon budget[6] -a limit on carbon dioxide emissions set to prevent global temperatures from exceeding the target of 1.5 degrees Celsius.[7]

II. Global Warming and Climate Change

Due to the important consequences of anthropogenic climate change such as sea level rise and likely increases in the number and severity of extreme weather events (e.g., torrential rainfalls, strong winds and extreme hot days) in many countries (including Turkey), it is estimated that ten or even hundreds of millions of people (and of course of a dozen of countries) have been exposed to climate change related risks and dangers. Furthermore, due to the accelerated sea level rise it is foreseen that many countries are likely to lose substantial landmass and some of the world's island nations even may disappear in this century. Given these considerations, climate change has become a major global crisis of the modern world,[8] affecting developed, developing and underdeveloped countries.[9]

Human-induced temperature increase has now become a global problem. Today, it has reached a point where it can affect and destroy all countries and the ecosystem of the planet, from the level of influencing one or a

5 ibid.

6 "The idea of a 'carbon budget' that ties an amount of future warming to a total amount of CO2 emissions is based on a strong relationship between cumulative emissions and temperatures in climate models" Zeke Hausfather, 'Analysis: How Much "Carbon Budget" Is Left to Limit Global Warming to 1.5C? - Carbon Brief <https://www.carbonbrief.org/analysis-how-much-carbon-budget-is-left-to-limit-global-warming-to-1-5c/> accessed 4 April 2023.

7 Because of the Paris Agreement

8 Kutluhan Bozkurt, *Avrupa Birliği Politikaları ve Düzenlemeleri Kapsamında Göç Hukuku, Mülteci Statüsü ve Sığınma* (Legal Yayınları 2018) 113–114; John A Church and others, 'Sea Level Change' in Intergovernmental Panel on Climate Change and others (eds), *Climate Change 2013: The Physical Science Basis. Contribution of Working Group I to the Fifth Assessment Report of the Intergovernmental Panel on Climate Change* (1st edn, Cambridge University Press 2014) <https://www.cambridge.org/core/product/identifier/CBO9781107415324A034/type/book_part> accessed 17 April 2023; Susmita Dasgupta and others, 'The Impact of Sea Level Rise on Developing Countries: A Comparative Analysis' (2007) 93 Climatic Change 379, 1–51.

9 Kutluhan Bozkurt, 'Uluslararası Düzenlemeler Kapsamında Küresel Isınma ve Türkiye'deki Mevcut Durum', *1. Bozok Uluslararası Siyaset Bilimi Kongresi, Geçmişten Günümüze Yerel, Bölgesel ve Küresel Krizler* (2018) 21–22.

few countries. Global warming causes climatic changes affecting different components of climate system such as cryosphere and thus the melting of glaciers, which eventually results in sea level rise.[10] Therefore, important cities of many countries are in danger of being flooded and hundreds of millions of people living in these regions are at risk of becoming homeless.[11] In this respect, climate change has triggered people's migration from areas affected by rising water and unstable weather[12], causing new currents and crises, serious economic losses, collapse of infrastructures of countries, emergence of political-economic crises and widespread and serious health problems such as epidemics and diseases. These changes have resulted in increased concerns among the developed countries and others.

The climate crisis is not only threatening people's life, it also puts many living species on the planet in danger of extinction. Unfortunately, the balance and connection ties within the ecosystem are in the process of breaking. This process requires the establishment and implementation of correct and consistent climate policies at the national and international level. At this point, it should be said that the IPCC plays an important and key role. It is possible to say that as of 2020, countries have approached the issue more sensitively and climate awareness has begun to emerge. Serious, effective and productive international studies are carried out in this field as well.[13]

Given that global warming is one of the important parameters of the climate change and that it consists of different elements, in this paper energy axis regarding carbon-based energy, in particular in relation to the global warming and climate change, will be taken into account.

---

10 Barbara Neumann and others, 'Future Coastal Population Growth and Exposure to Sea-Level Rise and Coastal Flooding - A Global Assessment' (2015) 10 PLOS ONE e0118571.

11 Kutluhan Bozkurt and Deniz Bozkurt, 'Küresel Isınma ve İklim Değişikliği Ekseninde Uluslararası İklim Politikaları ve Düzenlemeleri ve Türkiye'deki Mevcut Durum' in Y Yoldaş (ed), *Türkiye'de İç ve Dış Politikanın Geleceği, Doç. Dr. Özlem Becerik Yoldaş'a Armağan* (DER Yayınları 2021) 177–178.

12 Nuray Ekşi, 'İklim Mültecileri' [2016] Göç Araştırmaları Dergisi 10, 10–58.

13 'Climate Change Performance Index, CCPI Results 2020' <https://ccpi.org/> accessed 22 March 2023.

III. The Link Between Carbon-Based Energy as well as Its Production and Global Warming

It is important to note that energy, which is the source of life and our existence, is a phenomenon encountered in all areas of life and its sustainability is very important. Moreover, in the process from the discovery of energy to its inclusion in daily life, human beings have managed to survive by using many different energy resources.[14] It should be emphasized that over time, the depletion of traditional fossil resources has become an important problem to overcome in terms of energy needs of the whole world. Agricultural activities and the use of fossil resources rather than food, which is the most basic resource we need to survive, cause the formation of greenhouse gases such as carbon dioxide (CO2), methane (CH4), nitrous oxide (N2O), hydro fluoride carbons (HFCs), which in turn causes global warming and triggers crises that threaten the future.[15]

It has now become a necessity to abandon the carbon energy sources on which the classical economy is based, and instead to switch to a new economic system where nature-friendly and alternative energy sources are the main actors in production. At this point, there is a need for correct, applicable and auditable climate policies and practices on an international scale.[16] For these reasons, "Climate Change" is a global problem. The search for an international agreement on the subject began with the Kyoto Protocol (1997) and has eventually led to many international meetings and initiatives (e.g., Copenhagen Agreement, Cancun / Mexico, Durban / South Africa, Doha / Qatar meetings and summits), and reached an important point with Paris Climate Treaty (2015).

The former President of the United States of America announced that he withdrew from this agreement during his term,[17] but after the election in the USA, the new President returned to the Paris Climate Agreement, which is an important international document for the Climate Change and

14 Deren Fırat, Yılsev Hoca and Kutluhan Bozkurt, 'Avrupa Birliği Politikaları Çerçevesinde Yenilenebilir Enerji ve Türkiye' (2021) 18 Yeditepe Üniversitesi Hukuk Fakültesi Dergisi 743, 744.

15 H Naci Bayraç, 'Enerji Kullanımının Küresel Isınmaya Etkisi ve Önleyici Politikalar' (2010) 11 Eskişehir Osmangazi Üniversitesi Sosyal Bilimler Dergisi 229, 229.

16 Bozkurt and Bozkurt (n 11) 177–178.

17 'Climate Change: US Formally Withdraws from Paris Agreement' *BBC News* (4 November 2020) <https://www.bbc.com/news/science-environment-54797743> accessed 6 April 2023.

Protection Law.[18] In the long run, it will affect and shape the domestic law of many countries. Therefore, legal regulations and policies to prevent global warming emerge as a necessity in terms of regional, national and international (including the EU) levels.

IV. Climate Change and Turkey

The Mediterranean Basin, in which Turkey is located, is among the regions that will be most affected by climate change and global warming. In this context, several studies showed that the rate of observed temperature in Turkey will increase in worst-case scenarios, resulting in drought and desertification problems in many areas.[19]

Obviously, Turkey, like many EU countries, supplies most of her energy from outside with carbon-based energy resources such as oil and natural gas. These fossil resources not only harm the nature, but also put countries in an economically difficult situation because of dependence on carbon-derived energy. Due to factors such as the reduction of fossil fuel reserves because of excessive use and major damage to the environment, the importance of alternative energy sources has been accepted and new searches have been started.[20]

Much of Turkey's progress on Climate Change and Protection Issue is made within the framework of the European Union of negotiations on "environment and energy" regulations. It should be noted that Turkey follows a dual path regulating this article, using both EU law and international law. From the perspective of international law, Turkey has been actively participating in both the Kyoto Protocol and the Paris Climate Agreement.

In addition, Turkey has prepared a "Climate Change Action Plan" and "Turkey's Climate Change Adaptation Strategy and Action Plan" (Turkey's Climate Changes Action Plan 2011-2023, Turkey's Climate Change Adapta-

18 'The U.S. Is Back in the Paris Agreement. Now What? - The Paris Climate Agreement' <https://news.climate.columbia.edu/2021/02/04/u-s-rejoins-paris-agreement/> accessed 6 April 2023.

19 Barış Önol and others, 'Evaluation of the Twenty-First Century RCM Simulations Driven by Multiple GCMs over the Eastern Mediterranean–Black Sea Region' (2014) 42 Climate Dynamics 1949; please see also; Deniz Bozkurt and Ömer Lütfi Şen, 'Climate Change Impacts in the Euphrates–Tigris Basin Based on Different Model and Scenario Simulations' (2013) 480 Journal of Hydrology 149, 3–7.

20 Fırat, Hoca and Bozkurt (n 14) 744.

tion Strategy and Action Plan) for the years 2011-2023.[21] It is clear that new primary (constitutional level and also level codes) and secondary regulations (regulations, directives etc.) will be required in this area. All these possible new regulations will have to comply with international law as well as EU law due to the accession negotiations.

As a result, countries make regulations regarding the use of renewable energy in their domestic laws. In addition, the declarations and directives issued by the European Union in terms of member countries and candidate countries are also very important in this context. That's why it should be focused on the European Union's energy policy and the EU Directive on climate change, energy and renewable energy sources in the light of the content evaluated in the national legislation in Turkey. On the other hand, Turkey shall also focus on global warming and climate changes on the carbon energy axis, in the light of international law regulations that also effect the Turkish legal system and regulations.

V. Legal Aspect in Turkey

Legal dimension and tools are one of the important parameters against global warming and climate change. Without effective climate policies and legal regulations concerning in the fight against climate change, nature will have less chance and will not be able to turn from negative developments to positive ones. At this point, it is needed to have very effective and correct legal policies and regulations at both international and domestic levels.

It should be underlined that a legal view of climate change in Turkey should be divided into three sub-fields: the EU and the aspects of EU law, the aspects of the international law and finally the case law aspect.

21 Please see 'Turkey's Climate Changes Action Plan 2011-2023 and Turkey's Climate Change Adaptation Strategy and Action Plan' <https://webdosya.csb.gov.tr/db/iklim/editordosya/iklim_degisikligi_eylem_plani_EN_2014.pdf> accessed 29 March 2023; 'Turkey's National Climate Change Adaptation Strategy and Action Plan 2011–2023' <https://webdosya.csb.gov.tr/db/iklim/editordosya/uyum_stratejisi_eylem_plani_EN(2).pdf> accessed 28 March 2023.

1.The EU and EU Law Aspect

It should be noted that the process of becoming a full member of the European Union (EU) is not easy for Turkey given that Turkey's desire to join the EU took more than half a century.[22] Undoubtedly, the accession process of Turkey to the EU has brought with it different challenges and turmoil such as readmission and visa liberalization agreement, negotiation, custom union, refugee problem, and others. As a candidate member state, Turkey is under the influence of EU law and system. Since 2016, it has been observed that the relations of the parties contain a high level of stress and tension from the above point of view.[23] (However, the concept of fighting against climate change can be a dynamo in EU-Turkey relations. Due to Turkey's accession negotiations process, EU standard and regulations should be taken into account, particularly primary (treaties and agreements of the EU) and secondary sources (regulations, directive and decisions) in the light of chapters for full membership.[24]

For analyzing the impact of the EU law on Turkish law, the policies and regulations of protection of the environment, energy, renewable energy, as well as the policies and regulations of the EU on fighting against climate change and global warming must be considered. These considerations will affect the Turkish domestic law and law policies in the coming years. In order to have a full membership, Turkey has to adopt the EU acquis Communautaire into national law and its applications.

New regulations or directives of the EU on protection of the nature, renewable energy and climate change must be considered by Turkey, and thus Turkey should prepare a new, correct and efficient national strategy, legal text and code on climate. Currently, Turkey is focusing on a new climate code.[25]

---

22 Kutluhan Bozkurt, 'The EU-Turkey Relationships and Evaluation of Human Rights Axis of the Relationship' [2022] eNOULAIR 15–29 <http://dspace.onua.edu.ua/bitstream/handle/11300/23270/Bozkurt%20K.%20The%20EU%e2%80%93Turkey%20relationships%20and%20evaluation%20of%20human%20rights%20axis%20of%20the%20relationship.pdf?sequence=1&isAllowed=y> accessed 29 March 2023.

23 Kutluhan Bozkurt, Turkey- EU Relations: A Short Overview and Impact of the Refugee Crisis on the EU- TURKEY Accession Negotiations, (2017) Legal Albania, ISSN:2519-9102, Volume:2, 41.

24 Klaus-Dieter Borchardt, *The ABC of European Union Law* (2017) 89–110.

25 A climate (draft) law has been submitted to Turkish Parliament. The Ministry of Environment, Urbanisation and Climate Change has said the law will help Turkey become resilient against the destructive effects of climate change-induced disasters, encourage nature-friendly production by promoting renewable energy sources, and

The content of draft -code- text will be very important. During this procedure, the EU standards and regulations should be adopted. In order to have an efficient regulation it needs a GAP analysis regarding legal aspect of climate and energy issues.

This paper also focuses on current legal regulations of Turkey, concerning renewable energy and climate protection. For this purpose, Turkish constitution, codes, presidential degrees, regulations and laws regarding the legal fight against climate change and alternative energy sources will be reviewed during the preparation of a new climate code in Turkey. For the sake of analysis of these categories, EU policies and legal regulations must also be reviewed.

Renewable energy and climate change aspect can be a driving force in the EU-Turkey relations and for that reason, Turkey should focus specifically on this area to re-start the negotiations with the EU. Harmonization processes of Turkish national law into the acquis Communautaire at the level of central governments/authorities and regional or local authorities regarding climate change and energy will determine the EU-Turkey relations in the future.

Reviewing the EU progress reports of the last five years, it can be that there is a stagnation and negative situation in EU-Turkey relations. For the last five years, there has been a minimal and highly limited dialogue between the parties and relations have been frozen.[26] In the latest reports it has been observed and emphasized that the Turkish economy prefers a development-based, mainly on carbon (hydrocarbons), in other words fossil

---

protect biodiversity and green areas. It will also increase water and food security and local and national action plans will be prepared with the law proposal. This includes arrangements to minimise the impact of the climate crisis on the economy, cities, and critical sectors, especially agriculture and food. Risk assessment, monitoring, information and early warning systems will be developed to minimise losses and damages caused by disasters. The environmentally friendly production process will be legally secured to increase the international competitiveness of the sectors. Please see; <https://csb.gov.tr/turkiye-nin-ilk-iklim-kanunu-neler-getiriyor-bakanlik-faaliyetleri-40594> accessed 11 April 2025. However, the public has criticised the draft law for not doing enough to tackle climate change. It does not address how to solve the crisis, when to shut down thermal power plants, how to improve existing policies on energy, transport, agriculture and urbanisation that increase greenhouse gasses, or the need for a just transition and binding targets for the energy transition. It is not enough to mention emission trading in the draft. Please see Gürbüz, 'İklim Kanunu ve iklim inkârcıları' <https://www.birgun.net/makale/iklim-kanunu-ve-iklim-inkarcilari-614087> accessed 11 April 2025.

26 Bozkurt, 'The EU-Turkey Relationships and Evaluation of Human Rights Axis of the Relationship' (n 22) 15–29.

fuel, economy.[27] On the other hand, some critics claim that Turkey has achieved some level of preparation in the area of horizontal legislation and has an Environmental Impact Assessment (EIA) legislation, which is mostly aligned with the EU EIA Directive.[28] However, the EU emphasizes that the procedures for transboundary consultations are not aligned with the EIA and the Strategic Environmental Assessments (SEA) Directives.[29]

In the last report, the EU claims that there has been no progress made by Turkey on climate change over the reporting period, contrary to the expectations following the ratification of the Paris Agreement in October 2021 and the announcement that Turkey would aim at reaching net-zero emissions by 2053.[30] However, Turkey has accepted ratification process of the Paris Agreement after this progress report. The EU criticises additionally that in Turkey a climate law and the Emissions Trading System legislation are still to be adopted.

Finally, Turkey announces its intention of a nationally determined contribution (INDC)[31] before the COP27 to submit an enhanced,[32] which is a pretty and positive development regarding Turkey's duties on climate change.

---

27 'Commission Staff Working Document Türkiye 2022 Report' 111–113 <https://neighbourhood-enlargement.ec.europa.eu/system/files/2022-10/T%C3%BCrkiye%20Report%202022.pdf> accessed 1 April 2023; Please see also 'Commission Staff Working Document Turkey 2021 Report' 102–104 <https://www.ab.gov.tr/siteimages/birimler/kpb/turkey-report-2021-v2.pdf> accessed 1 April 2023; 'Commission Staff Working Document Turkey 2020 Report' 83–85 <https://www.ab.gov.tr/siteimages/trkiye_raporustrateji_belgesi_2020/turkey_report_2020.pdf> accessed 1 April 2023.

28 'Commission Staff Working Document Türkiye 2022 Report' (n 26) 115.

29 ibid.

30 ibid.

31 It should be emphasized that in accordance with decisions 1/CP.19 and 1/CP.20, the Republic of Turkey hereby presents its Intended Nationally Determined Contribution (INDC) towards achieving the ultimate objective of the United Nations Framework Convention on Climate Change that is set out in its Art 2 and clarifying information. That's way Turkey aims to contribute to the collective efforts to combat climate change in line with its national circumstances and capabilities. Please see 'Republic of Turkey Intended Nationally Determined Contribution' <https://unfccc.int/sites/default/files/NDC/2022-06/The_INDC_of_TURKEY_v.15.19.30.pdf> accessed 6 April 2023.

32 'Commission Staff Working Document Türkiye 2022 Report' (n 26) 115.

2. International Law Aspect

Turkey's responsibilities and duties are not only in the EU dimension. Turkey should also take into account international agreements on climate change and energy. Recently, Turkey has withdrawn her objections and joined the Paris Agreement, and this process also needs national regulations in the coming years. According to the Turkish Constitution, (Art. 90 and Art. 90, par. 5),[33] there is a hierarchy between provisions of Turkish codes and provisions of international treaties, if there happens a conflict. In this scenario, national authorities should consider the international treaties' provision(s), instead of conflicted provision of a code. However, the argument of this article is not clear for all treaties, but only for those on fundamental rights and freedoms meanwhile climate change treaties can be accepted as a fundamental rights and freedoms treaty. According to the Turkish Constitution, this has no answer and maybe it also needs a new constitutional amendment regarding international treaties and agreements on climate change.

After the signing of the Paris Agreement by Turkey, some questions must be asked: How will it affect the Turkish national law? Regarding central and local authorities, how should they be considered in the national law pertaining to the Paris Agreement? Does it need any domestic regulation(s)? Should national courts also apply provisions of the agreement? And how will it be? Responding to these questions will be depended on Turkey's law-making processes and policies. At the current state of affairs, it does not seem to be elementary to supply a perspective on it.[34]

The UN regulations and resolutions regarding climate change and renewable energy should be taken into consideration by Turkey for a national

---

33 Art. 90 par. 5: *"International agreements duly put into effect have the force of law. No appeal to the Constitutional Court shall be made with regard to these agreements, on the grounds that they are unconstitutional. In the case of a conflict between international agreements, duly put into effect, concerning fundamental rights and freedoms and the laws due to differences in provisions on the same matter, the provisions of international agreements shall prevail"*, please see 'Turkey's Constitution of 1982 with Amendments through 2017' <https://www.constituteproject.org/constitution/Turkey_2017.pdf?lang=en> accessed 1 April 2023.

34 The natural catastrophe, earthquake, in the southern Turkey on February 6th, 2023 had an impact of change on the agenda of Turkey, due to the loss of tens of thousands of lives, not reaching tens of thousands of people under the debris, injuries of hundreds of thousands of people and millions of people losing their homes and job. In addition, in two months Turkey will have an election of critical value. Under such circumstances, the climate change and global warming issue has unfortunately lost its significance in Turkey for the year 2023.

climate strategy. The UN regulations and resolutions, which are related to the climate change and friendly energy sources, should be taken into account by Turkey, since the UN climate change and global warming policies play a significant role for national laws. As a member of international community, Turkey should take the UN climate policies and perspectives into the account and include them in the Turkish national law in order to have efficient and necessary regulations.

3. Case Law Aspect

In recent years, judicial decisions both in national[35] and international levels are of special importance in the protection of nature and the fight against climate change and global warming. The judiciary has a dynamic role both in the implementation of existing regulations and in the formulation of new regulations and provisions in areas where they are deficient or insufficient.[36] In this context, the International Court of Justice (ICJ), Court of Justice of the European Union (CJEU) and European Court of Human Rights (ECHR) can be taken into special consideration.

It is important to stress that Turkey should take into account primarily the ruling of European Court of Human Rights-ECHR given that Turkey is a founding member of the **Council of Europe**. Rulings on climate change, protection of environment and the Convention for the Protection of Human Rights and Fundamental Freedoms, which are known as the European Convention on Human Rights,[37] must be obeyed by the member states of the Council of Europe.

The European Convention on Human Rights does not directly address climate protection and global warming. However, the Court discusses directly or indirectly the phenomenon of climate change, protection of environment

35 See '"Urgenda Case", ECLI:NL:HR:2019:2007' <https://www.urgenda.nl/wp-content/uploads/ENG-Dutch-Supreme-Court-Urgenda-v-Netherlands-20-12-2019.pdf> accessed 2 April 2023. For another example, see; '"The Case of the Century", N°1904967, 1904968, 1904972, 1904976/4-1' <http://paris.tribunal-administratif.fr/content/download/179360/1759761/version/1/file/1904967190496819049721904976.pdf> accessed 2 April 2023.

36 Volodymyr Ladyka and others, 'Directions and Risks of Legal Rights Enforcement by Territorial Communities after the Opening of the Agricultural Land Market in Ukraine' (2022) 20 Problems and Perspectives in Management 291, 297.

37 'European Convention on Human Rights - Official Texts, Convention and Protocols' <https://www.echr.coe.int/Pages/home.aspx?p=basictexts&c> accessed 2 April 2023.

in some of its judgments on the right to life,[38] right to respect for private and family life,[39] freedom of assembly and association,[40] and the individual applications at the ECHR sent by the citizens of Turkey against the state of Turkey.[41] The ECHR found a violation of right under Article 8 of the European Convention on Human Rights in the case of *Taşkın and Others Against Turkey* [42] under Aarhus Agreement which Turkey was/is not a signatory state of this agreement and did not joint to this agreement. However, the ECHR did not take into account the situation of Turkey and the Court interpreted Aarhus Agreement as a cross-border agreement and found a violation of Article 8 of the European Convention on Human Rights according to Aarhus Agreement's provisions. For that reason, *Taşkın and Others v. Turkey* Application constitutes a substantial value, as the cross-border agreement applied by the Court in this case was a positive development, in terms of considering the protection of the nature and the environment.

In the case of *Öneryıldız v. Turkey Application*[43] as well, the Court found a violation of the right under the Article 2 of the European Convention on Human Rights. Similarly, the Court did take into account a cross-border convention, which is the Convention on the Protection of the Environment through Criminal Law,[44] signed by fourteen States so far respectively.[45] Turkey is not a signatory state of the Convention on the Protection of the Environment through Criminal Law. Nevertheless, the Court applied

---

38 Article 2, Right to life, 'European Convention on Human Rights' <https://www.echr.coe.int/documents/convention_eng.pdf> accessed 2 April 2023.

39 Article 8, Right to respect for private and family life, ibid.

40 Article 11, freedom of assembly and association, ibid.

41 Nükhet Y Turgut, 'Çevreyi Koruyucu Uluslararası Sözleşmelerin Yadsınamaz Önemi', *Uluslararası Çevre Koruma Sözleşmeleri* (2nd edn, Türkiye Barolar Birliği 2014) 17–18.

42 *Taşkin and Others v Turkey* [2004] ECtHR 46117/99.

43 *Öneryildiz v Turkey* [2004] ECtHR [GC] 48939/99. Please also see *Demir and Baykara v Turkey* [2008] ECtHR [GC] 34503/97.

44 Obviously, the Convention on the Protection of the Environment through Criminal Law is the first international convention to criminalise acts causing or likely to cause environmental damage. Thus, it is a significant event in the development of environmental criminal law, ETS no. 172 – Strasbourg, 4 November 1998. Please see 'The Convention on the Protection of the Environment Through Criminal Law' <https://huespedes.cica.es/gimadus/06/THE%20CONVENTION%20ON%20THE%20PROTECTION%20OF%20THE%20ENVIRONMENT%20THROUGH%20CRIMINAL%20LAW.htm> accessed 3 April 2023.

45 'Convention on the Protection of the Environment through Criminal Law' <https://www.ecolex.org/details/treaty/convention-on-the-protection-of-the-environment-through-criminal-law-tre-001292/> accessed 6 April 2023.

cross-border convention through the Article 2 of the European Convention on Human Rights.[46]

It is clear that since Turkey is not full member of the EU, she remains outside the jurisdiction of the judiciary of the CJEU. However, as a candidate state to join the EU, Turkey shall take into account case laws and ruling of the CJEU for the accession negotiation process with the EU. At this point, it can be notably highly useful and positive if Turkey takes ruling of the CJEU regarding protecting of the climate and taking global warming specifically into account. Certainly, Turkey should implement domestic law in the light of rulings of the CJEU, if Turkey wishes to join the EU.

Lastly, Turkey, as a member of international community, shall/would be also taken into consideration of ruling of the International Court of Justice (ICJ) regarding climate change and global warming, if Turkey wants to have an efficient regulation regarding protection of the climate change and stopping global warming.

VI. Conclusion

The 21st century highlights itself as a century in which human beings, the dominant species on the planet, are at the point of significantly destroying the future of the planet and countless living organisms on the planet. At this point, it is not possible to state that the existing policies and regulations aimed at reducing and finally giving an end to global warming and preventing climate change are sufficient, since the rapid warming of the planet and the negative course of climate change continue to increase significantly. The necessity for more radical, effective and accurate climate policies and regulations has emerged. It is crucially urgent to control (and to end) the carbon- and fossil fuels-based production system and to switch to nature and planet-friendly, renewable energy sources at a major rate.

The giving a legal personality to the planate and the recognition of the planet's right to self-determination and the planet's right to life, similarly the recognition of this right as a superior value is an important goal for universal and effective climate policies and legal regulations.[47] The international community and states should work towards this goal and cooperate to define

46 *Öneryildiz v. Turkey* (n 42).

47 Kutluhan Bozkurt and Yasemin Özbilgin, 'İklim Mültecileri: İklim Adaleti Perspektifinde İklime Bağlı Göç Hareketleri ve Uluslararası Hukuk Bağlamında Yeni Düzenleme Gerekliliği' in Şükrü Karatepe (ed), *İklim Adaleti* (İdealkent Yayınları 2023) 411.

ecocide crimes. One of the most essential steps to be taken in defining ecocide crimes, halting global warming and preventing climate change will be the drafting of the Universal Declaration of the Rights of the Planet and the granting a legal personality to the planet, as the ongoing problem by now requires the protection of the planet's right to life and the recognition of its rights.

Turkey is in an interesting paradox (or in other words, as a cause-and-effect relationship) as it is one of the countries that is both rapidly growing in the increase of carbon emissions which adds up to the increase of global warming and at the same time, one of the countries that will be most affected by global warming and climate change. Growing with a high carbon economy does not seem to be a correct choice and option. It has become very clear that Turkey needs the accurate climate policies and regulations, both in terms of EU law and international law.

In the fight against global warming and climate change, Turkey must overcome the discrepancies between its rhetoric and practices. For this reason, she must both ensure that the climate law and other legislation to be prepared are effective, accurate and adequate and that they are implemented without compromise. Otherwise, Turkey will be a candidate country to experience severe problems in migration movements, access to clean water and the implementation of the right agricultural policies due to global warming and climate change. It is highly likely that many climate lawsuits will be filed in the coming years due to climate change and global warming.

In the EU accession process, Turkey has no chance to avoid the EU's climate policies and carbon emission ban regulations.

References

Bayraç HN, 'Enerji Kullanımının Küresel Isınmaya Etkisi ve Önleyici Politikalar' (2010) 11 Eskişehir Osmangazi Üniversitesi Sosyal Bilimler Dergisi 229

Borchardt K-D, *The ABC of European Union Law* (2017)

Bozkurt D and Şen ÖL, 'Climate Change Impacts in the Euphrates–Tigris Basin Based on Different Model and Scenario Simulations' (2013) 480 Journal of Hydrology 149

Bozkurt K, *Avrupa Birliği Politikaları ve Düzenlemeleri Kapsamında Göç Hukuku, Mülteci Statüsü ve Sığınma* (Legal Yayınları 2018)

——, 'Uluslararası Düzenlemeler Kapsamında Küresel Isınma ve Türkiye'deki Mevcut Durum', *1. Bozok Uluslararası Siyaset Bilimi Kongresi, Geçmişten Günümüze Yerel, Bölgesel ve Küresel Krizler* (2018)

——, 'Turkey- EU Relations: A Short Overview and Impact of the Refugee Crisis on the EU- TURKEY Accession Negotiations' (2017)

——, 'The EU-Turkey Relationships and Evaluation of Human Rights Axis of the Relationship' [2022] eNOULAIR <http://dspace.onua.edu.ua/bitstream/handle/11300/23270/Bozkurt%20K.%20The%20EU%e2%80%93Turkey%20relationships%20and%20evaluation%20of%20human%20rights%20axis%20of%20the%20relationship.pdf?sequence=1&isAllowed=y> accessed 29 March 2023

Bozkurt K and Bozkurt D, 'Küresel Isınma ve İklim Değişikliği Ekseninde Uluslararası İklim Politikaları ve Düzenlemeleri ve Türkiye'deki Mevcut Durum' in Y Yoldaş (ed), *Türkiye'de İç ve Dış Politikanın Geleceği, Doç. Dr. Özlem Becerik Yoldaş'a Armağan* (DER Yaynları 2021)

Bozkurt K and Özbilgin Y, 'İklim Mültecileri: İklim Adaleti Perspektifinde İklime Bağlı Göç Hareketleri ve Uluslararası Hukuk Bağlamında Yeni Düzenleme Gerekliliği' in Şükrü Karatepe (ed), *İklim Adaleti* (İdealkent Yayınları 2023)

Church JA and others, 'Sea Level Change' in Intergovernmental Panel on Climate Change and others (eds), *Climate Change 2013: The Physical Science Basis. Contribution of Working Group I to the Fifth Assessment Report of the Intergovernmental Panel on Climate Change* (1st edn, Cambridge University Press 2014) <https://www.cambridge.org/core/product/identifier/CBO9781107415324A034/type/book_part> accessed 17 April 2023

'Climate Change Performance Index, CCPI Results 2020' <https://ccpi.org/> accessed 22 March 2023

'Climate Change: US Formally Withdraws from Paris Agreement' *BBC News* (4 November 2020) <https://www.bbc.com/news/science-environment-54797743> accessed 6 April 2023

'Commission Staff Working Document Turkey 2020 Report' <https://www.ab.gov.tr/siteimages/trkiye_raporustrateji_belgesi_2020/turkey_report_2020.pdf> accessed 1 April 2023

'Commission Staff Working Document Turkey 2021 Report' <https://www.ab.gov.tr/siteimages/birimler/kpb/turkey-report-2021-v2.pdf> accessed 1 April 2023

'Commission Staff Working Document Türkiye 2022 Report' <https://neighbourhood-enlargement.ec.europa.eu/system/files/2022-10/T%C3%BCrkiye%20Report%202022.pdf> accessed 1 April 2023

'Convention on the Protection of the Environment through Criminal Law' <https://www.ecolex.org/details/treaty/convention-on-the-protection-of-the-environment-through-criminal-law-tre-001292/> accessed 6 April 2023

Dasgupta S and others, 'The Impact of Sea Level Rise on Developing Countries: A Comparative Analysis' (2007) 93 Climatic Change 379

Ekşi N, 'İklim Mültecileri' [2016] Göç Araştırmaları Dergisi 10

'European Convention on Human Rights' <https://www.echr.coe.int/documents/convention_eng.pdf> accessed 2 April 2023

'European Convention on Human Rights - Official Texts, Convention and Protocols' <https://www.echr.coe.int/Pages/home.aspx?p=basictexts&c> accessed 2 April 2023

Fırat D, Hoca Y and Bozkurt K, 'Avrupa Birliği Politikaları Çerçevesinde Yenilenebilir Enerji ve Türkiye' (2021) 18 Yeditepe Üniversitesi Hukuk Fakültesi Dergisi 743

Gürbüz, Ö, ‘İklim Kanunu ve iklim inkârcıları’, <https://www.birgun.net/makale/iklim-kanunu-ve-iklim-inkarcilari-614087> accessed 11 April 2025

Hausfather Z, ‘Analysis: How Much “Carbon Budget” Is Left to Limit Global Warming to 1.5C? - Carbon Brief’ <https://www.carbonbrief.org/analysis-how-much-carbon-budget-is-left-to-limit-global-warming-to-1-5c/> accessed 4 April 2023

‘İklim krizi: Türkiye’nin sera gazı salımları neden artıyor, tehlikeli F-gazları niçin kullanılıyor?’ (*BBC News Türkçe*, 3 April 2023) <https://www.bbc.com/turkce/articles/cjkyzkvxvglo> accessed 4 April 2023

‘Küresel Fosil Yakıtlar Veri Tabanı: Türkiye’nin 2040’a kadar kömür üretimini yüzde 73 oranında azaltması gerekiyor’ (*BBC News Türkçe*, 22 September 2022) <https://www.bbc.com/turkce/articles/cn0ve1veq4yo> accessed 4 April 2023

Ladyka V and others, ‘Directions and Risks of Legal Rights Enforcement by Territorial Communities after the Opening of the Agricultural Land Market in Ukraine’ (2022) 20 Problems and Perspectives in Management 291

Neumann B and others, ‘Future Coastal Population Growth and Exposure to Sea-Level Rise and Coastal Flooding - A Global Assessment’ (2015) 10 PLOS ONE e0118571

Önol B and others, ‘Evaluation of the Twenty-First Century RCM Simulations Driven by Multiple GCMs over the Eastern Mediterranean–Black Sea Region’ (2014) 42 Climate Dynamics 1949

‘Republic of Turkey Intended Nationally Determined Contribution’ <https://unfccc.int/sites/default/files/NDC/2022-06/The_INDC_of_TURKEY_v.15.19.30.pdf> accessed 6 April 2023

‘“The Case of the Century”, N°1904967, 1904968, 1904972, 1904976/4-1’ <http://paris.tribunal-administratif.fr/content/download/179360/1759761/version/1/file/1904967190496819049721904976.pdf> accessed 2 April 2023

‘The Convention on the Protection of the Environment Through Criminal Law’ <https://huespedes.cica.es/gimadus/06/THE%20CONVENTION%20ON%20THE%20PROTECTION%20OF%20THE%20ENVIRONMENT%20THROUGH%20CRIMINAL%20LAW.htm> accessed 3 April 2023

‘The U.S. Is Back in the Paris Agreement. Now What? - The Paris Climate Agreement’ <https://news.climate.columbia.edu/2021/02/04/u-s-rejoins-paris-agreement/> accessed 6 April 2023

‘TÜİK Kurumsal’ <https://data.tuik.gov.tr/Bulten/Index?p=Sera-Gazi-Emisyon-Istatistikleri-1990-2021-49672> accessed 4 April 2023

The Ministry of Environment, Urbanisation and Climate Change, ‘Türkiye ‘nin ilk iklim kanunu neler getiriyor?’ <https://csb.gov.tr/turkiye-nin-ilk-iklim-kanunu-neler-getiriyor-bakanlik-faaliyetleri-40594> accessed 11 April 2025

Turgut NY, ‘Çevreyi Koruyucu Uluslararası Sözleşmelerin Yadsınamaz Önemi’, *Uluslararası Çevre Koruma Sözleşmeleri* (2nd edn, Türkiye Barolar Birliği 2014)

‘Turkey’s Climate Changes Action Plan 2011-2023 and Turkey’s Climate Change Adaptation Strategy and Action Plan’ <https://webdosya.csb.gov.tr/db/iklim/editordosya/iklim_degisikligi_eylem_plani_EN_2014.pdf> accessed 29 March 2023

‘Turkey’s Constitution of 1982 with Amendments through 2017’ <https://www.constituteproject.org/constitution/Turkey_2017.pdf?lang=en> accessed 1 April 2023

'Turkey's National Climate Change Adaptation Strategy and Action Plan 2011–2023' <https://webdosya.csb.gov.tr/db/iklim/editordosya/uyum_stratejisi_eylem_plani_EN(2).pdf> accessed 28 March 2023

'"Urgenda Case", ECLI:NL:HR:2019:2007' <https://www.urgenda.nl/wp-content/uploads/ENG-Dutch-Supreme-Court-Urgenda-v-Netherlands-20-12-2019.pdf> accessed 2 April 2023

Demir and Baykara v Turkey [2008] ECtHR [GC] 34503/97

Öneryildiz v Turkey [2004] ECtHR [GC] 48939/99

Taşkin and Others v Turkey [2004] ECtHR 46117/99

Climate Change and its legal impact: The status and rights of climate refugees in Turkey

*Ayşe Yasemin Aydoğmuş Giroldi**

Abstract

One of the most important problems of today's global world is climate change. Together with its effects on the environment, consequently it is also affecting the lives of human beings. Many individuals have voluntarily or compulsorily started to move within their countries or to other countries. A major immigration wave is on the way and this situation requires some legal regulations. Within this context the main focus of this article will be the human mobility caused by climate change and Turkey's legal approach to this mobility.

Keywords: Climate change, human mobility, displacement of people, refugee, climate refugee The green new concepts on the market

I. Introduction

Climate change, commonly covered in the media through as global warming, currently affects only some parts of the world, but it is soon to have extensive effects and to change the lives of more people around the world[1]. Nowadays mostly affected countries and international organizations are working on climate change and its consequences[2]. In this article I will focus on an important consequence of the climate change: human mobility. In the first part of this paper I will explain briefly what climate change is and its legal impacts. I will determine that human mobility is one of the biggest problems resulting from climate change and I will examine this conceptually. In the second part of the paper I will talk about refugees and particularly climate

---

* Associate Professor, Private International Law Department, Faculty of Law., Istanbul University.

1 Lancet and University College London Institute for Global Health Commission, Managing the Health Effects of Climate Change, P. 1, http://www.thelancet.com/pdfs/journals/lancet/PIIS0140-6736(09)60935-1.pdf (last visited 17.2.2017).

2 For example taking urgent action against climate change is one of the 17 sustainable development goals of UN. See http://www.un.org/sustainabledevelopment/climate-change-2/ (last visited 4.2.2017). Also see http://www.unep.org/climatechange/ for the work of UNEP on the climate change (last visited 4.2.2017). For Turkish government's work on climate change see http://www.csb.gov.tr/projeler/iklim/index.php?Sayfa=haberdetay&Id=15637 (last visited 4.2.2017).

refugees. Here the sources of Turkish Law will be examined in detail and accordingly the status and rights of climate refugees will be put forth for consideration. Lastly I will conclude with some proposals for new regulations.

A. Climate Change and Its Legal Impact

1. Concept of Climate Change

Climate change means the statistically significant current or prospective changes in climate lasting for the long term due to natural causes such as rising temperature and floods, and human activities such as deforestation, bad urbanization, and social and economic problems[3]. Nowadays climate change is most commonly known as "global warming". The most significant result of global warming is rising temperatures, which causes melting of the glaciers and ice caps. As a result the sea level rises and more floods and extreme weather events happen around the world, especially in the Asia - Pacific region[4]. Consequently some islands face the risk of submergence, which would result in the community living there losing their homeland. Whist rising sea levels causes problems in low-lying coastal areas of the world, including some of the islands of Tuvalu, Kiribati, Maldives and Bangladesh[5], other parts of the world, such as Morocco, Tunisia, Egypt and Libya, face

3 For the definition in article 1 of the UNFCC see http://unfccc.int/files/essential_background/convention/background/application/pdf/convention_text_with_annexes_english_for_posting.pdf (last visited 4.2.2017), for IPCC definition see https://www.ipcc.ch/ipccreports/tar/wg1/518.htm (last visited 4.2.2017).

4 UN Economic and Social Commission for Asia and the Pacific, The Economics of Climate Change in the Asia-Pacific Region, 2016, P. 1.

5 Wong, P.P., I.J. Losada, J.-P. Gattuso, J. Hinkel, A. Khattabi, K.L. McInnes, Y. Saito, A. Sallenger, 2014, Coastal systems and low-lying areas. In: Climate Change 2014: Impacts,Adaptation, and Vulnerability. Part A:
Global and Sectoral Aspects. Contribution of Working Group II to the Fifth Assessment Report of the Intergovernmental Panel on Climate Change [Field, C.B., V.R. Barros, D.J. Dokken, K.J. Mach, M.D. Mastrandrea, T.E. Bilir, M. Chatterjee, K.L. Ebi, Y.O. Estrada, R.C. Genova, B. Girma, E.S. Kissel, A.N. Levy, S. MacCracken, P.R. Mastrandrea & L.L.White (eds.)]. Cambridge University Press, Cambridge, United Kingdom and New York, NY, USA, P. 361-409, especially P. 367-368.

drought[6]. These conditions can make people's lives extremely difficult or even unsustainable, as has happened in some parts of Tuvalu and Kiribati[7].

2. Legal Impacts of Climate Change

a. International Organizations and Conventions

Since 1970's international community started to work on environmental issues and climate change. In 1972 UNEP has been established to coordinate environmental agenda and environmental policies[8]. Later on the World Meteorological Organization and UNEP established the IPCC in 1988 for providing people to decide on environmental policies with regular scientific assessments, statistics and evaluations regarding the future of the climate change[9]. Besides these large scale worldwide organizations several regional organizations and programs in smaller scales like Sierra Nevada Alliance Regional Climate Change Program and Climate Action Network Australia have been established too.

International community not only organized plans and programs but also prepared legal documents to take serious measures against climate change. Most important ones of these are UNFCCC, Kyoto Protocol, and Paris Agreement.

6 Niang, I., O.C. Ruppel, M.A. Abdrabo, A. Essel, C. Lennard, J. Padgham, P. Urquhart, 2014, Africa. In: Climate Change 2014: Impacts, Adaptation, and Vulnerability. Part B: Regional Aspects. Contribution of Working Group II to the Fifth Assessment Report of the Intergovernmental Panel on Climate Change [Barros, V.R., C.B. Field, D.J. Dokken, M.D. Mastrandrea, K.J. Mach, T.E. Bilir, M. Chatterjee, K.L. Ebi, Y.O. Estrada, R.C. Genova, B. Girma, E.S. Kissel, A.N. Levy, S. MacCracken, P.R. Mastrandrea & L.L.White (eds.)]. Cambridge University Press, Cambridge, United Kingdom and New York, NY, USA, P. 1199-1265.

7 See the refugee application of the citizens of Tuvalu mentioned in the part II. Who Is A Climate Refugee and What Are The Differences Between Climate Refugees and Other Refugees of this article.

8 UNEP Organization Profile, P. 3 http://www.unep.org/PDF/UNEPOrganizationProfile.pdf (last visited 17.10.2016).

9 http://www.ipcc.ch/news_and_events/docs/factsheets/FS_what_ipcc.pdf (last visited 17.10.2016).

b. Examples of Countries Suffering From Climate Change

Negative effects of climate change are being noticed around the world in several ways. Carteret Islanders of Papua New Ginea are the first climate refugees on the world[10]. International community is aware of the fact that Carteret Islanders are trying to find a place to live since the conditions in their land are extremely difficult both in terms of environment and economy[11]. On the other hand Tuvalu has become a symbol for the disappearing islands. Due to climate change rise of sea level, floods, storm surges and coastal erosion are observed in Tuvalu[12]. Tuvalu's extreme position against climate change is a highlighting topic in the international community. Tuvaluan governors has been sharing their worries about future several times during the meetings of UN agencies[13]. In those statements it has been said that developed countries have to help reduce the negative effects of climate change since they are the biggest greenhouse gas producers, today the problem in Tuvalu is not economic but it is a matter of life, Tuvaluan people are facing vital problems due to climate change and lack of action against it. Kiribati and Maldives are other examples of countries facing rising sea level while Egypt, China, Morocco is dealing with the problem of desertification.

3. An Important Outcome of Climate Change: Human Mobility and Climate Refugees

Climate change is a phenomenon having impacts on various things like environment, economy, politics and sociology. Obviously one of the biggest impacts is on the human lives. Today climate change's negative impacts on environment and economy cause to the movement of human beings. Human mobility is a general term including several types of movements of individuals.

---

10 For related news see http://earthfirstjournal.org/newswire/2014/04/06/first-official-climate-change-refugees-evacuate-their-island-homes-for-good/ (last visited 20.2.2017).

11 http://www.abc.net.au/news/2016-08-07/carteret-climate-refugees-new-home/7693950 (last visited 20.2.2017).

12 Carol Farbotko, Wishful Sinking: Disappearing Islands, Climate Refugees and Cosmopolitan Experimentation, Asia Pacific Viewpoint, Vol. 51, No. 1, April 2010, P. 48 - 49.

13 For the Prime Minister Bikenibeu Paeniu's statement in UNFCC – Conference of Parties 3 in 8.12.1997 see http://www.tuvaluislands.com/kyoto-panieu.htm, Ambassador/Permanent Representative of Tuvalu Afelee F Pita's statement at the Special Session of the Security Council on Energy, Climate and Security in 17.4.2007 see http://www.tuvaluislands.com/un/2007/un_2007-04-17.html (last visited 20.2.2017).

Human mobility caused by climate change can either be due to a sudden onset disaster such as tsunami or drought, or due to a slow onset disaster such as sea level rises, desertification or social-economic problems resulting from these disasters[14]. Human mobility can be categorized according to the duration of the migration as either permanent or temporary, and according to the number of migrants, for example individual or group migration[15]. On the other hand mobility can be either internal or external.

The term "human mobility" sometimes causes misunderstandings due to the problem of terminology. However, when we look at the mainstream divisions we can identify two main types of mobility: one is the displacement of people – i.e. the forced movement of individuals to leave their habitual residence whether or not it is the homeland; the other is migration, which is a voluntary movement of people or planned relocation[16], maintained and carried on upon the request or consent of those who are the subject of the relocation[17]. In this article I will be focusing on environmentally displaced individuals who have had to leave their countries and are often referred to as "climate refugees".

First, I will explain that the term "climate refugee" is in popular usage but it is inaccurate and misleading since the term "refugee" is a legal term defined in international documents and national laws. When we refer to environmentally displaced people as climate refugees, this may cause misunderstandings since the 1951 Convention Relating to The Status of Refugees

14 Olivia Dun, François Gemenne, Defining "Environmental Migration", Forced Migration Review, 31.10.2008, p. 10, Benoit Mayer, Climate Change, Migration and International Law in Southeast Asia, P.1, http://www.benoitmayer.com/files/Climate%20Change%20Migration%20and%20International%20Law%20in%20SE%20Asia.pdf (last visited 12.2.2017), (published in Koh Kheng Lian et al. (eds.), Climate Change Adaptation: ASEAN and the World (World Scientific, 2015), 337-358). http://www.benoitmayer.com/files/Climate%20Change%20Migration%20and%20International%20Law%20in%20SE%20Asia.pdf (last visited 4.2.2017).

15 For the categorization of human mobility see António Guterres, Migration, Displacement and Planned Relocation, 31.12.2012, http://www.unhcr.org/news/editorial/2012/12/55535d6a9/migration-displacement-planned-relocation.html (last visited 29.1.2017).

16 According to article 3(d) of Resettlement Law numbered 5543 (Official Gazette dated 26.9.2006 and numbered 26301) immigrants are the people whose ancestors are Turkish and who are bound with Turkish culture, arrived to Turkey individually or within a group and whose immigrant status has been accepted in accordance with this Law.

17 *Recommendations From the Advisory Group on Climate Change and Human Mobility COP 20 Lima, Peru*, Human Mobility in the Context of Climate Change, P. 3 https://www.iom.int/files/live/sites/iom/files/pbn/docs/Human-Mobility-in-the-context-of-Climate-Change.pdf (last visited 4.2.2017) .

(the "Convention") does not include environmental factors as one of the reasons for gaining the status of refugee[18]. Therefore, in order to distinguish climate refugees from traditional refugees we will look at the status of refugee in Turkish law.

B. Refugees and Especially Climate Refugees in Turkey

1. Definition of Refugee in Turkish Law

Nowadays the term "climate refugee" is highly popular but is it accurate? In order to answer this question we first have to see who can be a refugee. In Turkish Law the term "refugee" has been defined through international agreements and domestic legislation.

a. 1951 Convention Relating to The Status of Refugees

People normally have the diplomatic protection of the country of which they are nationals[19]. However when the basic human rights of a national are not protected in their homeland they may need to move to another country and ask for the help of the international community[20]. After World Wars I and II, the lack of a mechanism to protect people who were in urgent need of legal protection became apparent[21]. Therefore the international community developed regulations providing protection for people in need of help by guaranteeing their basic human rights[22]. In 1951 the comprehensive Convention Relating to the Status of Refugees was prepared and signed. The term

---

18 Kara K. Moberg, Extending Refugee Definitions to Cover Environmentally Displaced Persons Displaces Necessary Protection, 94 Iowa Law Review, 1107, 2008 - 2009, P. 1113. For further information on scholars view regarding the same see Aurelie Lopez, The Protection of Environmentally Displaced Persons in International Law, 37 Environmental Law, Spring 2007, P. 391 – 392.

19 Aysel Çelikel, Günseli Öztekin Gelgel, Yabancılar Hukuku, 22nd ed., 2016, P. 11, Bülent Çiçekli, Yabancılar ve Mülteci Hukuku, 6th ed., 2016, P. 51, Ergin Nomer, Türk Vatandaşlık Hukuku, 22nd ed., 2016, P. 24-25, B. Bahadır Erdem, Vatandaşlık Hukuku, 5th ed., 2016, P. 21.

20 The 1951 Conventıon Relating to the Status of Refugees and its 1967 Protocol, UNCHR, Geneva, 2011, p. 2 (http://www.unhcr.org/about-us/background/4ec262df9/1951-convention-relating-status-refugees-its-1967-protocol.html (last visited 03.10.2016).

21 Çiçekli, Mülteci, P. 215 – 217.

22 Id. at P. 216 – 218.

"refugee" is defined in the article 1 of the Convention. According to article 1/A a person who has been considered a refugee under the Arrangements of 12 May 1926 and 30 June 1928 or under the Conventions of 28 October 1933 and 10 February 1938, the Protocol of 14 September 1939 or the Constitution of the International Refugee Organization; Decisions of non-eligibility taken by the International Refugee Organization during the period of its activities shall not prevent the status of refugee being accorded to persons who fulfil the conditions of paragraph 2 of this section or as a result of events occurring before 1 January 1951 and owing to wellfounded fear of being persecuted for reasons of race, religion, nationality, membership of a particular social group or political opinion, is outside the country of his nationality and is unable or, owing to such fear, is unwilling to avail himself of the protection of that country; or who, not having a nationality and being outside the country of his former habitual residence as a result of such events, is unable or, owing to such fear, is unwilling to return to it. In the case of a person who has more than one nationality, the term "the country of his nationality" shall mean each of the countries of which he is a national, and a person shall not be deemed to be lacking the protection of the country of his nationality if, without any valid reason based on well-founded fear, he has not availed himself of the protection of one of the countries of which he is a national[23].

---

23 Turkey has a reservation for this article. Turkey considers that the term "events occurring before 1 January 1951" refers to the beginning of the events. Consequently, since the pressure exerted upon the Turkish minority in Bulgaria, which began before 1 January 1951, is still continuing, the provision of this Convention must also apply to the Bulgarian refugees of Turkish extraction compelled to leave that country as a result of this pressure and who, being unable to enter Turkey, might seek refuge on the territory of another contracting party after 1 January 1951. The Turkish Government will, at the time of ratification, enter reservations which it could make under article 42 of the Convention. Reservation and declaration made upon ratification: No provision of this Convention may be interpreted as granting to refugees greater rights than those accorded to Turkish citizens in Turkey; The Government of the Republic of Turkey is not a party to the Arrangements of 12 May 1926 and of 30 June 1928 mentioned in article 1, paragraph A, of this Convention. Furthermore, the 150 persons affected by the Arrangement of 30 June 1928 having been amnestied under Act No.3527, the provisions laid down in this Arrangement are no longer valid in the case of Turkey. Consequently, the Government of the Republic of Turkey considers the Convention of 28 July 1951 independently of the aforementioned Arrangements. The Government of the Republic understands that the action of "re-availment" or "reacquisition" as referred to in article 1, paragraph C, of the Convention–that is to say: "If (1) He has voluntarily re-availed himself of the protection of the country of his nationality; or (2) Having lost his nationality, he has voluntarily reacquired it"–does not depend only on the request

In accordance with its reservation on the article 1/B((a) Turkey stated that "*events occurring before 1 January 1951*" in article 1, section A, shall be understood as "*events occurring in Europe before 1 January 1951*"[24].

b. 1967 Protocol Relating to the Status of Refugees

The 1951 Convention was only covering people who can be refugees as the result of events occurring before 1 January 1951. As new situations may arise that may result in refugees, a new regulation was needed in order to ensure equivalent protection for people suffering for the same reasons but after the deadline of 1 January 1951 as determined in the 1951 Convention. The 1967 Protocol Relating to the Status of Refugees was therefore prepared and signed[25]. Turkey is party to the Protocol[26]. In this way, Turkey lifted the time restriction and maintained only the geographical limit for gaining refugee status.

c. Law on Foreigners and International Protection Numbered 6458[27]

In Turkish domestic law the term "refugee" is defined in the Law on Foreigners and International Protection numbered 6458, which entered into force in 2014. This law, similarly to the international regulations discussed above, defines "refugee" in article 61 as "*a person who as a result of events occurring in European countries and owing to a well-founded fear of being persecuted for reasons of race, religion, nationality, membership of a particular social group or political opinion, is outside the country of his citizenship and is unable or, owing to such fear, is unwilling to avail himself or herself of the protection of that country; or who, not having a nationality and being outside the country of his former residence as a result of such events, is unable or, owing to such fear, is unwilling to return to it, shall be granted refugee status upon*

---

of the person concerned but also on the consent of the State in question. See Official Gazette dated 5.9.1961 and numbered 10898.

24 For the list of reservations see (https://treaties.un.org/doc/Publication/MTDSG/Volume%20I/Chapter%20V/V-2.en.pdf, 03.10.206).

25 For detailed information and a list of signatory parties see https://treaties.un.org/Pages/UNTSOnline.aspx?id=2&clang=_en (last visited 11.2.2017).

26 For the Council of Ministers' decision dated 1.7.1968 and numbered 6/10266 see Official Gazette dated 05.08.1968 and numbered 12968.

27 Official Gazette dated 11.4.2013 and numbered 28615.

completion of the refugee status determination process". Under article 62, it is stated that people suffering from same reasons that come from countries outside Europe can be conditional refugees. As is clear from the above, these regulations are focused on providing international protection for individuals who are facing or are in severe risk of facing discrimination or persecution because of their race, religion, nationality or social or political membership of a group. At this point we need to examine whether people who lost, or have a high risk of losing, their basic human rights – such as the right to life, the right to a healthy environment, and the right to food and health care – due to environmental causes can be categorized as refugees.

2. Who Is A Climate Refugee and What Are The Differences Between Climate Refugees and Other Refugees

Climate refugees (environmental refugees), better referred to as environmentally displaced persons, are individuals who must leave their homeland because of the negative effects of climate change[28]. Environmental causes of the displacement of people can be both natural events, such as droughts, floods and earthquakes, as well as human activities such as greenhouse gases, cutting down forests or economic problems following environmental events. As noted above, climate change-induced migration can be either internal or external. Here I will be focusing only on external migration, meaning climate change-induced migration where individuals cross borders.

As previously explained the traditional term "refugee" does not cover climate refugees. Even if climate refugees are in a situation closer to traditional refugees than ordinary migrants who voluntarily change their homelands, they still do not qualify as refugees[29]. In today's world the requirements for benefiting from the international protection for refugees cannot be satisfied if someone has only suffered, or would only suffer, damage as a result of environmental factors and they may face being sent back to their homeland[30]. The difference between traditional refugees and climate refugees has been discussed also before national authorities of New Zealand. In a case brought before NZRSAA Tuvaluan citizen appellant's case was based on the

---

28 *Moberg*, Refugee Definitions, P. 1109 – 1111, Benoit Mayer, The International Legal Challenges of Climate-Induced Migration: Proposal for an International Legal Framework, 22:3 Colorado Journal of International Environmental Law and Policy, 2011, P. 362.

29 *Mayer,* Refugee Definitions, P. 380 – 381.

30 *Mayer,* Refugee Definitions, *P.* 382.

environmental and economic difficulties in Tuvalu[31]. The appellant was a man born in Kiribati, but an ethnic Tuvaluan, when the colony of Gilbert and Ellice Islands split into two independent nations of Kiribati and Tuvalu he went to live in Tuvalu. He has been educated, worked and married in Tuvalu. He has four daughters. All of his family except his youngest daughter who is born in New Zealand have applied for refugee status[32].

Appellant after arriving in New Zealand in 1998 applied for refugee status in 2000, his application was denied by the relevant authority. Furthermore this decision has been appealed. Here it is said that appellant's fear is focused on environmental and economic difficulties that he faced in Tuvalu. Appellant says that his house in Tuvalu is five feet from the sea and when the tide is high the land can be submerged in the water. In addition to the environmental problems there is shortage of drinkable water and medicine, problem of unemployment and weak education opportunities. He stated that he was highly worried about the future of his daughters since there were weak educational and medical opportunities in Tuvalu and one of them was born with serious hearing difficulties. Therefore he asked for granting refugee status for himself.

Appeal Authority stated that since New Zealand is party of 1951 Convention granting of refugee status has to be examined accordingly. The authority decides to make a two-tier analysis in terms of the Convention. Firstly looks at the facts of the case whether there is a real chance of the appellant being persecuted if he returns back to Tuvalu. Secondly if the answer of the first question is yes the authority checks whether the risk of persecutions is arising out of one of the five reasons mentioned in the Convention. In conclusion the authority stated that the facts which appellant based his application on are not one of the five reasons mentioned in the Convention, according to Convention the status of refugee can be granted only on the ground of race, religion, nationality, membership of a particular group and political opinion, here the appellant does not face risk of persecution due to one of these factors, all citizens of Tuvalu face same problems, therefore the request for granting the status of refugee has been declined. In this way the authority of New Zealand interpreted 1951 Convention and stated that being citizen

31 For the case Refugee Appeal No 72313 [2000] NZRSAA 491 (19.10.2000) before NZRSAA see http://www.nzlii.org/nz/cases/NZRSAA/2000/ (13.2.2017).

32 Together with him also his family applied for refugee status and also their cases have been brought before NZRSAA. See cases Refugee Appeal No 72314 [2000] NZRSAA 492 (19.10.2000), 72315 [2000] NZRSAA 493 (19.10.2000), 72316 [2000] NZRSAA 494 (19.10.2000) http://www.nzlii.org/nz/cases/NZRSAA/2000/ (last visited 13.2.2017).

of a country where environmental problems and consequential economic difficulties affect practice of human rights badly is not considered a reasons sufficient for gaining the status of refugee.

In another case before New Zealand Refugee Status Appeals Authority three appellants who belong to same family applied for refugee status based on the fact that Tuvaluan economy was very small, there is problem of unemployment, water pollution, shortage of food and drinkable water, lack of medical treatment and educational facilities, and sea level was rising, since their house is close to the water line there was the risk of house to be submerged[33]. The appellants stated that because of these reasons they had to leave Tuvalu and had no other chance than applying for refugee status. It is also stated that all of these problems amounted to the appellants being persecuted by the government of Tuvalu, the government consciously choose not to spend money on developing facilities that are urgently needed by the citizens, government's this attitude and economic plans show that there is discrimination and persecution against some citizens of Tuvalu, governors had a better standard of living in terms of economy and environment due to the taken measures and this situation is evidence of the persecution against the appellants.

Again Appeal Authority made the two-tier analysis. Firstly examined objectively, is there a real chance of the appellants being persecuted in case they go back to Tuvalu and secondly if the answer of first question is yes does the reason for persecution is one of the reasons mentioned in the 1951 Convention. Authority stated that environmental and economic problems are not one of the reasons mentioned in the Convention. General lack of medical, educational and transportation facilities, shortage of food and drinkable water cannot be considered as any of the Convention reasons where the appellants can be said to be differentially at risk of harm amounting to persecution. Lack of important facilities and shortage of vital needs Tuvalu are the same for all Tuvaluan citizens. All Tuvaluans face the problems arising out of climate change, poor economic conditions in Tuvalu to all Tuvaluan citizens. Therefore the reasons of applying to the refugee status by the appellants cannot be considered as forms of harm directed at the appellants for reason of their civil or political status as mentioned in the Convention.

It is stated that even if the appellants claim that because of their belonging to a lower socio-economic group in Tuvalu they are differentially at risk

33 For the case Refugee Appeal No 72179 [2000] NZRSAA 385 (31.08.2000) before NZRSAA see http://www.nzlii.org/nz/cases/NZRSAA/2000/385.html (last visited 19.2.2017).

of harm and their economic status makes them more vulnerable in terms of being persecuted none of the facts mentioned in the application can be considered as a particular social group which members of that group can be said to be persecuted in terms of the Convention. In order to be considered as a member of the said particular social group there have to be a link between the said membership of a particular social group and the persecution feared. Besides there is no evidence to prove that the appellants are subject to discriminations and can be subject to persecutions because of their belonging to the said group. On those grounds the Authority rejected the refugee status applications. Here we have to say that there are too many similar cases before the same Authority and its approach of excluding environmental and consequential economic problems from five reasons providing refugee status according to the Convention is the same as the cases mentioned here.

3. Status and Rights of Climate Refugees in Turkey

As seen before according to Turkish Law Turkey grants the status of refugee in case a person who owns reasonable fear of being persecuted for reasons of race, religion, nationality, membership of a particular social group or political opinion, is outside the country of his nationality and is unable or, owns such fear, is unwilling to avail himself of the protection of that country; or who, is having a nationality and being outside the country of his former habitual residence as a result of such events, is unable or, owns to such fear, is unwilling to return to it as a result of events occurring in Europe. Considering the precedent from the New Zealand Authority, we may consider that if a similar case were brought before the Turkish authorities, they may come to the same conclusion.

In the aforesaid cases applications have been examined through a two-tier analysis. Firstly it is examined whether the person who applied for refugee status is really facing a risk of persecution in case he/she returns back to his country and secondly it is responded if the answer of the first question is yes does the ground for persecution is one of the five reasons mentioned in the Convention. In the cases it is clearly stated that even if the applicant face important problems regarding housing, nutrition and health the grounds for refugee status are determined in the Convention and there is no place for any discretion of authorities that may lead us to reach to a conclusion that environmental factors can be considered as one of the said grounds. This approach can be criticized as interpreting the Convention only with the literal meaning of the articles and disregarding the aim behind the Convention. Examples of some other international documents protecting right to live in satisfactory environment can be shown as evidence of the international communities' goal to provide environmentally safe habitat for everyone and is can be claimed that if the 1951 Convention was prepared under today's conditions it would definitely mention environmental problems as a reason for gaining refugee status. However today we cannot take this criticism as an instrument to interpret the Convention, nobody can aspect a country to interpret said articles according to the principles dominantly finding in other international documents. International authorities state that the risk is very high and observed impacts of climate change is faster that it was anticipated[34]. In today's world it is stated that there are more climate refugees than political refugees trying to survive from wars, discrimination and other conflicts to be considered as reasons for obtaining refugee status[35]. Therefore we need to work on new statuses within the concept of environmental displacement.

C. Conclusion

The current situation regarding climate refugees is highly concerning. In today's conditions the legal framework for the status of refugee is not wide enough to assist environmentally displaced people, or so-called "climate refugees". However, we have seen that these people face severe risks to their right to life, clean water, food security and health. We should keep in mind that such climate refugees urgently need the help of the international community but there is currently a lack of regulation. UN and other international organizations have conducted studies and a Draft Convention on the International Status of Environmentally Displaced Persons has been prepared by CIDCE[36].

---

34 IPCC Special Report, Managing the Risks of Extreme Events and Disasters to Advance Climate Change Adaptation, Field, C.B., V. Barros, T.F. Stocker, D. Qin, D.J. Dokken, K.L. Ebi, M.D. Mastrandrea, K.J. Mach,
G.-K. Plattner, S.K. Allen, M. Tignor, and P.M. Midgley (Eds.), 2012, http://www.ipcc.ch/pdf/special-reports/srex/SREX_Full_Report.pdf (16.10.2016), https://www.greencrossaustralia.org/our-work/climate-adaptation/sea-levels-rising-faster-than-expected.aspx (20.2.2017).

35 http://nationalgeographic.org/encyclopedia/climate-refugee/ (06.10.2016)

36 CIDCE is an International Non-Governmental Organization which is composed of environmental lawyers and helps preparing international and national regulations regarding environmental strategies. https://cidce.org/presentation-presentation/ (20.2.2017).

Third version of Draft Convention[37] has been published in the May 2013. In the preamble and objective of the Convention it has been said that considering the dangerous effects of climate change and people who's right to life, health and dignity is injured and had to displace by the environmental problems and taking into account that international community tries to recognize a legal status for environmentally displaced persons and accordingly increased their activities in order to help those people this Convention has been prepared to establish a legal framework that guarantees the rights of environmentally displaced persons and to organize their reception to other countries as well as their eventual return. Since Turkey is working hardly on traditional refugee status and party to the all-important international documents regarding refugees status and it is highly possible that it may be up against the issue of climate refugees it is important for Turkey that it involves in international working groups and on the other hand revises national regulations accordingly. Hopefully we may have a regulation developing a framework for applying to all the situations of external displacements caused by environmental reasons respecting human rights, dignity and accepted by the international law.

Bibliography

António Guterres, Migration, Displacement and Planned Relocation, 31.12.2012, http://www.unhcr.org/news/editorial/2012/12/55535d6a9/migration-displacement-planned-relocation.html.

Aurelie Lopez, The Protection of Environmentally Displaced Persons in International Law, 37 Environmental Law, Spring 2007, p. 365 – 409.

Aysel Çelikel & Günseli Öztekin Gelgel, Yabancılar Hukuku, 22nd ed., 2016.

B. Bahadır Erdem, Vatandaşlık Hukuku, 5th ed., 2016.

Benoit Mayer, Climate Change, Migration and International Law in Southeast Asia, Koh Kheng Lian et al. (eds.), Climate Change Adaptation: ASEAN and the World (World Scientific, 2015), 337-358.

Benoit Mayer, The International Legal Challenges of Climate-Induced Migration: Proposal for an International Legal Framework, 22:3 Colorado Journal of International Environmental Law and Policy, 2011, p. 357 – 416.

Bülent Çiçekli, Yabancılar ve Mülteci Hukuku, 6th ed., 2016.

---

37 For the text of third version of Draft Convention on the International Status of Environmentally Displaced Persons see https://cidce.org/wp-content/uploads/2016/08/Draft-Convention-on-the-International-Status-on-environmentally-displaced-persons-third-version.pdf (20.2.2017).

Carol Farbotko, Wishful Sinking: Disappearing Islands, Climate Refugees and Cosmopolitan Experimentation, Asia Pacific Viewpoint, Vol. 51, No. 1, April 2010, p. 47 – 60.

Ergin Nomer, Türk Vatandaşlık Hukuku, 22nd ed., 2016.

http://unfccc.int

http://nationalgeographic.org.

https://cidce.org.

IPCC Special Report, Managing the Risks of Extreme Events and Disasters to Advance Climate Change Adaptation, Field, C.B., V. Barros, T.F. Stocker, D. Qin, D.J. Dokken, K.L. Ebi, M.D. Mastrandrea, K.J. Mach, G.-K. Plattner, S.K. Allen, M. Tignor, and P.M. Midgley (Eds.), 2012.

Kara K. Moberg, Extending Refugee Definitions to Cover Environmentally Displaced Persons Displaces Necessary Protection, 94 Iowa Law Review, 2008 – 2009, p. 1107 – 1136.

Lancet and University College London Institute for Global Health Commission, Managing the Health Effects of Climate Change, http://www.thelancet.com/pdfs/journals/lancet/PIIS0140-6736(09)60935-1.pdf.

Niang, I., O.C. Ruppel, M.A. Abdrabo, A. Essel, C. Lennard, J. Padgham & P. Urquhart, 2014, Africa. In: Climate Change 2014: Impacts, Adaptation, and Vulnerability. Part B: Regional Aspects. Contribution of Working Group II to the Fifth Assessment Report of the Intergovernmental Panel on Climate Change [Barros, V.R., C.B. Field, D.J. Dokken, M.D. Mastrandrea, K.J. Mach, T.E. Bilir, M. Chatterjee, K.L. Ebi, Y.O. Estrada, R.C. Genova, B. Girma, E.S. Kissel, A.N. Levy, S. MacCracken, P.R. Mastrandrea & L.L.White (eds.)]. Cambridge University Press, Cambridge, United Kingdom and New York, NY, USA.

Olivia Dun & François Gemenne, Defining "Environmental Migration", Forced Migration Review, 31.10.2008, p. 10 – 11.

Olcay Ziya, Mülteci-Göçmen Belirsizliğinde İklim Mültecileri, TBB Dergisi, 2012(99), p. 229 – 240.

Recommendations From the Advisory Group on Climate Change and Human Mobility COP 20 Lima, Peru, Human Mobility in the Context of Climate Change, https://www.iom.int/files/live/sites/iom/files/pbn/docs/Human-Mobility-in-the-context-of-Climate-Change.pdf.

Wong, P.P., I.J. Losada, J.-P. Gattuso, J. Hinkel, A. Khattabi, K.L. McInnes, Y. Saito & A. Sallenger, 2014, Coastal systems and low-lying areas. In: Climate Change 2014: Impacts, Adaptation, and Vulnerability. Part A: Global and Sectoral Aspects. Contribution of Working Group II to the Fifth Assessment Report of the Intergovernmental Panel on Climate Change [Field, C.B., V.R. Barros, D.J. Dokken, K.J. Mach, M.D. Mastrandrea, T.E. Bilir, M. Chatterjee, K.L. Ebi, Y.O. Estrada, R.C. Genova, B. Girma, E.S. Kissel, A.N. Levy, S. MacCracken, P.R. Mastrandrea & L.L.White (eds.)]. Cambridge University Press, Cambridge, United Kingdom and New York, NY, USA.

www.csb.gov.tr

www.greencrossaustralia.org

www.nzlii.org

www.tuvaluislands.com

www.un.org
www.unep.org
www.unhcr.org

Draft Convention on the International Status of Environmentally-Displaced Persons

Nuray Ekşi, Marmara University Faculty of Law (r.)

Abstract

International agreements do not provide adequate protection for environmentally displaced persons. As a result, various solutions have been proposed to address their protection. One such proposal is the drafting of a specific convention that addresses all aspects of environmental displacement, whether internal or international. At the initiative of a group of academics from the University of Limoges, the Draft Convention on the International Status of Environmentally Displaced Persons was developed. This article will briefly outline the issue of environmental displacement, highlight the reasons why international agreements fail to protect environmentally displaced persons, and explain the provisions of the Draft Convention.
Keywords: Climate refugees, environmental refugees, climate migrants, internally displaced persons, environmentally-displaced persons, environmentally-induced migration, environmentally induced displacement, environmental migrant, ecological migrants, climate refugees, environmental refuges, ecological refugees, humanitarian protection, climate change displacement, DPs.

I. Overall Assessment of Environmentally-Displaced Persons

A. Environmentally-Displaced Persons in General

The concept of "refugee" is defined by the *1951 Convention relating to the Status of Refugees,*[1] and with 146 states party to it, general uniformity in understanding this concept is established. However, since the entry into force of the 1951 Geneva Convention, new concepts and categories have emerged in asylum law. Despite this, these emerging categories have not been adequately protected under existing international law. Among them, "environmentally displaced persons" have become a central topic of discussion in various circles.

Different classifications of natural disasters have been made.[2] Natural disasters, regardless of their nature, are a leading cause of displacement,

---

1 United Nations Treaty Series, 1954, Vol. 189, pp. 151-185.

2 For these classifications, *see* SCOTT Matthew, Natural Disasters, Climate Change and *Non-Refoulement*: What Scope for Resisting Expulsion under Articles 3 and 8 of the European Convention on Human Rights?, 26(2014)3 International Journal of Refugee Law, p. 407.

resulting in both internal and international migration.[3] These displacements, compounded by the effects of disappearing small islands, coastal erosion, water and food shortages, extreme weather events, armed conflict, and political instability due to dwindling natural resources,[4] have led to the emergence of new terms such as "environmentally-displaced persons", "environmentally-induced migration", "environmentally induced displacement", "environmental migrant", "ecological migrants", "climate refugees", "environmental refuges" or "ecological refugees".[5]

International agreements do not offer adequate protection to environmentally displaced persons. As a result, various actors have proposed a range of solutions to address their protection. One proposed solution is the creation of a specific convention that addresses all aspects of environmental displacement, whether internal or international. A group of academics from the University of Limoges, France, took the initiative to draft a text after conducting negotiations. Initial work focused on a project concerning the rights of environmentally displaced persons, which was later transformed into a convention. The first draft of the *Convention on the International Status of Environmentally Displaced Persons* was published in 2006. The text was then revised twice, in 2008[6] and 2013, respectively. The third version[7] was

3 MOBERG K. Kara, Extending Refugee definitions to Cover Environmentally Displaced Persons Displaces Necessary Protection, 94(2009) Iowa Law Review, p. 1111.

4 Book Review, Reviewed by Carl Söderbergh, Laura Westra, Environmental Justice and the Rights of Ecological Refugees, London 2009, 2(2010) Climate and Development, p. 295.

5 JACOVELLA Giulia, International Law and the (De)Politicisation of Climate Change and Migration: Lessons from the Pacific, 2(2015)1 SOAS Law Journal, p. 82. The concept of "environmental refugee" was firstly created by Lester Brown of World Watch Institute (WWI) in 1970. It was later adopted by the International Institute for Environment and Development (IIED) in 1984, the UN Environment Programme (UNEP) in 1985, and featured in the 1992 Agenda 21. However, since climate or environmental refugees are not meet the requirements of refugee definition of the 1951 Geneva Convention, the UNHCR, the IOM, and the Refugee Policy Group (RPG) prefer not to use the term "refugee" and suggest alternatives such as "environmental migrants", "climate change migrants", or "environmentally displaced persons" (ISLAM Rafiqul, Climate Refugees and International Refugee Law, *(in)* An Introduction to International Refugee Law, Editors Jahid Hossain Bhuiyan/M. Rafiqul Islam, Leiden 2013, p. 217-218).

6 For the text of 2008 version the Draft Convention, *see* Draft Convention on the International Status of Environmentally-Displaced Persons, 12(2008)4 Revue Européenne de Droit de l'Environnement, pp. 395-406.

7 For the text of the 2013 version of the Draft Convention, *see* https://cidce.org/wp-content/uploads/2016/08/Draft-Convention-on-the-International-Status-on-environmentally-displaced-persons-third-version.pdf (accessed 15.02.2025).

published in 2013. This study will focus solely on the third version of the Draft Convention.

B. International Treaties Fail to Provide Specific Protection for Environmentally Displaced Persons

Nishimura draw the picture of the legal gap in protection of environmentally-displaced persons as follows:

> "No international agreement exists that explicitly accounts for climate change-induced migration. Nor is there academic consensus on how to characterize and treat climate change migrants. Debate centres on whether climate change migrants can be considered a legally distinct group; whether and, if so, how to expand existing international refugee or environmental law to encompass climate change migrants; and whether a new international framework or agreement is needed. Proposed solutions and calls for action have yet to produce meaningful agreement on how to proceed. Instead, states and international decision makers are at an impasse, and the legal gaps in protection remain".[8]

As *Nishimura* rightly emphasized, efforts to either expand existing conventions to cover environmentally displaced persons or to draft a specific convention addressing their needs have not been successful thus far. However, initiatives and efforts to create a convention are still ongoing.[9] The only success that has been achieved is in regional level and covers internally displacement in Africa. The *African Union Convention for the Protection and Assistance of Internally Displaced Persons in Africa* is the first legally binding instrument addressing internal displacement. It is widely praised

---

8 NISHIMURA, Lauren 'Climate Change Migrants': Impediments to a Protection Framework and the Need to Incorporate Migration into Climate Change Adaptation Strategies, 27(2015)1 International Journal of Refugee Law, p. 108.

9 *Docherty* and *Giannini* argue that creating a new, stand-alone convention is the best way to protect climate refugees, and outlines the normative and institutional framework for the proposed convention. *See* DOCHERTY Bonnie/GIANNINI Tyler, Confronting a Rising Tide: A Proposal for a Convention on Climate Change Refugees, 33(2009) Harvard Environmental Law Review, pp. 349-403. *Hodgkinson/Anderson/Young* also propose a single, stand-alone convention to address the problem of climate change displacement (HODGKINSON David/BURTON Tess/ANDERSON Heather/YOUNG Lucy, The Hour When the Ship Comes in: A Convention for Persons Displaced by Climate Change, 36(2010) Monash University Law Review, p. 81 et seq.).

and acknowledged as a crucial step in addressing legal gaps related to the protection and assistance of internally displaced persons. The convention covers all causes and stages of internal displacement.[10] Besides the African Union Convention, the *Guiding Principles on Internal Displacement*, adopted by the United Nations General Assembly in 1998, are also noteworthy. Both instruments focus solely on internal displacement, excluding internationally displaced persons from their scope.

Article 1A(2) of the 1951 Geneva Convention Relating to the Status of Refugees provides that a refugee is someone who is unable or unwilling to return to their country of origin owing to a well-founded fear of being persecuted for reasons of race, religion, nationality,[11] membership of a particular social group, or political opinion. In order to be considered a refugee, a person must show well-founded fear of persecution for one of the reasons stated in Article 1A(2) of the 1951 Geneva Convention.[12] It is irrelevant whether the persecution stems from any single one of these reasons or from a combination of two or more.[13] According to paragraph 39 of the *UNHCR's Handbook on Procedures and Criteria for Determining Refugee Status under the 1951 Convention and the 1967 Protocol*, the concept of "persecution" excludes such persons that are victims of famine or natural disaster.[14] States parties are obligated to apply the 1951 Geneva Convention solely based on one of its five grounds.

---

10 ABEBE Allehone Mulugeta, The African Union Convention on Internally Displaced Persons: Its Codification Background, Scope, and Enforcement Challenges, 29(2010)3 Refugee Survey Quarterly, s. 28-29.

11 "74. The term "nationality" in this context is not to be understood only as "citizenship". It refers also to membership of an ethnic or linguistic group and may occasionally overlap with the term "race". Persecution for reasons of nationality may consist of adverse attitudes and measures directed against a national (ethnic, linguistic) minority and in certain circumstances the fact of belonging to such a minority may in itself give rise to well-founded fear of persecution" (Procedures and Criteria for Determining Refugee Status under the 1951 Convention and the 1967 Protocol relating to the Status of Refugees HCR/IP/4/Eng/REV.1 Reedited, Geneva, January 1992, UNHCR 1979).

12 For the background of the refugee definition, *see* GLYNN Irial, The Genesis and Development of Article 1 of the 1951 Refugee Convention, 25(2012)1 Journal of Refugee Studies, p. 134-145.

13 Procedures and Criteria for Determining Refugee Status under the 1951 Convention and the 1967 Protocol relating to the Status of Refugees HCR/IP/4/Eng/REV.1 Reedited, Geneva, January 1992, UNHCR 1979. http://www.unhcr.org/publ/PUBL/3d58e13b4.pdf (accessed 15.2.2025).

14 Handbook on Procedures and Criteria for Determining Refugee Status under the 1951 Convention and the 1967 Protocol relating to the Status of Refugees, HCR/IP/4/Eng/REV.1 Reedited, Geneva, January 1992, UNHCR 1979.

As mentioned, natural disasters or climate change is not accounted among the grounds listed in the 1951 Geneva Convention. Despite being labeled as "environmental refugees" or "climate change refugees", there is a protection gap within the meaning of the 1951 Geneva Convention for those environmentally displaced.[15] Climate change refugees or environmental refugees are not considered "refugees" within the meaning of the 1951 Geneva Convention in judgments made by various countries' courts. Scholars generally agree that persons displaced by climate change would not be the subject of protection under the 1951 Geneva Convention and there is a legal gap in the protection of those environmentally displaced across borders.[16] Moreover, international

---

15 SKINNER Jennifer, The State Responsibility in the Face of Environmentally Displaced Persons, 42(2014)4 Wake Forest Journal of Law & Policy, p. 417-418; MAYER Benoit, The International Legal Challenges of Climate-Induced Migration: Proposal for an International Legal Framework, 22(2011) Colorado Journal of International Environmental Law and Policy, pp. 380-381.

16 JACOVELLA, 84; SKINNER, 418; HODGKINSON/BURTON/ANDERSON/YOUNG, 75; WILLIAMS Angela, Turning the Tide: Recognizing Climate Change Refugees in International Law, 30(2008) Law and Policy, p. 508; LOPEZ Aurelie, The Protection of Environmentally-Displaced Persons in International Law, 37(2007) Environmental Law, p. 387. However, *Heather/Jonathan* are of the view that 1951 Geneva Convention is applicable to submerged or uninhabitable states. *"In order to legally grant asylum to the displaced inhabitants of completely submerged or uninhabitable states, we need not advocate for an expansion of refugee law to cover all climate migrants, nor need we twist the characterization of persecution so that displaced islanders somehow count as persecuted by their own submerged countries. We need only bear in mind that it is fundamental lack of basic national protection, rather than persecution that is at the heart of the 1951 Convention"* (HEATHER Alexander/JONATHAN Simon "Unable to Return" in the 1951 Refugee Convention: Stateless Refugees and Climate Change, 26 (2014) Florida Journal of International Law, p. 573). *Marcs* make a distinction between the naturally occurring environmental disasters and artificial environmental harm. He presents an argument that while purely natural environmental disasters are not sufficient to establish refugee status an applicant who can show deliberately inflicted severe environmental harm in the absence of state protection will have a strong claim to refugee status pursuant to an evolutionary interpretation of the 1951 Geneva Convention definition (MARCS Carly, Spoiling Movi's River: Towards Recognition of Persecutory Environmental Harm within the Meaning of the Refugee Convention, 24(2008) American University International Law Review, p. 71). *Cooper* also claims that climate refugees are particular social group and therefore they are covered by the definition of the 1951 Geneva Convention (COOPER B. Jessica B., Environmental Refugees: Meeting the Requirements of the Refugee Definition, 6(1998) New York University Environmental Law Journal, p. 535-526). *Falstrom* disagrees with *Cooper* and argues that environmentally displaced persons do not constitute a distinct social group and generally do not meet the traditional definition, unless they fulfill the criteria based on grounds other than environmental factors (FALSTROM Dana Zartner, Stemming

organizations working in the field of migration and asylum, such as UNHCR, IOM, and the Refugee Policy Group, have also expressed reluctance to include environmentally displaced persons as refugees.[17] However, as *Lopez* points out that "nothing actually prevents a country from granting refugee status to a person persecuted through environmental damage for one of the reasons enumerated in the 1951 Refugee Convention".[18]

Since climate refugees are not considered conventional refugees, solutions are being sought through other conventions to provide them with the best possible protection. Three conventions are viewed as potential remedies to address the legal gap in the protection of environmentally displaced persons: (1) The 1984 Convention against Torture and Other Cruel, Inhuman or Degrading Treatment or Punishment ("the Torture Convention"); (2) the 1966 International Covenant on Civil and Political Rights ("the ICCPR"), and (3) International Covenant for Economic, Social and Political Rights ("the ICESCR"). However, no specific protection is offered to environmentally displaced persons under the 1984 Convention against Torture, nor under the ICCPR or the ICESCR.

The United Nations Framework Convention on Climate Change ("the UNFCCC") to which 193 States are parties has been in force since 21 March 1994.[19] Both the UNFCCC and its Kyoto Protocol do not address the issue of international protection for climate refugees.

The question of whether there is a connection between climate change and the full enjoyment of human rights is another important issue that needs to be addressed. Articles 2 and 3 of the European Convention on Human Rights

---

the Flow of Environmental Displacement: Creating a Convention to Protect Persons and Preserve the Environment, 13(2002) Colorado Journal of International Environmental Law and Policy, p. 13 and 16). In order to fill the protection gap *Markovich/ Annandale* there is an emerging argument suggesting that the definition of a refugee is being extended in customary law, or from a more speculative perspective, that the existing definition already permits claims from environmental refugees (MARKOVICH Vivian/ANNANDALE David, Sinking without a Life jacket? Sea Level Rise and the Position of Small Island States in International Law, 5(2000)2 Asia Pacific Journal of Environmental Law, p. 151-154).

17 BARISIC Angela/INCI Dilan, Environmentally Displaced People in the Hands of International Legal Protection or Left to Their Fate?, Karlstad University Legal Science C Independent Study, 15 ECTS, 24.5.2013, p. 21: http://www.diva-portal.org/smash/get/diva2:633332/ATTACHMENT01.pdf (accessed 15.2.2025); LOPEZ, 388.

18 LOPEZ, 387.

19 For the text of UN Framework Convention on Climate Change, *see* United Nations Treaty Series, 1994, Vol. 1771, p 107.

prohibit countries from returning individuals to a risk of arbitrary deprivation of life, the death penalty, torture, or cruel, inhuman, or degrading treatment or punishment. These articles could potentially protect climate refugees from being deported to countries facing natural disasters.[20] Therefore, it is suggested that alternative protection could be offered under the principle of *non-refoulement*.[21]

II. Draft Convention on the International Status of Environmentally-Displaced Persons

A. Background and General Framework of the Convention

1. The Reasons Behind Drafting the Convention

Migration experts state that environmental migration is mostly internal.[22] Since this issue is under the realm of the principle of states' sovereignty it is highly difficult to daft an international convention for providing protection to internally displaced persons. However, a set of guiding principles adopted as soft law address internally displaced persons. The *Guiding Principles on Internal Displacement* (the Guiding Principles)[23] were officially adopted by the United Nations General Assembly in 1998, and consist of thirty recommendations upholding the human rights of IDPs.[24] The Guiding Principles

---

20 *Scott* is of the view that Articles 3 and 8 of the ECHR could serve as obstacles to expulsion, helping to fill some protection gaps that states may otherwise overlook in cases of natural disasters (SCOTT, 404-432).

21 NISHIMURA, 115.

22 HODGKINSON/ANDERSON/YOUNG, 82. For the Mongolia's and Northern Uganda's internal environmental displacement, *see* MAYER Benoit, The Rights of Mongolia's Internal Migrants under International Law: Climatic, Domestic and Commercial Responsibilities, 7(2014) Journal of East Asia and International Law, p. 197-219; OOSTEROM A. Marjoke, Internal Displacement, the Camp and the Construction of Citizenship: Perspectives from Northern Uganda, 29(2016)3 Journal of Refugee Studies, p. 363-387; KOLMANNSKOG Vikram, Climate Change, Environmental Displacement and International Law, 24(2012) Journal of International Development, p.1072.

23 United Nations Commission on Human Rights, 'Report of the Representative of the Secretary-General on Internally Displaced Persons: Guiding Principles on Internal Displacement': Un doc E/CN.4/1998/53/Add.2, 1998.

24 For more information, *see* GEMENNE François/BRÜCKER Pauline, From the Guiding Principles on Internal Displacement to the Nansen Initiative: What the Governance of Environmental Migration Can Learn from the Governance of Internal Displacement,27(2015)2 International Journal of Refugee Law, p.245-263.

neither bind states nor impose positive obligations on them. Although they can be considered a starting point, they are far from being a comprehensive instrument for protecting environmentally displaced persons.[25] Despite their soft law nature it should not be undermined that the Guiding Principles are increasingly being incorporated into national laws.[26] Another regional instrument regarding internally displacement is the *African Union Convention for the Protection and Assistance of Internally Displaced Persons in Africa* which is shortly known as "Kampala Convention".

To address the gap in the protection of environmentally displaced persons, various approaches exist. The first is to amend the 1951 Refugee Convention; the second is to add a protocol to the 1992 United Nations Framework Convention on Climate Change; and the third is to create a new international treaty.[27]

A range of actors have advocated for a new international treaty on climate change displacement, or a protocol to the 1951 Geneva Convention, to establish a new category of refugee-like protected persons.[28] A person fleeing their country due to environmental reasons does not meet the criteria to be considered a refugee under Article 1 of the 1951 Geneva Convention, as it would be impossible for them to demonstrate a well-founded fear of persecution based on any of the grounds listed in the Convention.[29] Despite numerous attempts, no specific convention or protocol annexed to the 1951 Geneva Convention or the ECHR has been concluded to protect those affected by climate change.

There are various suggestions how to frame a new convention. *Falstrom* argues that the 1984 Convention against Torture could serve as a model for a new convention on the protection of environmentally displaced persons.[30] He suggests that by adopting the structure of the Convention against Torture, a

---

25 JACOVELLA, 85; KOLMANNSKOG, 1072-1073.

26 KOLMANNSKOG, 1073; LEAL-ARCAS Rafael, Climate Migration and International Trade, 6(2012) Vienna Journal on International Constitutional Law, p. 417; BETTS Alexander, Towards a 'Soft Law' Framework for the Protection of Vulnerable Irregular Migrants, 22(2010)2 International Journal of Refugee Law, p. 224.

27 JACOVELLA, 86.

28 McADAM Jane, Swimming against the Tide: Why a Climate Change Displacement Treaty is Not the Answer, 23(2011)1 International Journal of Refugee Law, p. 6.

29 ATAPATTU Sumudu, Climate Change, Human Rights, and Forced Migration: Implications for International Law, 27(2009-2010)3 Wisconsin International Law Journal, p. 617.

30 FALSTROM, 18-23.

new convention could be drafted to address the specific issue of environmentally displaced persons.[31]

It has also been noted that current international legal instruments addressing human rights fail to protect climate refugees. As a result, the protection of climate refugees is left to domestic laws, which, however, do not include effective provisions on this matter.[32]

A group of academics from the University of Limoges, France have prepared the *Draft Convention on the International Status of Environmentally-Displaced Persons*.[33] Initially, the members of Interdisciplinary Centre of Research on Environmental, Planning and Urban Law (CRIDEAU) who particularly specialized in environmental law had been conducting a project relating to the rights of environmentally displaced persons. Some academics from University of Limoges, Faculty of Law and Faculty of Economics specialized in human rights joined the Project.[34] A colloquium on ecological refugees held at Limoges in 2005 and the papers presented in the colloquium were published. The colloquium brought the idea to draft a convention. A group of researchers was constituted in 2007 and they submitted a first draft in 2008. A second version of the draft convention was prepared by the Limoges group of researchers in 2010.[35] The third version of the *Draft Convention on the International Status of Environmentally-Displaced Persons* shared with the public in 2013.

2. General Structure of the Convention

The draft Convention contains preamble and 36 articles under eight chapters. Chapter one deals with objective, definitions and scope of application (Articles 1-3). Chapter two deals with the principles applicable to environmentally displaced persons. These principles are principle of solidarity (Article 4), principle of common but differentiated responsibilities (Article 5), principle of effective protection (Article 6), principle of non-discrimination (Article 7)

---

31 FALSTROM, 21. For the other suggestions to draft a single stand-alone convention dealing with the protection and assistance provisions as well as administrative, financial and institutional aspects of internal and international environmentally displacement, *see* HODGKINSON/ANDERSON/YOUNG, 77 et seq.

32 MOBERG, 1117.

33 McADAM, 7. *See* also PRIEUR Michel, Draft Convention on the International Status of Environmentally-Displaced Persons, 43(2010-2011) Urban Lawyer, p. 247.

34 PRIEUR, 248.

35 PRIEUR, 248.

and principle of non-expulsion (Article 8). Chapter three and four addresses the rights guaranteed to persons threatened with displacement Articles 9-10) as well as rights guaranteed to displaced persons (Articles 12-13). Chapter four introduces provisions as to recognition of the status of an environmentally-displaced person and criminal immunity of environmentally-displaced person who illegally enters the country of a contracting state (Articles 14-19).

The draft Convention set up certain institutions responsible for monitoring implementation and application of the Convention by contracting states. Those institutions are World Agency for Environmentally-Displaced Persons (WAEP), High Authority and World Fund for the Environmentally-Displaced (WFED). Articles 25 to 27 in Chapter seven deal with the measures of the implementation of the Convention. Under the title of "final provisions" Chapter eight, Article 28 to 36, set rules concerning reservations, signature, ratification, acceptance or approval and entry into force. The Draft Convention is a stand-alone instrument designed to address all issues related to both internal and international displacement. *Cudiamat* is rightly states that, although the ultimate goal of the Draft Convention is to protect environmentally displaced persons, it is too advanced a step for the international community to accept.[36]

3. Scope of the Convention

The Draft Convention defines both the normative and institutional dimensions of protection and assistance for environmentally displaced persons. According to Article 3, the Draft Convention aims to address both internal and international displacement.[37] However, due to the principle of sovereignty, the application of the Draft Convention to internal displacement may be removed from the text.

Lopez says that "environmental disasters are traditionally classified into four categories: (1) long-term environmental degradation, including global warming, deforestation, land erosion, salinity, siltation, waterlogging, and

36 CUDIAMAT Nicole Angeline, Displacement Disparity: Filling the Gap of Protection for the Environmentally Displaced Person, 46(2011-2012) Valparaiso University Law Review, p. 930.

37 BIRRIEL Thais Pinheiro, Climate Change, Environmentally Displaced Persons and post Sovereignty: An Assessment of Normative Gaps and Potential Solutions in International Law, November, 2019, DePaul University College of Liberal Arts & Social Sciences Theses and Dissertations 281, pp. 63-64: https://via.library.depaul.edu/cgi/viewcontent.cgi?article=1287&context=etd (accessed 15.2.2025).

desertification, (2) sudden natural environmental disruptions, including earthquakes, droughts, floods, hurricanes, monsoons, tidal waves, tornadoes, and volcanic eruptions, 3) accidents, including both industrial and chemical disasters, and 4) armed conflicts".[38] However, three and four categories are encompass by one and two. Therefore, basically environmental disasters are grouped into two categories. The first is "sudden-onset events/sudden environmental disaster" and the second is "slow-onset events/gradual environmental disaster". "Slow-onset events are those that occur gradually and include, *inter alia*, drought, desertification, rising sea levels, and land and forest degradation. Sudden-onset events, such as flooding, hurricanes, earthquakes, and cyclones, are distinct occurrences that have and will always occur, but which can be amplified by existing land degradation".[39] The Draft Convention covers both categories.

Article 3 expands the scope of the Draft Convention by including environmental displacements caused by armed conflicts or acts of terrorism. Armed conflicts and acts of terrorism are not natural environmental events, but rather man-made disasters. Environmental migration is triggered by both natural and anthropogenic factors, such as development projects including dam and infrastructure construction, intensive agriculture, deforestation, and the emission of aerosols and greenhouse gases.[40] The Draft Convention addresses all types of disasters, whether of natural or anthropogenic origin.[41]

4. Fundamental Principles of the Convention

Under Articles 4 to 8, each contracting state agrees to implement the Convention based on the principles of joint responsibility, solidarity, common but differentiated responsibilities, effective protection, non-discrimination, and non-expulsion.[42]

---

38 LOPEZ, 369. *See* also LEAL-ARCAS, 413.

39 NISHIMURA, 112. *See* also McCUE Gregory, Environmental Refugees: Applying International Environmental Law to Involuntary Migration, 6(1993)1 Georgetown International Environmental Law Review, p. 160; FALSTROM, 4.

40 JACOVELLA Giulia, International Law and the (De)Politicisation of Climate Change and Migration: Lessons from the Pacific, 2(2015)1 SOAS Law Journal, p. 83.

41 PRIEUR, 253.

42 For information about the principles of the Draft Convention, *see* BIRRIEL, 64-65.

5. Reservations and Entry into Force

The contracting states are not allowed to make reservation to any provisions of the draft Convention and protocols (Article 33). Article 35 provides that the Draft Convention will entry into force the 30-day following the date of deposit of the tenth instrument of ratification, acceptance or approval.

6. Non-Effectiveness Clause of the Convention

Article 28 of the Draft Convention gives the priority to the conventions which are more favorable to environmentally-displaced persons. Article 28 provides that "the provisions of the present Convention cannot be interpreted as affecting the rights and guarantees that are more favorable to environmentally-displaced persons included in other binding national and international instruments that are or will enter into force, notably those concerning minorities and aboriginal peoples". According to the same Article the provisions of the Draft Convention do not affect the right to seek asylum or to benefit from other forms of national or international protection.

B. Rights Guaranteed to Persons Threatened with Displacement and Displaced Persons

1. Rights Guaranteed to Persons Threatened with Displacement

One of the rights granted to individuals threatened with displacement under the Draft Convention is the right to obtain information and participate in any policies or programs related to environmental disasters. "Each person, each family, groups and each population has the right of access to information relating to environmental threats and critical situations implied by these threats" as well as "to participate in the determination of policies and programs to prevent environmental disasters and to take charge, at the outset or throughout, of the consequences" (Article 9/1-2). Contracting states are also obligated to make legal arrangements that allow people living in their country to benefit from the rights to information and participation (Article 9/3-4).

Article 10 of the Draft Convention grants the right to displacement to all individuals, families, groups, and populations facing sudden or gradual environmental degradation that inevitably affects their living conditions.

Those affected by environmental disasters have the right to move either within or outside their home state. Contracting states must not hinder, attempt to hinder, or allow any hindrance to this displacement. Displacement should occur with the consent of the relevant individuals; however, in cases of grave and imminent danger, displacement can occur without their consent. (Article 11).

2. Rights Guaranteed to Displaced Persons

Persons may be displaced either internally or internationally, and the Draft Convention grants the same rights to both groups. Article 12 specifies that every environmentally displaced person is entitled to assistance, access to water and food aid, healthcare, legal recognition, civil and political rights, housing, the right to return, respect for family life, the right to work, education and training, the preservation of cultural identity, rights related to property and personal possessions, and the right to maintain connections with pets.

Internationally environmentally displaced persons have the right to conserve the nationality of his or her state of origin affected by an environmental disaster. If requested, the host state shall facilitate his or her naturalization (Article 13).

C. Procedure to Claim the Status of an Environmentally-Displaced Person

Article 15 of the Draft Convention stipulates that contracting states shall not impose criminal sanctions on an environmentally displaced person who, having left their habitual residence, enters or remains illegally within the territory of a state party, provided the person reports to the police within one month of arrival. Victims of environmental disasters are entitled to claim the status of an environmentally displaced person. However, to be granted this status upon request, the individual must meet the definition of an environmentally displaced person. As a general principle, the procedure for claiming the status of an environmentally displaced person will be determined by the contracting parties (Article 16/1). Notwithstanding the obligation of contracting states to draft procedural instruments, Article 16 also introduces certain procedural guarantees. A person claiming the status of an environmentally displaced person is granted a temporary residence permit until a final decision is made by the National Commission on Environmental Displacements, or, in the case of an appeal, until the decision of the High

Authority. During the application process, the environmentally displaced person may, if necessary, receive translation or interpretation services at no cost. The other procedural guarantees provided in Article 16(4)(5)(6) are as follows:

The decision to accept or to reject a claim for the status of an environmentally displaced person is rendered by a National Commission on Environmental Displacements. The Commission can render a decision only after having held a adversarial and public hearing during which the person claiming the status of an environmentally-displaced person and a representative of the State Party have had the opportunity to make submissions. At the hearing the person claiming the status of an environmentally-displaced person may be represented by a counsel of his or her own choosing or, if needed, appointed by the Commission. The person has the right to the services of an interpreter if he or she does not understand or does not speak the language of the proceedings.

Claims for the status of an environmentally-displaced person based on the same environmental disaster can be heard together. In such cases, the group of claimants may be represented or assisted by one or more counsels of their own choosing or that are appointed by the Commission. Claimants and their counsels shall have access free of cost to the assistance of interpreters-translators at the various stages of the procedure. The existence of a group of claimants does not preclude individual claims or other subsequent group claims for the same environmental disaster.

In all cases, the decision to accept or reject a claim for the status of an environmentally-displaced person is made on an individual basis for each claimant. Reasons for a decision must be given.

D. Termination of the Status of Environmental Displaced Person

Under the title of "termination of status" Article 19 stipulates that "the protection granted by the status shall cease when the conditions for its recognition no longer exist. Any environmentally-displaced person can extend his or her stay after the termination of status. In this situation the State shall facilitate the stay of the relevant person on its territory".

E. Institution Created by the Convention

The Convention requires contracting states to establish certain institutions. These institutions are National Commission on Environmental Displacements (NCED), the High Authority, World Agency for Environmentally-Displaced Persons (WAEP) and World Fund for the Environmentally-Displaced (WFED).

The States parties to the Convention, following the entry into force of the Convention, shall create a national commission on environmental-displacements to hear status claims. Each commission shall consist of nine independent members, experts in the field of human rights, the environment and peace. The members shall be appointed by the highest judicial authorities of the country (Article 17).

In accordance with Article 20 the contracting States will create the High Authority and elect its members. Article 22 provides that each State Party can present two candidates. The High Authority is composed of 21 persons recognized in the fields of human rights, environmental protection and peace. The selection shall be based on equitable geographic distribution. NGOs can present a total of 5 candidates. The members of the High Authority serve in their personal capacity. They elect from among themselves a Chair. Members of the High Authority are elected for a term of 6 years. The decisions of the NCED can be appealed to the High Authority within one month following notification to the concerned parties. A claimant's appeal from a judgment for the status of an environmentally-displaced person has a suspensive effect on that judgment and the temporary residence permit previously granted to the claimant is extended. The High Authority shall hear any Contracting Party, any State not Party to the present Convention, and any concerned NGO and, on invitation by the President of the High Authority, any individual can submit written submissions and participate to the hearings. The procedural guarantees provided for in paragraphs 3 to 6 of Article 16 of the Draft Convention are applicable to the appeal process.

The WFED's mission is to provide financial and material assistance for the receipt and return of the environmentally-displaced (Article 23). The WAEP's duties are accounted in Article 21 and it is mainly responsible for monitoring the implementation of the Convention.

F. Measures of Implementation

1. Cooperation

Article 25 stipulates that the implementation of the Draft Convention primarily relies on the institutions it establishes, with active participation from international and regional organizations, as well as the secretariats and committees of international agreements related to environmental protection and human rights. Article 20 also stipulates that, no later than one year after the Convention's entry into force, State Parties shall hold a conference. Subsequently, the Parties are required to meet regularly, at least once every two years. An extraordinary meeting can be held at the request of at least one-quarter of the State Parties. The Conference of the Parties designates the members of the Executive Council of the World Agency for Environmentally-Displaced Persons (WAEP), of the Word Fund for the Environmentally-Displaced (WFED) and elects the members of the High Authority (Article 20/3).

2. Bi-lateral or Regional Agreements

Article 26 invites State Parties to conclude bilateral or multilateral agreements on a regional scale to fulfill their obligations under the Draft Convention.

3. National Implementation Reports

Each State Party shall continuously review the implementation of the Convention and prepare national reports.

Conclusion

The Draft Convention offers extensive protection and grants rights to environmental refugees that are nearly on par with those of citizens. In some aspects, it even provides more protective provisions than the 1951 Geneva Convention. Recent developments, particularly the Syrian crisis, have led to an increase in the number of refugees. However, due to ongoing political and economic instability worldwide, it is unlikely that states will ratify the Draft Convention. Furthermore, many states are hesitant to even recognize refugee status for those covered by the 1951 Geneva Convention, let alone agree to a new convention that could increase their burdens. As a result, it appears that the Draft Convention is likely to remain just that a draft.

Bibliography

ABEBE Allehone Mulugeta, The African Union Convention on Internally Displaced Persons: Its Codification Background, Scope, and Enforcement Challenges, 29(2010)3 Refugee Survey Quarterly, pp. 28-57.

ATAPATTU Sumudu, Climate Change, Human Rights, and Forced Migration: Implications for International Law, 27(2009-2010)3 Wisconsin International Law Journal, pp. 607-636.

BARISIC Angela/INCI Dilan, Environmentally Displaced People in the Hands of International Legal Protection or Left to Their Fate?, Karlstad University Legal Science C Independent Study, 15 ECTS, 24.5.2013: http://www.diva-portal.org/smash/get/diva2:633332/ATTACHMENT01.pdf (accessed 15.2.2025).

BETTS Alexander, Towards a 'Soft Law' Framework for the Protection of Vulnerable Irregular Migrants, 22(2010)2 International Journal of Refugee Law, pp. 209-236.

BIRRIEL Thais Pinheiro, Climate Change, Environmentally Displaced Persons and post Sovereignty: An Assessment of Normative Gaps and Potential Solutions in International Law, November, 2019, DePaul University College of Liberal Arts & Social Sciences Theses and Dissertations 281, https://via.library.depaul.edu/cgi/viewcontent.cgi?article=1287&context=etd (accessed 15.4.2021).

---Book Review, Reviewed by Carl Söderbergh, Laura Westra, Environmental Justice and the Rights of Ecological Refugees, London 2009, 2(2010) Climate and Development, pp. 295-298.

COOPER B. Jessica B., Environmental Refugees: Meeting the Requirements of the Refugee Definition, 6(1998) New York University Environmental Law Journal, pp. 480-530.

CUDIAMAT Nicole Angeline, Displacement Disparity: Filling the Gap of Protection for the Environmentally Displaced Person, 46(2011-2012) Valparaiso University Law Review, pp. 891-938.

---Draft Convention on the International Status of Environmentally-Displaced Persons, 12(2008)4 Revue Européenne de Droit de l'Environnement, pp. 395-406.

DOCHERTY Bonnie/GIANNINI Tyler, Confronting a Rising Tide: A Proposal for a Convention on Climate Change Refugees, 33(2009) Harvard Environmental Law Review, p. 349-403.

FALSTROM Dana Zartner, Stemming the Flow of Environmental Displacement: Creating a Convention to Protect Persons and Preserve the Environment, 13(2002) Colorado Journal of International Environmental Law and Policy, pp. 1-130.

GEMENNE François/BRÜCKER Pauline, From the Guiding Principles on Internal Displacement to the Nansen Initiative: What the Governance of Environmental Migration Can Learn from the Governance of Internal Displacement,27(2015)2 International Journal of Refugee Law, pp. 245-263.

GLYNN Irial, The Genesis and Development of Article 1 of the 1951 Refugee Convention, 25(2012)1 Journal of Refugee Studies, p. 134-145.

HEATHER Alexander/JONATHAN Simon "Unable to Return" in the 1951 Refugee Convention: Stateless Refugees and Climate Change, 26 (2014) Florida Journal of International Law, pp. 531-574.

HODGKINSON David/BURTON Tess/ANDERSON Heather/YOUNG Lucy, The Hour When the Ship Comes in: A Convention for Persons Displaced by Climate Change, 36(2010) Monash University Law Review, pp. 69-120.

ISLAM Rafiqul, Climate Refugees and International Refugee Law, *(in)* An Introduction to International Refugee Law, Editors Jahid Hossain Bhuiyan/M. Rafiqul Islam, Leiden 2013.

JACOVELLA Giulia, International Law and the (De)Politicisation of Climate Change and Migration: Lessons from the Pacific, 2(2015)1 SOAS Law Journal, pp. 76-109.

KOLMANNSKOG Vikram, Climate Change, Environmental Displacement and International Law, 24(2012) Journal of International Development, pp. 1071-1081.

LEAL-ARCAS Rafael, Climate Migration and International Trade, 6(2012)3-4 Vienna Online Journal on International Constitutional Law, pp. 410-440.

LOPEZ Aurelie, The Protection of Environmentally-Displaced Persons in International Law, 37(2007) Environmental Law, p. 365-410.

MARCS Carly, Spoiling Movi's River: Towards Recognition of Persecutory Environmental Harm within the Meaning of the Refugee Convention, 24(2008) American University International Law Review, pp. 31-72.

MARKOVICH Vivian/ANNANDALE David, Sinking without a Life Jacket? Sea Level Rise and the Position of Small Island States in International Law, 5(2000)2 Asia Pacific Journal of Environmental Law, pp.135-154.

MAYER Benoit, The International Legal Challenges of Climate-Induced Migration: Proposal for an International Legal Framework, 22(2011) Colorado Journal of International Environmental Law and Policy, pp. 357-416.

MAYER Benoit, The Rights of Mongolia's Internal Migrants under International Law: Climatic, Domestic and Commercial Responsibilities, 7(2014) Journal of East Asia and International Law, pp. 197-219.

McADAM Jane, Swimming against the Tide: Why a Climate Change Displacement Treaty is Not the Answer, 23(2011)1 International Journal of Refugee Law, pp. 2-27.

McCUE Gregory, Environmental Refugees: Applying International Environmental Law to Involuntary Migration, 6(1993)1 Georgetown International Environmental Law Review, pp. 151-190.

MOBERG K. Kara, Extending Refugee definitions to Cover Environmentally Displaced Persons Displaces Necessary Protection, 94(2009) Iowa Law Review, pp. 1107-1136.

NISHIMURA, Lauren 'Climate Change Migrants': Impediments to a Protection Framework and the Need to Incorporate Migration into Climate Change Adaptation Strategies, 27(2015)1 International Journal of Refugee Law, pp. 107-134.

OOSTEROM A. Marjoke, Internal Displacement, the Camp and the Construction of Citizenship: Perspectives from Northern Uganda, 29(2016)3 Journal of Refugee Studies, pp. 363-387.

---Procedures and Criteria for Determining Refugee Status under the 1951 Convention and the 1967 Protocol relating to the Status of Refugees HCR/IP/4/Eng/REV.1 Reedited, Geneva, January 1992, UNHCR 1979. http://www.unhcr.org/publ/PUBL/3d58e13b4.pdf (accessed 15.2.2025).

PRIEUR Michel, Draft Convention on the International Status of Environmentally-Displaced Persons 42-43(2010-2011)4 Urban Lawyer, pp. 247-257.

SCOTT Matthew, Natural Disasters, Climate Change and *Non-Refoulement*: What Scope for Resisting Expulsion under Articles 3 and 8 of the European Convention on Human Rights?, 26(2014)3 International Journal of Refugee Law, pp. 404-432.

SKINNER Jennifer, The State Responsibility in the Face of Environmentally Displaced Persons, 42(2014)4 Wake Forest Journal of Law & Policy, pp. 417-434.

---United Nations Commission on Human Rights, 'Report of the Representative of the Secretary-General on Internally Displaced Persons: Guiding Principles on Internal Displacement': Un doc E/CN.4/1998/53/Add.2, 1998.

WILLIAMS Angela, Turning the Tide: Recognizing Climate Change Refugees in International Law, 30(2008) Law and Policy, pp. 502-529.

Climate Refugees in a Nutshell

Nuray Ekşi, Marmara University Faculty of Law (r.)

Abstract

Environmental disasters or climate changes have caused migration and, as a result of internal and international displacement, the emergence of a group of people often called "climate refugees" or "environmental refugees". Although they are often called "climate refugees" or "environmental refugees" they do not fall within the definition of refugee under the 1951 Geneva Convention on the Legal Status of Refugees. International agreements provide no adequate protection for climate or environmental refugees. In this article, following the explanation of definition of climate refugees, the reasons why the international agreements fail to protect climate refugees will be explained and the proposed solutions for climate refugees will be underlined.

Keywords: Climate refugees, environmental refugees, climate migrants, internally displaced persons, IDPs, humanitarian protection, climate change displacement

Abbreviations

Colo. J. Int'l Envtl. L.&Pol'y	Colorado Journal of International Environmental Law and Policy
DPs	Displaced Persons
Envtl. L.	Environmental Law
ECHR	Europan Convention on Human Rights
GEP	Global Environmental Politics
HELR	Harvard Environmental Law Review
ICCPR	International Covenant on Civil and Political Rights
ICESCR	International Covenant for Economic, Social and Political Rights
IDPs	Internally Displaced Persons
Int'l J. Refugee L.	International Journal of Refugee Law
Iowa L. Rev.	Iowa Law Review
İKÜHFD	İstanbul Kültür Üniversitesi Hukuk Fakültesi Dergisi
J. Int. Dev.	Journal of International Development
LFIP	Turkish Law on Foreigners and International Protection
NZCA	New Zealand Court of Appeal
NZIPT	New Zealand Immigration and Protection Tribunal
OJ	Official Journal of the European Union
RRTA	Refugee Review Tribunal of Australia

SOAS L.J.	SOAS Law Journal
UNFCCC	United Nations Framework Convention on Climate Change
UNHCR	United Nations High Commissioner for Refugees
UNTS	United Nations Treaty Series
Wis. Int'l L.J.	Wisconsin International Law Journal

I. The Concept of "Climate Refugees"

Among the many reasons for migration, natural disasters are the leading cause of displacement.[1] As a result of natural disasters people displaced either internally or internationally. In addition to economic refugees, disappearing small islands and costal states, water and food shortages, extreme weather events, armed conflict and political instability due to diminishing natural sources[2] have created new concept of "climate refugees", "environmental refuges" or "ecological refugees".[3] However, natural disasters are not accounted for in the refugee definition of the 1951 Geneva Convention Relating to the Status of Refugees. Article 1A(2) of the 1951 Geneva Convention provides that a refugee is someone who is unable or unwilling to return to their country of origin owing to a well-founded fear of being persecuted for reasons of race, religion, nationality, membership of a particular social group, or political opinion. In order to be considered a refugee, a person must show well-founded fear of persecution for one of the reasons stated in Article 1A(2) of the 1951 Geneva Convention. It is immaterial whether the persecution arises from any single one of these reasons or from a combination of two or more of

1 MOBERG K. Kara, Extending Refugee definitions to Cover Environmentally Displaced Persons Displaces Necessary Protection, 94(2009) Iowa L. Rev., p. 1111.

2 Book Review, Reviewed by Carl Söderbergh, Laura Westra, Environmental Justice and the Rights of Ecological Refugees, London 2009, 2(2010) Climate and Development, p. 295.

3 The concept of "environmental refugee" was firstly created by Lester Brown of World Watch Institute (WWI) in 1970, which was subsequently used by International Institute for Environment and Development located in London in 1984 and the UN Environment Programme-UNEP in 1985 and its 1992 Agenda 21. However, since climate or environmental refugees are not meet the requirements of refugee definition of the 1951 Geneva Convention, the UNHCR, the IOM, and the Refugee Policy Group (RPG) prefer not to use the term "refugee" and suggest alternatives such as environmental migrants, climate change migrants, or environmentally displaced persons" (ISLAM Rafiqul, Climate Refugees and International Refugee Law, (in) An Introduction to International Refugee Law, Editors Jahid Hossain Bhuiyan/M. Rafiqul Islam, Leiden 2013, p. 217-218).

them[4]. The reasons for persecution are (1) race, (2) religion, (3) nationality[5], (4) membership of a particular social group or (5) political opinion.

According to paragraph 39 of the UNHCR's Handbook on Procedures and Criteria for Determining Refugee Status under the 1951 Convention and the 1967 Protocol, the concept of "persecution" excludes such persons that are victims of famine or natural disaster.[6] A variety of actors have called for a new international treaty on climate change displacement, or a Protocol to the 1951 Geneva Convention to create a new class of refugee-like protected persons.[7] However, the increase in the number of refugees and environmental disasters moved the issue of the drafting of a new treaty for the protection of climate refugees away from the agenda of states.

Tuvalu and Kiribati are just two examples of many countries that are losing inhabitable land.[8] Tuvaluans depend on farming and fishing as their means of survival.[9] Due to the increase in salt in their soil, increasingly severe storms and rising sea levels, the ability of the Tuvalu to farm has been negatively impacted. Each year many Tuvaluans try to migrate, particularly to New Zealand and Australia. Knowing that the eventual submersion of its homeland is inevitable, the Tuvalu Government has unsuccessfully sought agreements with Australia and New Zealand that would allow Tuvaluans to migrate to these countries if an emergency evacuation is necessary.[10] While the numbers of "climate change refugees", "ecological refugees" or "environmental

4 Procedures and Criteria for Determining Refugee Status under the 1951 Convention and the 1967 Protocol relating to the Status of Refugees HCR/IP/4/Eng/REV.1 Reedited, Geneva, January 1992, UNHCR 1979. http://www.unhcr.org/publ/PUBL/3d58e13b4.pdf (accessed 27.7.2016).

5 "74. The term "nationality" in this context is not to be understood only as "citizenship". It refers also to membership of an ethnic or linguistic group and may occasionally overlap with the term "race". Persecution for reasons of nationality may consist of adverse attitudes and measures directed against a national (ethnic, linguistic) minority and in certain circumstances the fact of belonging to such a minority may in itself give rise to well-founded fear of persecution" (Procedures and Criteria for Determining Refugee Status under the 1951 Convention and the 1967 Protocol relating to the Status of Refugees HCR/IP/4/Eng/REV.1 Reedited, Geneva, January 1992, UNHCR 1979).

6 Handbook on Procedures and Criteria for Determining Refugee Status under the 1951 Convention and the 1967 Protocol relating to the Status of Refugees, HCR/IP/4/Eng/REV.1 Reedited, Geneva, January 1992, UNHCR 1979.

7 McADAM Jane, Swimming against the Tide: Why a Climate Change Displacement Treaty is Not the Answer, 23(2011)1 Int'l J. Refugee L., p. 6.

8 MOBERG, 1110.

9 MOBERG, 1109-1110.

10 MOBERG, 1109; LOPEZ Aurelie, The Protection of Environmentally-Displaced Persons in International Law, 37(2007) Envtl. L., p. 372-373.

refugees" have been constantly increasing, no adequate protection is provided to them under any international treaty.

II. No Adequate Protection for Climate Refugees under National Laws

Save as certain countries such as Sweden, climate refugees will not receive protection under the national laws as well. The Swedish Law on Foreigners provides protection to "persons otherwise in need of protection" in addition to refugees. The concept of "persons otherwise in need of protection" does cover environmental refugees. Chapter 4 Section 2 of the Swedish Law on Foreigners provides that a "person otherwise in need of protection" is a foreigner who is outside their home country because they (1) feel a well-founded fear of suffering the death penalty or being subjected to corporal punishment, torture or other inhumane or degrading treatment or punishment, (2) need protection because of external or internal armed conflict or, because of other severe conflicts in their country of origin, feel a well-founded fear of being subjected to serious abuses, or (3) is unable to return to their country of origin because of an environmental disaster. Section 2 is mainly reflection of non-refoulement principle.

In the EU Directive on temporary protection[11], no specific reference is made to natural or environmental disasters.[12] But Article 7 gives discretion to the member states to extend temporary protection to additional categories of displaced persons ("DPs").

The current trend that provides no protection to the climate refugees is followed by Turkey. In 2013, Turkey enacted a new law entitled the "Law No. 6458 on Foreigners and International Protection" ("LFIP").[13] Provisions of the LFIP regarding the administrative structure and the appointment of personnel came into force on the date of publication of the Law in

11 Council Directive 2001/55/EC of 20 July 2001on Minimum Standards for Giving Temporary Protection in the event of a mass influx of displaced Persons and on Measures Promoting a Balance of Efforts between Member States in Receiving such Persons and Bearing the Consequences thereof, OJ 7.8.2011 L 212 p. 12-23.

12 *"As far as environmentally-displaced persons are concerned, however, an extensive interpretation of the directive may not reasonably include this category of displaced persons"* (LOPEZ, 399).

13 Official Gazette Dated 11.4.2013 No. 28615. The unofficial English translation of the Law on Foreigners and International Protection was published by the Republic of Turkey's Ministry of Interior Directorate General of Migration Management, Publication Number: 6, April 2014.

the Official Gazette, namely 11 April 2013. Other provisions of the LFIP have been in force since 11 April 2014. That means that the entirety of the provisions of the LFIP has been in effect only since 11 April 2014. The LFIP redesigns the administrative structure of migration and international protection. The LFIP sets forth the procedures and principles regarding the visa, entrance and residence permits of foreigners. It also addresses expulsion of foreigners as well as international protection. Additionally, the LFIP contains provisions concerning the administrative review of and the judicial challenges to decisions made under the LFIP concerning regular and irregular migration as well as international protection.[14]

It is worth mentioning, however, that the LFIP does *not* provide for the protection of *internally* displaced persons. The LFIP only provides protection to displaced persons who have left their country due to the reasons listed in Article 63. Environmental reasons are not accounted for among the grounds for protection listed in Article 63 of the LFIP. Article 63 of the LFIP does, however, provide protection to people, *regardless of their country of origin*, that are displaced and flee their country because they face: (1) the death penalty or execution; (2) torture or inhumane or degrading treatment or punishment; (3) serious threat to their person by reason of indiscriminate violence in situations of international or internal armed conflict upon return to their country of origin or country of habitual residence. Although Article 63 does not cover climate refugees we can say that the LFIP goes far beyond protections provided under the Geneva Convention and the domestic laws of many other States because of its coverage of foreigners under threat of indiscriminate violence in situations of international or internal armed conflict.

14 For more information about the LFIP *see* EKŞİ Nuray, The New Turkish Law on Foreigners and International Protection: An Overall Assessment, Schriften zum Migrationsrecht 17, Nomos Verlagsgesellschaft, Baden-Baden, Germany 2014; EKŞİ Nuray, Yabancılar ve Uluslararası Koruma Hukuku [Foreigners and International Protection Law], 3rd edition, Istanbul 2015. For the negotiation and drafting process of the LFIP as well as the corresponding provisions of EU legislation and the impact of the ECtHR judgments on the LFIP *see* EKŞİ Nuray, Yabancılar ve Uluslararası Koruma Kanunu Tasarısı, [Draft Law on Foreigners and International Protection] Istanbul 2012, p. 5-110.

III. International Treaties Fail to Protect Climate Refugees

A. No Protection under 1951 Geneva Convention for Climate Refugees

Climate refugees are not considered "refugees" within the meaning of the 1951 Geneva Convention in judgments made by various countries' courts. In most cases, climate refugees move internally within their own countries ("IDPs"– Internally Displaced Persons). As they have not left their own country and are not in danger of persecution per se, they do not fall within scope of the 1951 Geneva Convention.

Tuvalu and Kiribati citizens are examples of climate refugees. However, the Refugee Status Appeals Authority of New Zealand[15] and the Australian Refugee Review Tribunal[16] refused to grant refugee status to people from

---

15 Refugee Appeal Nos. 72189/2000, 72190/2000, 72191/2000, 72192/2000,72193/2000, 72194/2000 & 72195/2000, Nos. 72189/2000, 72190/2000,72191/2000, 72192/2000, 72193/2000, 72194/2000 & 72195/2000, New Zealand: Refugee Status Appeals Authority, 17 August 2000, available at: http://www.refworld.org/docid/4d08cf7f2.html [accessed 18 May 2014]. For other cases *see* JACOVELLA Giulia, International Law and the (De)Politicisation of Climate Change and Migration: Lessons from the Pacific, 2(2015)1 SOAS L.J., p. 88-91.
For the Turkish translation of the decision dated 17 August 2000 *see* EKŞİ Nuray, Turkish Translation of the Decision of Refugee Status Appeals Authority New Zealand to Decline the Granting of Refugee Status in Case of Environmental Problems and Economic Difficulties, X(2011)1 İKÜHFD, p. 219-224.
In the case of *Teitiota v Chief Executive of the Ministry of Business, Innovation and Employment*, the New Zealand Court of Appeal ("NZCA") ruled that *"the appellant raised an argument that the international community itself was tantamount to the 'persecutor' for the purposes of the Refugee Convention. This completely reverses the traditional refugee paradigm. Traditionally, a refugee is fleeing his own government or a non-state actor from whom the government is unwilling or unable to protect him. Thus, the claimant is seeking refuge within the very country that is allegedly 'persecuting' him. No one should read this judgment as downplaying the importance of climate change. It is a major and growing concern for the international community. The point this judgment makes is that climate change and its effect on countries like Kiribati is not appropriately addressed under the Refugee Convention"* [New Zealand Court of Appeal, *Teitiota v Chief Executive of the Ministry of Business, Innovation and Employment* [2014] NZCA 173 (8 May 2014)].
As the Washington Post dated 14.8.2014 rightly stated that the tribunal avoided a clear decision on whether climate change can or cannot be reason enough for refugees to be granted residency [http://www.washingtonpost.com/blogs/worldviews/wp/2014/08/07/has-the-era-of-the-climate-change-refugee-begun/(accessed 2.8.2016)].

16 RRT Case No. 0907346, [2009] RRTA 1168, Australia: Refugee Review Tribunal, 10 December 2009: http://www.refworld.org/docid/4b8fdd952.html (accessed 12.8.2016). For the Turkish translation of the decision dated 10 December 2009 *see* MOLU Esra, Turkish Translation of the Decision of the Australian Refugee Review Tribunal Dated

Tuvalu and Kiribati as they do not meet the requirements described in Article 1A of the 1951 Geneva Convention.[17] According to the Refugee Review Tribunal of Australia "there appears no doubt that the circumstances the applicant, and others living in Kiribati, face are serious and deserving of significant governmental consideration and attention. They are not matters against which, however, the Refugees Convention as it applies in Australia is able to provide protection. The applicant does not hold well-founded fear of being persecuted for reasons of race, religion, nationality, membership of any particular social group or political opinion should he return to Kiribati now, or in the foreseeable future". The summary of the case and the decision of the Refugee Review Tribunal of Austria dated 10 December 2009 are as follows:

> "The applicant is a national of Kirabati. He is married and has one adopted daughter. His wife is still in Kiribati and his daughter is married and resides in the United States. The applicant has previously traveled to Australia to study and work, but his most recent entry was in March 2007 and he has not departed Australia since that date. The applicant's claims are that he can not return home to his country, Kirabati, which has been significantly affected by climate change and is likely to be non habitable in the foreseeable future. Kirabati is a collection of small Islands in the Pacific Ocean; it is halfway between Australia and Hawaii. Most of the country's remaining land is less than 2 meters above sea level. The applicant resided in a village prior to coming to Australia. This has been badly affected by sea water and regular wild storms. The crops are ruined and there is no fresh drinking water.

10 December 2009 to Decline Granting of Refugee Status to the Kiribati Citizens Due to the Climate Change, X(2011)1 İKÜHFD, p. 225-238.

17 However, in 2014, the New Zealand Immigration and Protection Tribunal ("NZIPT") agreed to issue a residence permit on humanitarian grounds to the Tuvaluan family who left their country due to climate change and whose refugee application was dismissed and whose original appeals against dismissal were turned down by the court. According to the NZIPT, "*the appellants claim that if deported to Tuvalu they will be separated from the husband's family, all of whom are living in New Zealand as either citizens or residents, and with whom they have particularly close bonds. The appellants also claim that they will be at risk of suffering the adverse impacts of climate change and socio-economic deprivation. The primary issue for determination is whether these factors, either alone or in combination, amount to exceptional circumstances of a humanitarian nature. The Tribunal is satisfied that this is the case and that it would not be contrary to the public interest to allow the appellants to remain in New Zealand. They, and their two children, are each to be granted residence visas*" [New Zealand Immigration and Protection Tribunal, AD (Tuvalu) [2014] NZIPT 501370 (4 June 2014)]. For a similar decision of NZIPT, *see* New Zealand Immigration and Protection Tribunal, AC (Tuvalu) [2014] NZIPT 800517 (4 June 2014).

Living in the village has become extremely difficult and it is anticipated that all the people of that village will have to relocate as they will not have any food, water or shelter. Relocation within Kirabati itself is difficult, as it is all a matter of short time before people are again affected by rising sea levels and have to relocate again. There is already a serious shortage of food, fresh water, shelter and energy and this must urgently be addressed now before the Island of Kirabati is completely submerged, which some estimate could be as early as 2050, according to a IPCC report. Climate change is a reality and the effects of carbon dioxide emission is most greatly felt in the pacific and small islands such as Kiribati are bearing the brunt of these changes to the environment, consequently the people of Kiribati will become displaced and it is extremely important that developed countries in the pacific recognise the effect of climate change on the people of Kiribati and have in place measures to accommodate the refugees affected by climate change. Can Australia's existing laws accommodate climate change refugees? Under existing laws, climate people affected by climate change are not recognised as a cognisable group of people in need of protection. It is submitted however, that existing protection visa laws can, and should, be creatively interpreted to accommodate climate change refugees in the absence of specific provisions in the Migration Act. Under the Migration Act, s.36(2) (a), persons to whom Australia has protection obligations are entitled to "a protection visa". As a party to the refugee convention Australia owes protections to any person who: 'owing to well-founded fear of being persecuted for reasons of race, religion, nationality, membership of a particular social group or political opinion, is outside the country of his nationality and is unable or, owing to such fear, is unwilling to avail himself of the protection of that country; or who, not having a nationality and being outside the country of his former habitual residence, is unable or, owing to such fear, is unwilling to return to it". The applicant is outside his home country of Kiribati. The applicant's claims are grounded in events that are currently taking place now and will take place in the future in their home country, including rising sea levels, salination and floods. It is submitted that climate change should be seen as a form of persecution which involves serious harm. While it may be difficult to define climate change as persecution having regard to current international and domestic law, it would not be difficult to satisfy the requirement of serious harm as defined in s.9lR(1)(c) and s.9 in the Migration Act, in that people affected by climate change will suffer significant economic hardship, as they will be denied the capacity to earn a livelihood and that such hardship threatens the applicant's capacity to subsist. Furthermore, the government of Kirabati is unable to protect people such as the applicant from the persecution...It is further submitted that the people of Kirabati, especially people such as the applicant, who come from parts of the island that is heavily affected by rising sea levels and salination, are a cognizable social group, and can be defined as members of 'a particular social group'. It is submitted that the applicant's fear is well founded. There is a large body of evidence available to indicate that carbon dioxide emissions are bringing about radical and fast approaching climate change. In recent years many of the pacific islands have submerged deeper under water and most of the Island of Kiribati is less than 2 or so meters above sea level, making it highly vulnerable to sea level change, violent storms and eventually full submersion. Australia's current policy clearly indicates that the government accepts the reality and the effect of climate change on the region. It is submitted that the applicant is a person to whom Australia has protection obligations, as he has a well-founded fear of persecution in Kiribati for reasons of membership of a particular social group: namely, people from Kirabati and/or from the Island of Kiribati who have lost the capacity to earn a livelihood as a result of climate change. It is acknowledged that Australian laws, as currently interpreted, might not provide the perfect legal framework within which people such as the applicant can claim protection, however, it is submitted that in such circumstances, and in the absence of specific legislation to deal with this, the laws should be interpreted in a creative way to allow people such as the applicant to be recognized as refugees...The difficulty with this application in the Tribunal's view, is that the Tribunal does not believe the applicant fears persecution for reasons of race, religion, nationality, membership of a particular social group or political opinion as required by the Refugees Convention. Although it is not necessary that those who would persecute proceed from a basis of malignity, it is well established that persecution within the meaning of the Convention must involves a discriminatory element...It is the view of the Tribunal that the applicant does not hold well-founded fear of being persecuted for reasons of race, religion, nationality, membership of any particular social group or political opinion should he return to Kiribati now, or in the foreseeable future. On this basis, he is not a person owed protection obligations by Australia nor is he the member of the same family unit as such a person. This being the case, he cannot satisfy essential prescribed criterion for a Class XA visa contained at s.36 of the Act. He must, therefore, be refused the grant of such a visa under s.65 of the Act. The delegate's decision to this effect should be affirmed".

The decisions made by the Refugee Review Tribunal of Australia concerning exclusion of the climate refugees from the scope of conventional refugee definition are gained stability. In another decision made in 2012, the Refugee Review Tribunal of Australia affirms the decision not to grant a Japanese citizen a protection.[18] The applicant, who claims to be a citizen of Japan, arrived in Australia and applied to the Department of Immigration and Citizenship for "the protection visa". Her visa application was refused on the basis that the applicant is not a person to whom Australia has protection obligations under the Refugees Convention. The applicant applied to the Refugee Review Tribunal. Under s.65(1) a visa may be granted only if the decision maker is satisfied that the prescribed criteria for the visa have been satisfied. The criteria for a protection visa are set out in s.36 of the Act and Part 866 of Schedule 2 to the Migration Regulations 1994 (the Regulations). An applicant for the visa must meet one of the alternative criteria in s.36(2)(a), (aa), (b), or (c). That is, the applicant is either a person to whom Australia has protection obligations under the 1951 Convention relating to the Status of Refugees as amended by the 1967 Protocol relating to the Status of Refugees or on other 'complementary protection' grounds, or is a member of the same family unit as a person to whom Australia has protection obligations under s.36(2) and that person holds a protection visa. Australia is a party to the Refugees Convention and generally speaking, has protection obligations to people who are refugees as defined in Article 1 of the Convention. Refugee Review Tribunal of Australia stated that there are four key elements to the Convention definition. First, an applicant must be outside his or her country. Second, an applicant must fear persecution. Third, the persecution which the applicant fears must be for one or more of the reasons enumerated in the Convention definition –race, religion, nationality, membership of a particular social group or political opinion. Fourth, an applicant for refugee status must be unable or unwilling to avail himself of the protection of his home country.

Refugee application of a person fleeing from Fukushima disaster was also rejected by Australia. The facts of the case are as follows: The applicant is from Ibarag/Ibaraki which was radiation-affected from Fukushima disaster in Japan due to a magnitude-9 earthquake in northeastern Japan together with tsunami on 11 March 2011. At her hearing, the applicant said that she

18 1111982 [2012] RRTA 218 (5 April 2012).

was afraid to go back to Japan because the area where she had been living which was near Fukushima had been flooded after the tsunami in 2011 and also radiation-affected. She had nowhere to live. She will therefore be facing "a humanitarian challenge situation in Japan". The applicant says that in Japan more than 28,000 people have been confirmed dead or listed as missing since the Japanese disaster in March 2011, and that Japan is now affected by high levels of radioactive substances. The applicant says that the Japanese Government lied about the radiation count present in the water, food and air. The applicant says that a growing number of commentators have employed the notion of "environmental refugees" or "climate refugees", though the UNHCR has serious reservations about this terminology and says that such terms have no basis in international refugee law. The applicant says that the circumstances of her case are of such a compelling nature that it is in the public interest to grant her a Protection Visa in Australia; she says it is not feasible for her to move back to Japan. The applicant says her home and everything has been destroyed and she could not reach her house; she got no help from anyone; the Japanese Government does not provide assistance to people from affected areas and she strongly believes that there is danger to her life if she returns.

The Tribunal took into account various reports drafted independent institution which indicated that radiation levels were within safe limits. The Tribunal reached that conclusion that the applicant would be able to meet the criteria either for a Convention refugee, or for complementary protection. It did not appear to the Tribunal that there was a real chance or a real risk, that she would face either Convention persecution or significant harm if she went back to Japan. The applicant has also claimed previously, although not at her Tribunal hearing, that she was discriminated against in employment as a female in Japan. The Tribunal is not satisfied that the evidence she gave about this claim indicates that it reached the level of persecution in a Convention sense or of "significant harm", as required by the legislation on complementary protection. The applicant did not put this forward at her Tribunal hearing as a reason why she was afraid to go back to Japan, and the Tribunal does not accept that, even if she were discriminated against in the future as she has claimed to be in the past, this would amount to either persecution or significant harm. On the evidence before it, the Tribunal finds that the applicant, if she were to return to Japan, would not be required to live in any area of Japan which might be harmful to her. She does not own or lease any accommodation in Japan, having most recently lived in employer-provided rent-free accommodation. She has no immediate family anywhere in Japan or any ongoing ties to a particular location in Japan, not having lived there for at least some two and a half years. She has traveled extensively outside Japan in the past ten years, according to her evidence, and has not been employed in Japan for the past five years. The applicant at her Tribunal hearing was unable to explain how she has been able to live for the past five years, or to travel to Australia without being employed, beyond saying that she has been able to rely on friends in Australia. In these circumstances the extent of the economic hardship which the applicant might suffer in Japan has not been demonstrated to be such that her capacity to subsist might be threatened. On the evidence before it, the Tribunal is not satisfied that there is a real chance that the applicant will face 151 Geneva Convention-based persecution if she returns to Japan in the foreseeable future.

B. No Protection under the 1984 Convention against Torture and 1966 International Covenant on Civil and Political Rights

As the climate refugees are not conventional refugees, solutions are searched through other conventions in order to provide them with the best possible protection. It has been argued that Article 6(1) of the 1966 International Covenant on Civil and Political Rights ("the ICCPR")[19] and Article 1 of the International Covenant for Economic, Social and Political Rights ("the ICESCR")[20] do not contain effective instruments to protect environmentally displaced people; that it is not possible to accord adequate protection under international human rights law to such people because climate change results from a multiplicity of factors and it is impossible to identify a given factor that causes displacement; and that because the ICCPR and ICESCR and other similar treaties on human rights provide protection after a violation of a fundamental right, it is impossible to protect the environmentally displaced people before they lose their homes and living spaces.[21]

In addition to the 1951 Geneva Convention, Tuvalu citizens claim protection not only under the 1984 Convention against Torture and Other Cruel, Inhuman or Degrading Treatment or Punishment but also under the ICCPR.

19 For the ratification law of the ICCPR *see* Official Gazette Dated 21.7.2003 No. 25175. For the ratification of the Protocol for ICCPR Convention *see* Official Gazette Dated 5.8.2006 No. 26250.

20 For the ratification law of the ICESCR *see* Official Gazette Dated 11.8.2003 No. 25196.

21 MOBERG, 1116-1117.

In its recent decision dated 4 June 2014[22], the Immigration and Protection Tribunal of New Zealand ("the NZIPT") dismissed an appeal which was based on three conventions all together. The appellants claimed that there were substantial grounds for believing that they would be in danger of being arbitrarily deprived of their lives or in danger of being subjected to cruel treatment if returned to Tuvalu because of the effects of climate change in Tuvalu. The NZIPT ruled that the central issue to be determined by the Tribunal was whether the Government of Tuvalu could be said to be failing to take steps within its power to protect the appellants' lives from the effects of climate change such that their lives could be said to be in danger and whether or not the harm they feared amounted to cruel treatment as that term is defined under the Act. The NZIPT found out that appellants' claims derived to a significant extent from the geophysical characteristics in Tuvalu. The NZIPT reached the conclusion that the appellants were not refugees within the meaning of the 1951 Geneva Convention. The NZIPT also found that they were not protected persons within the meaning of the 1984 Convention against Torture or the 1966 ICCPR.[23]

C. No Protection under the United Nations Framework Convention on Climate Change and Kyoto Protocol

Although there are two main international instruments concerning "climate change" none of them provide protection to the people displaced from their homes because of environmental-related reasons. The United Nations Framework Convention on Climate Change ("the UNFCCC") to which 193 States are parties was accepted on 9 May 1992 and has been in force since 21 March 1994.[24] The UNFCCC encourages cooperation among the States relating to climate change and draws a framework for the future. The Kyoto Protocol to the UNFCCC commits the State Parties to reduce their collective emissions of greenhouse gases. However, neither of these instruments deals with the aspect of international protection of climate refugees.

---

22 Immigration and Protection Tribunal New Zealand [2014] NZIPT 800517-520.

23 Falstrom argues that 1984 Convention against Torture can be a model to a new convention on the protection of environmentally displaced persons (FALSTROM Dana Zartner, Stemming the Flow of Environmental Displacement: Creating a Convention to Protect Persons and Preserve the Environment, 13(2002) Colo. J. Int'l Envtl. L.&Pol'y, p. 18-23).

24 UN Framework Convention on Climate Change, 1771 UNTS 107.

D. Implications of Climate Change for the Enjoyment of Human Rights under the ECHR

The question of whether there is any kind of relationship between climate change and the full enjoyment of human rights is another topic that must be addressed. Article 2 and 3 of the ECHR preclude countries from returning people to a risk of arbitrary deprivation of life, the death penalty, torture, or cruel, inhuman or degrading treatment or punishment. Both articles may help climate refugees not to be deported to their countries which face natural disasters.

IV. Proposed Solutions for Protection of Climate Refugees

A person fleeing his/her country due to environmental reasons does not satisfy the conditions necessary to be considered a refugee under the definition in Article 1 of the 1951 Geneva Convention because it would be impossible for him/her to establish a well-founded fear of persecution based on any of the grounds enumerated in the Convention.[25] Moreover, despite many attempts, no specific convention or protocol annex to the 1951 Geneva Convention or the ECHR has been concluded to protect the people affected from climate change.

It has also been noted that the current international legal instruments dealing with human rights fail to protect climate refugees. This means that the protection of climate refugees is left to domestic laws, but domestic laws do not contain effective provisions on this matter.[26] It must be underlined that although the 1951 Geneva Convention does not cover climate refugees, there is nothing that prevents State Parties to the Convention from following a broad interpretation of the concept of refugee and extending protection to climate refugees. However, States tend to stick to a narrow interpretation of the definition of refugee and thereby to limit the number of foreigners receiving protection within their territories. Fortunately, there have been calls from various circles for the preparation of a treaty, or an additional protocol to the 1951 Geneva Convention, which would provide people who left their places because of environmental or climate-related reasons with a status similar to that of refugees.

25 ATAPATTU Sumudu, Climate Change, Human Rights, and Forced Migration: Implications for International Law, 27(2009-2010)3 Wis. Int'l L.J. p. 617.

26 MOBERG, 1117.

Some commentators have proposed the preparation of the Protocol on the Recognition, Protection, and Resettlement of Climate Refugees as an addendum to the UNFCCC.[27] A group of academics from the University of Limoges have prepared the Draft Convention on the International Status of Environmentally-Displaced Persons.[28] Further, some commentators have proposed the preparation of a new convention that will deal exclusively with the treatment of climate refugees.[29] The Council of Europe Parliamentary Assembly's Committee on Migration, Refugees and Population has recommended the adoption of a protocol, to be added to the ECHR, to address the right to a safe and healthy environment and to provide protection to climate refugees.[30]

The UNHCR data show that currently there are around 10 million refugees and 43 million forcefully displaced people in the world. To justify the adoption of a new treaty and the assumption of new responsibilities by the states to address the rights of climate refugees even though the problems of these refugees and forcefully displaced have not yet been resolved at national level, *McAdam* points to the conversion of the individual burden into international burden sharing.[31]

Already some small island states such as Carteret Islands, Tokelau, and Vanuatu have begun to permanently resettle people[32]. Certain countries which are strongly affected by climate changes have been challenging to find an appropriate solution. For example, "Tuvalu threatened to file legal action against the United States and Australia for their contribution to global warming which, in turn, is causing the sea levels to rise. Tuvalu also discussed the issue of immigration policies with New Zealand and Australia. Currently, New Zealand accepts 75 citizens between the age of 18-45 years annually from Tuvalu under its labor migration program. Thus, it is apparent that New

27 BIERMANN Frank/BOAS Ingrid, Preparing for a Warmer World: Towards a Global Governance System to Protect Climate Refugees', 10(2010)1 GEP, p. 60.

28 McADAM, 7. *See* also PRIEUR Michel, Draft Convention on the International Status of Environmentally-Displaced Persons 42/43 Urb. Law. 247 (2010-2011).

29 DOERTY B./GIANNINI T., Confronting a Rising Tide: A Proposal for a Convention on Climate Change Refugees, (2009)33 HELR, 349 *et seq.*

30 McADAM, 7. The Council of Europe Parliamentary Assembly, Committee on Migration, Refugees and Population, 'Environmentally Induced Migration and Displacement: A 21st Century Challenge' Doc. 11785, 23 Dec. 2008.

31 McADAM, 16-17.

32 ATAPATTU, 633.

Zealand has not opened its doors to climate refugees. Furthermore, Australia has no current plans to admit climate immigrants into its borders”.[33]

V. Conclusion

As can be inferred from the previous explanations and jurisprudence, no burden arises under international law as well as national laws for the countries to provide protection to climate change refugees. Being victims of environmental disasters are not only the result of natural events but also act of human beings. Consequently, it is high time for all the countries to change their policy towards climate refugees. Taking into account of their contribution to the occurrence of environmental disasters particularly industrialized countries should play a leading role for taking necessary measures for protection of climate refugees. Instead of leaving the climate refugees alone with their destiny, efforts should be made to conclude an international treaty which provides refugee-type protection and commitment of sharing the burden of environmental disasters.

Bibliography

ATAPATTU Sumudu, Climate Change, Human Rights, and Forced Migration: Implications for International Law, 27(2009-2010)3 Wis. Int'l L.J.

BIERMANN Frank/BOAS Ingrid, Preparing for a Warmer World: Towards a Global Governance System to Protect Climate Refugees', 10(2010)1 GEP.

---Book Review, Reviewed by Carl Söderbergh, Laura Westra, Environmental Justice and the Rights of Ecological Refugees, London 2009, 2(2010) Climate and Development.

---Council Directive 2001/55/EC of 20 July 2001on Minimum Standards for Giving Temporary Protection in the event of a mass influx of displaced Persons and on Measures Promoting a Balance of Efforts between Member States in Receiving such Persons and Bearing the Consequences thereof, OJ 7.8.2011 L 212 p. 12-23.

---Council of Europe Parliamentary Assembly, Committee on Migration, Refugees and Population, 'Environmentally Induced Migration and Displacement: A 21st Century Challenge' Doc. 11785, 23 Dec. 2008.

DOERTY B./GIANNINI T., Confronting a Rising Tide: A Proposal for a Convention on Climate Change Refugees, (2009)33 HELR.

33 ATAPATTU, 633.

EKŞİ Nuray, Turkish Translation of the Decision of Refugee Status Appeals Authority New Zealand to Decline the Granting of Refugee Status in Case of Environmental Problems and Economic Difficulties, X(2011)1 İKÜHFD.

EKŞİ Nuray, Yabancılar ve Uluslararası Koruma Kanunu Tasarısı, [Draft Law on Foreigners and International Protection] Istanbul 2012.

EKŞİ Nuray, The New Turkish Law on Foreigners and International Protection: An Overall Assessment, Schriften zum Migrationsrecht 17, Nomos Verlagsgesellschaft, Baden-Baden, Germany 2014.

EKŞİ Nuray, Foreigners and International Protection Law, 3rd edition, Istanbul 2015.

FALSTROM Dana Zartner, Stemming the Flow of Environmental Displacement: Creating a Convention to Protect Persons and Preserve the Environment, 13(2002) Colo. J. Int'l Envtl. L.&Pol'y.

ISLAM Rafiqul, Climate Refugees and International Refugee Law, (in) An Introduction to International Refugee Law, Editors Jahid Hossain Bhuiyan/M. Rafiqul Islam, Leiden 2013.

McADAM Jane, Swimming against the Tide: Why a Climate Change Displacement Treaty is Not the Answer, 23(2011)1 Int'l J. Refugee L.

MOLU Esra, Turkish Translation of the Decision of the Australian Refugee Review Tribunal Dated 10 December 2009 to Decline Granting of Refugee Status to the Kiribati Citizens Due to the Climate Change, X(2011)1 İKÜHFD.

LOPEZ Aurelie, The Protection of Environmentally-Displaced Persons in International Law, 37(2007) Envtl. L., p. 372-373.

MOBERG K. Kara, Extending Refugee definitions to Cover Environmentally Displaced Persons Displaces Necessary Protection, 94(2009) Iowa L. Rev.

PRIEUR Michel, Draft Convention on the International Status of Environmentally-Displaced Persons 42/43 Urb. Law. 247 (2010-2011).

---Procedures and Criteria for Determining Refugee Status under the 1951 Convention and the 1967 Protocol relating to the Status of Refugees HCR/IP/4/Eng/REV.1 Reedited, Geneva, January 1992, UNHCR 1979. http://www.unhcr.org/publ/PUBL/3d58e13b4.pdf (accessed 27.7.2016).

IV. Challenge Green Investment

The Approach of the Turkish Model Bilateral Investment Treaty to the envtionamental protection in Investment Law

*Melis Avşar**

Abstract

The Bilateral investment treaties on the reciprocal encouragement and protection of investment (BITs) determine how investments are made between the two states. These agreements mainly deal with what should be evaluated within the scope of investment and how to resolve a dispute between the investor and the contracting (host) state. In addition to these, since the 1990s, regulations on labor rights, consumer rights, health, and environmental protection have been introduced in the BITs. This change stems from the importance of recognizing the regulatory powers of the state on a few key issues, rather than attracting investors to the country at all costs. The Model BIT, which was prepared in 2011 according to this trend in Turkey, included regulations for environmental protection both in the beginning part and Article 5 (general exemptions). In this study, Turkey's Model BIT and the arrangements in the treaties in which this model is used will be examined.

Keywords: Environmental Protection, Bilateral Investment Treaties, Turkey's Model BIT, Investment, Environment, ICSID.

I. Introduction

1. Throughout history, the biggest issue in investment law has been seen as the protection of investors. The scope of this protection is not limited to regulations in the laws of host states; additionally, many bilateral or multilateral agreements have been concluded between states in this regard. Using bilateral investment treaties (BITs) is a popular method that states use to regulate their country's investment regime. Today, many states are preparing model treaty texts to be used in future bilateral investment treaties.
2. Investor protection is generally achieved by protecting the property rights of investors in the host state and ensuring that they receive fair and equitable treatment as domestic investors. However, this concern is beginning to change. Besides the protection of investors, the protection of consumer rights, environment and, labor laws in the host state has been gained some importance. Of course, the notion of investor protection did not lose its

* Assistant Professor, Private International Law Department, Istanbul University Faculty of Law

importance. Nevertheless, other concerns, such as environmental protection, are starting to be recognized as one of the issues in investment law.

3. The relationship between environmental protection and investment law is interesting. Investment is considered as a civil law matter in principle because when the investor makes a capital investment in the host state, this investment also exhibits the characteristics of being a commercial activity. On the other hand, environmental protection is a subject of public law, as the primary concern in this context is the protection of *ordre public*. Therefore, the relationship between investment activity and environmental protection, and its effect on the regulations in investment law, constitute an extremely important issue that needs to be examined.
4. In this study, firstly, information will be given about the concept of BIT and the BITs used by Turkey. Then, it will be examined how the regulations regarding the protection of the environment took place in BITs throughout historical process. In this context, the model prepared by Turkey and the provisions related to the protection of the environment in this model will be examined. Lastly, it will be briefly discussed to what extent the states can intervene in the investments of investors to protect the environment.

A. An Overview of Bilateral Investment Treaty

A Bilateral Investment Treaty is a treaty signed between two states to attract investors to their countries and to regulate general principles of investment regimes. Most of them include dispute resolution mechanisms on how to resolve investment disputes. The primary purpose of these treaties is to protect investors and promote investment in host states countries.[1]

Before World War II, the concept of investment protection was not a major concern for states. During this era, the only concern regarding investment protection was the protection of property.[2] From the end of World War II until the collapse of the Soviet Union, states entered into numerous multilateral and bilateral agreements to regulate both investment and trade.

1 United Nations Conference on Trade and Development (UNCTAD), Trends in International Investment Agreements: An Overview, UNCTAD Series on Issues in International Investment Agreements, (Trends in International Investment Agreements), United Nations, New York, and Geneva, 1999, p. 15.

2 For the history of international trade law, see *R. A. Brand*, Sustaining The Development of International Trade And Environmental Law, Vermont Law Review 1997 (21), p. 823, 824.

The most popular agreements during this period, known as the colonial era, were the FCN (friendship, commerce, and navigation) agreements. These FCN agreements addressed a wide range of issues, including investment protection, trade, and human rights.[3]

However, after a while, FCN agreements did not provide adequate protection for the investor's investment in the host states' countries. This was primarily due to socialist states expropriating investments without compensating the investors. As a result, the non-socialist developed countries sought solutions to such expropriations because the FCN agreements and other United Nation agreements were insufficient to prevent this problem.[4] In response, Germany made the first BIT in history with Pakistan and the Dominican Republic in 1969. Subsequently, other European countries followed this trend.[5]

The implementation of BITs in developed countries aimed to provide protection against expropriation without compensation. Conversely, developing countries sought to attract foreign investors to their countries through BITs.[6] As a result, making BITs began to serve an important function for both developed and developing countries.

The free-market ideology has gained importance since the 1980s. After the collapse of the Soviet Union, the idea of liberalization began to spread all over the world. Starting from the 2000s, the purposes of making BITs began to change. This change was driven by the shifting distinction between 'developed country' and 'developing country'. While developing countries used to import capital, they have now also started to export capital. During this period, there has been a significant increase in the number of BITs, a consequence of the evolving definitions of developed-developing countries and the capital needs of states. Another crucial reason is the increase in the capital needs of the states. Since the economic crisis was experienced all over the world, private

3 *S. Rose-Ackerman & J. Tobin*, Foreign Direct Investment and the Business Environment in Developing Countries: The Impact of Bilateral Investment Treaties, 2005, p. 6.

4 *K. J. Vandevelde*, Model Bilateral Investment Treaties: The Way Forward, Southwestern Journal of International Law 2011 (18), p. 307, 308.

5 France in 1960, Switzerland in 1961, the Netherlands in 1963, Italy and Belgium-Luxembourg Union in 1964, Sweden and Denmark in 1965 and Norway in 1966 made its first BIT. Also *see K. J. Vandevelde*, A Brief History of International Investment Agreements, U.C. Davis Journal of International Law 2005 (12), p. 157, 169.

6 *C. Sacchidananda & D. Mukherjee*, Relationship between Trade, Investment and Environment: A Review of Issues, 2010, p. 11.

lending and national resources of the developed states began to be insufficient as a source of capital.[7]

This change was also reflected in the preparation process of BITs. In the past, the BITs were prepared only by developed countries, which generally used their own model drafts. Additionally, most developing countries had to accept the terms set by the developed countries. The only exception to this situation was resource-rich countries. Since these states did not need to attract investors to their countries, they were not obliged to accept such agreements imposed unilaterally. However, they had to accept these BITs, especially when competing with other countries for the attention of similar investors.[8]

Today, developing countries such as Turkey have their own model BIT. This is because, in the globalized era, it is not possible to think of states separately from each other. Turkey signed its first BIT with Germany in 1962. The BIT with the U.S. followed this in 1986. Turkey's total number of BITs is 108 by the year 2022.[9] 93.9 percent of the Turkish direct investments in the world are within the scope of BITs. 90.7 percent of foreign investments in Turkey are covered by BITs. As can be seen, Turkey frequently uses BITs in the field of investment law. In this context, Turkey prepared a model BIT for the first time in 2011.[10] Turkey's model BIT consists of a preamble section and 13 articles. Most of the rules in this model are the same as those used by Turkey in the previous BITS that already concluded. However, there are two important innovations brought by the model. These are the preamble section and the fifth article of the model (general exceptions clause). Turkey has signed ten BITs using this model. These are the BITs signed with Nigeria in 2011 (*not in force*), Kosovo in 2012, Montenegro in 2012, the Republic of Djibouti (Cibuti) in 2015, the Republic of Mauritius in 2016 (*not in force*), the Republic of Belarus in 2018 (*not in force*), Mali in 2018 (*not in force*), Kyrgyzstan in 2018, the State of Palestine in 2018 (*not in force*), and Burkina Faso in 2019 (*not in force*).[11]

---

7 *Vandevelde, supra* note 5 at p. 177.

8 *G. Verhoosel*, Foreign Direct Investment and Legal Constraints on Domestic Environmental Policies: Striking a "Reasonable" Balance Between Stability and Change, Law & Policy in International Business 1998 (29), p. 451, 460.

9 This data was obtained from the website of Republic of Turkey Ministry of Industry and Technology. ‹https://www.sanayi.gov.tr/anlasmalar/yktk› accessed 01.01.2022.

10 The draft has not been published. In this study, this draft was obtained from by Prof. Dr. Faruk Kerem Giray.

11 This data was obtained from the website of Republic of Turkey Ministry of Industry and Technology. ‹https://www.sanayi.gov.tr/anlasmalar/yktk/a116020› accessed 01.01.2022.

B. The Development of the Environmental Proetection Clauses in BITs in the Historical Process

1. An Overview

1. Environmental regulations in the countries are an important factor for investors when choosing a country to invest in.[12] Underdeveloped countries provide advantages to investors due to the low standards sought in regulations on labor, health, and environment. These advantages are simply related to the reduction of production costs. Thus, investment and production costs can be lower in investments made in underdeveloped countries. However, the mentality of lowering basic standards in this way to attract investors had to start changing. There are two reasons for this change. First, it is now recognized in many international agreements/directives, such as ILO or OECD Guidelines, that the companies must respect human rights, labor regulations, and the environment. Second, the U.S. and Canada faced multiple lawsuits for the violations of NAFTA. Some were directly related to the measures taken by states to protect the environment. In these cases, the judges concluded that the state's actions regarding environmental protection counted as expropriation. States are therefore obliged to pay compensation for the measures they take to protect the environment. Such decisions have diminished the authority of the host states to take any measure to protect the environment.[13]

Environmental protection clauses are more commonly used in FTAs (Free Trade Agreements) than in BITs.[14] This is because FTAs are made more publicly than BITs.[15] Only 6.5% of BITs have such protection clauses. The first example of such provisions being included BITs was in the BIT signed between China and Singapore. Today, many developed and developing countries have their own model BITs, which include environmental protection regulations. Although most states have already signed BITs with each

12 *Verhoosel, supra* note 8 at p. 461; *R. Mabey & N. Mcnally*, Foreign Direct Investment and the Environment: From Pollution Havens to Sustainable Development, 1999, p. 45.

13 *H. Z. Nalçacıoğlu Erden*, Milletlerarası Yatırım Hukukunda Dolaylı Kamulaştırma, 2015, p. 356.

14 *K. Gordon & J. Pohl*, International Environmental Concerns in International Investment Agreements, 2011, p. 5.

15 *T. Wälde & A. Kolo*, Environmental Regulation, Investment Protection and "Regulatory Taking" in International Law, ICLQ 2001 (50), p. 811, 814.

other, many of these BITs will expire in the coming years.[16] However, some developed countries, such as the Germany Model BIT (2008)[17], did not include such clauses.

Current models were mostly influenced by the U.S. Model BIT.[18] Both U.S. and Canada have extensively included the environmental issues in their models. However, not all of them are based on the U.S. Model BIT. For example, unlike the U.S. Model BIT, in the Belgian Model BIT, it is stated that a state can only take environmental measures by law, and the scope of the right to regulate the environmental matters right is defined narrowly.

The Turkish Model BIT dated 2011 was influenced by the U.S. Model BIT. However, in the Turkish model, the scope of the right to regulate environmental protection is considered much narrower and more limited than in the American model.

2. Position of Turkey

In Turkish Model BIT, there are several regulations regarding the protection of the environment.

The first of these regulations is in the Preamble section. According to the preamble of Turkish Model BIT, "*... convinced that these objectives can be achieved without relaxing health, safety, and environmental measures of general application as well as internationally recognized labor rights, ...*" While it is debatable among scholars whether the Preamble can be considered as a part of the Treaty, it is widely accepted in the doctrine that the Preamble section can be used as a tool for interpreting the Treaty.[19]

Secondly, it is recognized that the right of the host state to regulate environmental protection matters is outside the scope of the rules on investor

16 *M. E. Footer*, Bits and Pieces: Social and Environmental Protection in the Regulation of Foreign Investment, Michigan State Journal of International Law 2009 (18), p. 33, 46.

17 <https://investmentpolicy.unctad.org/international-investment-agreements/treaty-files/2865/download> accessed 01.01.2022.

18 *Vandevelde, supra* note 4 at p. 312.

19 *M. H. Hulme*, Preambles in Treaty Interpretation, University of Pennsylvania Law Review 2016 (164), p. 1281, 1312.

protection in the BIT.[20] According to the article 5 titled General Exceptions,[21] "... *Nothing in this Agreement shall be construed to prevent a Contracting Party from adopting, maintaining, or enforcing any non-discriminatory legal measure: a) designed and applied for the protection of human, animal or plant life or health, or the environment; b) related to the conservation of living or non-living exhaustible natural resources.*" As it can be seen, the measurements taken by the host state to protect the environment cannot be considered as a violation of investment.

Last but not least, article 6 titled Expropriation and Compensation stated that: "... *2. Non-discriminatory legal measures designed and applied to protect legitimate public welfare objectives, such as health, safety and environment, do not constitute indirect expropriation.*" Even if the measures to be taken by the host state regarding the protection of the environment constitute an intervention to the investment, the investor will not be able to argue that the investment has been indirectly expropriated.

In summary, direct and binding regulation of environmental protection clauses was preferred in the Turkish Model BIT. The Model Treaty aims to achieve environmental protection by recognizing the host state's right to take legal measures. The definition of the legal measures is not included in the Model Treaty. It can be said that all measures cover any laws, regulations, or administrative actions.[22]

3. Aims of Regulation Regarding Environmental Protection in the BITs

1. As mentioned above, the perception of 'attracting investors no matter what' has changed since the 2000s. The disputes relating to the environmental issues that arose between the US and Canada were among the first disputes in this matter.[23] In these cases, it was discussed whether a state should compensate the investor for the measures it has taken to protect the environment.

---

20 *B. Şit Köşkeroğlu*, Model İkili Yatırım Anlaşmaları ve Türkiye'nin Model İkili Yatırım Anlaşması Taslağı, TBB Dergisi 2013 (107), p. 143, 158.

21 Detailed information for general exception clauses and interpretation of general exception clauses, *see A. Newcombe*, General Exceptions in International Investment Agreements, Sustainable Development in World Investment Law 2011 (30), p. 355, 363.

22 United Nations Conference on Trade and Development (UNCTAD), Trends in International Investment Agreements: An Overview, UNCTAD Series on Issues in International Investment Agreements, United Nations, New York, and Geneva, 1999, p. 96.

23 *A. Romson*, Environmental Policy Space & International Investment Law, 2015, p. 26.

It can be argued that the main purpose of such clauses in BITs is to avoid a possible dispute over whether an action of the host state can be considered as a compensable expropriation. However, from the investor's point of view, investors want to invest in more stable countries. On the other hand, developing countries are constantly changing their environmental regulations.[24] As a result, balancing investor protection with other public policies has become an important issue in investment law.[25] Moreover, developed countries have their own agenda in this matter. Now that they are also considered as capital importing states, they want to protect their countries and, above all, maximize their state's regulatory power.

These clauses can take different forms.[26] The most important ones are: 'not lowering environmental standards', 'right to regulate' and, 'general exceptions'. The clause 'not lowering environmental standards' is a clause that encourages states not to lower their environmental protection standards to attract investors. Both the U.S. and Canada's Model BIT had adopted this clause.

With the 'general exceptions' clause, a state can reserve the right to regulate certain matters. Along with other states, Turkey has also used this clause in its model BIT. According to article 5 of the Turkish Model BIT: "*Nothing in this Agreement shall be construed to prevent a Contracting Party from adopting, maintaining, or enforcing any non-discriminatory legal measure: a) designed and applied for the protection of human, animal or plant life or health, or the environment...*"

Environmental protection clauses in the BITs are not limited to these two clauses.[27] For example, in the Turkish Model BIT, some issues related to environmental protection are regulated in the preamble. According to the preamble: "*...Contracting parties convinced that these objectives*[28] *can be achieved without relaxing health, safety and environmental measures of*

24 *Verhoosel, supra* note 8 at p. 454.

25 United Nations Conference on Trade and Development, Recent Developments in International Investment Agreements, 2008, p. 5.

26 See for details United Nations Conference on Trade and Development, Bilateral Investment Treaties 1995-2006, New York, 2007, p. 94-96.

27 *Footer, supra* note 15 at p. 42-46.

28 Promote greater economic cooperation between parties, particularly with respect to investment by investors of one Contracting Party in the territory of the other Contracting Part; to recognize that agreement upon the treatment to be accorded such investment will stimulate the flow of capital and technology and the economic development of the Contracting Parties; Agree that fair and equitable treatment of investments is desirable in order to maintain a stable framework for investment and

general application as well as internationally recognized labor right." The Austrian Model BIT has a similar regulation in its preamble. Neither of these regulations creates a demandable liability for the parties. However, many ICSID cases have shown that the preambles of the treaties are important tools for the interpretation of the treaties.

Another example is Article 5 of the Belgian Model BIT. This article states that policy space is protected, and its language is not strict. States are not obliged to do anything. In my opinion, the existence of such regulations blocks investor's compensation claims. Otherwise, states do not need to include such regulations in their BITs; they already have the right to regulate restrictions on the grounds of common welfare if they provide proper compensation. However, that does not mean that a state can take any measure as long as its environment related. If certain conditions occurr, it may be considered an indirect expropriation.

4. Limits of the State's Right to Make Regulations on Environmental Protection

There is a growing trend in investor-state relations to balance the protection of the investor's property rights with the host state's right to regulate social and environmental protection issues.[29]

All states have the right to regulate environmental matters as a natural consequence of statehood.[30] However the actions and the regulations of the states can be subject to arbitration in investment law. In order to eliminate the liability for compensation, host states include provisions in their model BITs that the possibility of regulating environmental issues will be reserved. However, whether these provisions in the BITs are capable of removing states' liability for compensation is contradictory among many scholars.

It is important to determine when an action will be considered an indirect expropriation. This determination can be made using the criteria of proportionality, non-discrimination, and predictability.[31] However, it is difficult the say in advance which actions are non-compensable.

---

will contribute to maximizing effective utilization of economic resources and improve living standards.

29 *Footer, supra* note 15 at p. 63.

30 It should not normally entitle investors to compensation. See *J. M. Wagner*, International Investment, Expropriation and Environmental Protection, Golden Gate University Law Review 1999 (23), p. 465, 527.

31 *Wälde & Kolo, supra* note 14 at p. 814.

The main problem for investors is not that the environmental protection standards of the host country are high, but that the standards are changed after the investments are made.[32] The second argument in favor of the investors is that it would be unfair to put all the losses and risks on the investor himself.[33]

In terms of the host state, it can be said that according to the "polluter pays" rule[34], which is one of the most accepted principles in environmental law, the corporations have to bear all the consequences that will harm the environment. Another justification is that all states have the right to sovereignty. It is unacceptable for states to be liable for compensation for the action they have made using their sovereign rights.

C. Conclustions

Bilateral investment treaties are very popular tools used by states to regulate investment regimes. The relationship between environmental law and investment law has been increasing since the late 90s. Many countries have environmental protection clauses in their model BITs. The state's right to regulate environmental matters interferes with investment protection. As a rule, states can take environmental protection actions without paying compensation. However, I think that the limit of this right should be determined by indirect expropriation.

On the other hand, regulations specific to the sectors that are more likely to harm the environment should be included in bilateral or multilateral investment treaties. Therefore, on a global scale, host states should be constrained by these rules in terms of lowering environmental protection standards as they compete to attract investors.

Bibliography

Vandevelde, Kenneth J.: Model Bilateral Investment Treaties: The Way Forward, Southwestern Journal of International Law 2011 (18), p. 307.

32 *Verhoosel, supra* note 8 at p. 478; *Wälde & Kolo, supra* note 14 at p. 816. For the relationship between the environmental protection clauses and stabilization clauses in BITs, *see T. Wälde & G. Ndi*, Stabilizing International Investment Commitments: International Law Versus Contract Interpretation, Tex. Int'l LJ 1996 (31-2), p. 215.

33 *Wälde & Kolo, supra* note 14 at p. 845.

34 *C. Stevens*, Interpreting the Polluter Pays Principle in the Trade and Environment Context, Cornell International Law Journal 1994 (27-3), p. 577.

Rose-Ackerman, Susan & *Tobin*, Jennifer: Foreign Direct Investment and the Business Environment in Developing Countries: The Impact of Bilateral Investment Treaties, 2005.

Verhoosel, Gaetan: Foreign Direct Investment and Legal Constraints on Domestic Environmental Policies: Striking a "Reasonable" Balance Between Stability and Change, Law & Policy in International Business 1998 (29), p. 451.

Mabey, Richard & *Mcnally*, Nick: Foreign Direct Investment and the Environment: From Pollution Havens to Sustainable Development, 1999.

Nalçacıoğlu Erden, Hümeyra Zeynep: Milletlerarası Yatırım Hukukunda Dolaylı Kamulaştırma, 2015.

Gordon, Kathyrn & *Pohl*, Joachim: International Environmental Concerns in International Investment Agreements, 2011.

Wälde, Thomas & *Kolo*, Abba: Environmental Regulation, Investment Protection and "Regulatory Taking" in International Law, ICLQ 2001 (50), p. 811.

Stevens, Candice: Interpreting the Polluter Pays Principle in the Trade and Environment Context, Cornell International Law Journal 1994 (27-3), p. 577.

Wälde, Thomas *&* *Ndi*, George: Stabilizing International Investment Commitments: International Law Versus Contract Interpretation, Tex. Int'l LJ 1996 (31-2), p. 215.

J. M. Wagner, International Investment, Expropriation and Environmental Protection, Golden Gate University Law Review 1999 (23), p. 465, 527.

Romson, Asa: Environmental Policy Space & International Investment Law, 2015.

Newcombe, Andrew: General Exceptions in International Investment Agreements, Sustainable Development in World Investment Law 2011 (30), p. 355.

Şit Köşkeroğlu, Banu: Model İkili Yatırım Anlaşmaları ve Türkiye'nin Model İkili Yatırım Anlaşması Taslağı, TBB Dergisi 2013 (107), p. 143.

Hulme, Max H.: Preambles in Treaty Interpretation, University of Pennsylvania Law Review 2016 (164), p. 1281.

Footer, Mary E.: Bits and Pieces: Social and Environmental Protection in the Regulation of Foreign Investment, Michigan State Journal of International Law 2009 (18), p. 33.

Brand, Ronald A.: Sustaining the Development of International Trade and Environmental Law, Vermont Law Review 1997 (21), p. 823.

Vandevelde, Kenneth J.: A Brief History of International Investment Agreements, U.C. Davis Journal of International Law 2005 (12), p. 157.

Sacchidananda, Chakraborty & *Mukherjee*, Debashis: Relationship between Trade, Investment and Environment: A Review of Issues, 2010.

Environmental Issues in International Investment Law

*Miray Azaklı Köse**

I. Introduction

Investment arbitration is based on international investment agreements that provide foreign investors to file a claim against a State due to the violation of a treaty obligation. These treaties typically aim to protect investors rights against unlawful interference of the host State. Early examples of investment treaties are merely focused on protecting private interests of the investors. However this trend has changed over time due to the change in international economic relations. In the past, only developed countries were able to make transboundary investment in developing countries. In order to attract foreign investments, developing countries tended to exclude clauses protecting public interest. Therefore, at that time the main object was to protect the investments of the nationals of the developed countries.[1] In recent years, since investment flow in both directions, developed countries have increasingly become capital importers and regulating host States police powers in order to protect their population and territory has become necessary.

Environmental disputes involve a direct conflict between competing obligations of the State to promote foreign investment and protect its population and territory from environmental harm.[2] As a result, it is based on a conflict between private business interests and public interests. Since states have exclusive sovereignty over their territory, they also possess legislative and executive powers on any subject. International investment agreements may limit the use of these powers, however States may also be bound by obligations arising from international treaties regarding environmental protection. In such cases, there are two competing obligations of a State both stemm from international treaties.

* Assistant Professor, Department of International Law, Istanbul Medeniyet University.

1 Ole Kristian Fauchald, International Investment Law and Environmental Protection, Yearbook of International Environmental Law, 17/2006, p. 7-8.

2 Christina L. Beharry/Melinda E. Kuritzky, Going Green: Managing the Environment Through International Investment Arbitration, American University International Law Review, 30/2015, p. 387.

International investment agreements are basically the creatures of public international law. International Center for Settlement of Investment Disputes (ICSID) Convention Art. 42 regulates the applicable law to the merits of international investment disputes. Principally, the tribunals shall decide a dispute in accordance with the rules agreed by the parties.[3] In the absence of such an agreement, in investor-state disputes the tribunals shall apply the law of the host state and rules of international law as may be applicable.[4] As a consequence, even if no environmental clauses exist in an investment agreement, the Tribunal still may apply international environmental law rules related to dispute theoratically. However in the case-law of investment arbitration, the fact that the applicable law to the merits of an investor-State dispute may also include international rules on the protection have not considered relevant.[5] Since the tribunals are reluctant to apply international environmental law rules, the inclusion of environmental clauses in international investment agreements is required. In the present article, firstly these environmental clauses that exist in bilateral and multilateral investment agreements and the classification of them will be examined. Then jurisprudence of investment tribunals on environmental issues will be summarized and assessed. Finally a brief, overall assessment of the situation of environmental considerations in international investment law will be provided.

A. Environmental Clauses in International Investment and Free Trade Agreements

The most important sources of international investment law are bilateral investment treaties (BITs), sectoral and regional treaties such as the Energy Charter Treaty (the ECT)[6] and the North American Free Trade Agreement (NAFTA)[7] and other free trade agreements with chapters on investment.

3 ICSID Convention, Art. 42(1): "The Tribunal shall decide a dispute in accordance with such rules of law as may be agreed by the parties." For the text of the Convention in English see https://icsid.worldbank.org/sites/default/files/documents/ICSID_Convention.pdf

4 ICSID Convention, Art. 42(2).

5 Pia Acconci, The integration of non-investment concerns as an opportunity for the modernization of international investment law: Is a multilateral approach desirable?, in General Interests of Host States in International Investment Law, 2014, p. 176.

6 For the text of the ECT see: https://www.italaw.com/sites/default/files/laws/italaw6101%2821%29_0.pdf

7 For the text of the NAFTA see: https://www.nafta-sec-alena.org/Home/Texts-of-the-Agreement/North-American-Free-Trade-Agreement

The ICSID Convention is also one of the main sources, but it only provides procedural norms and does not contain substantive obligation.

Beginning with the NAFTA in the early 1990s, investment treaties have begun to address environmental issues.[8] Among other environment related norms included in NAFTA, it contains general language in its preamble:

> "Undertake each of the preceding in a manner consistent with environmental protection and conservation; ... strenghten the development and enforcement of environmental regulation."

Investment chapter of NAFTA also provides environmental reference under performance requirements[9], a provision that reserves parties' right to take environmental measures in accordance with the provision of the chapter[10] and a clause preventing parties from the relaxation of environmental measures in order to attract investment[11].

The ECT provides references to environmental concerns and addresses multilateral environmental agreements in its preamble and specific environmental provisions in its articles. On the other hand, standard BITs generally do not explicitly mention environmental issues[12]:

According to a recent survey conducted by the Organisation for Economic Coopearation and Development, language referring to environmental concerns is rare in BITs (only 6.5% of the BITs contain), but more common in non-BIT international investment agreements.[13] On the other hand,

---

8 *Fauchald*, International Investment Law, p. 3.

9 See Art. 1106(2) (6): "Provided that such measures are not applied in an arbitrary or unjustifiable manner, or do not constitute a disguised restriction on international trade or investment, nothing in paragraph 1(b) or (c) or 3(a) or (b) shall be construed to prevent any Party from adopting or maintaining measures, including environmental measures:
(a) necessary to secure compliance with laws and regulations that are not inconsistent with the provisions of this Agreement;
(b) necessary to protect human, animal or plant life or health; or
(c) necessary for the conservation of living or non-living exhaustible natural resources.

10 Art. 1114(1): "Nothing in this Chapter shall be construed to prevent a Party from adopting, maintaining or enforcing any measure otherwise consistent with this Chapter that it considers appropriate to ensure that investment activity in its territory is undertaken in a manner sensitive to environmental concerns."

11 Art. 1114(2): "The Parties recognize that it is inappropriate to encourage investment by relaxing domestic health, safety or environmental measures. ... "

12 *Fauchald*, International Investment Law, p. 4.

13 Kathryn Gordon & Joachim Pohl, Environmental Concerns in International Investment Agreements: A Survey, OECD Working Papers on International Investment

environmental language is becoming more common in recent treaties. Nearly 50% of the treaties concluded since 2005 contain environmental reference.[14] Additionally the survey shows that environmental language adresses seven distinct policy purposes including: general language in preambles, reserving policy space for environmental regulation for the entire treaty, reserving policy space for environmental regulation for specific subject matters (such as performance requirements and national treatment), precluding non-discriminatory environmental regulation as a basis for claims of indirect expropriation, non lowering environmental standards to attract investment, recoursing to environmental experts by arbitration tribunals and finally, general promotion of progress in environmental protection and cooperation.[15]

B. Jurisprudence of Investment Tribunals on Environmental Issues

One of the consequences of an unlawful act is generally compensation. If a State successfully invokes environmental clauses in a case, it is possible to escape liability and compensation. Therefore States have often relied on environmental considerations in numerous cases.

Investment tribunals generally have considered environmental issues as factual rather than legal matters.[16] These tribunals examine the facts in order to determine whether the State in question has violated a treaty obligation. As noted above, an environmental clause may take place in various treaty provisions such as general exceptions, expropriation, fair and equitable treatment, performance requirements etc. Generally states rely on environmental considerations to defend a measure's legality and its compliance with the treaty obligations. For instance a State may rely on environmental considerations in order to prove that the measure in question does not amount to an expropriation.

In early awards the tribunals dismissed the relevance of environmental concerns. Therefore environmental considerations had not much effect on

2011/01. (The survey analyses the use of references to environmental concerns in a sample of 1,623 international investment agreements across 49 countries. 8.2% of the sample of non-BIT international investment agreements contain a reference to environmental concerns.)

14 *Gordon/Pohl*, Environmental Concerns, p. 5.

15 *Gordon/Pohl*, Environmental Concerns, p. 5-6.

16 *Beharry/Kuritzky*, Going Green, p. 396, 402.

the results of the cases. For instance, in *Santa Elena v. Costa Rica*[17] the tribunal concluded that even takings justified on environmental grounds must be compensated as they are similar to any other expropriatory measures that a state may take in order to implement its policies.[18]

In *Methanex Corp. v. United States*[19], the tribunal adopted a competely different approach. The respondent (the US) based its argument on environmental considerations in order to defend California's ban on the sale and use of a chemical methyl tertiary-buthyl ether (MTBE). According to Methanex, MTBE is a safe, effective and economic component of gasoline and does not pose a risk to human health or the environment.[20] It further claims that the true motive behind the measures was to create a local ethanol industry in California.[21] Among other claims, the Methanex alleged that such measures amount to expropriation and violate the relevant provision of NAFTA.[22] The US argued that the MTBE posed an environmental threat to groundwater and drinking water.[23] The Tribunal concluded that the California ban was made for a public purpose, was non-discriminatory and was accomplished with due process.[24] Therefore it was a lawful regulation and not an expropriation. Furthermore the Tribunal concluded that : "it is a

17 Santa Elena v. Costa Rica, ICSID Case No. ARB/96/1 (Award, 17 February 2000) http://www.italaw.com/documents/santaelena_award.pdf

18 Santa Elena v. Costa Rica, p.192, para. 71-72. The tribunal also states that: "...where property is expropriated, even for environmental purposes, whether domestic or international, the state's obligation to pay compensation remains."
The approach adopted by the tribunal is regarded as "prevailing thinking" of investment arbitration tribunals. In such cases there was an attempt at insulating investment protection from other values, such as the protection of the environment. See M. Sornarajah, Resistance and Change in The International Law on Foreign Investment, 2015, p. 334; fn 70.

19 Methanex Corp. v. US, UNCITRAL, (Award, 3 August 2005) http://www.italaw.com/sites/default/files/case-documents/ita0529.pdf

20 Methanex Corp. v. US, Part II Ch. D para 2

21 Methanex Corp. v. US, para 24

22 Methanex Corp. v. US, para 28 (The relevant provision of NAFTA is Article 1110 which provides: "No Party may directly or indirectly nationalize or expropriate an investment of an investor of another Party in its territory or take a measure tantamount to nationalization or expropriation of such an investment ("expropriation"), except:
(a) for a public purpose;
(b) on a non-discriminatory basis;
(c) in accordance with due process of law and Article 1105(1); and
(d) on payment of compensation in accordance with paragraphs 2 through 6.")

23 Methanex Corp. v. US, para 15

24 Methanex Corp. v. US, Part IV Ch. D para 15

principle of customary international law that, where economic injury results from a bona fide regulation within the police powers of a State, compensation is not required."[25] The US did not pay compensation due to the effects of its measures on a foreign investor.

In *Chemtura v. Canada*[26] The Pest Management Regulatory Agency (PMRA) was a federal agency of Canada which was responsible for the regulation of pest control products in order to prevent unacceptable risks to people and the environment from the use of pest control products.[27] The PMRA by relying on the Special Review that assesses the risks of lindane, announced that the risk assessment findings warranted regulatory action by way of suspension or termination of lindane registrations.[28] Chemtura –a US chemical manufacturer- challenged that federal measure before arbitration tribunal. Canada argued that the conduct of the PMRA was a valid exercise of police powers. Consequently the Tribunal stated that[29]:

> "the Tribunal considers in any event that the measures challenged by the Claimant constituted a valid exercise of the Respondent's police powers. As discussed in detail in connection with Article 1105 of NAFTA, the PMRA took measures within its mandate, in a non-discriminatory manner, motivated by the increasing awareness of the dangers presented by lindane for human health and the environment. A measure adopted under such circumstances is a valid exercise of the State's police powers and, as a result, does not constitute an expropriation."

The tribunal also made a reference to *Saluka v. Czech Republic*[30] in support of its view. In that case, the Tribunal held that[31]:

> "In the opinion of the Tribunal, the principle that a State does not commit an expropriation and is thus not liable to pay compensation

---

25 But the Tribunal also noted that compensation would be required "if specific commitments had been given by the regulating government to the then putative foreign investor contemplating investment that the government would refrain from such regulation. Methanex Corp. v. US, Part IV Ch. D para 7

26 Chemtura v. Canada, UNCITRAL, (Award, 2 August 2010) http://www.italaw.com/sites/default/files/case-documents/ita0149_0.pdf

27 Chemtura v. Canada, para 10

28 Chemtura v. Canada, para 29

29 Chemtura v. Canada, para 266

30 Saluka v. Czech Republic, UNCITRAL, (Partial Award, 17 March 2006) http://www.italaw.com/sites/default/files/case-documents/ita0740.pdf

31 Saluka v. Czech Republic, para 262. The rule is stated without exceptions. *Sornarajah*, Resistance and Change, p. 337, fn 74

> to a dispossessed alien investor when it adopts general regulations that are 'commonly accepted as within the police power of States' forms part of customary international law today."

As seen from the recent awards, the arbitral tribunals adopted *the police powers doctrine* while dealing with issues concerning environmental measures. Furthermore the police powers doctrine is recognized as a part of customary international law. However the case-law does not provide objective and normative standards by which to review regulations adressing public health and the environment.[32] The evaluation of a governmental conduct is entirely left to the discretion of the tribunals.

One recent award has a special importance, since it reflects a progressive approach going beyond the police powers doctrine. *Perenco v. Ecuador*[33] case was related to the environmental impact of oil extraction activities conducted by Perenco in Ecuador. Ecuador brought a counterclaim and the tribunal has found Perenco liable. The tribunal stated that:

> "The Tribunal agrees that if a legal relationship between an investor and the State permits the filing of a claim by the State for environmental damage caused by the investor's activities and such a claim substantiated, the State is entitled to full reparation in accordance with the requirements of the applicable law.
>
> The Tribunal further recognises that a State has a wide latitude under international law to prescribe and adjust its environmental laws, standards and policies in response to changing views and a deeper understanding of the risks posed by various activities ..."[34]

Perenco v. Ecuador has been considered a change of mindset and a footprint of normalisation.[35] Since environmental considerations are not integrated into the reasoning as an extraneous factor, but they are simply adressed as a requirement of normal operations in the extractive industries.[36]

---

32 *Sornarajah*, Resistance and Change, p. 338; *Beharry/ Kuritzky*, Going Green, p. 403.

33 Perenco v. Ecuador, ICSID Case No. ARB/08/6, (Interim Decision on the Environmental Counterclaim, 11 August 2015) http://www.italaw.com/sites/default/ files/ case-documents/italaw6315.pdf

34 Perenco v. Ecuador, para.34-35

35 Jorge E. Vinuales, Foreign Investment and the Environment in International Law: The Current State of Play, C-EENRG Working Papers, 2016, p. 20 https://www.ceenrg.landecon.cam.ac.uk/system/files/documents/wp05.pdf

36 *Vinuales*, Foreign Investment, p. 20.

C. Conclusion

International investment law is no longer an isolated area that ignores environmental concerns. Particularly after 1990s environmental clauses have been increasingly included in international investment agreements. Environment-related disputes before arbitral tribunals increased due to the rise of these clauses. Since private interests of the foreign investors are in conflict with public interests of the states in such disputes, the task of a tribunal is balancing treaty obligations of the States and the investors.

Although environmental concerns has been taken into account by arbitral tribunals, international investment law and international environmental law are not still on equal footing. The tribunals mindset has significantly changed over time and the tribunals improved new doctrines in order to deal with environmental issues. While early awards left no place to environmental considerations, some recent awards adressed environmental conflicts as normative conflicts. Previously, those were seen just kind of legitimacy problems and factual issues that are subordinated to investment law concepts: The tribunals had used them merely to determine whether a governmental measure is legitimate. However more recent case-law shows that, environmental rules are recognized as a normative set of rules.

Most investment agreements do not contain policy space provisions, while others have a general wording far from guiding arbitrators. Therefore detailed environmental clauses that cover appropriate, objective standards are required in investment agreements. At present, interpretation of the environmental clauses is left to the discretion of the tribunals. If well-established exception clauses determining the extent of a state's regulatory powers play a part in treaties; tribunals may evaluate governmental measures more effectively.

Bibliography

Acconci, Pia: The integration of non-investment concerns as an opportunity for the modernization of international investment law: Is a multilateral approach desirable?, in General Interests of Host States in International Investment Law, 2014.

Beharry, Christina L./ Kuritzky, Melinda E. : Going Green: Managing the Environment Through International Investment Arbitration, American University International Law Review, 30/2015.

Fauchald, Ole Kristian: International Investment Law and Environmental Protection, Yearbook of International Environmental Law, 17/2006.

Gordon, Kathryn/Pohl, Joachim: Environmental Concerns in International Investment Agreements: A Survey, OECD Working Papers on International Investment 2011/01.

Sornarajah, M.: Resistance and Change in The International Law on Foreign Investment, 2015.

Vinuales, Jorge E.: Foreign Investment and the Environment in International Law: The Current State of Play, C-EENRG Working Papers, 2016.https://www.ceenrg.landecon.cam.ac.uk/system/files/documents/wp05.pdf

Cases

Chemtura v. Canada, UNCITRAL, (Award, 2 August 2010) http://www.italaw.com/sites/default/files/case-documents/ita0149_0.pdf

Methanex Corp. v. US, UNCITRAL, (Award, 3 August 2005) http://www.italaw.com/sites/default/files/case-documents/ita0529.pdf

Perenco v. Ecuador, ICSID Case No. ARB/08/6, (Interim Decision on the Environmental Counterclaim, 11 August 2015) http://www.italaw.com/sites/default/ files/case-documents/italaw6315.pdf

Saluka v. Czech Republic, UNCITRAL, (Partial Award, 17 March 2006) http://www.italaw.com/sites/default/files/case-documents/ita0740.pdf

Santa Elena v. Costa Rica, ICSID Case No. ARB/96/1 (Award, 17 February 2000) http://www.italaw.com/documents/santaelena_award.pdf

Turkey's 'Mega' Challenges: An Outline of Megaprojects in National and International Environmental Law Framework

Nebile Pelin Mantı[*]

Abstract

Within the past few decades, Turkish government has launched many mega projects as a part of their political agenda. These projects have started wide discussions in Turkey, as many of these projects were not considered environmental-friendly, sustainable, nor necessary, and mostly because they are not responding directly the need for energy and sustainability, but bringing a huge burden on an economy in crisis, and as they underestimate the disaster risk, and especially difficulties arising because of the eroding principle of the rule of law in Turkey, in terms of environmental law and policy, posed a major concern for public.

This article aims to give an outline of Mega Projects in Turkey, particularly in Istanbul, and will try to evaluate the environmental effects, under Turkish Environmental Law and International Law.

Key Words: mega projects, construction, environment, Canal Istanbul, Urban transformation

I. Introduction

At the beginning of 2000s, the sustainable use of natural resources and the growing need for energy has become one of the crucial issues in Turkey. Environmental policies were one of the biggest challenges in front of Turkey's EU negotiation process for full membership[1].

---

* Research Assistant, Public International Law Department, Istanbul University Faculty of Law.

1 The EU points out the importance of a high level of environmental protection, including all aspects of nuclear safety in Principles governing the negotiations paper, Negotiating Framework, Luxembourg, 3 October 2005. (Available at: https://ec.europa.eu/neighbourhood-enlargement/sites/near/files/pdf/turkey/st20002_05_tr_framedoc_en.pdf)

In 2002, following the financial crisis[2] in 2001 and 3 years after the destruction of city centres by 1999 Great Marmara Earthquake[3], to rebuild the economy, newly elected ruling Justice and Development Party (*Adalet ve Kalkınma Partisi, shortly AKP*) took many steps, and one of the headlines was large scale construction projects. Mega Projects, in this regard, were presented as a development model, since the construction projects are usually transformative for an economy in decline.

As a part of their election propaganda, the Turkish government claimed to become one of the top economies in the world by 2023, which is the 100th anniversary of the foundation of the Turkish Republic and therefore, huge investments in several construction projects, covering transportation, energy production and urban transformation were initiated.

A. A Framework for Mega Projects:

Mega projects are not specific to the 21st century. Within the course of history, huge monuments, temples built on behalf of kings, the gods, pharaohs are the beginnings of mega projects. From Göbeklitepe in Şanlıurfa to Pantheon built by the Emperor Hadrian in Rome; God-kings and emperors, and even the dictators[4] of modern times, wanted to be remembered in history through these gigantic works, which would survive for centuries. And these projects

2 The Turkish government's fiscal deficit deteriorated significantly from 1995 to 2000. On February 19, 2001, a political crisis emerged involving Turkish Prime Minister Bulent Ecevit and President Ahmet Necdet Sezer. Sezer appears to have accused Ecevit of corruption, resulting in Ecevit demanding a public apology. This political rupture raised doubts that the government would adhere to the requirements of the IMF Program; this resulted in the stock market falling 14%, the overnight rate spiking to 6200%, and the recent IMF reserve additions evaporating as the central bank defended the crawling peg once again. Simon-Peter Noble, Turkey: The 2001 Financial Crisis, Seekinalpha, Oct. 18, 2018 (Available from: https://seekingalpha.com/article/4212301-turkey-2001-financial-crisis)

3 The Izmit earthquake (also known as the Kocaeli, Gölcük, or Great Marmara earthquake) took place on 17 August 1999, at 03:01:40 local time in northwestern Turkey. The shock had a moment magnitude of 7.6, and then 7.4, a maximum Mercalli intensity of IX (Violent), killing total of 17,479 people in Turkey, a 1000 of which died during the shock, as many buildings in Istanbul collapsed.

4 The mega projects of Hitler which he could not bring to life was Germania or New Berlin. Welthauptstadt, Capital of the World in other words, was Hitler's project for Berlin, which was wished to remain 1000 years. The project took start in 1937, and in this regard many sections of Berlin were evacuated, and this can also be considered as one of the reasons of the Holocaust.

require mobilization of enormous resources and labour, and their legitimacy were granted by the political / holy power behind them. On the other hand, these projects required enormous manpower and thousands of slaves were employed under inhuman conditions.

Today, the challenges are various. One of the most important issues for Turkey is the sustainable use of natural resources and growing need for energy. Therefore, following the elections in 2011, Turkish government has launched many (about 75) mega projects additionally, some of them were to ensure the wise use of energy and natural resources.

Mega projects are designed to respond the need for infrastructure and structure following 1999 earthquakes, and to manage the use of energy and natural resources wisely. They have a large budget, and they transform the landscape quickly. Megaproject construction sites cover a huge area, and displaces the soil and subsoil, thereby significantly altering the biological, geological, and physical features of the landscape. The contractors excavate mountains to fill the stream bed, they dug the harbours and divert rivers and aquifers, which were protected by artificial dikes, and in the end, land is cleared, levelled and the soil characteristics, landforms and habitat change drastically, which result also change in species' composition, and leave the territory with long-term effects, along with its effects on the economy, culture, and health. "Environment" is one of the biggest challenges in front of Turkey's EU negotiation process for full membership, is still the management and conservation of the environment and the sustainable use of natural resources, especially difficulties arising because of the eroding principle of the rule of law in Turkey in terms of environmental law and policy poses a major problem.

Defining mega projects legally is not an easy work, as most definitions given for megaprojects are inaccurate and only apply to certain types of projects. Mega projects are defined as the "large-scale, complex ventures that typically cost a billion dollars or more, take many years to develop and build, involve multiple public and private stakeholders, are transformational, and impact millions of people"[5]. Although considered crucial to the future of cities, states, and individual livelihoods, and considered economically transformative, the effects of "mega" projects on Istanbul, which have been planned and put into practice for more than a decade, are creating more discussion in terms of urban nature and identity, urban quality and urban memory.

5 Bent Flyvbjerg, What You Should Know About Megaprojects, and Why: An Overview, Project Management Journal, vol. 45, no. 2, April-May 2014, pp. 6-19, DOI: 10.1002/pmj.21409, p.3.

The problem is multi-dimensional and comprehensive. The Mega Projects which have started in near term, like the construction of the third airport in Istanbul, the construction of the third Bosphorus bridge, an increasing amount of natural gas exploration activities, the construction of large dams and hydroelectric power plants; rapidly privatized natural resources and construction of large hydroelectric power plants in eastern Turkey, etc. are mainly targeting the economic growth. However, these and other 'mega' investment projects have devastating effects on eco - system and most of them violate existing environmental law framework, as most of them were initiated without a proper environmental impact assessment. Particularly companies operating water resources are mostly originated from mining sector, and therefore they use heavily toxic substances and chemicals in their activities, and they pollute water, soil and air and cause an irreversible damage.

The EU acquis on the Turkish environmental law implementations have limited impact to minimize the destructive environmental effects of Mega Projects, mentioned by scientists and scholars and try to figure out which mechanisms and sanctions can be used to protect the natural environment and the resources against violations in the light of the protection provided by national and international agreements, firstly as the normative background is harmonized, implementation part lacks commitment.

In 2002, following a financial crisis, to rebuild the country's economy, ruling Justice and Development Party (AKP), took many steps which initiated great discussions. In terms of economic recovery, state assets have been privatised, and the government has used urban and rural interventions as profitable outlets for capital surplus investment to attract foreign direct investment (FDI).

Before elections, in 2011, as the economic situation mega projects are declared by former Prime Minister Recep Tayyip Erdoğan and are considered by Turkish government as one of the solutions to overcome the financial instability, and as a trump to use during Turkey's long-standing EU membership negotiation process.

In this scope, many mega projects were presented. Most of these were targeting Istanbul, as a mega city, and began in succession like Canal Istanbul, Urban Transformation, 3rd Airport, Yavuz Sultan Selim Bridge (Third Bosphorus Bridge), Eurasia Tunnel, an underwater railway connecting Europe and Asia sides of Istanbul with a tunnel passing under the Bosphorus, Istanbul-Izmir Highway, Ankara-Istanbul High Speed Train (YHT) line. And some focusing on energy production, like Marmara, Akkuyu and Sinop Nuclear Power Plants, etc.

Mega Projects caused a great concern in public, and environmental NGOs and other organisations reacted, emphasizing on the devastating effects of 'mega' investment projects, in terms of urban culture and urban structure of one of world's oldest cities with huge environmental problems, bearing in mind also the disaster risk and attended earthquake after 1999 Great Marmara earthquake.

The most striking point of mega projects are the huge traces of destruction and pollution they have left in nature that possible future effects cannot be systematically revealed.

Some of these projects are not implemented and neutralized in accordance with the Environmental Impact Assessment (shortly, EIA) process, and some are implemented without a proper EIA (for example, 3rd Bridge).

B. Istanbul Focus

1. The Law of Mega Projects

The sustainable use of natural resources and the growing need for energy has become one of the crucial issues in Turkey since 1980s. In the following years, environmental policies were one of the biggest challenges in front of Turkey's EU negotiation process for full membership. In 1999 Turkey faced a series of earthquakes, which caused a great destruction and changed the Marmara region entirely. Upon their election in 2002, new government started to implement some mega projects, to respond the need for infrastructure and structure which was destroyed in 1999 earthquakes and to manage the use of energy and natural resources wisely.

Following 1999 Great Marmara Earthquake, from the beginning of 2000s, Turkish Government, as a part of their politic and economic agenda, declared 34 great construction projects that 4 of them focus Istanbul in particular, namely the 3rd Istanbul airport, Eurasia Tunnel, a road tunnel which connects Anatolian and European sides of Istanbul, and the Yavuz Sultan Selim or Istanbul Bridge, the third bridge over Bosphorus and Urban Transformation.

The first steps for the protection of the environment in Turkey were taken in 1980s, and following its 1987 application for EU membership, and in furtherance of the long-lasting accession talks that commenced in 2005, many secondary legislations passed by The Grand National Assembly of Turkish Republic (Assembly).

Turkey has ratified many international conventions and bilateral agreements for the protection of environment. Turkey is currently a party to many environmental international agreements, conventions, and protocols and that are relevant to major projects and to which your jurisdiction is a signatory? To what extent have they been implemented into national law?

The main legislation for the protection of the environment in Turkey, is the Environmental Law No 2872 (Environmental Law), which came into force in 1983, and was revised in accordance with EU legislation in 2006.

Under Turkish Law, projects and facilities are subject to two main environmental review and permit procedures:

- The environmental impact assessment (EIA) procedure.
- The environmental permit and licensing procedure.

Those two main environmental review and permit requirements are regulated by two separate regulations issued by the Ministry of Environment and Urbanisation (MEU) under the Environmental Law, which are namely, The Regulation on Environmental Impact Assessment (EIA Regulation) governs the EIA procedure and The Regulation on Permits and Licences[6].

Turkey ranks third in the world in terms of earthquake-related casualties and eighth regarding the total number of people affected. Every year, the country experiences at least one 5+ magnitude earthquake – which renders the proper management and coordination of disasters crucial.

Turkey's disaster policy dates to the aftermath of the 1939 Erzincan earthquake, which claimed nearly 33.000 lives and left at least 100.000 injured. Two decades later, the Turkish Parliament adopted the Law on Precautions to be Taken due to Disaster Affecting Public Life and Assistance to be Provided (No.7269) to fulfill the long-existing legal void. The legislative effort on disaster continued with the 1988 by-law on the Principles of the Organization and Planning of Emergency Assistance Regarding Disasters.

6 Published in the *Official Gazette* No 29115 on 10 September 2014, (Permit and Licence Regulation) governs the permit and licensing procedure. In addition, other relevant environmental laws and regulations that set out criteria for audits and inspections within the scope of the Environmental Law include the: Forestry Law No 6831. Regulation on the Conservation of Wetlands (published in the *Official Gazette* No 28962 of 4 April 2014). Waste Management Regulation (published in the *Official Gazette* No 29314 of 2 April 2015). Regulation on Environmental Inspection (published in the *Official Gazette* No 27061 of 21 November 2008). Industrial Air Pollution Control Regulation (published in the *Official Gazette* No 27277 of 3 July 2009). Air Quality Regulation (published in the *Official Gazette* No 26898 of 6 June 2008). Noise Control Regulation (published in the *Official Gazette* No 26809 of 7 March 2008). Water Pollution Control Regulation (published in the *Official Gazette* No 25687 of 31 December 2004). Waste Oil Regulation (published in the *Official Gazette* No 26952 of 30 July 2008).

2. Istanbul and Urban Transformation

Urban transformation can be defined as a process including "demolishing illegal housing, unpermitted buildings and the buildings that do not comply with the planning regulations of the city and create new urban settlement areas that comply with the planning regulations".

Istanbul is one of the most effected cities from this uncontrolled development being the demographic, economic, and cultural capital of Turkey. Currently the fifth largest city in the World, and home to more than 15 million inhabitants, bridging East and West, Istanbul has long stood as a critical crossroads for commerce, innovation, and cultural exchange.

After Great Marmara[7] (İzmit-Gölcük) Earthquake on 17 August 1999 and Bolu Düzce Earthquake on 12 November 1999. In Marmara region, main initiative is used, not as to restauration of what has been lost, but for the reconstruction of a new, better, solid buildings, to solve the great infrastructure problem. As a part of their election propaganda in 2002, the newly elected Turkish government claimed to become one of the top ten economies in the world by 2023, which is the 100th anniversary of the foundation of Turkish Republic. Therefore, huge investments in many megaprojects, including large scale infrastructure, energy, defence, and transportation sectors are declared as the core element of this strategy.

Disaster Act No.6306 requires the *"transformation of the areas under disaster risk"* and was regulating the areas under "disaster risk", the Ministry of Environment and Urbanisation is entitled to declare areas where *"the public order or security is challenged," "the infrastructure services are inadequate"* and *"the buildings are unlicensed"* as the areas that are under risk.

The urbanization process in Turkey accelerated in the 1950s with industrialization, and western cities started to grow uncontrollably such as Ankara, Istanbul, Bursa and Izmir became particularly intensive areas. One of the important factors of uncontrolled development in cities has been the devel-

7 Great Marmara, or İzmit-Gölcük, Earthquake took place at 3:02 a.m. local time. The northwest Turkey was shaken by a magnitude 7.4 earthquake, catching most people in their sleep. A total of 120,000 poorly engineered houses were damaged beyond repair, 30,000 houses were heavily damaged, 2,000 other buildings collapsed, and 4,000 other buildings were heavily damaged. More than 300,000 people were left homeless after the earthquake. Earthquake was felt in the entire Marmara Region, from Ankara to Izmir. According to official reports, 17 thousand 840 people were killed, and 43 thousand 935 people were injured. 505 people were disabled. 285 thousand 211 housing, 42 thousand 902 business sites were damaged. The earthquake caused a tsunami in the Sea of Marmara that was about 2.5 meters high, which also caused the deaths of 155 people.

oping slum areas due to the lack of housing features to respond the rapid urbanization. In the 1970s, while urbanisation continued in the big cities, and satellite cities began to form on the other hand.

By the 1980s, while urbanization and urban slum areas were transformed, urban areas and urban areas were transformed into urban areas. Urban transformation concept which is used to express the government policies developed for the solution of the urban problems; including development, renovation, revitalization, concepts of reproduction, developed cities like in the US and UK.

Urban Transformation has different appearances in Turkey as Urban Renewal (Kentsel Yenileme), Regeneration (Yeniden Üretim), Conservation/Preservation (Koruma); Rehabilitation (Sağlıklılaştırma-Eski Haline Getirme); Revitalization (Yeniden Canlandırma); Redevelopment (Yeniden Geliştirme) and Gentrification (Soylulaştırma).

Urban renewal, with the help of public initiative or with the help of the public, cleaning of poor neighbourhoods, improvement of buildings, protection, better sheltering, working and resting conditions, for the purpose of providing public structures, in accordance with the local designs and regulations, all or part of the cities and urban elements, Better changing conditions

The Government's agenda is hardly criticized for "being far from a pluralistic process, to deny any opposition or criticism coming either from the opposition party or civil society". Therefore, the main source of this initiative is the political authority, and justification of this huge transformation is made under an eventual earthquake risk. However, the implementation of urban transformation is criticized as ended with an unjust rent transfer, displacement, social exclusion and thus gentrification.

The most critical issues regarding urban transformation process includes property rights of the owners and different legislations, as well as differences of implementation by local authorities as to construction plans, priorities and competences are causing multi-dimensional problems as to determination of objective criteria and judicial review of these decisions.

The provision of Article 129/5 of the 1982 Constitution mentions that the compensation cases arising from the fault committed by civil servants and other public officials while exercising their powers can only be brought against the administration, provided that they are brought before Courts and judicial remedy is open against all kinds of actions and actions of the administration.

A local's house in Fikirtepe neighbourhood, within the construction site. The owner refused to sign an agreement with the construction company for 4 years.

The house was demolished in August 2014, as the owner signed an agreement that made him an owner of 5 flats.

3. Istanbul`s Third Airport

Istanbul's third airport, set to be one of the largest in the world in terms of passenger capacity, is under construction in the Arnavutkoy district of Istanbul. Tendered to a consortium of five Turkish companies, Cengiz-Kolin-Limak-Mapa-Kalyon, for EUR 22 billion in May 2013, the airport project will be realized through the built-operate-transfer method and is currently expected to cost an additional EUR 10 billion to complete.

Once complete, Istanbul's third airport will relieve the heavily congested Ataturk Airport, becoming both the main hub of Turkish Airlines (THY) and a new layover location for a multitude of airline companies given its prime location between Europe, Asia, Africa and the Middle East.

Over 500.000 trees in one of the world's oldest forests are being cut down, important migration routes for birds will be forlorn and many animals, will lose their natural habitat. The large-scale urban development plans in Istanbul are also followed by marginalization of local communities: Many people, including poor Roman families, are forced into giving up their homes.

Ongoing construction in northern Istanbul is having a devastating effect on the environment: More than 2 million trees were cut down in one of the world's oldest forests; important bird migration routes are destroyed; and many animals, such as wild pigs, have lost their natural habitat.

4. Canal Istanbul Project

The Turkish Straits are a unique system of waterways consisting of two straits, which are connecting the Mediterranean Sea and Aegean Sea to the Marmara Sea with Çanakkale Strait and then to the Black Sea through Istanbul Strait, as Turks call it the Bosphorus.

The Bosphorus divides Istanbul from the middle is the narrowest gateway for international maritime transport and large-tonnage vessels are a danger during their transit.

The navigation through Turkish Straits is regulated by Montreux Convention of 1936. Since the conclusion of the Monteux Convention, the maritime traffic through both straits intensified and the risk also increased depending various factors, some of which are the populated areas close to the Bosphorus, augmenting naval traffic[8] and the constructural properties and cargo of the navigating vessels, which are changing and becoming more dangerous[9].

Canal Istanbul Project, also called as "crazy project" by Erdoğan during press conference in 2011, during his prime ministry, after a cargo ship rammed into the shore of the Bosphorus and caused extensive damage to one of the historic mansions in the shoreline and offers to reduce the pressure on the strait while adding to Turkey's economy, and to ensure the security of the Bosphorus. This artificial sea-level waterway will be built parallel to the Bosphorus and will connect the Black Sea to the Sea of Marmara. At a planned 47 kilometers in length and 150 meters in width, main aim is to provide relief for shipping traffic, particularly oil tanker traffic, passing through the Bosphorus. The canal has a designed capacity of 160 vessels a day and is scheduled to be completed by 2023 at a cost of USD 15 billion.

8 The natural waterway cuts through Turkey's Istanbul and divides the country between two continents – Europe and Asia. It is a corridor for commuters, travellers, merchant vessels, and residents who are overflowing city.

9 Cahit Istikbal, a pilot and president of the Turkish Maritime Safety Association said "The Bosphorus' vital route is generally congested and of strategic importance. It is a difficult-to-navigate waterway. The difficulty comes from its narrowness and sharp curves," (Available at: "https://www.scmp.com/news/world/europe/article/2149028/erdogans-kanal-istanbul-may-save-ships-crashing-critics-say-its" \t "_blank")

The passage requires special attention because of the physical properties of the lane. The widest part of the Bosphorus is with a very curved structure of 3.6 kilometers, the narrowest is 698 meters and its length is 29.9 kilometers. It is the only way out of the Black Sea, which is fed by three big streams and many small waters like Tuna, Dnieper and Don, and it is located in a higher position from the Black Sea and higher than the Sea of Marmara, which causes severe currents on the surface and at the bottom. This is the most important factor that increases the danger during passage.

The Bosphorus is one of the busiest maritime passages and is also one of the most strategic waterways of the world in the world. With nearly 43,000 vessels passing through in 2017, the Bosphorus sees nearly three times the traffic of the Suez Canal and is considered as one of the most strategically significant and busiest waterways of the world.

The EIA Report of Canal Istanbul Project was published in 23.12.2019[10], and was open to public comments for 10 days. On January 17, 2020, Minister of Environment and Urbanization announced that the EIA report of Canal İstanbul is approved.

It is stated in the EIA Report that the project route will be completed in 7 years. In this long process, both the environment and human life will be adversely affected. In the report, it is stated that dust, polluted air and greenhouse gas emissions will be affected throughout all stages of the process. As it has been determined, the topographic structure will change, and agricultural activities will be adversely affected.

The area where the project will be implemented is on the earthquake zones. Considering that the construction and population will increase in the region within the scope of the project, there is a danger of significant loss of life and property. In addition, with the project, state forest areas, natural and archaeological sites, nature parks, national parks, wetlands, etc. protected areas will disappear. Forest, pasture, river and marine ecosystems will be damaged and adversely affected throughout the project area. With the failure of Terkos Lake and Sazlıdere Dam, which are important water resources of Istanbul and Marmara region, a significant water problem and scarcity will be encountered. In addition, this project will create problems in the natural balance of the Marmara Sea and the Black Sea. Long term effects will be more devastating.

10 1.595 paged EIA Report with Annexes 12.208 pages and was open to comments for 10 days. (Available at: http://eced.csb.gov.tr/ced/jsp/ek1/21257)

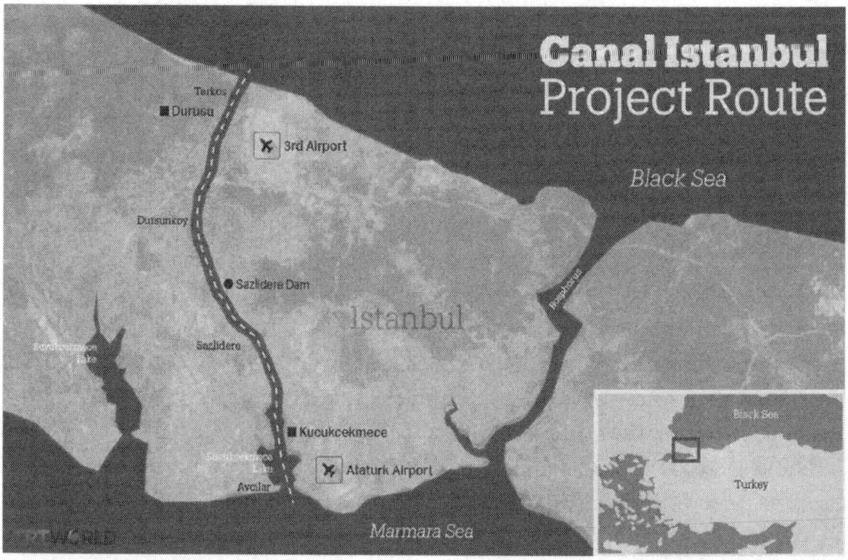
Canal Istanbul
Project Route
Black Sea
Terkos
Durusu
3rd Airport
Dursunkoy
Sazlidere Dam
Istanbul
Sazlidere
Bosphorus
Kucukcekmece
Ataturk Airport
Avcilar
Marmara Sea
Black Sea
Turkey

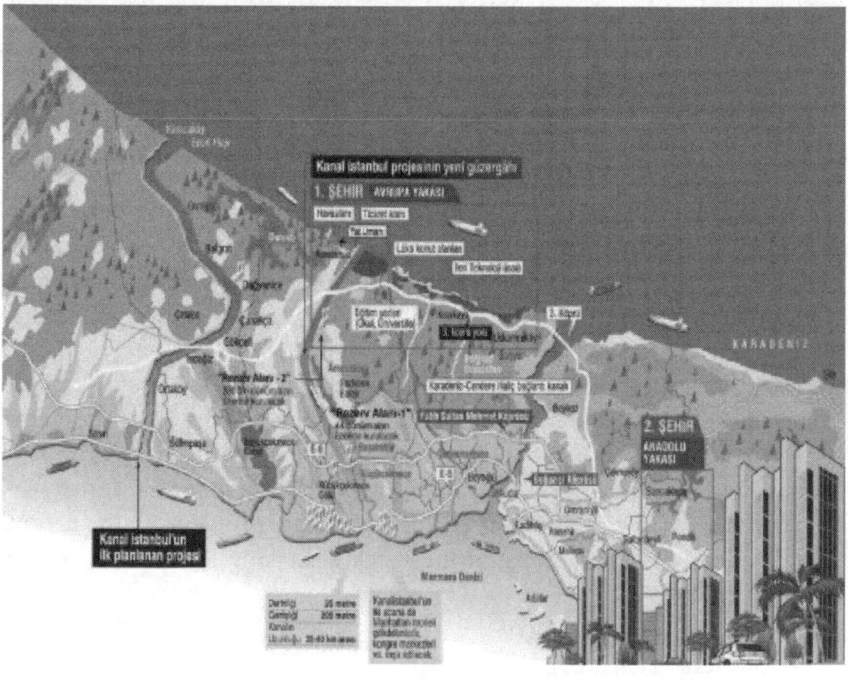
Kanal İstanbul projesinin yeni güzergâhı
1. ŞEHİR
AVRUPA YAKASI
KARADENİZ
2. ŞEHİR
ANADOLU YAKASI
Kanal İstanbul'un ilk planlanan projesi

5. Istanbul Airport Project

One of the most prominent examples of megaprojects is Istanbul's third airport, Istanbul Airport, which will be located to the north of Istanbul, on a close area to the Black Sea and Lake Terkos. According to the declared information, the airport will be close to villages and will cost the destruction of forested areas and basins which will have negative effects on the air quality for the city.

It is supposed to become one of the largest worldwide, dispatching over 150 million passengers every year. The construction in the north of Istanbul affects the environment dramatically: Over 2 million in one of the world's oldest forests are being cut down, important migration routes for birds will be forlorn and many other animals, such as wild boars, will lose their natural habitat. The large-scale urban development plans in Istanbul are also followed by marginalisation of local communities: Many people, for example poor Roman families, are forced into giving up their homes.

The projects are pushed forward without any considerations of the public health and human rights or the state of natural environment.

Natural resources in the east of Turkey become privatized and large energy plants are being constructed. A lot of the companies that own and work with the water resources come from the mining sector. They pollute water, land and air with toxic materials and gases. In addition, an increased amount of shale gas extraction, the construction of small scale but many dams and hydropower plants, as well as aggressive deforestation are intensifying the problems. The Turkish government is planning to build about 75 new coal fired power plants until 2020 (currently, there are 55 coal power plants in Turkey). The emissions from these plants pose a supplementary threat to human health and the climate.

In addition, water from dozens of canals from large and small ponds will be released into the Black Sea, which will cause an environmental disaster in the Thrace Region, according to environmentalists. Seventy wetlands feeding the Terkos Basin, which is vital for meeting Istanbul's water needs, will dry up, they say.

The airport also sits on a vital bird migration route, the Istanbul Bird Watching Group says. This also poses a security issue. The group highlighted the fact that hundreds of thousands of birds migrate through the region in the spring and autumn, leading to a greater risk of a bird flying into a plane's engine.

Roughly 2.5 million trees will be cut down by the end of the project, negatively impacting the region's ecosystem.

As a result, many of these megaprojects have a negative impact on the public health and living conditions of the local population, leading in some cases to expropriation of land and displacement of local communities. The proposed coal power plants make Turkey a ticking climate bomb: the country is expected to double its emissions until 2030.

6. Environmental Protection and The Rule of Law in Turkey

The main question that comes into mind is, what these megaprojects are good for and how more constructions will solve the infrastructure and deforestation problems?

Environmental action started in the early 1980s and Turkish Government has since been enacting laws and regulations to protect environment and in order to manage the use of natural resources. In this context first legislations were enacted to prevent and eliminate environmental pollution and following Turkey's EU membership candidacy, management of natural resources and the protection of land environment have also become important chapters.

The environmental problems arising from these megaprojects are linked to the lack of operation of rule of law in the country. In theory, the Turkish constitution ensures the protection of the environment in articles 56 within the Constitution and with local legislation. However, there is a huge gap between the legal provisions and what is happening in practice. The Turkish government is disrespecting the prevailing law systematically and at the same time considering the introduction of new amendments to the constitution, which might weaken the environmental standards in the country. The executive has increased its authority over the last years, while the independence of the judicative has been pushed back. Patronage and understaffed environmental protection agencies have worsened the situation.

Besides the eroding rule of law, there is also a lack of transparency and accountability, which is especially evident in the procedure of environmental impact assessments (EIA). The amendments to the EIA law in the past years have magnified the problems. Many infrastructural projects are now arbitrarily exempted from the EIAs. As a result, information is not shared with the public, deadlines are changed hidden, meetings are held in secret and civil society is kept out from the decision boards and public hearings, while at the same time, the investing companies are dominating these meetings.

The official accession negotiations between the EU and Turkey started in 2005. Chapter 27 on Environment and Climate Change was opened in 2009. However, the environmental chapter is not among the politically sensitive ones compared to other issues such as justice and home affairs, Turkey´s relations with Cyprus and Turkey's role the refugee crisis.

Urban planners criticize that none of these projects will substantially solve traffic problems in Istanbul, but rather induce additional traffic through the existing opportunity structures.

Turkey has to revise the negative changes in its environmental law from the past years and show significant and visible progress in areas such as the implementation of horizontal legislation, access to justice, transparency provisions, environmental impact safeguards and water legislation.

The primary concerns focus on transparency. The progress is necessary and important; however, it is clear that the problems in the field of environment are deeply interlinked with other social and justice issues. Violations of environmental standards directly affect other issues such as peace, justice, human rights, migration, or energy. Another big challenge is that the 28 EU member states have very divergent national strategies and priorities in their relations with Turkey, making it difficult for the EU institutions to speak with one voice during the negotiations and define a clear position, which takes into consideration the whole complexity of the situation.

The environmental problems in Turkey should not be neglected for the sake of other geopolitical goals, such as the tackling of the EU refugee crisis.

The EU has the tools influence the reform process in Turkey through the accession negotiations. Turkey is the largest recipient of funding from the European Bank of Reconstruction and Development (EBRD) and the European Investment Bank (EIB); therefore, many European banks invest in some of the Turkish megaprojects. These European banks are involved in co-funding megaprojects, which are not in line with EU climate and environmental policies. Besides, the definition of a "sustainable" project is not clear .

EU institutions, which are often shareholders in these banks or are able to influence their mandates, can approach financiers, when legislation is weak, or to the NGOs in Europe and Turkey, which may help to develop public pressure, as in the case of EBRD and the World Bank to pull out of a controversial refinery project near Izmir.

C. Conclusion

Mega projects received many reactions from public, since the effects of the projects in terms of urban nature, urban quality and urban memory are considered destructive. Even though it has been planned and implemented for more than ten years, the effects of these transformation and construction projects in Istanbul, have not been publicly discussed.

Although the term environmental justice has different connotations, reconsidering the human and environment relations becomes crucial. Impacts of climate change are growing unexpectedly: heat waves, followed by long-term droughts, and in another part of the world severe storms, heavy rain and floods are more frequent, like wildfires, which are increasing deforestation, threatening human and animal lives...

The projects risk creating great burdens on society, as they require huge economic investments and mainly since most of them have been initiated without having environmental impact analyses done, and therefore their medium- and long-term social, cultural, economic and ecological negativities were not properly evaluated or discussed. Environmental justice is one means to combat this, a quest for the legal and social empowerment of the poor and trying to weather the inequities that result from entrenched and unsustainable forms of resource use. Bearing in mind the earthquake risk in North-Western Anatolia, the mega construction projects, must be assessed in a wiser manner, by considering both positive and negative outcomes for long terms.

Since the beginning of Turkey's EU negotiations in 2005, and chapter 27 on Environment and Climate Change was also launched in 2009. However, Turkey's issues are growing, and Turkey needs to undo the negative changes made in the environmental legislation in recent years, as well as make serious and visible progress in areas such as the implementation of horizontal legislation, access to justice, transparency provisions, measures for environmental impact and as to water legislation.

V. Additional Environmental Subjects

The Concept of Just Transition and Its Prospective Reflections in Türkiye

Özge Yıldız Hakkakul[*]

Abstract

Climate change, considered apart from digitalisation and automation to be one of the prospective problems that workers will confront, will affect issues regarding Labour Law. It is argued that the new regulations restricting emissions can affect workers negatively by causing redundancy or a decrease in the labour costs. Therefore, a just transition strategy is crucial to protect workers in cases of job losses during the transition of the economy.

This paper explores the nexus between employment and climate change within the framework of just transition with the perspectives of the United Nations (UN), International Labour Organisation (ILO) and European Union (EU). The prospective reflections of just transition in Türkiye are also examined within the study. It is concluded that Turkish legislation regarding unemployment insurance, training and skills development, pension, occupational health and safety, and collective voice should be reviewed and probably revised.

Keywords: Just transition, Labour Law, Environmental Law, climate change, trade unions

Introduction

The intersection of Labour Law and Environmental Law has not been extensively researched. The intersection is clear, for example, when the trade unions fight not only for controls on harmful substances in the organised workplaces but also for greater controls on the use of those substances in production[1]. In this way, the trade unions and their members/workers are dealing with an issue regarding Environmental Law by having a voice in the implications of the use of hazardous substances on the whole society and they may even change the whole supply chain and political economy ultimately[2]. Some environmental issues and regulations fall also within the

---

* Research Assistant, Department of Labour and Social Security Law, Istanbul University Faculty of Law.

1 Dimitris Stevis, Unions and the Environment: Pathways to Global Labor Environmentalism, Working USA: The Journal of Labor and Society, Vol. 14, June 2011, pp. 155-156; David Doorey, Law of Just Transitions?: Putting Labor Law to Work on Climate Change, Osgoode Legal Studies Research Paper Series 164, 2016, pp. 21-22.

2 Stevis, pp. 155-156.

scope of Labour Law, most obviously occupational health and safety laws controlling exposure to and use of detrimental substances in the workplaces[3].

Since the objectives of Labour Law and Environmental Law are mainly different, the intersection of these disciplines could have been limited to Occupational Health and Safety Law, unless some crucial problems affecting the whole world such as climate change had occurred. Labour Law pursuing to balance the interests of employers and employees aims mainly to protect employees performing work in legal subordination, whereas Environmental Law strives to decrease pollution and damages caused by climate[4]. Nevertheless, climate change and related policies such as adjustments to it or reduction of the greenhouse gas emissions will affect labour markets[5]. It is stated that the effect of the new regulations restricting emissions or requiring green production equipment or techniques on the production system can cause redundancy or a decrease in the labour costs[6]. Indeed, the transition to a carbon-neutral economy will have an impact on every aspect regarding the production of goods, provision of services, consumption, etc.[7]. Climate change considered affecting Labour Law in several ways may bring these two fields together[8] and force scholars of the two fields to work together. This paper will explore the nexus between employment and climate change within the framework of just transition.

3 Doorey, p. 21.

4 Doorey, p. 24.

5 Anabella Rosemberg, Building a Just Transition: The linkages between climate change and employment, International Journal of Labour Research, 2 (2), p. 140, https://www.ilo.org/wcmsp5/groups/public/---ed_dialogue/---actrav/documents/publication/wcms_153352.pdf (accessed 25 July 2023).

6 Doorey, p. 22.

7 Béla Galgóczi, Just Transition Towards Environmentally Sustainable Economies and Societies for All- ILO ACTRAV Policy Brief, 2018, p. 1, https://www.ilo.org/wcmsp5/groups/public/---ed_dialogue/---actrav/documents/publication/wcms_647648.pdf (accessed 25 July 2023).

8 Doorey, p. 24; See also Navraj Singh Ghaleigh, Just Transition for Workers: When Climate Change Met Labour Justice, Edinburgh School of Law Research Paper No. 2019/30, p. 4.

A. The Concept of Just Transition

Occurring as an early trade union demand[9], just transition has become a generally accepted policy tool implemented by international institutions and treaties[10]. The Paris Agreement under the United Nations Framework Convention on Climate Change (UNFCCC) regarded as a landmark in the multilateral climate change, mentions just transition in the Preamble by stating that 'taking into account the imperatives of a just transition of the workforce and the creation of decent work and quality jobs in accordance with nationally defined development priorities'. The Conference of the Parties (COP) in Paris also adopted a work programme[11] comprising 'just transition of the workforce, and the creation of decent work and quality jobs'[12]. Accordingly, a technical paper on a just transition of the workforce, and the creation of decent work and quality jobs was prepared[13]. The Solidarity and Just Transition Silesia Declaration[14] adopted at COP24 in 2018 is regarded as 'a significant milestone, sending a crucial message that workers will not be sacrificed in an effort to cut emissions and mitigate climate change, and that the low-carbon economy will be fair and inclusive'[15]. The Glasgow

9 The first mention of 'just transition' is attributed to the president of Oil, Chemical and Atomic Workers Union Tony Mazzocchi. Mazzocchi proposed a 'superfund for workers', which would provide financial support and an opportunity for higher education for workers displaced on grounds of environmental protection policies. The name of the plan was later changed to 'just transition' because of the complaints of environmentalists regarding the negative connotations of the word 'superfund'. See Galgóczi, p. 1; also "Just Transition" – Just What Is It?- An Analysis of Language, Strategies, and Projects, A Joint Project of Labor Network for Sustainability and Strategic Practice: Grassroots Policy Project, p. 7, https://www.labor4sustainability.org/wp-content/uploads/2016/07/JustTransitionReport-FINAL.pdf (accessed 25 July 2023).

10 Galgóczi, p. 1.

11 See UNFCCC Report of the Conference of the Parties on its twenty-first session, held in Paris from 30 November to 13 December 2015, https://unfccc.int/sites/default/files/resource/docs/2015/cop21/eng/10a02.pdf (accessed 25 July 2023).

12 See Ghaleigh, p. 17.

13 UNFCCC Just Transition of the Workforce, and the Creation of Decent Work and Quality Jobs-Technical Paper, https://unfccc.int/sites/default/files/resource/Just%20transition.pdf (accessed 25 July 2023).

14 See Ghaleigh, p. 19; also Kirsten E. H. Jenkins, Implementing Just Transition after COP24, Climate Strategies, 2019, p. 5, https://cris.brighton.ac.uk/ws/portalfiles/portal/5571030/Implementing_Just_Transition_after_COP24_FINAL.pdf (accessed 25 July 2023).

15 Jenkins, p. 3.

Climate Pact[16] agreed at COP26 in 2021 'emphasises the importance of human rights and collaboration across sectors and all parts of society to deliver effective climate action and a just transition'[17]. Recently, the Sharm el-Sheikh Implementation Plan[18] adopted at COP27 in 2022 stressed social dialogue in the implementation-pathways to just transition.

One definition of just transition in the academic literature[19] is 'the conceptual framework in which the labour movement captures the complexities of the transition towards a low-carbon and climate-resilient economy, highlighting public policy needs and aiming to maximize benefits and minimize hardships for workers and their communities in this transformation'.

The green job[20] strategy is promising and necessary for the future of the humanity and earth. However, trade unions are also aware of the importance of pursuing a just transition strategy that does not leave workers and communities behind[21]. International Trade Union Confederation defines the term as 'a tool the trade union movement shares with the international community, aimed at smoothing the shift towards a more sustainable society and providing hope for the capacity of a green economy to sustain decent jobs and livelihoods for all'[22]. There can be conflicts between the short-term interests of trade union members and the longer-term interests of a broader range of community in environmental protection from polluting substances

---

16 UN, Glasgow Climate Pact, https://unfccc.int/sites/default/files/resource/cop26_auv_2f_cover_decision.pdf (accessed 25 July 2023).

17 See COP26 Presidency Outcomes the Climate Pact, 2021, p. 24, https://ukcop26.org/wp-content/uploads/2021/11/COP26-Presidency-Outcomes-The-Climate-Pact.pdf (accessed 25 July 2023).

18 UN, Sharm el-Sheikh Implementation Plan, https://unfccc.int/documents/624444 (accessed 25 July 2023).

19 Rosemberg, p. 141; see also Ghaleigh, p. 4.

20 'Green jobs are decent jobs that contribute to preserve or restore the environment, be they in traditional sectors such as manufacturing and construction, or in new, emerging green sectors such as renewable energy and energy efficiency.' See ILO, 'What is a green job?', 2016, https://www.ilo.org/global/topics/green-jobs/news/WCMS_220248/lang--en/index.htm (accessed 25 July 2023).

21 For the approach of the trade unions on green jobs and just transition, see Stevis, p. 146 ff. For the criticism of national legal frameworks in Europe (especially United Kingdom) that do not support trade union engagement with environmental issues, see Tonia Novitz, Social Sustainability, Labour and Trade: Forging Connections, in Margherita Pieraccini and Tonia Novitz (eds.), Legal Perspectives on Sustainability, Bristol University Press, 2020, pp. 164-166, 180.

22 International Trade Union Confederation, A Just Transition: A Fair Pathway to Protect the Climate, 2009, https://www.ituc-csi.org/IMG/pdf/01-Depliant-Transition5.pdf (accessed 25 July 2023).

originating from a particular industry over retention of jobs in that industry[23]. Indeed, climate change is regarded as one of the prospective problems that workers will confront apart from digitalisation and automation[24]. It is emphasised that 'just transition means that no worker can be left behind, and new jobs should be created in the regions where jobs will be lost'[25].

B. The Approach of the ILO and the EU

The concept of just transition was first discussed within the framework of the ILO at the 102nd Session of the International Labour Conference in 2013, where a resolution and a set of conclusions concerning sustainable development, decent work and green jobs were adopted[26]. In 2015, following the decision of the Governing Body of the ILO, 'Tripartite Meeting of Experts on Sustainable Development, Decent Work and Green Jobs' was convened, and some guidelines were issued regarding the subject[27]. In the guidelines, the key policy areas to address environmental, economic, and social sustainability are stated as macroeconomic and growth policies, industrial and sectoral policies, enterprise policies, skills development, occupational safety and health, social protection, active labour market policies, rights, social dialogue, and

23 Tonia Novitz, The Paradigm of Sustainability in a European Social Context: Collective Participation in Protection of Future Interests?, The International Journal of Comparative Labour Law and Industrial Relations, 31 (3), 2015, p. 247; Novitz, Social Sustainability, p. 164.

24 Luca Visentini, 'Now independence goes together with no social protection'- Interview by Beatriz Rios, Euractiv Event Report: How to Protect Workers' Rights in a Volatile Labour Market?, 2018, p. 6, https://en.euractiv.eu/wp-content/uploads/sites/2/special-report/EURACTIV-Event-Report-How-to-protect-workers-rights-in-a-volatile-labour-market.pdf (accessed 25 July 2023).

25 Luc Triangle, The World(s) of Work in Transition- Conference Report , ETUI-ETUC Conference Brussels 27-29 June 2018, p. 32, https://www.etui.org/Publications2/Conference-reports/The-world-s-of-work-in-transition (accessed 25 July 2023).

26 ILO, Resolution and conclusions concerning sustainable development, decent work and green jobs, International Labour Conference, 102nd Session, 2013, https://www.ilo.org/wcmsp5/groups/public/---ed_norm/---relconf/documents/meetingdocument/wcms_223785.pdf (accessed 25 July 2023).

27 For the process, see ILO, Guidelines for a just transition towards environmentally sustainable economies and societies for all, 2015, p. 3, https://www.ilo.org/wcmsp5/groups/public/---ed_emp/---emp_ent/documents/publication/wcms_432859.pdf (accessed 25 July 2023).

tripartism[28]. The ILO activity in this area is evaluated to grow exponentially with the adoption of the guidelines[29].

In 2023, the International Labour Office prepared a report[30] presenting the first international definition of the concept of just transition[31]. According to this definition, 'a just transition means promoting a green economy in a way that is as fair and inclusive as possible to everyone concerned –workers, enterprises and communities– by creating decent work opportunities and leaving no one behind'[32].

The EU shall work for the sustainable development of Europe based on balanced economic growth and price stability, a highly competitive social market economy, aiming at full employment and social progress, and a high level of protection and improvement of the quality of the environment as stated in Article 3 (3) of the Treaty on European Union. The protection of the environment and sustainable development are regarded as the general objectives of EU law[33]. The Treaty of Maastricht, the Amsterdam Treaty and the Lisbon Treaty reflect this approach, and the effective support of the European Court of Justice on the issue should not be ignored[34].

In December 2019, the European Commission (EC) issued The European Green Deal[35], a set of policies with the aim of making the EU climate neutral by 2050. The Commission proposed the European Climate Law[36]

---

28 ILO, Guidelines, p. 7.

29 Novitz, Social Sustainability, p. 170.

30 ILO, ILC.111/Report VI, Achieving a just transition towards environmentally sustainable economies and societies for all, International Labour Conference, 111th Session, 2023, https://www.ilo.org/wcmsp5/groups/public/---ed_norm/---relconf/documents/meetingdocument/wcms_876568.pdf (accessed 25 July 2023).

31 See ILO, Green jobs, green economy, just transition and related concepts: A review of definitions developed through intergovernmental processes and international organizations 2023, p. 29, https://www.ilo.org/wcmsp5/groups/public/---ed_emp/---emp_ent/documents/publication/wcms_883704.pdf (accessed 25 July 2023).

32 ILO, Report VI, p. 12.

33 Beate Sjåfjell, The Very Basis of Our Existence: Labour and the Neglected Environmental Dimension of Sustainable Development, 2009, p. 4, http://ssrn.com/abstract=1517393 (accessed 25 July 2023).

34 See Sjåfjell, p. 5 ff.

35 EC, The European Green Deal, https://eur-lex.europa.eu/resource.html?uri=cellar:b828d165-1c22-11ea-8c1f-01aa75ed71a1.0002.02/DOC_1&format=PDF (accessed 25 July 2023).

36 Regulation (EU) 2021/1119 of The European Parliament and of the Council of 30 June 2021 establishing the framework for achieving climate neutrality and amending Regulations (EC) No 401/2009 and (EU) 2018/1999 ('European Climate Law'), https:/

to make this objective legally binding[37]. The Deal covering all sectors of the economy, 'outlines investments needed and financing tools available, and explains how to ensure a just and inclusive transition'[38]. The Commission also proposed a 'Just Transition Mechanism', 'a key tool to ensure that the transition towards a climate-neutral economy happens in a fair way, leaving no one behind'[39].

An example of a national approach to the issue in Europe is provided from Norway[40]. The Basic Agreement for Civil Service[41] concluded between the Norwegian Confederation of Trade Unions and the Confederation of Norwegian Enterprise includes an article falling under the provision of objectives stating that 'environmental and climate considerations are to be a part of the cooperation and co-determination between the parties, with the aim of sustainable development'[42]. This is regarded as an important 'first step', indicating that other kinds of objectives than the ones addressing traditional Labour Law issues have been introduced into the field of collective agreements[43]. Some collective agreements in Canada also include clauses regarding the issue, such as green training and education, workplace environmental committees, green procurement, workforce adjustment, and social responsibility[44].

A new institutional development regarding just transition is the establishment of 'Just Transition Commissions' at government level. The examples

/eur-lex.europa.eu/legal-content/EN/TXT/PDF/?uri=CELEX:32021R1119&from=EN (accessed 25 July 2023).

37 See EC, Climate Action and the Green Deal, https://ec.europa.eu/info/strategy/priorities-2019-2024/european-green-deal/climate-action-and-green-deal_en (accessed 25 July 2023).

38 See The EU Switch to Green Flagship Initiative, The EU Green Deal– a roadmap to sustainable economies, https://www.switchtogreen.eu/the-eu-green-deal-promoting-a-green-notable-circular-economy (accessed 25 July 2023).

39 EC, The Just Transition Mechanism: making sure no one is left behind, https://ec.europa.eu/info/strategy/priorities-2019-2024/european-green-deal/finance-and-green-deal/just-transition-mechanism_en (accessed 25 July 2023).

40 See Sjåfjell, p. 17

41 Basic agreements in Norway are regarded as one form of (national level) collective agreements in the general legal sense, see Sjåfjell, p. 17, fn. 75.

42 Sjåfjell, p. 17.

43 Sjåfjell, pp. 17-18.

44 See Green Agreements Library, https://www.zotero.org/green_agreements/items/4RD8VSP9/library (accessed 25 July 2023).

are given from Scotland and Spain[45]. The key roles of the Just Transition Commission of Scotland[46] are stated as 'to support the production and monitoring of key just transition plans, providing expert advice on their development', whereas in Spain a pact between the social partners and the Spanish government provides for €250 million to be invested in mining communities, as the country's coal mines are shut down soon[47].

C. *Labour Law Issues Regarding Just Transition and Turkish Law*

Türkiye has been endeavouring to adopt environmental regulations and standards acknowledged by the EU[48]. Some regulations adopted formerly, for instance[49], are the Regulation on the Control of Industrial Air Pollution and Zero Waste Regulation. The Ministry of Environment, Urbanisation and Climate Change[50] also announced a draft regulation called the Integrated Pollution Prevention and Control Regulation and issued the Regulation on the Export and Import of Some Hazardous Chemicals in January 2023. Türkiye has also made some modifications regarding the legislation to reduce green gas emissions and increase the use of clean and renewable energy resources in several fields, such as manufacturing, heating, waste,

---

45 See Ghaleigh, pp. 30-32. For the Canadian commission outside Europe, see Task Force: Just Transition for Canadian Coal Power Workers and Communities, https://www.canada.ca/en/environment-climate-change/services/climate-change/task-force-just-transition.html (accessed 25 July 2023). On the other hand, the Canadian government is severely criticised for providing support to the Canadian mining companies, which cause serious environmental harm in Latin America. See The Impact of Canadian Mining in Latin America and Canada's responsibility: Executive Summary of the Report submitted to the Inter-American Commission on Human Rights, Working Group on Mining and Human Rights in Latin America, pp. 10, 25, https://www.dplf.org/sites/default/files/report_canadian_mining_executive_summary.pdf (accessed 25 July 2023).

46 Scottish Government, Just Transition Commission, https://www.gov.scot/groups/just-transition-commission/ (accessed 25 July 2023).

47 ETUC, 'Spain guarantees a just transition for miners', https://www.etuc.org/en/spain-guarantees-just-transition-miners (accessed 25 July 2023).

48 For more information, see Ümit Hergüner/Deniz Tuncel/Zeynep Tor, Turkey, The Environment and Climate Change Law Review, Ed. Theodore L Garrett, Law Business Research, 2019, p. 184 ff. https://herguner.av.tr/wp-content/uploads/2019/02/LBR-The-Environment-and-Climate-Change-Law-Review.pdf (accessed 25 July 2023).

49 See Hergüner/Tuncel/Tor, p. 189.

50 The phrase 'Climate Change' has been added to the name of the Ministry in October 2021.

and transport[51]. Recently, in July 2021, the Ministry of Trade intending to comply with the European Green Deal prepared The Green Deal Action Plan, 'a roadmap aiming to support green transformation in all relevant policy areas'[52].

The just transition, aiming to protect and create good jobs, will necessarily involve lay-offs and requirements for new labour force skills and retraining[53]. In this regard, rules relating to unemployment insurance, pension, and freedom of association will have greater importance[54]. Turkish Labour Law will hereby be examined to evaluate whether current Turkish legislation provides adequate legal solutions to the prospective legal issues regarding just transition.

1. Unemployment Insurance

Considering the possible lay-offs, unemployment insurance laws will play a significant role in the process of the transition of the economy[55]. The Canadian Labour Congress, (the largest labour organisation in Canada) active in developing the concept of just transitions[56], emphasises the importance of effective unemployment insurance as a necessary foundation for an effective just transition programme and states that 'An effective unemployment insurance program is one which provides an adequate degree of income replacement, has reasonable qualifying requirements, provides for a benefit period sufficient to support most adjustment needs and is sufficiently flexible to permit recipients to engage in activities relevant to employment adjustment while receiving benefits'[57].

In Türkiye, the Unemployment Insurance Act No. 4447 adopted the principle of compulsory insurance, which enables the employees to be included

51 See Hergüner/Tuncel/Tor, p. 192.
52 See E. Benan Arseven/C. Hazal Baydar, Turkey Adopts Action Plan To Comply With European Green Deal, 2021, https://www.mondaq.com/turkey/climate-change/1106412/turkey-adopts-action-plan-to-comply-with-european-green-deal (accessed 25 July 2023). See also Republic of Turkey Climate Change Strategy 2010-2023, https://webdosya.csb.gov.tr/db/iklim/editordosya/iklim_degisikligi_stratejisi_EN(2).pdf (accessed 25 July 2023).
53 Doorey, p. 41, 43.
54 See Doorey, p. 43.
55 Doorey, p. 43.
56 See Doorey, p. 34, fn. 124.
57 See Doorey, p. 43, fn. 148.

within the scope of the insurance automatically once they start working under the employment contract[58]. In order to be eligible for unemployment benefit, it is required to have work insured and paid insurance premium for a minimum of 600 days in the last three years before the termination of the employment contract. The minimum duration to receive unemployment benefit is 180 days, whereas the maximum duration is 300 days (Art. 50).

Because of the prospective importance of the unemployment insurance regarding just transition, some amendments on the qualifying requirements and the degree of income support as well as the benefit period might be necessary in Turkish Law. Indeed, some amendments have already been made regarding the qualifying requirements. Previously, it was required to work 'continuously' by paying the insurance premium in the last 120 days before the termination of the employment contract to be entitled to unemployment benefit.This requirement drew criticism owing to its restrictive impact on the eligibility for unemployment benefit[59]. Now it is sufficient to be subject to the employment contract in the last 120 days before the termination of the contract to be entitled to unemployment benefit (in addition to a minimum of 600 days of working and premium paying requirement in the last three years). Such amendments may be crucial in the process of just transition, enabling the unemployed to receive unemployment benefit effectively for the duration of unemployment.

2. Training and Skills Development

Training and skills development are important means to prevent unemployment and create new jobs[60]. The workers should be trained for green jobs to have more opportunities in the labour market. In this context, educational leave for workers might be necessary to acquire new skills[61].

Under the Act No. 4447, studies shall be conducted in order to find a job for the insured unemployed, which is convenient for their profession with similar wage and working conditions[62]. Turkish Employment Agency entitled

58 A. Can Tuncay/Ömer Ekmekçi, Sosyal Güvenlik Hukuku Dersleri, Beta, 2021, p. 696; Tankut Centel, Turkish Social Law, Springer, 2021, pp. 220-221.

59 Tuncay/Ekmekçi, p. 709.

60 See Doorey, p. 46.

61 Rosemberg, p. 144; see also Technical Paper, p. 55.

62 See Centel, Social Law, p. 220.

to provide these kinds of services regarding unemployment insurance (Art. 46) is also in charge of providing the insured unemployed with the services of vocational training and skills development. Furthermore, it is prescribed by the Act that the Agency shall organise courses and programmes for the insured unemployed within the scope of active labour force services (Art. 48). It should be stated that social protection schemes, including active labour market policies, are regarded as key to ensure justice during the transition[63].

New skills development courses and programmes will be needed to provide the unemployed with assistance to find new and probably green jobs in the just transition process. Therefore, the quantity of training should be increased, and their content should be updated.

3. Pension

Pension laws might also play an important role in the phase of just transition by providing income security to older workers confronting the loss of their jobs[64]. Early retirement is defined as the retirement enabling workers to receive a pension before the chronological age prescribed by laws because of some promotive or drastic conditions. It is based on the principle of voluntariness and is used as a means of employment policy in many countries[65].

Under the Social Insurances and General Health Insurance Act No. 5510, the condition of age prescribed to receive a pension will increase gradually and will be 65 in 2048 both for women and men. When it comes to just transition, the importance of early retirement options increases. Therefore, such regulations might be adopted to minimise the damage of job losses.

4. Occupational Health and Safety

The importance of Occupational Health and Safety Law as the nexus of Labour Law and Environmental Law is obvious. In the process of just transition, occupational health and safety will play a more critical role

63 Rosemberg, p. 144; see also Technical Paper, p. 25.
64 Doorey, p. 47.
65 Tuncay/Ekmekçi, p. 526.

targeting unsafe workplaces, including old high carbon workplaces and new greener workplaces[66].

In Turkish Law, apart from the regulations, the main legal source to regulate the field is the Occupational Health and Safety Act No. 6331. Despite the connection with Environmental Law, comprehensive provisions regarding the issue do not fall within the scope of the Act. In the process of just transition, relevant provisions might be necessary.

In 2019, The Regulation on Prevention of Major Industrial Accidents and Reduction of Their Effects was adopted within the framework of conformity with the legislation of the EU, taking into consideration the Directive 2012/18/EU on the control of major-accident hazards involving dangerous substances. This can be regarded as an essential step for the establishment of a connection between Labour Law and Environmental Law.

5. Collective Voice

In the literature[67], freedom of association and the laws used to instantiate it are regarded as crucial since Just Transition Law is stated to 'promote collective voice and participation by civil society in the setting of transitional goals.' The examples are given regarding workplace closures, relocations, economic transitions, and it is indicated that participation and consultation processes regarding the issues might embrace environmental organisations, concerned citizens, community groups, etc. apart from the trade unions[68]. Therefore, regulations regarding notice and consultation requirements in cases of workplace closures or transitions and transfers of undertakings will be of great importance in the process of just transition[69].

In Turkish Law, transfer of undertakings is mainly regulated in Article 6 of the Labour Act No. 4857. Under the Article, the consents of the employees are unnecessary to carry out transfer of undertakings. The employees have the right to objection merely when transfer of undertakings takes place through the merger, division, and conversion of the commercial companies under the

66 Doorey, p. 47.
67 Doorey, p. 43; see also Ghaleigh, p. 32.
68 Doorey, p. 43.
69 See Doorey, p. 46.

Turkish Act of Commerce No. 6102[70]. That the information and consultation obligations imposed on the transferor and transferee under Article 7 of the Council Directive 2001/23/EC are not regulated in Article 6 of the Labour Act No. 4857 has drawn criticism[71].

The obligation of the employer to inform the trade union representatives is prescribed in Article 29 of the Labour Act No. 4857 regarding collective lay-off[72]. In the notice given by the employer, the trade union representatives, apart from the provincial directorate and Turkish Employment Agency, will be informed about the reasons of the collective lay-off, the number and groups of the employees who will be affected by the lay-off and period when the procedures regarding the lay-off will be carried out. Furthermore, the employer is obliged to negotiate with the trade union representatives on the lay-off. Nevertheless, the employer is not obliged to inform the trade union representatives in case of the workplace closure. The employer is only obliged to inform the provincial directorate and Turkish Employment Agency in that case.

As stated above, the obligation of the employer regarding information and consultation is limited under Turkish Law. However, information and consultation procedures will become crucial in the phase of just transition. Therefore, regulations on the issue should be reviewed and probably revised in conformity with the current developments.

Conclusion

In a country with a high rate of unemployment, the transition to a 'greener economy' because of climate change may be regarded as another reason for unemployment. The capacity of developing countries to deliver a just transition programme is deemed to be modest[73]. Providing workers with new jobs through training and skills development programmes seems thus fundamental for Türkiye.

70 See Sarper Süzek, İş Hukuku, Beta, 2021, pp. 204, 213-216; Tankut Centel, Introduction to Turkish Labour Law, Springer, 2017, pp. 55-57; Ömer Ekmekçi/Esra Yiğit, Bireysel İş Hukuku, Onikilevha, 2022, pp. 240-248.

71 Süzek, p. 204; Gülsevil Alpagut, İşyerinin Devri ve İş Sözleşmesini Fesih Hakkı, Beta, 2010, p. 186.

72 See Centel, Labour Law, pp. 183-184.

73 Rosemberg, p. 148.

Trade unions regarded as crucial to raising awareness of just transition among the workers will play a major role in the phase of the transition. Information and consultation procedures which are limited in Türkiye should be improved, enabling the trade unions to protect the rights of their members more effectively. It is also suggested that solutions should be put forward for the workers affected by the job losses because of ecological transitions to ensure acceptance of the transition[74].

The provisions regarding environmental issues in the Norwegian and Canadian collective agreements are inspiring. However, such provisions may seem unfamiliar to Turkish trade unions striving to acquire authorisation to conclude collective agreements in the workplaces of their members. Once they come through the hard procedure prescribed by the Act on Trade Unions and Collective Labour Agreement No. 6356, they aim to protect the rights of their members regarding traditional Labour Law issues, such as wages and working conditions to maintain their support for the next collective agreement authorisation process. Therefore, simplification of the regulations regarding the authorisation to conclude a collective agreement is crucial to just transition apart from other issues such as collective bargaining.

74 Triangle, pp. 32-33.

New Development and Future Prospects of Turkey's Environmental Law Policy

*Ayşe Nur Tütüncü**

Abstract

The paper discusses how the Turkish legislation responds to issues such as water use, water rights, environmental sustainability, waste management, and climate change, by considering the existing regulations in the environmental field in Turkey, general international law and the *European Union acquis* in this context and a general evaluation of future prospects is carried out.
Keywords: Environment; Turkey; European Union; Accession; Protection.

I. New Developments in Environmental Law in Turkey: General Assessment

A. Accession Procedure to the European Union

Let's start with remembering the due process to become a member of the European Union (EU)? Accession to EU is not automatic, since it requires an adequate preparation process for the applicant country and on the EU's capacity to integrate the new member.

The accession process involves compliance with the accession criteria, including adoption and implementation of the *Acquis*. These rules are divided into 35 different policy fields (chapters), such as environment, transport, energy, etc., each of which is negotiated separately. Throughout the negotiations, the Commission monitors the candidate's progress in applying EU legislation and meeting its other commitments, including any standard requirements.

The conditions and date of accession, any transition periods required and the adjustments to the Treaties on which the Union is founded must be agreed in the form of an accession treaty between the candidate country and the Member States. To give due form to the accession, this treaty is signed and ratified by all the Member States and the candidate country in accordance with their own constitutional rules. The European Parliament gives its consent.

---

* Head of Department of Public International Law, Faculty of Law, University of Istanbul.

B. Historical Background of Turkey's Accession Process

Turkey's involvement with European integration dates to 1959 and includes the Ankara Association Agreement (1963) for the progressive establishment of the Customs Union. In 1987, Turkey applied to join what was then the European Economic Community, and in 1997 it was declared eligible to join the EU. Turkey's accession would be different from previous enlargements because of the combined impact of Turkey's population, size, geographical location, economic and security concerns and military potential, as well as cultural and religious characteristics. Having opened EU accession talks in 2005, eight chapters have been frozen since 2006 due to Ankara's refusal to open its borders to the Greek part of Cyprus, which is a member of the EU. As to environmental points, Turkey and the European Union opened the environment chapter of negotiations.[1]

As a major emerging economy and a member of NATO and the G20, Turkey is recognised as an active regional foreign policy player, with a strategic location, and this was important for EU's energy security. The EU is therefore committed to intensify the political dialogue with Turkey on foreign policy issues of mutual interest.

C. Environmental Protection in Turkey

1. The Legal and Institutional Structure

The legal and administrative background of environmental protection is not very old in Turkey. In 1982, the right to environment was enshrined in the Constitution.[2] In 1983, the Environmental Act was promulgated.[3] The Environmental Act endorsed many additional measures. The aim of the Act was not limited to prevent and eliminate environmental pollution, but also to promote means that would allow the management of natural resources and the land. According to the basic principles that govern the application of the Environmental Act, as stated in the Constitution, citizens as well as the

1 William Chislett, Turkey's 10 Years of EU Accession Negotiations: No End in Sight, Elcano Royal Institute, Working Paper 14/2015 - 5/10/2015, p.5.

2 Article 56 reads: 'Everybody is entitled to live in a healthy and balanced environment, to preserve the healthiness of the environment and to prevent environmental pollution'.

3 Act no. 2872, 11 August 1983, Official Gazette, no. 18132. (Amended in 1984, 1986, 1988, and 1998, 2006).

state bear responsibility for the protection of the environment. It is also stated in the Act that in all economic activities every measure should be taken to minimise pollution.

In line with the Environment Act, several regulations have been issued since 1983: (*The following dates show their lastly amended status*)

- Air Quality Control Regulation (2008)
- Water Pollution Control Regulation (2004) lastly amended 2022
- Regulation on Environmental Noise Control (2022)
- Regulation on Waste Management (2015)
- Regulation on Environmental Impact Assessment (2022)
- Regulation on Control of Medical Waste (2017)
- Control of Toxic Chemical Substances and Products Regulation (1993) lastly amended 2001: Its name has been changed to "Hazardous Chemicals Regulation"
- Control of Hazardous Wastes Regulation (2005) lastly amended 2013 and Repealed by Regulation on Waste Management (2015)

Complementary to the Environmental Act and its regulations, other laws and international conventions governing the protection of the environment have been put into force.Within the framework of sustainable development, Turkey today faces the challenge of balancing economic growth with environmental progress. Several institutional and legislative elements of environmental reform have been put on the agenda as part of the environmental planning in the country. This will require strengthened environmental efforts and cooperation between the central government, municipalities and the private sector, which will create the necessary environmental infrastructure in urban and industrial areas. In following years, Turkey found and will find ways to implement environmental policies and to strengthen enforcement capabilities; to invest for the environmental infrastructure, to provide public participation and to increase public awareness regarding environmental problems public participation and increase public awareness of environmental problems; to integrate environmental concerns into economic decisions; all of which would be made to comply with the country's international commitments; and to complete harmonisation requirements harmonisation with EU standards. A Statutory Decree No. 443 established the Ministry of Environment in 1991[4] On 8 May 2003, the Ministry of Environment was

4 21 August 1991, Official Gazette, no. 20967: The Special Directorate of Environmental Protection Institution was connected to the Ministry of Environment.

merged with the Ministry of Forestry with the Law No.4856[5]. The new ministry was named as "The Ministry of Environment and Forestry. Lastly the Ministry was renamed to the current Ministry of Environment and Urban Planning in 2011[6].

For more than a decade, shortly the Ministry of Environment displayed a commendable activism. According to Article 2 of the Statutory Decree no. 636, the duties and responsibilities of the Ministry are drafting legislations concerning environment and urbanization and auditing their implementation, making policies to prevent pollution and determining standards for the protection of the environment, audit and impact assessment of facilities which may create pollution by leaving waste to receiving environment, making policies regarding global climate change, making urbanization policies and auditing their implementation. However, these advances are not enough to address the increased pressures from unregulated industrialization and unplanned urban growth.

2. Factors Affecting the Formation of Environmental Law in Turkey

In the formation and development of environmental policies, there are three major factors having stimulated the government in devising policies and enacting laws. The first is the European Union. The second is the integration of environmental policies with economic and political activities of major international organizations. And the third factor is that some NGOs and individuals that gathered together the bureaucratic support and formed various national environmental policies alone.

3. The European Union Factor

In this respect of Turkey's relations with the EU represents a great importance, as Turkey would have to adopt or change national laws, rules and procedures so that the requirements of the EU are fully incorporated into national legislation; provide the institutions and budgets needed to carry out these laws and regulations; provide the controls and penalties to ensure that the law is being complied with. In this context, Turkey is obliged to consider the provisions of the Customs Union Agreement and

5 8 May 2003, Official Gazette, no. 25102.
6 8 June 2011, Official Gazette, no. 27958 (bis).

should harmonise its legislation with the *Acquis.* To this end, Turkey has undertaken some important commitments, such as to adopt legislations, to reach agreements, and to apply relevant provisions whereas the latter is a political commitment to be made on the way to full membership. Let us now discuss these issues separately[7]. After the entry into force of the Decision on the Customs Union, it has become compulsory for Turkey to initiate a program for the harmonization of the EC environmental law. The Decision 1/95 on the Customs Union is concerned entirely with the free movement of goods and related issues. After the entry into force of the Decision on the Customs Union, it has become compulsory for Turkey to initiate a program for the harmonization of its own legislation to the EC environmental law. Otherwise, free movement provisions work one-sided. For example, if genetically modified food is not clearly distinguished and marked, and if custom officers do not inspect whether they are exported in the light of CITES provision[8], then this will amount to breach of EC law. The EU Commission may ban Turkish goods for their failure in EC norms. If Turkish goods are not allowed to carry ISO 9000, ISO 14000 and CE signs, the provisions of the Custom Union will not in favour of Turkey. Another factor that forces Turkey to consider the prerequisites of EU environmental law is the obligation to incorporate the *Acquis,* which has two types: A and B categories. From the genesis of the EC Law up until the present time, the Union's environmental policy has been composed of two kinds of measures by which a state intending to join the Community should abide: first (A), Community's own legislation (e.g. regulations and directives), and second (B) the treaties to which the Community is party[9].The EU is a noticeable

7 See similar view in DİNÇER, M., **Çevre Gönüllü Kuruluşları** [Environmental NGOs], The Environment Foundation of Turkey, Ankara, 1996, p.96; SÜMER ÇAKIR Gülizar, "Türkiye'de Çevre Bilincinin Gelişimine Katkıları Bakımından Türkiye Çevre Vakfı [Turkish Environmental Foundation from the Perspective of Its Contributions to the Development of Level of Environmental Consciousness in Turkey], Süleyman Demirel Üniversitesi İktisadi İdari Bilimler Fakültesi Dergisi, 2007, V.12, No.2, p.279.

8 CITES (the Convention on International Trade in Endangered Species of Wild Fauna and Flora) is an international agreement between governments. Its aim is to ensure that international trade in specimens of wild animals and plants does not threaten their survival. Turkey has been a Party to the CITES since 1996.

9 Although there was no clear reference to the protection of the environment in the 1957 Rome Treaty, EC environmental law has developed from 1957 onwards by utilizing two indirect provisions of the EEC Treaty: Article 100 and 235. The Single European Act of 1987 introduced a new 'Environment Title', which provided the first legal basis for a common environment policy with the aims of preserving the quality of the

figure in international environmental relations. The EU, together with the Member States, has become party to numerous international environmental agreements. International treaties to which the Community is party are an integral part of the Community's legal system and those such agreements include the so-called mixed agreements to which both the Community and the Member States are parties. Regarding the case when the EU is party to an international treaty, the EU can fulfil its obligation under the treaty either by Community measures (e.g. regulations and directives) or by satisfying itself that all Member States have adopted the measures necessary to ensure their fulfilment, or by taking a position between halfway[10]. Another problem is that low environmental standards in Turkey will lead to one-sided competition in favour of Turkey, where national companies would not have to pay for anti-pollution equipment and would be free to impose the costs of pollution on the public.[11] Being in breach of competition rules will result as Turkey's infringement of EC legislation. To prevent this, ever since the beginning of the 1960s, Turkey attempted to harmonize its national legislation with that of the EU. Turkey's main challenges[12] in the environmental field are apart

environment, protecting human health, environment and ensuring a rational use of natural resources. Subsequent Treaty revisions strengthened Europe's commitment to environmental protection and the role of the European Parliament in its development. The Treaty of Maastricht (1993) made the environment an official EU policy area, introduced the co-decision procedure and to integrate environmental protection into all EU sectorial policies with a view to promoting sustainable management development. 'Combating climate change' became a specific goal with the Lisbon Treaty (2009) as did sustainable development in relations with third countries. A new legal personality enabled the EU to conclude international agreements. The area of EU environmental law has expanded exponentially and is the subject of its own dedicated literature. For a brief introduction on the part of the law of the European Union that refers to the protection of the environment for further discussion of EU environmental law, see: DOUMA, Wybe Th., "*European Environmental Law after Lisbon: an introduction*", T.M.C. Asser Institute-European Environment Law, Introduction, http://www.asser.nl/eel/dossiers/ eel-introduction/european-environmental-law-after-lisbon-an-introduction/ (20.08.2017). Also, see VEDDER, Hans, "The Treaty of Lisbon and European Environmental Policy", Social Science Research Network, for electronic copy see: http://ssrn.com/abstract=1310190 (20.08.2017). SANDS, P., Principles of International Environmental Law, Third edition, Cambridge University Press 2012.

10 LANG, T. J., "*Implications of the European Community's Environmental Policy for Turkey*", European Law Review, 13(6), 1988, 404.,

11 Id. at p.409.

12 Some of the main challenges in the environmental sector are: improving and extending water supply networks; improving and extending wastewater collection and treatment plants; ensuring that air emissions from large combustion plants are reduced; improving air quality in many urban centres; ensuring that dangerous substances released from

from further transposition of the Community *Acquis*, implementation related matters such as, administrative capacity, monitoring and enforcement of environmental legislation.

4. Relations with International Organizations

Turkey has involved dynamically in the activities of many well-known regional or global intergovernmental organizations[13]. Turkey, as a member of these organizations, is required to take part in this greening process. Turkey should corollary take part in CoE's activities so that the low environmental profile should not hamper Turkey's full EU membership process. An important motivating factor to be in line with environmental policies of international organizations is the chance of receiving financial assistance for the projects to be carried out in Turkey. In this context, the World Bank, UNDP, the EU, Global Environment Facility (GEF), the Islamic Development Bank and the IMF by using their funds forced to Turkey to ratify lots of conventions related to environment.

5. The Influence of NGO`s in the Formation of National Policies

Environmental protection activities mostly seen in the last decade have led to the development of many national and regional environmental non-governmental institutions in Turkey. The main national NGOs, which are actively involved in many environmental problems to create public awareness consciousness and to encourage public participation, aim to propose efficient solutions providing a basis as a pressure group on the decision-making process. The rise of a new genre of activist NGOs with a range of interest areas,

installations are controlled and risks of accidents are minimized; collecting, treating and disposing of waste from households, industry and hospitals; cleaning up contaminated land and rivers where water quality is unacceptable; protecting ecosystems, habitats and species from economic and environmental pressures; reducing emissions of pollutants from economic sectors; and ratifying the Aarhus Convention and implementing its provisions.

13 E.g. on November 1995, Turkey was elected to membership on the Governing Council of UNEP for the period of 1996-2000. It is apt to note that Turkey is a member of the Council of Europe, NATO, WTO, OSCE, the Black Sea Economic Cooperation (BSEC), and the Economic Cooperation Organization (ECO). As a founding member of the UN, Turkey participates in the activities of UN subsidiary bodies and specialized agencies such as UNCTAD, UNCHE, UNCED, UNEP, UNDP, UNECE, UNESCO, IMO, FAO, IAEA, WHO, ICAO, IBRD, IMF, ILO.

-one hopes- is to form a long-term national environmental policy based on scientific data and real political interest. For example, the Society for the Protection of Natural Environment, TEMA and the Environment Foundation of Turkey are involved in activities ranging from the monitoring of waterfowl and the preservation of biodiversity to the formation of public opinion.

6. Contemporary Practice of Turkey Relating to International Environmental Law

Turkish authorities started signing and ratifying a few treaties since the beginning of the difficult journey for Europe. Turkey's interest in participating in international conservation treaties goes back to the early 1960s. It was only after the early 1970s that Turkish authorities approached environmental issues as a long-term state policy. Turkey has signed and ratified many of important international conventions, agreements and protocols on fauna and flora, cultural property, regional seas, the atmosphere, the ozone layer, waste management. Recent years marked the success of bilateral negotiations on cooperation on environmental protection. Turkey has been actively involved in international cooperation efforts to address environmental problems that are complex and mostly related to socio-economic issues. Turkey, considering its national interests and socio-economic conditions, has become party to many conventions both at the global and regional level, with a view to contribute the solution of environmental problems and they have become part of the Turkish positive law. The environment legislation covers horizontal issues (Environmental Impact Assessment (EIA), access to environmental information), as well as the arrangements regarding the air quality, water quality, waste management, nature protection, industrial pollution control, chemicals, noise and climate change. Furthermore, several international conventions, as well, are included by the Turkish environmental *Acquis*. Turkey acceded early treaties that refer, in varying degrees, regarding waste management, namely, the OECD Convention on Third Party Liability in the Field of Nuclear Energy[14], Treaty Banning Nuclear Weapon Tests in the Atmosphere, in Outer Space and Under Water Treaty on the Prohibition of the Emplacement of Nuclear Weapons and Other Weapons

14 29 January 1960, Protocol Amending the Treaty (28 January 1964): Official Gazette, 13 June 1967,

of Mass Destruction on the Seabed and Ocean Floor and in the Subsoil Thereof[15], Convention on the Prohibition of the Development, Production and Stockpiling of Bacteriological (Biological) and Toxic Weapons, and on Their Destruction, and the Convention on Early Notification of Nuclear Accidents[16]. Some of the other more recent waste management conventions are the Basel Convention on the Control of Transboundary Movements of Hazardous Wastes and their Disposal, which became effective for Turkey on 20 September 1994[17], Nuclear Safety Convention[18] and lastly the International Convention on Oil Pollution Preparedness, Response and Cooperation[19]. In the matter of the atmospheric pollution, Turkey refused to sign for years the UN Framework Convention on Climate Change (UNFCC) and its Kyoto Protocol related with the atmospheric pollution. The Climate Change Convention and Protocol was finally ratified[20]. UNFCC and Kyoto Protocol to the UN Framework Convention on Climate Change contain provisions regarding procedural rights. As these instruments are part of the *Acquis*, Turkey should do its best to comply with their provisions. Thus Turkey also ratified the Paris Agreement at the 76th General Assembly of the United Nations on September 21, 2021. announcing with 2053 net zero emissions target.In addition, our Certificate of Ratification and National Statement regarding the Paris Agreement were deposited on 11 October 2021 with the United Nations Secretary-General, who is the Depositary of the Agreement. The 30-day depository period of the Agreement expired on 10 November and Turkey became a party to the Paris Agreement on this date.[21] To determine its greenhouse gas emissions, an obvious and self-evident reporting mechanism should be developed. Aside from the climate change problem, Turkey is party to other conventions on the atmospheric pollution. One of the major hazards that will affect the future generations is air pollution. Air pollution in the world has reached a risky level for human life, particularly due to the rapid industrial development. In recognition of this fact, the countries over the world entered several international conventions, the first of which was concluded in 1979, to prevent air pollution. Turkey has become party to

15 Official Gazette, 13 May 1965.
16 Official Gazette, 3 September 1990.
17 Official Gazette, 15 May 1994. Turkey ratified the amendments to the Convention (Articles 4A and 7) bis, in 2003 (2003/5909 CMR, Official, Gazette, 28 July 2003).
18 Official Gazette, 14 January 1995.
19 Official Gazette, 18 September 2003.
20 Official Gazette, 18 December 2003. Official Gazette, 13 May 2009.
21 Official Gazette, 7 October 2021.

some of these conventions and made them an integral part of its domestic law in accordance with the Article 90 of its Constitution, which states that " International treaties duly put into effect have the force of law.The first convention Turkey became party in this regard was the 1979 Geneva Convention on Long-Range Transboundary Air Pollution (LRTAP)[22], and its protocols except the 1984 Protocol on Long-Term Financing of the Co-operative Programme for Monitoring and Evaluation of the Long-Range Transmission of Air Pollutants in Europe were not ratified[23]. To comply with its provisions, in 2008, the Assessment and Management of Air Quality Regulation was promulgated[24]. It was followed by the Vienna Convention for the Protection of Ozone Layer[25] and The Montreal Convention[26]. In the case of the Ozone Depletion, Turkey ratified the Vienna Convention for the Protection of the Ozone Layer and the Montreal Protocol on Substances that Deplete the Ozone Layer in 1990[27]. On 25 July 1999, a regulation was enacted with a view to implementing the Convention[28]. Regarding nature protection, some environmental treaties, ratified by Turkey also contain provisions regarding procedural rights. These treaties are Convention on Biological Diversity[29], Cartagena Protocol on Biosafety to the Biological Diversity[30]. Due to dangerous and noxious substances, land-based pollution and international maritime traffic, the pollution of the regional seas is a major concern. The main legislation dealing with the pollution of the Turkish seas are the Environmental Act of 1983, the Ports Act 1941[31], the Sea Products Act of 1971[32] and the Coastal Act of 1990[33]. The Coastal Security Headquarters has been assigned to monitor and prevent acts that are contrary to the provisions of international treaties. The first international treaty ratified by Turkey dealing with the marine pollution through transportation is the OECD Convention

22 Official Gazette, 23 March 1983.
23 Official Gazette, 23 July 1985.
24 Official Gazette, 06 June 2008.
25 Vienna 1985 accepted by Turkey on 08.09.1990.
26 Montreal 16.09.1987, accepted by Turkey in 1990.
27 Official Gazette, 8 September 1990.
28 Official Gazette, 12 November 2008.
29 Official Gazette, 27 December 1996.
30 Official Gazette, 11 August 2003.
31 Act no. 618, 20 April 1941, Official Gazette 20.04.1925, amendment in Official Gazette 16.07. 2008, 09.07.2024.
32 Official Gazette 04.04.1971, amendments in Official Gazette 15.05.1986; 22.07.2003.
33 Official Gazette 17.4.1990, amendments 1992, 2003, 2005, 2008 lastly amended 2024.

on Third Party Liability in the Field of Nuclear Energy[34]. Secondly, Turkey ratified, in 1989–90, the International Convention for the Prevention of Pollution from Ships (MARPOL) and its 1978 Protocol together with Annexes I, II, V, amendments, and I dated 1984, 1985 and 1987[35] and Annexes III, IV[36] and VI[37] Turkey also ratified the 1978 Convention on Standards of Training, Certification and Watch Keeping for Seafarers in 1989[38]; 1978[39] and 88[40] Protocols of International Convention for the Safety of Life at Sea 1974 (Protocol 78 SOLAS 74), International Regulations for Preventing Collisions at Sea 1972 (COLREG 1972)[41], The Protocol on Preparedness, Response and Co-operation to pollution Incidents by Hazardous and Noxious Substances (OPRC-HNS 2000)[42]. In these conventions, there are provisions on environmental protection. Nevertheless, there are some international conventions and protocols that still wait for ratification on marine pollution, air pollution, biodiversity, UNECE Treaties, Council of Europe Treaties.

D. Conclusion

Turkey has been actively involved in international cooperation efforts to address environmental problems that are complex and mostly related to socio-economic issues. Turkey, considering its national interests and socio-economic conditions, has become party to several conventions both at the global and regional level, with a view to contribute to address environmental problems. Turkey's vigilance in safeguarding its environment will be the key

34 Opened for signature in Paris, 26 June 1960; entered in force on 17 June 1962. Turkey ratified it with the Act no. 299, on 9 May 1961. Additional Protocol dated 28 January 1964 was ratified on 1 June 1967 with the Act no. 878.

35 London, 12 International Legal Materials (ILM) 1319 (1973). The Protocol was prepared on 17 February 1978 – before the Convention was in force. It entered in force on 2 October 1983. 17 ILM 546 (1978). Entry into force for Turkey is on 13 September 1989, (CMR 89/44517), Official Gazette, 21935: Annex I was in force on 2 October 1983, Annex II was in force on 6 April 1987, Annex V in force on 31 December 1988: Turkey ratified these instruments with CMR no. 90/442, dated 3 May 1990: Official Gazette, 24 June 1990, no. 20558.

36 Annexes III, IV, Official Gazette, 23 May 2014.

37 Annex VI Official Gazette, 11 September 2013.

38 Entered in force on 28 April 1984. Turkish accession took place on 28 April 1989, Official Gazette, no. 20152.

39 Official Gazette, 27 June 2013.

40 Law admitted 29.05. 2013. But still not in force.

41 Official Gazette, 23.05.2014.

42 Official Gazette, 27.06.2013.

to the continuance of its economic development. Beside the international efforts, the EU accession process gives Turkey some responsibilities to introduce a series of fundamental reforms. In this framework, special projects focusing on drafting new legislation, reviewing of compliance of national legislation to EU legislation and evaluation of investment requirements in the field of environment have been carried out. In the past years, there was some progress, mainly in increasing capacity in waste management and waste-water treatment, whereas enforcement and implementation remains weak, especially on waste management and industrial pollution. More ambitious and better coordinated environment and climate policies still need to be established and implemented.

Analysis of the Turkish Draft Law on Biodiversity

Galip Engin Şimşek[*]

Abstract

In this article, the Draft Turkish Law on Biodiversity is analyzed in comparison with relevant international conventions and EU laws in order to show the degree of harmonization between them. It also contains some references to relevant Turkish laws and court decisions to provide a complete picture of the protection status of biodiversity in Turkish legal system.

Key Words: Turkish law, biodiversity, EU *acquis*, Turkish Constitutional Court

I. Introduction

Türkiye's accession into EU requires the acceptance of certain laws with regard to *acquis communitare*.[1] One of these is a law on the protection of biodiversity in Türkiye,[2] which is also needed to implement the commitments

---

* Associate Professor, Department of International Law, Istanbul University Faculty of Law.

1 The Chapter on Environment was opened to accession negotiations at the Intergovernmental Conference which was held in Brussels on December 21, 2009. EU Integrated Approximation Strategy (UÇES) (2007-2023) contains detailed information concerning the technical and institutional infrastructure to be developed as well as environmental improvements and arrangements to be carried out in Turkey in order to ensure alignment with the EU's environmental acquis and its effective implementation which all-together constitute a precondition for accession to the EU. For this purpose, UÇES sets out objectives, targets, strategies and activities to be undertaken in Türkiye in the priority areas, including water, solid waste, air, industrial pollution control, nature protection and horizontal sector, see www.joi.or.jp/modules/investmentcustom/documents/TUR_EU_INTEGRATED_ENVIRONMENTAL_APPROXIMATION_STRATEGY.pdf.
In this regard, see also the latest (the 8th) Environment Action Programme of the EU, which aims to achieve the UN's 2030 Agenda, https://environment.ec.europa.eu/strategy/environment-action-programme-2030_en.

2 One of the the purposes of the UÇES is to improve the conditions of natural flora and fauna together with their ecosystems, taking into account the balance between sustainable use and conservation. It aims to raise the ratio of the protected areas to the total country area to 10 %. However, it is pointed out that due to the redundancy of protection regulations coming under the responsibility of different institutions and the lack of qualified personnel, the effective management of the areas has become difficult. Turkish National legislation is considered as insufficient in identification and classification of habitat types and animal and plant species, which have special significance; forming a network of

under the Biodiversity Convention and the other relevant protocols.[3] Preparations for this law was started by the Ministry of Forestry and Agriculture in 2003, together with relevant civil society groups and three different drafts were considered in this fashion. In subsequent meetings, however, civil society groups were left outside the negotiations and the government continued the preparations on its own. In this new format, more drafts have been considered. In this article, I will give the general outlines of the last Draft prepared in 2021.

A. General Outlines oft he Draft Law

The 2021 Draft Law on the Protection of Biodiversity begins with a general preamble and, then, continues with text of various articles and the rational for each article.[4] Altogether, there are 22 articles. The preamble of the Draft submits that the it aims to fill the legal gap, which is necessary to supply the basis for the secondary regulations on the designation and monitoring of biodiversity, protection of species, habitats and genetic resources, access to genetic resources and benefit-sharing, information sharing about biodiversity, prevention of biopiracy, as well as providing a sanctioning power during the implementation phase. In other words, it aims to bring a holistic view into the legal protection area.[5] Another aim is to deliver Türkiye's commitments

---

protected areas; preparing an inventory about habitats and species; taking into consideration of flora and fauna, as well as their living environments in spatial plans; establishing management plans and a monitoring system. Moreover, it is also pointed out to the need for establishing a new scientific and administrative center for the implementation of CITES and a rescue center for sheltering the confiscated live samples, as well as a guidebook for the identification of species and a system of branding. For the latest developments in most of these topics, see Turkish National Biodiversity Action Plan (2018-2028), including National Sea Research Strategy, prepared by the Ministry of Forestry and Agriculture in pursuance of Article 6 of Biodiversity Convention and 2020 Aichi Biodiversity Targets, see http://extwprlegs1.fao.org/docs/pdf/tur208837Tur.pdf.

3 Türkiye ratified the Biodiversity Convention in 14.02.1997 and the Cartagena Protocol on Biosafety in 24.11.2003. Türkiye is not a party to the Nagoya Protocol on Access and Benefit-sharing.

4 https://gaib.org.tr/tr/hububat/duyurular/biyolojik-cesitliligi-koruma-kanun-teklifi-taslagi-hk-3007.html

5 Some of the relevant laws, by-laws and decisions in Turkish law for the protection of nature are as follows: The Environmental Law, Official Gazette (OG)/1983 No. 18132; The Law on National Parks, OG/1983 No. 18132; The Law on Land Hunting, OG/2003 No. 25165; The Forest Law, OG/1956 No. 9402; The Law on the Protection of

under UN Biodiversity Convention and various other international treaties and to harmonize Turkish law vis-a-vis EU laws[6] and programs.[7]

Cultural and Natural Properties, OG/1983 No. 18113; The Agriculture Law, OG/2006 No. 26149; The Law on Aquaculture, OG/1971 No.13799; The Law Approving The Cartagena Protocol on Bio-safety (2003); The Animal Protection Law, OG/2004 No. 5199; The Law on Animal Health and Surveillance, OG/1986 No. 19109; The Law on Veterinary Services, Plant Health, Food and Feed Staff, OG/2010 No. 27610; The Anti-Smuggling Law, OG/2007 No. 26479; Cabinet Decree 88/12839 on scientific research and filing by foreigners; Law on the Right to Information, OG/2003 No. 25269; By-law on The Environmental Impact Assessment, OG/2022 No.31907; By-law on the Strategic Environmental Assessment, OG/2017, No. 30032; By-law of the Practices in National Parks, OG/1986 No.19309; By-law of Hunting, Wild Animals and Stock, Production and Trade of Their Products, OG/ 2005 No.25847; By-law of Hunting and Wild Animals and Production Facilities and Stations and Rescuing Centers, OG/2004 No.25656; By-law on the Basic principles of Hunting Education and Certificate, OG/2004 No.25687; By-law on the Basic principles of the Establishment, Management and Inspection of Hunting Areas, OG/2004 No.25464; By-law on the Basic Principles of the Duties and Practices of Central Hunting Commission and Hunting Commission of Provinces OG/2004 No. 25455; By-law on Hunting of Local or Foreign Hunters in the Extent of Hunting Tourism, OG/2005 No.25694; By-law on the Election, Education, Duties and Responsibilities of Volunteer Hunting Inspectors, OG/2004 No.25511; By-law on the Procedures and Principles of the Designation, Registration and Approval of Protected Areas, OG/2012 No. 28358; Decision of Principle on the Conditions of Protection and Use of Natural Site Areas, OG/2019 No. 3097; By-law on the National Implementation of CITES, Official Gazette/2001 No. 24623; By-law of the Protection of Wild Life and the Development of Wild Life Sites, OG/2004 No.25637; By-law on the Basic Principles of the Protection of Wild Animals and Their Life Sites and Contention with the Harmful Animals, OG/2005 No.25976; By-law on the Establishment of Zoos and the Procedures and Principles on Their Working, OG/2007 No. 26610; By-law on the Genetically Modified Organisms and Their Products, OG/2010 No. 27671; By-law on the Principles and Methods of Organic Agriculture, OG/2010 No. 27676; By-law on the Protection of the Domestic Animal Genetic Resources, OG/2011 No.28150; By-law on the Collection, Preservation and Utilization of Plant Genetic Variety, OG/1992 No.21316; By-law on the Removal, Production and Foreign Trade of Natural Flower Bulbs, OG/2012 No.28358; By-law on Plant Quarantine, OG/2011 No. 28131; By-law on Aquaculture, OG/1995 No.22223 and 5/1-2 Notices on the Hunting of Aquaculture Products, OG/2020/20-21; By-law on Using Aquaculture Resources for Research and Their Import or Export, OG/2015 No. 29381; By-law on the Registration of the Genetic Resources of Aquaculture Products, OG/2012 No. 28328; By-law on the Conservation of Wetlands, OG/2014 No. 28962; Notification on the Regulation of Commercial Fishing No. 2012/65; Notification on the Regulation of Amateur Fishing No. 2012/66.

6 The relevant EU *acquis,* which are to be implemented in national law, include: Council Directive 79/409 (EEC) on the conservation of wild birds; Council Directive 92/43 (EC) on the conservation of natural habitats and of wild fauna and flora; Council Regulation 97/338 (EC) on the protection of species of wild fauna and flora by regulating trade therein; Commission Regulation 98/2473 (EC) suspending the introduction into the Community of specimens of certain species of wild fauna and flora; Commission

For the protection of nature, the Draft requires the Ministry to prepare lists for protected species and habitats, to declare species and habitat protection areas, to prepare protection action plans, to create ecological corridors and a "Biodiversity Protection Web" mechanism, which aims to forge a link between the habitats of protected species. The Draft also allows the sustainable economic use of biodiversity for national development purposes[8] and gives the Ministry to permit activities in species or habitat protection areas, after the preparation of an ecological or environmental impact assessment, depending on the type of the area in question. It also gives the President the power to permit activities in such areas without any assessment for some exceptional purposes. Finally, the draft mentions that the Ministry, as a principle, is to let the public to participate the decision making process on the administration of nature and biodiversity.

Regulation 97/2307 (EC) replacing the Council Regulation 97/338 (EC); Commission Regulation 97/939 (EC) laying down detailed rules concerning the implementation of Council Regulation 97/338 (EC); Commission Regulation 97/2551 (EC) suspending the introduction into the Community of specimens of certain species of wild fauna and flora; Commission Regulation 98/767 (EC) replacing the Commission Regulation 97/939 (EC); Commission Regulation 99/1968 (EC) on suspending the introduction into the Community of specimens of certain species of wild fauna and flora; Commission Regulation 2001/1808 (EC) laying down detailed rules concerning the implementation of Council Regulation 97/338 (EC); Council Regulation 91/3254 (EC) prohibiting the use of leg-hold traps and the introduction into the Community of pelts and manifactured goods of certain wild animal species originating in countries which catch them by means of trapping methods which do not meet international humane trapping standards; Council Decision 97/602 (EC) pertaining to the article 1(1)a of the Commission Regulation 97/35 (EC) and the second paragraph in the article 3(1) of the Regulation 91/3254 (EEC); Commission Regulation 97/35 (EC) laying down provisions on the certification of pelts and goods; Council Directive 99/22 (EC) relating to the keeping of wild animals in zoos.

7 See Natura 2000 Program, which was launched by the Commission Decision 97/266 (EC), to establish a network of core breeding and resting sites for rare and threatened species, and some rare natural habitat types, which are protected in their own right, http://ec.europa.eu/environment/nature/natura2000/index_en.htm.

8 In this respect, see the Natura 2000 Program, which does not involve a system of strict nature reserves, from which all human activities would be excluded. The conservation and sustainable use of the Natura 2000 areas is based on the idea of people working with nature rather than against it. Member States must ensure that the sites are managed in a sustainable manner, both ecologically and economically.

B. Analysis of Articles

As for the individual articles of the Draft, Article 1 defines the goal and scope of the code as follows: protection, improvement and sustainable use of biological riches of the country, sustainable use of biodiversity and sharing of the benefits arising from genetic resources. Article 2 gives the definitions of certain terms, like biodiversity, ecological corridor, ecological impact assessment, sustainable use, ecosystem, habitats, genetic resource, protected area, favourable protection level, strictly protected species, invasive species, endangered species etc. These definitions are largely based on those of relevant conventions and EU directives. The main principles that should be taken into account in the protection and sustainable use of nature and biodiversity are listed in Article 3. These are listed as follows: pursuing the balance between protection and use; taking necessary measures against the threats that might cause serious or irreparable damage to biodiversity; protecting, improving and maintaining the sustainability of important species and habitats; protecting ecological balance, as well as landscape and natural ecosystem values; ensuring transparency, informing public and encouraging their participation in the management and decision-taking processes; determining the country's biodiversity for all ecosystems and designating protected species and habitats; considering local peoples' traditional activities, while protecting biodiversity.

Under Article 4, the Ministry is entrusted with the following duties:[9] to prepare the lists of protected species and habitats,[10] to prepare species protection action plans for the species that are chosen to be protected strictly,[11]

9 By virtue of Presidential Decree on Presidential Organization, Section 14, Article 410, the Ministry of Forestry and Agriculture has already been commissioned for the development of policies of nature protection, designation of protected areas, protection of biodiversity and taking measures for the implementation of international agreements on nature protection, see https://www.resmigazete.gov.tr/eskiler/2018/07/20180710-1.pdf. For the numbers, sizes and examples of protected areas designated by the Ministry, see the National Biodiversity Action Plan (2018-28), http://extwprlegs1.fao.org/docs/pdf/tur208837Tur.pdf.

10 The Preamble of the Article mentions that Ministry will prepare the list of protected species and habitats taking into account the protection status of those under the Law on Land Hunting and the Law of Aquaculture. For this purpose, also see other laws and by-laws mentioned in footnote 5 above.

11 In this regard, in the annexes of the Council Directive 92/43 (EC), over 1.000 animal and plant species, as well as 200 habitat types are protected in various ways. Also in the European Red Lists of Threatened Species, developed by the IUCN, an overview of the conservation status of 10,000 European species are provided, so that appropriate action

to take measures for the protection of migratory species' stop over and reproduction areas, to create biodiversity protection webs and ecological corridors.[12] According to the Article, the Ministry has the power to declare species or habitat protection areas, which conserve them in favourable protection levels; and to prepare administration plans in order to intervene, take measures and to monitor these areas. However, in the Article, the categories of areas that need to be protected are not expressly defined. In this regard, the relevant categories can be found in Biodiversity, CITES, Bern, Barcelona, Ramsar and other conventions.[13] For this purpose, in our

---

can be taken to protect those threatened with extinction, https://www.eea.europa.eu/data-and-maps/data/european-red-lists-7.

12 Establishment of a biodiversity protection web is required by EU's Natura 2000 program and the relevant EU directives. The web aims at connecting ecologically important and geographically close protected areas via ecological corridors for facilitating the interaction of species and habitats. In this regard, Natura 2000 program requires States to choose sites according to precise, scientific criteria. However, the selection procedure varies depending on which of the two nature directives – Birds or Habitats – warrants the creation of a particular site. Under the Habitats Directive (Art. 3 and 4), Member States designate Special Areas of Conservation (SACs) to ensure the favourable conservation status of each habitat type and species throughout their range in the EU. The choice of sites must ensure that the natural habitat types listed in the Directive's Annex I and the habitats of the species listed in its Annex II are maintained or, where appropriate, restored to a favourable conservation status in their natural range. Moreover (in Arts. 3 and 10), Member States shall endeavour to encourage the management of features of the landscape, which are of major importance for wild fauna and flora, with a view to improve the ecological coherence of the Natura 2000 network. Such features include those, which are essential for the migration, dispersal and genetic exchange of wild species, by virtue of their linear and continuous structure (such as rivers with their banks or the traditional systems for marking field boundaries) or their function as stepping stones (such as ponds or small woods). On the other hand, under the Birds Directive (Art. 4), the network must include Special Protection Areas (SPAs) designated for particularly threatened species and all migratory bird species. In this respect, they must ensure that all the 'most suitable territories', both in number and surface area, are designated. For more information, see http://ec.europa.eu/environment/nature/natura2000/sites/index_en.htm. For the question of ecological coherence, www.iucn.org/sites/dev/files/legal_aspects_of_connectivity_conservation_a_concept_pape.pdf.
For the official launching of Natura 2000 in Türkiye, see http://www.milliparklar.gov.tr/anasayfa/resimlihaber/16-04-13/NATURA_2000_ PROJES%C4%B0_RESM%C4%B0_OLARAK_BA%C5%9ELADI.aspx?sflang=tr; and see https://rec.org.tr/2017/09/12/natura-2000-ve-biyolojik-cesitlilik-icin-ulusal-veritabani-egitimleri. See also, Özüdoğru&Duygu, Türkiye'nin Avrupa Birliği ile Katılım Müzakereleri Sürecinde Natura 2000 Korunan Alanlar Ekolojik Ağının Değerlendirilmesi, http://dergiler.ankara.edu.tr/dergiler/47/1037/12516.pdf.

13 For example, the Ministry has designated gene protection and administration areas for the protection of species, including endemic and threatened ones within the

legal system, one should look at the Forest Law, National Parks Law, the By-law on National Parks, Land Hunting Law, Environmental Law, By-law on the Conservation of Wetlands,[14] and the By-law on the Procedures and Principles of the Designation, Registration and Approval of Protected Areas. Particularly, in the last By-law, most of the categories of protected areas that exist in various other laws are defined and regulated.[15] In this respect, first of all, it includes a definition of natural site areas, which are divided into strictly protected sensitive areas, qualified protected areas and sustainable protection and controlled use areas, then it provides other categories like special environment protection areas, wetlands, national parks, nature parks, monuments and caves. The By-law provides that the Ministry, by its own initiative or upon a request, will designate and register such areas, parks and monuments, as well as their boundaries.[16] If the area or the wetland in

---

scope of the Biodiversity Convention; biogenetic reserve areas for the protection of habitats and ecosystems within the scope of Bern Convention; biosphere reserve areas for the protection of various ecosystems and landscapes within the scope of UNESCO Biosphere Protection Areas Action Plan; wetland protection areas within the scope of Ramsar Convention; key diversity areas, including sea turtles nesting areas, Mediterranean monk seal areas and important bird, plant and forest areas within the scope of CITES, Bern and Barcelona Conventions; zero extinction areas within the scope of IUCN red list; special conservation interest areas within the scope of Bern Convention; geological heritage areas within the scope of World Heritage Convention. For further information and the examples of some of these areas, see Demirel, Pirselimoğlu et al., Ülkemizde Uluslararası Koruma Statüleri Kapsamında Korunan Alanlar, Korunan Doğal Alanlar Sempozyumu, 8-10 Eylül 2005, SDÜ, Isparta.

14 Under the Article 4 of the Forest Law, forests are divided into three categories: protection forests (damaged or burned forests, national parks and production forests). The National Parks Law and the By-law on National Parks include definitions on national parks, nature parks, nature monuments and nature protection areas. The Land Hunting Law includes a definition on wildlife protection and development areas. The Environmental Law includes a definition on special environmental protection areas, the Law on the Protection of Cultural and Natural Assets includes definitions on natural sites, protection areas and natural assets and the By-law on the Conservation of Wetlands provides types of protection areas, like strict protection area, sensitive protection area, sustainable use area, controlled use area and Ramsar area, see OG/2014 No. 28962. For further analysis, see Yılmaz E., Ülkemizdeki Orman İşlevleri ve Tahsis Kriterleri, Doğu Akdeniz Ormancılık Araştırma Müdürlüğü Dergisi, 2004 Sayı 10, s. 1-25.

15 See OG/2012 No. 28358, as amended in 2020, OG/2020 No.31070 and in 2022, OG/2022 No. 31769.

16 In cases of natural site areas and natural monuments, these have to be announced to the public just after the decision of registration. The latest amendment to the By-law provides that public could object to the registration within 60 days after the announcement and any error of facts needs to be evaluated by the relevant institution.

question is outside of forest areas or if it is going to be a special environment protection area, the designation will be made by the President upon the recommendation of the Ministry of Environment.[17] According to the By-law, in strictly protected sensitive areas, only scientific and educational activities are allowed. On the other hand, qualified protected areas can be used for non-industrial traditional agricultural, husbandry and fishing purposes. Moreover, some other projects like irrigation dams, roads, camping areas, car parks, electric energy stations and transmission lines are also permitted. In sustainable protection and controlled use areas, however, in addition to the economic activities and projects, which are permitted in qualified protected areas, integrated industrial agricultural and husbandry plants, touristic facilities and residential activities are also allowed.[18]

One must notice that despite mentioning it in Article 3 as a principle, the current version of Article 4 is lacking a provision on public participation into the protection decision-making process, which was included in the earlier version of the draft article.[19]

According to the Draft Article 5, releasing foreign species into the nature is subject to the permission of the Ministry. The Article also regulates the measures that should be taken to prevent the invasive species' entry into the

17 Administration of this type of areas and the economic activities allowed (including residential and agricultural buildings, touristic facilities, stone quarries etc) in them are subject to the Law on the Establishment of the Agency for the Protection of Special Areas, OG/1989 No. 383. Power and responsibilities of the Agency later transferred to the General Directorate of Cultural and Natural Heritage, see OG/2011 No. 648

18 For a detailed information on the activities permitted in these areas, see the Decision of Principle on the Conditions of Protection and Use of Natural Site Areas, OG/2019 No. 30971. See also By-law on Making Plans in Protected Areas, OG/2012 No. 28242 and By-law on the Change of Immovable Properties with Building Ban in Natural Site Areas and Special Environment Protection Areas with Treasury Properties, OG/2013 No. 28727.

19 According to the earlier version, the Ministry was required to inform the public and the local people about the importance of protection and resource value of an area and consult them by means of at least one public meeting before the designation and reevaluation of the status of a protected area. For the purposes of protection and sustainable use of nature and biodiversity, the Ministry would cooperate with local authorities, universities, research institutions, civil society and private sector. In this regard, establishing a National Biodiversity Advisory Committee was also envisaged. In this respect also see, Article 30 of Turkish Environment Law No. 2872; Directive 2003/4 (EC); Decision 2005/370 (EC); Directive 2003/35/EC; Regulation 2006/1367(EC) and UNECE Convention on Access to Information, Public Participation in Decision Making and Access to Justice in Environmental Matters (Aarhus Convention), https://www.unece.org/env/pp/treatytext.html;

nature or their elimination. For this purpose, the Ministry should prepare a list of invasive species. In a similar fashion, Articles 6, 7 and 8 entrust the Ministry with the task to reinstate local wild species that became or are in danger of extinction into their natural habitats, to establish facilities for their reproduction and rehabilitation, to take them under protection in arboretums, aquariums, natural life parks and gene banks,[20] and to protect and improve the conditions of degenerated landscape and habitats.[21]

Article 9 of the draft deals with the ecological impact assessment and the grounds for its exclusion in certain activities.[22] It is provided that any activity in the protected areas, that might have a possible impact on the favourable protection level of the species, or in habitat protection areas is subject to ecological impact assessment. It also provides that if the activity in question is subject to environmental impact assessment (ie., protected areas outside the forest regimes), then, ecological and environmental assessments should be conducted together.[23] The preamble of the article explains that the aim of ecological impact assessment process is to determine the impacts of planned activities upon the species and habitats with scientific methods and to prevent or minimise these impacts in order to guarantee the basic needs of current and coming generations. This rational is in accord with the Article 6 of EU's Habitats Directive.[24] Nevertheless, Article 9 provides some exceptions to the

---

20 See Article 22 of the EU Habitats Directive.

21 For some information regarding states' duties with respect to degenerated habitats and landscape, see ECJ's Cascina Tre Pini case, where the Court stated that 'the failure of a Member State to fulfil the obligation of protecting a particular site does not necessarily justify the declassification of that site. On the contrary, it is for that state to take the measures to safeguard that site', see Case C-301/12 Cascina Tre Pini (2013), para. 32.

22 For the criticism of this article as replacing already established system of environmental impact assessment with that of ecological impact assessment, see Alıca G., "Tabiatı ve Biyolojik Çeşitliliği Koruma Kanunu Tasarısı'nın Doğa Koruma Kanunu Mevzuatı Çerçevesinde Değerlendirilmesi", Ankara Barosu Dergisi 2012/3, pp.194-95. It is argued that despite the ambiguous nature of ecological impact assessment process, environmental impact assessment process and the system of rules and court decisions developed around this concept established a regime of protection which included both national laws and international treaties.

23 By-law on Environmental Impact Assessment, OG/2022 No.31907. In the fifth supplement of this By-law, almost all categories of protected areas designated as such in Turkish legal system or considered as such according to certain international conventions are declared as sensitive areas, whose legal status should to be taken into account during the preparations of the assessment, see https://www.resmigazete.gov.tr/eskiler/2022/07/20220729-2-1.pdf

24 In this regard, Article 6.4 of Habitats Directive and ECJ's relevant case law require a balance of interests between the conservation objectives and the achievement of long

duty to conduct ecological impact assessment. In this regard, it gives the President the authority to permit activities, if necessary for public security, natural disasters or public health, without any assessment in species and habitat protection areas.

In the earlier version of this article, it was stated that if the assessment shows negative impacts and no alternative solutions exist to cancel these impacts, but overriding public interest requires the approval of the project, the Ministry should take all the necessary preventive or compensatory measures in connection with the project to offset the negative impacts.[25] Considering this earlier version,[26] the reason for the omission of compensatory measures in case of negative impacts in the latest version requires an interpretation. In this respect, I would argue that the current article has to be interpreted in conjunction with the definition of ecological impact assessment in the Draft Article 2, the By-law on Environmental Impact Assessment,[27] the By-law on the Procedures and Principles of the Designation, Registration and Approval of Protected Areas, and the By-law on the Conservation of Wetlands. In all these document, it is required that the assessment should include preventive or compensatory measures against negative impacts. Therefore, it is fair to conclude that the Ministry has to implement these measures recommended in the assessment or have them implemented by the contractors of the projects.

Article 10 deals with the research in and access to genetic materials. It provides that research and development in biodiversity resources, collecting the individuals of endemic species or their genetic material out of their habitats, taking or selling them out of the country, use of genetic materials and the traditional knowledge about them, sharing of knowledge with foreigners obtained by scientific research on biodiversity and patenting or licensing of

---

term public interest of a social or economic nature, see Council Directive 92/43 (EC). Also see, Directive 2011/92 (EU) (known as 'Environmental Impact Assessment' – EIA Directive) and Directive 2001/42 (EC) (known as 'Strategic Environmental Assessment' – SEA Directive). For an important case on this issue, see Case C-258/11 Peter Sweetman and Others v. Ann Bord Pleanala (2013).

25 It was also stated that if the area in question enclosed a priority habitat type or a priority species, then overriding public interest would include only public health, public security or benefits for the environment.

26 This version was in Accord with Article 6 of the Habitats Directive, which provides that if a plan or project must nevertheless be carried out for imperative reasons of overriding public interest, including those of a social or economic nature, the Member State shall take all compensatory measures necessary to ensure that the overall coherence of Natura 2000 is protected.

27 The By-law on Environmental Impact Assessment includes a detailed article on informing the public and access to the asessment process.

products derived from genetic materials are subject to the permission of the Ministry. Moreover, before the permission given, a written contract, setting forth the conditions of sharing the material and non-material benefits that could be derived from the research or commercialization of genetic materials, has to be concluded with the persons applying for the permission. On the other hand, no permission is required for the following situations: research on human genes, traditional knowledge that is very well known and not specific to a certain region, non-commercial use of traditional knowledge by the local people, research and development in national defence industry. The preamble of the Article mentions that the permission requirement in the cases listed are compatible with our country's powers and responsibilities under the Biodiversity Convention, Nagoya Protocol on Access to Genetic Resources and Sharing of Benefits and EU Regulation 2014/511.

Article 10 also provides that the Ministry (together with the ministries of commerce, interior and industry) should establish control points to fight against biopiracy.[28]

Article 23 provides the creation of an inventory containing the data related with biodiversity and set out monitoring parameters and monitoring plans.[29]

The final section of the Draft deals with the prohibited activities, the sanctions and the obligation to restore. Prohibited activities under Article 12 cover hunting, killing or disturbing, collecting eggs, destroying nests, selling and buying of animal species in the lists; and cutting, collecting, uprooting, buying and selling of plant species.[30] However, the Ministry could give permission to these activities for research or reproduction purposes.[31] Articles

---

28 Ministry has established a Database and a Guide to Fight against Biopiracy to help the law enforcement personnel. There is also a draft law prepared for this purpose. For the current implementation methods on the basis of Environmental Law and Misdemeanor Law, see Güler&Mutlu, Türkiye'de Biyokaçakçılık Sorunu: Küre Dağları Milli Parkı Örneği, Kırıkkale Üniversitesi İktisadi ve İdari Bilimler Fakültesi 12. Uluslararası Kamu Yönetimi Sempozyumu, Bildiriler El Kitabı, 2018, s. 505-7.

29 For the ongoing inventory project, see http://www.milliparklar.gov.tr/envanter/index.htm. For the biodiversity database, see http://www.nuhungemisi.gov.tr/Giris/index.aspx. For the ongoing DNA barcoding, environmental DNA, gene banks, synthetic-biology, biosensors projects, see http://extwprlegs1.fao.org/docs/pdf/tur208837Tur.pdf.

30 See the By-law on the Conservation of Wetlands, Article 12. Also see Articles 12-15 of the EU Habitats Directive and Bern Convention, Article 22.

31 According to Article 16 of the Habitats Directive, derogations from articles prohibiting certain activities are allowed, under strictly supervised conditions, on a selective basis, to a limited extent, in limited numbers, only in the interest of protecting wild fauna and flora and conserving natural habitats; or to prevent serious damage, in particular to

13 and 14 provide administrative fines, judicial fines and prison sentences for the violations of various sub-articles of Articles 5 and 10, and for the activities prohibited under Article 12. According to Article 15, equipment or species obtained from people involved in the illegal activities would be confiscated and sold. The living species acquired in this way should be returned back to its natural habitats, if this is not possible, then, they would be sold or delivered to a research institution, or destroyed in case of invasive species. Under Article 17, people who damage species or habitats as a result of illegal activities are under the obligation to restore them, or if this is not possible, they have to pay compensation. Finally, Articles 18 and 19 provides a list of monetary resources coming from various permits, fines and confiscated equipment, these resources should be primarily used for the protection and improvement of biodiversity, or spend on projects and education programs on biodiversity protection and ecosystem improvement.

C. Turkish Constitutional Court`s Relevant Case Law

Before concluding this paper, Turkish Constitutional Court's attitude on this issues deserves to be mentioned. According to the case law of the Court, under Article 56 and 63 of the Constitution, the state is responsible to take all the measures to develop the environment, prevent its pollution and conserve historical, cultural and natural assets and valuables. In this regard, the Court has decided that wild animals and their natural habitat are also natural assets that need to be protected under Article 56.[32] The Court has also stated that Article 56 requires the protection of natural beauty and the prevention of air and water pollution through an environmental impact assessment process of certain activities, which might have adverse effects on the environment,

crops, livestock, forests, fisheries and water and other types of property; or in the interests of public health and public safety and other imperative reasons of overriding public interest, including those of a social or economic nature or for the beneficial consequences of primary importance for the environment; and finally, for the purpose of research and education, repopulating and re-introducing these species and breeding operations, including the artificial propagation of plants.

32 Constitutional Court Decision, E. 2010/51, OG/2012 No. 28184. However, the Court has considered that the protection and management of forest areas does not come under article 56, but article 169, which directly provides for the protection and development of forests, E. 2003/100, OG/2004 No. 25408. For the suitability of allocation of forest areas for touristic use, see E. 2008/51, OG/2011 No. 27934.

like mining, development plans or urban renewal.[33] Unfortunately, in none of these cases, the Court took into account any international instrument regulating these issues.

D. Conclusion

On the basis of the analysis of the articles above, it is fair to conclude that, to a large extent, the Draft Law meets the requirements of Biodiversity Convention, EU's regulations and other relevant international agreements. However, the allocation of powers between ministries for the determination, registration and administration and various protection categories defined in different laws are confusing and need to be harmonized. Moreover, the lack of an article dealing with public information, participation, cooperation in the decision-making process is also liable to criticism, especially considering the international standards set by the Aarhus Convention. Finally, the Draft article regulating ecological impact assessment and environmental impact assessment requires an interpretation in conjunction with relevant laws, by-laws and Constitutional Court's relevant case law.

---

33 28 E. 2011/110, OG/2012 No. 28360. See also, E. 2006/129, OG/2010 No. 27456; E. 2001/106, OG/2013 No. 28606 and E. 2010/82, OG/2013 No. 28716. In an earlier case, the Court had also stated that the constitutional right to a healthy environment could not be dispensed with due to economic justifications and certain activities should not be permitted without considering their environmental impact. Consequently, the Court found an article of the Turkish Environmental Law, which allowed certain energy and mining projects to be realized without a prior environmental impact assessment, as against article 56 of the Constitution, E. 2006/99 , OG/2009 No. 27282. In another case, however, the Court did not find that the relevant article of the Coastal Law, which allows draining or filling in sea, lake or river areas, was in violation of article 56, E. 1990/23, OG/1992 No. 21120, In a recent decision, the Court emphasized the importance of renewable energy in terms of the climate change and the protection of environment, E. 2011/27, OG/2012 No. 28433. For further analysis of the case law, see Y. Semiz, Anayasa Mahkemesi'nin Çevre Hakkı Perspektifi, Hacettepe HFD, 4(2) 2014.

Environmental legal protection in Germany – legal foundations and current discussions on restrictions

*Dr. Maximilian Schmidt**

I. Introduction

Environmental legal protection in the sense of access to justice in environmental matters is - especially in interaction with other instruments of control such as access to information and public participation[1] - a central element of environmental law. The practical effectiveness of environmental law depends essentially on the mechanisms of law enforcement. The warranty and institutional safeguarding of neutral control by courts is indispensable, especially in connection with the authorisation of environmentally relevant projects, and ultimately serves justice in environmental matters[2] .

This article[3] provides an insight into environmental legal protection in Germany by first giving an overview of the relevant legal foundations (A.). Secondly, selected current discussions on restrictions of environmental legal protection are examined for compatibility with these legal foundations (B.) and thirdly a conclusion is drawn (C.).

A. Overview of legal foundations

Even an overview of the legal basis of environmental legal protection in Germany cannot be limited to national regulations. The German regulations are based almost entirely on provisions of International law, which have also found their way into European law. For this reason, the jurisdiction of the European Court of Justice (ECJ) is an important source of information and insight regarding the content and scope of environmental law protection.

* Lawyer, Kapellmann und Partner Rechtsanwälte mbB, München.

1 Together, these elements form the three pillars of the Aarhus Convention (see in more detail under B. I.).

2 See for all *Kahl/Gärditz,* Umweltrecht, 11th edition 2019, § 5 no. 1; cf. *Ehemann,* Umweltgerechtigkeit, 2020, p. 195.

3 Originally this article was composed in German and is therefore mainly based on German bibliographic sources.

Following the hierarchy of norms and, to a certain extent, the chronology of modern environmental law protection the relevant provisions of International law (I.), then of European law (II.) and finally of German law (III.) are presented in the overview below.

1. International law

The central regulation on access to justice in environmental matters at the level of International law is Art. 9 of the "Convention on Access to Information, Public Participation in Decision-making and Access to Justice in Environmental Matters", also known as the Aarhus Convention (AC)[4]. The legal protection in environmental matters forms the third of three pillars of this international convention signed in June 1998 by 37 states in the Danish city of Aarhus[5]. The first pillar is access to environmental information (Art. 4 and 5 AC); the second one is public participation in environmental decision-making procedures (public participation, Art. 6 to 8 AC)[6]. Initially Article 9 establishes a link to these first two pillars by guaranteeing the judicial assertion of the right to access to information contained in Art. 4 para. 1 AC (Art. 9 para. 1 AC) as well as the right to public participation standardised in Art. 6 AC[7]. In addition to this procedural reinforcement of the first two pillars, paragraph 2 of Article 9 contains the following obligation: Parties of the convention shall ensure that members of the public concerned (see below) who have a sufficient interest or, alternatively, maintain impairment of a right (where the administrative procedural law of a party of the convention requires this as a precondition), have access to legal protection against environmentally signi-

4 The agreement is located as a pan-European process at the level of the United Nations Economic Commission for Europe - UNECE (*Lutz/Sauer*, Neuigkeiten zur Aarhus-Konvention – die 6. Vertragsstaatenkonferenz in Montenegro, EurUP 2018, 118; see also https://www.bmuv.de/themen/bildung-beteiligung/umweltinformation/die-aarhus-konvention).

5 The agreement entered into force on 30.10.2001 (for the current status of implementation see: https://unece.org/environment-policy/public-participation/aarhus-convention/status-ratification).

6 On the three pillars of the Aarhus Convention, see e.g. *Federal Environment Agency (Umweltbundesamt - UBA)*, Beteiligungsrechte im Umweltschutz, Was bringt Ihnen die Aarhus-Konvention?, 2018, p. 1; *Fischer-Hüftle*, Beteiligungs- und Klagerechte im Naturschutz, NuR 2018, 735, 736.

7 *Wegner*, Subjektiv-rechtliche Ansätze im Völkerrecht zum Schutz biologischer Vielfalt, 2018, p. 449; *Federal Environment Agency (UBA)*, Beteiligungsrechte im Umweltschutz, Was bringt Ihnen die Aarhus-Konvention?, 2018, p.4.

ficant activities (decisions, acts or omissions) within the meaning of Art. 6 para. 1 AC and - if Contracting States so provide - against the violation of other relevant provisions of the Aarhus Convention[8]. Environmentally significant activities with the meaning of Art. 6 para. 1 AC are decisions on whether to permit proposed activities listed in Annex 1 of the Aarhus Convention[9] as well as decisions on proposed activities not listed therein, which may have a significant effect on the environment. Generally, it is a matter of permitting decisions by state bodies (authorities) on environmentally relevant projects. The "Public concerned" means in accordance with Art. 2 No. 5 AC "the public affected or likely to be affected by, or having an interest in, the environmental decision-making". It goes on to say that such an interest is given in the case of "non-governmental organizations promoting environmental protection and meeting any requirements under national law". This extends the legal protection conveyed by Art. 9 para. 2 AC to environmental organisations[10], which in practice are of particular importance for the protection of environmental rights[11]. The basic idea of being concerned or affected is therefore the existence of a particularly condensed relationship between the state administration and the persons affected by administrative decisions[12]. In addition to a factual concern, the normative element of a (significant) interest also constitutes a concern, which is furthermore always considered to be per se given for environmental organisations[13].

More generally and subordinate[14] to this requirement relating to the public concerned, Art. 9 para. 3 AC then requires that members of the public (not limited to parts concerned), be given legal remedies to review the environ-

8 *Wegner,* Subjektiv-rechtliche Ansätze im Völkerrecht zum Schutz biologischer Vielfalt, 2018, p. 454; *Kahl/Gärditz,* Umweltrecht, 11th edition 2019, § 5 no. 13.

9 Annex 1 contains a list of various industrial plants, plants for agriculture, plants for energy production as well as energy transport, infrastructure plants and other categories.

10 Named as environmental organisations or environmental associations in the following.

11 Cf. *Wegner,* Subjektiv-rechtliche Ansätze im Völkerrecht zum Schutz biologischer Vielfalt, 2018, p. 407 („das bestimmende Zuordnungssubjekt für die Rechtspositionen der Aarhus-Konvention").

12 *Guckelberger,* Formen von Öffentlichkeit und Öffentlichkeitsbeteiligung im Umweltverwaltungsrecht, VerwArch 2012, 31, 38; *Wegner,* Subjektiv-rechtliche Ansätze im Völkerrecht zum Schutz biologischer Vielfalt, 2018, p. 406.

13 *Wegner,* Subjektiv-rechtliche Ansätze im Völkerrecht zum Schutz biologischer Vielfalt, 2018, p. 406; *Guckelberger,* Aarhus-Konvention und Unionsrecht als Faktoren für die Verbandsklage, NuR 2020, 149, 150; *Schenderlein,* Rechtsschutz und Partizipation im Umweltrecht, 2013, p. 133.

14 See in this regard, for example, ECJ, Judgment of 20 December 2017, C-664/15, para. 41 et seq.

mental law applicable in the respective Contracting State provided they fulfil criteria laid down in their national law[15]. Further paragraphs of Art. 9 AC (para. 4 and 5) do not contain any independent guarantees but adress the effectiveness of legal protection according to the procedures of paragraphs 1 to 3[16].

2. European law

The former European Community (EC) – now the European Union (EU) – approved the Aarhus Convention by decision in 2005[17]. Thus, the provisions of the Convention became an integral part of the European legal order (see Art. 216 para. 2 TFEU[18])[19]. The implementation of the Aarhus Convention and its provisions is served by various Union legal acts. With the so-called Aarhus Regulation[20], for example, legal protection against measures of Union institutions was extended beyond the provisions of Art. 263 TFEU[21]. The obligations of Art. 9 para. 2 AC (public concerned) were implemented at European level by Art. 11 of Directive 2011/92/EU (EIA Directive)[22] and Art. 25 of Directive 2010/75/EU (Industrial Emissions Directive)[23], in each case for the

15 *Kahl/Gärditz,* Umweltrecht, 11th edition 2019, § 5 No. 13; *Fischer-Hüftle,* Beteiligungs- und Klagerechte im Naturschutz, NuR 2018, 735, 738.

16 *Wegner,* Subjektiv-rechtliche Ansätze im Völkerrecht zum Schutz biologischer Vielfalt, 2018, p. 450.

17 Council Decision of 17 February 2005 on the conclusion, on behalf of the European Community, of the Convention on access to information, public participation in decision-making and access to justice in environmental matters, (2005/370/EC), OJ EU No. L 124, 17 May 2005, p. 1.

18 Treaty on the Functioning of the European Union (TFEU), consolidated version of 26 October 2012, OJ EU No. C 326 of 26 October 2012, p. 47.

19 ECJ, Judgment of 08 March 2011, C-240/09, para. 30; *Fischer-Hüftle,* Beteiligungs- und Klagerechte im Naturschutz, NuR 2018, 735, 736.

20 Regulation (EC) No 1367/2006 of the European Parliament and of the Council of 6 September 2006 on the application of the provisions of the Aarhus Convention on Access to Information, Public Participation in Decision-making and Access to Justice in Environmental Matters to Community institutions and bodies, OJ EU No L 264, 25 September 2006, p. 13.

21 *Kahl/Gärditz,* Umweltrecht, 11th edition 2019, § 5 no. 15.

22 Directive 2011/92/EU of the European Parliament and of the Council of 13 December 2011 on the assessment of the effects of certain public and private projects on the environment, OJ EU No. L 26, 28 January 2012, p. 1.

23 Directive 2010/75/EU of the European Parliament and of the Council of 24 November 2010 on industrial emissions (integrated pollution prevention and control), OJ EU No. L 334, 17 December 2010, p. 17.

scope of application of the aforementioned Directives[24]. Via a reference in Art. 23 lit. b of Directive 2012/18/EU (Seveso Directive)[25], they also apply with regard to the scope of this Directive[26]. Art. 9 para. 3 AC has not been implemented at the level of European law. However, according to the ECJ, the fact that the European Union has ratified the Aarhus Convention obliges Member State courts to interpret national law in such a way that it is as consistent as possible with the objectives of Art. 9 para. 3 AC to allow a wider access to justice[27].

3. German law

The Code of Administrative Court Procedure (Verwaltungsgerichtsordnung - VwGO)[28] contains general provisions on legal protection against state approvals and on administrative disputes in general. The German model of legal protection in administrative law is based on the system of infringement action, that means only people who assert the infringement of a subjective public right are authorised to file an action (§ 42 para. 2 VwGO)[29]. The scope of legal protection thus depends on whether the case in question involves the violation of a norm that serves to protect the person seeking legal protection ("Schutznormtheorie"/protective norm theory)[30]. However, this system is insufficient for adequate legal protection in environmental matters, as environmental protection regulations (such as species or area protection law) often

---

24 *Kahl/Gärditz,* Umweltrecht, 11th edition 2019, § 5 no. 14.

25 Directive 2012/18/EU of the European Parliament and of the Council of 4 July 2012 on the control of major-accident hazards involving dangerous substances, amending and subsequently repealing Council Directive 96/82/EC, OJ EU No. L 197, 24 July 2012, p. 1.

26 *Kahl/Gärditz,* Umweltrecht, 11th edition 2019, § 5 no. 14; similarly Art. 13 Directive 2004/35/EC (Environmental Damage Directive).

27 ECJ, Judgment of 08 March 2011, C-240/09, para. 50 et seq.; *Franzius,* Verbandsklage im Umweltrecht, NuR 2019, 649, 650.

28 Verwaltungsgerichtsordnung as promulgated on 19 March 1991 (BGBl. I S. 686), as last amended by Article 2 of the Act of 8 October 2021 (BGBl. I S. 4650).

29 *Kahl/Gärditz,* Umweltrecht, 11th edition 2019, § 5 no. 2; generally *Wahl/Schütz,* in: Schoch/Schneider, VwGO, 07/2021, § 42 no. 5 et seq.

30 *Kahl/Gärditz,* Umweltrecht, 11th edition 2019, § 5 no. 2; fundamentally on the protective norm theory ("Schutznormtheorie"), for example BVerwG, Judegement of 15 November 1985, 8 C 43/83, juris no. 15 with reference to BVerwG, Judgement of 25 February 1977, IV C 22.75; see also *Wysk,* in: Wysk, VwGO, 3rd edition 2020, § 42 no. 113 et seq.

lack this subjectivisable protective norm character[31]. It is therefore to a certain extent superimposed and supplemented by environmental-specific special administrative procedural law, in particular[32] in the form of the "Umweltrechtsbehelfsgesetz (UmwRG)[33]". This forms the central set of rules for the implementation of the International and European legal requirements already described, which consequently also have decisive significance for the interpretation of the provisions of the UmwRG[34]. Material scope of application of the UmwRG are legal remedies by private individuals and environmental organisations against certain decisions conclusively listed in § 1 para. 1 sentence 1 UmwRG[35]. Environmental organisations acknowledged under § 3 UmwRG may bring forth an action irrespective of the violation of their own rights (§ 2 UmwRG)[36]. The prerequisite for this, however, is in particular the assertion that a decision within the meaning of § 1 para. 1 sentence 1 UmwRG or its omission contradicts legal provisions which may be of significance for the decision (§ 2 para. 1 sentence 1 no. 1 UmwRG) and affects the association in its statutory area of responsibility (§ 2 para. 1 sentence 1 no. 2 UmwRG). § 4 UmwRG enables the judicial assertion of certain procedural errors. This is interesting insofar as, according to the traditional understanding of legal protection in administrative law in Germany, procedural rules can in principle not confer legal standing due to their lack of protective normative character[37].

The UmwRG is regularly enhanced and, as an act of implementation in relation to higher-ranking law, is characterised by ECJ jurisdiction on the relevant European law, which in turn is primarily based on requirements of

31 See, for example, with regard to territorial protection law: BVerwG, Judgement of 17 February 2021, 7 C 3/20, juris no. 7 et seq.; generally *Kahl/Gärditz,* Umweltrecht, 11th edition 2019, § 5 no. 2.

32 In addition, § 64 of the "Bundesnaturschutzgesetz" (Federal Nature Conservation Act) contains a special legal remedy provision relating to recognised nature conservation organisations (for more details see, for example, *Steiger/Kramp,* Grüne Liga gegen Tesla - Kann und soll das Verbandsklagerecht eingeschränkt werden?, ZUR 2020, 358, 362 f.).

33 Umwelt-Rechtsbehelfsgesetz as promulgated on 23 August 2017 (BGBl. I S. 3290), as last amended by Article 8 of the Act of 25 February 2021 (BGBl. I S. 306).

34 *Schlacke,* Die Novelle des UmwRG 2017, NVwZ 2017, 905, 908; *Franzius,* in: Schink/Reidt/Mitschang, UVPG/UmwRG, 2018, § 1 UmwRG no. 4 et seq.

35 *Franzius,* in: Schink/Reidt/Mitschang, UVPG/UmwRG, 2018, § 1 UmwRG no. 1

36 Regarding acknowledgement see § 3 UmwRG.

37 *Kahl/Gärditz,* Umweltrecht, 11th edition 2019, § 5 no. 24; see also *Franzius,* Verbandsklage im Umweltrecht, NuR 2019, 649, 653.

the Aarhus Convention (see above)[38]. The implementation by the UmwRG is sometimes criticised as insufficient in various respects[39].

B. Current duscussion regardin limitations on environmental legal protection

At present, demands for acceleration of planning and permitting for infrastructure projects as well as industrial plants can be heard quite clearly[40] - not only in Germany[41]. The call for acceleration is particularly loud and understandable with regard to renewable energy plants (especially wind turbines). A timely expansion of the corresponding production capacities is indispensable to achieve the political and legal climate protection goals[42]. Furthermore the independence of energy production made possible for Germany by renewable energies and the associated issue of energy supply security have recently become even more important[43].

---

38 *Fischer-Hüftle,* Beteiligungs- und Klagerechte im Naturschutz, NuR 2018, 735, 736.

39 For example, the scope of application falls short of the requirements of International and European law (e.g. *Franzius,* in: Schink/Reidt/Mitschang, UVPG/UmwRG, 2018, § 1 UmwRG no. 8; *Schlacke,* Die Novelle des UmwRG 2017, NVwZ 2017, 905, 908); Art. 9 para. 3 AC was insufficiently implemented (e.g. *Fischer-Hüftle,* Beteiligungs- und Klagerechte im Naturschutz, NuR 2018, 735, 736); see also *Franzius,* Verbandsklage im Umweltrecht, NuR 2019, 649.

40 Representative of many: *Federal Ministry for Economic Affairs and Climate Protection,* Eröffnungsbilanz Klimaschutz, 2022, p. 9.

41 See for example *European Commission,* Communication from the Commission to the European Parliament, the European Council, the Council, the European Economic and Social Committee and the Committee of the Regions, REPowerEU: A Common European Approach for More Affordable, Secure and Sustainable Energy, COM(2022) 108 final, p. 11.

42 For example, § 3 para. 1, 2 "Klimaschutzgesetz (KSG)" (Climate Protection Act); for the European level: Amended proposal for a Regulation of the European Parliament and of the Council establishing a framework for achieving climate neutrality and amending Regulation (EU) 2018/1999 (European Climate Change Act), COM(2020) 563 final; for the international level: Paris Agreement based on the United Nations Framework Convention on Climate Change of 12 December 2015.

43 See, for example, *Federal Ministry for Economic Affairs and Climate Protection,* Gesetz zu Sofortmaßnahmen für einen beschleunigten Ausbau der erneuerbaren Energien und weiteren Maßnahmen im Stromsektor, legal act from 20 Juli 2022; *Federal Ministry for the Environment, Nature Conservation, Nuclear Safety and Consumer Protection/ Federal Ministry for Economic Affairs and Climate Protection,* Beschleunigung des naturverträglichen Ausbaus der Windenergie an Land, Eckpunktepapier of 04 April 2022, p. 2; cf. also COM(2022) 108 final, p. 1.

Juridical discussions in this context not only revolve around the legal requirements and framework conditions for the actual planning and permitting process, but also include the level of legal protection. The realisation of such projects is delayed not only by lengthy and complex permitting procedures, but also by legal disputes (e.g. over granted or refused permits). Against this backdrop, various demands for restrictions on legal protection are being put forward. In the following, selected proposals of this kind are going to be examined for their compatibility with the requirements of International and European law[44]. As a higher-ranking law, these requirements can limit the scope of the German legislature for possible required adjustments. An important source of knowledge in this regard is the relevant case law of the European Court of Justice (ECJ).

1. Restrictions of environmental organisations' right of legal standing

It is precisely the far-reaching legal protection opportunities of environmental associations that are a thorn in the side of some; possibly already because it used to be different and extensions in German administrative procedural law (in particular § 2 UmwRG) perceived as too far-reaching were only carried out following a rebuke by the ECJ[45]. Sometimes there are even calls for the abolition of the right of associations to file an action[46]. However, it is more than obvious that such a demand is in conflict with higher-ranking law. The public concerned in the sense of Art. 9 para. 2 AC as well as Art. 11 EIA Directive and Art. 25 Industrial Emissions Directive also include organisations ("non-governmental organisations promoting environmental protection", according to Art. 11 EIA Directive) explicitly.

At its 32nd party convention the Christian Democratic Union of Germany (CDU) decided to limit the right of organisations to file an action at least to cases where the interests of the organisation in question are directly con-

44 This does not imply any claim to completeness.

45 Starting with ECJ, Judgment of 12 May 2011, C-115/09; see *Franzius,* Verbandsklage im Umweltrecht, NuR 2019, 649, 650 f.; *Guckelberger,* Aarhus-Konvention und Unionsrecht als prägende Faktoren für die Verbandsklage im UmwRG, NuR 2020, 149, 149 et seq.; for more on the criticism of organisations' actions also see *Steiger/Kramp,* Grüne Liga gegen Tesla - Kann und soll das Verbandsklagerecht eingeschränkt werden?, ZUR 2020, 358, 360 et seq.

46 *Christian Democratic Union (CDU),* Sammlung der Anträge und Empfehlungen der Antragskommission, 32nd Party Congress of the CDU of Germany, 22-23 November 2019, Application no. C 235.

cerned or where the organisation was not properly involved (in the meaning of participation) in the procedure of approval[47]. A restriction in the form of direct concern is probably aimed at depriving environmental organisations of the opportunity to complain about the violation of such regulations that exclusively serve the public interest. In principle, this would correspond to the legal situation before the creation of the UmwRG (pure infringement action), which is, however, rightly and with good cause outdated in the context of legal protection in environmental matters. Admittedly, Art. 9 para. 2 sentence 1 AC forces the access to justice for members of the public concerned who have a sufficient interest or alternatively assert an infringement of rights, provided that the procedural law of the respective Contracting State requires it. The second alternative could indicate the possibility of a certain restriction of access to justice in the sense of being affected in the form of a violation of one's own individual rights[48]. However, this possibility is restricted by Art. 9 para. 2 sentence 2 AC insofar as the restriction of the violation of rights (as well as of the sufficient interest) must be in line with the objective of granting the public concerned broad access to courts. And this public concerned also includes, via Art. 2 No. 5 AC, environmental organisations which fulfil any possible requirements of a Contract state's law (§ 3 UmwRG, for example, requires acknowledgement, see below). Already in 2011 the ECJ explicitly clarified that it must be possible for environmental organisations to also assert the violation of such substantive norms that protect the environment solely in the interest of the general public[49]. It is precisely in this assertion of general and not merely individual interests that the primary purpose of the representative action does lie[50]. Concern within the meaning of the Aarhus Convention does explicitly not require factual concern or the state of being affected, but is also given in the case of a sufficient interest, which is furthermore fictitious in relation to environmental associations (see already under B. I.).

47 *CDU*, Other Resolutions of the 32nd Party Congress of the CDU of Germany, 22-23 November 2019, p. 50; *CDU*, Nachhaltigkeit, Wachstum, Wohlstand – die Soziale Martkwirtschaft von Morgen, Resolution of the 32nd Party Congress of the CDU of Germany, 22-23 November 2019, p. 14. In contrast, the CDU's election manifesto for the Bundestag elections only mentioned streamlining the organisations' right of legal standing (*CDU*, Das Programm für Stabilität und Erneuerung - Gemeinsam für ein modernes Deutschland, 2021, p. 36).

48 Cf. *Wegner*, Subjektiv-rechtliche Ansätze im Völkerrecht zum Schutz biologischer Vielfalt, 2018, p. 458.

49 ECJ, Judgment of 12 May 2011, C-115/09 para. 44; *Wegner*, Subjektiv-rechtliche Ansätze im Völkerrecht zum Schutz biologischer Vielfalt, 2018, p. 468.

50 *Heß*, Aktivierung der Umweltverbandsklage, ZUR 2018, 686, 687.

The sometimes proposed restriction thus violates higher-ranking law and would be inadmissible. The restriction of relevant associations in Art. 2 No. 5 AC to those which fulfil all requirements under national law also does not provide a gateway for this. The Aarhus Convention Compliance Committee (ACCC)[51] requires in this respect that the requirements are clearly defined, do not constitute an unreasonable burden and are not applied in a way that significantly shortens the access of such organisations to justice[52]. The requirements for the hereunto based recognition of an environmental association, which is required in Germany, must be neither too high nor purely politically motivated[53].

Equally inadmissible, as it contradicts higher-ranking law, is the aforementioned proposal limiting the right of organisations to file an action to cases in which the association concerned has not been properly involved. Rather, the jurisdiction of the ECJ indicates that environmental organisations can in principle invoke all procedural violations, without the subjective-legal quality of the procedural provision being in any way relevant[54]. For the sake of completeness, however, it should be mentioned at this point that the ECJ does not require the annulment of procedurally defective decisions without any exception. In this respect, it depends on whether the error had an effect on the result (then annulment) or not (see also § 4 UmwRG)[55].

2. Minimum number of members for environmental organisations

Time and again there are discussions about the minimum number of members that an environmental organisation must have. The sizes in question range from 25 to 40 or even 100 individuals[56]. Legally, this could be imple-

51 The ACCC is not an original body of the Aarhus Convention but was created by decision of the Meeting of the Parties at the first Conference of the Parties (*Lustz/Sauer,* Neuigkeiten zur Aarhus-Konvention – die 6. Vertragsstaatenkonferenz in Montenegro, EurUP 2018, 118, 119).

52 ACCC/C/2008/31 (Germany), para. 71; so also *Wegner,* Subjektiv-rechtliche Ansätze im Völkerrecht zum Schutz biologischer Vielfalt, 2018, p. 408.

53 *Wegner,* Subjektiv-rechtliche Ansätze im Völkerrecht zum Schutz biologischer Vielfalt, 2018, p. 407 (with further references).

54 ECJ, Judgment of 07 November 2013, C-72/12, para. 36 et seq.; *Wegner*, Subjektiv-rechtliche Ansätze im Völkerrecht zum Schutz biologischer Vielfalt, 2018, p. 472 et seq.

55 ECJ, Judgment of 07 November 2013, C-72/12, para. 49; for example, *Wegner,* Subjektiv-rechtliche Ansätze im Völkerrecht zum Schutz biologischer Vielfalt, 2018, p. 473.

56 Promoting an orientation in the range between 25 and 50 members: *Schieferdecker,* in: Hoppe/Beckmann/Kment, UVPG, § 3 UmwRG no. 40; promoting a minimum number

mented in the form of a requirement for acknowledgement under § 3 UmwRG. The requirement of acknowledgement as such is also compatible with higher-ranking law. Art. 2 No. 5 AC only includes among the public concerned such non-governmental environmental organisations that fulfil all the requirements under domestic law. With regard to the number of members, § 3 para. 1 sentence 1 no. 3 UmwRG currently only provides for the guarantee of an appropriate fulfilment of tasks ("Gewähr für eine sachgerechte Aufgabenerfüllung"), from which a certain lower limit can be derived, at least on an abstract level[57]. There are also no specific statements on a required number of members at the level of European or International law. The ECJ has considered a required minimum size of at least 2,000 members to be inadmissible on the grounds that this would result in an excessive restriction of access to courts[58]. In doing so, the ECJ emphasised that the EIA Directive also covers small-scale matters which could be better dealt with by organisations at a local level[59]. Therefore, minimum admissible sizes are likely to be far below the objectionable threshold; probably 25 to 40 rather than 100 individuals[60]. The decisive factor is that they must not impede the access of the public concerned to judicial review pursuant to Art. 11 EIA Directive[61].

3. Reintroduction of substantive preclusion

Preclusion basically aims at enabling the submission of objections only for a certain period of time. Belated objections are no longer taken into account and are, so to speak, excluded or precluded. A distinction can be made between formal (procedural) and substantive preclusion. While formal preclusion means that belated objections are only excluded for the relevant (administrative or judicial) proceeding, substantive preclusion means that be-

---

of 100 members in territorial states: *Louis*, Die Anerkennung von Naturschutzverbänden, NuR 1994, 381, 384; against a link to an abstract number of members: *Fellenberg/Schiller*, in: Landmann/Rohmer, Umweltrecht, 09/2021, § 3 UmwRG no. 25.

57 Cf. BVerwG, Judgment of 06 December 1985, 4 C 55/82, juris no. 14.

58 ECJ, Judgment of 15 October 2009, C-263/08, para. 47 et seq.

59 ECJ, Judgment of 15 October 2009, C-263/08, para. 50.

60 Thus *Schieferdecker*, in: Hoppe/Beckmann/Kment, UVPG/UmwRG, 5th ed. 2018, § 3 UmwRG no. 42 (rather between 25 and 50 members).

61 *Franzius*, in: Schink/Reidt/Mitschang, UVPG/UmwRG, 2018, § 3 UmwRG no. 11.

lated objections are also excluded in subsequent judicial proceedings[62]. While there are still some regulations that provide for formal preclusion (in immission control licensing procedures, cf. § 10 para. 3 sentence 5 BImSchG[63], in administrative court proceedings, cf. § 6 UmwRG[64]), substantive preclusion does no longer exist in Germany[65]. Until 2017, however, § 2 para. 3 UmwRG still provided for such a preclusion in relation to environmental organisations for various constellations (including wind energy projects subject to EIA)[66]. In 2015, though, the ECJ declared this to be incompatible with Article 11 of the EIA Directive and Article 25 of the Industrial Emissions Directive, as it represented an excessive restriction of legal protection[67]. In response to that, this provision of substantive preclusion was deleted from the German law[68].

Nevertheless, there are still voices in favour of substantive preclusion and calling for a return to it in the pursuit of procedural acceleration[69]. Referring to later case law of the ECJ[70], proponents do not see a fundamental rejection of substantive preclusion[71]. It is correct that the ECJ, against the background of the facts underlying the decision in question, did at least indicate which legal requirements a preclusion rule would have to fulfil[72]. However, to see

62 On this, for example, *Weiß*, in: Schoch/Schneider, VwVfG, § 73 no. 281 et seq.; *Wegner*, Subjektiv-rechtliche Ansätze im Völkerrecht zum Schutz biologischer Vielfalt, 2018, p. 495.

63 Bundes-Immissionsschutzgesetz (Federal Immission Control Act) as promulgated on 17 May 2013 (BGBl. I S. 1274; 2021 I S. 123), as last amended by Art. 1 of the Act of 24 September 2021 (BGBl. I S. 4458).

64 For more details on remaining preclusion provisions, see *Schlacke*, Die Novelle des UmwRG 2017, NVwZ 2017, 905, 909 et seq.; for more details on § 6 UmwRG, see *Guckelberger*, Die Begründetheit von Umweltrechtsbehelfen von Verbänden seit der UmwRG-Novelle 2017, NuR 2020, 655, 655 et seq.

65 See at most in relation to certain plans and programmes: § 7 para. 3 UmwRG.

66 *Guckelberger*, Aarhus-Konvention und Unionsrecht als Faktoren für die Verbandsklage, NuR 2020, 149, 151.

67 ECJ, Judgment of 15 October 2015, C-137/14, para. 68 et seq., esp. para. 75 et seq.

68 BT-Drs. 18/9526, p. 39.

69 *Durner*, Nationale Spielräume für eine Wiedereinführung der Präklusion, VerwArch 2020, 162, 163; *Durner*, in: BMVI, Rechtsgutachten zur Wiedereinführung der Präklusion, 2019, p. 3 (with further references).

70 ECJ, Judgment of 20 December 2017, C-664/15.

71 *Durner*, in: BMVI, Rechtsgutachten zur Wiedereinführung der Präklusion, 2019, p. 50; *Durner*, Nationale Spielräume für eine Wiedereinführung der Präklusion, VerwArch 2020, 162.

72 ECJ, Judgment of 20 December 2017, C-664/15 para. 90 et seq.; *Gärditz*, Kurzgutachten: Zulässigkeit und Zweckmäßigkeit der materiellen Präklusion im Umweltrechtsschutz,

this as a complimentary ticket for the reintroduction of substantive preclusion would go way too far. For one thing, the ECJ decision in question was restricted to the scope of application of Art. 9 para. 3 AC (parts of the public not concerned)[73]. For another thing, the ECJ has meanwhile explicitely clarified that a substantive preclusion of objections through the relevant sections of the public concerned by a project (Art. 9 para. 2 AC) is inadmissible[74]. Jurisdiction clearly states a strict prohibition of preclusion in this respect[75]. Possible positive effects in terms of legal policy or practice (acceleration of proceedings) do not change this procedural inadmissibility. In 2015, the ECJ had already clearly perceived that the first-time submission of an objection before the court could impede the course of proceedings but rejected this argument because it was incompatible with the legal protection provisions of Art. 11 EIA Directive and Art. 25 Industrial Emissions Directive[76].

Consequently, the legislator's scope for the (re-)introduction of substantive preclusion is small at best. Such a (re-)introduction is possible with the ECJ, for example, in relation to parts of the public not concerned (Art. 9 para. 3 AC), unless the non-participation in the proceedings is not (justifiably) reproachable as to the person seeking legal protection[77]. However, sections of the public that are not concerned should lack the right to sue anyway (§ 42 para. 2 VwGO), so that substantive preclusion would be superfluous or at least have a manageable effect. Furthermore, substantive preclusion would still be admissible - apart from certain constellations in planning procedures (see already § 7 para. 3 UmwRG) - in cases of the abuse of rights. On the one hand,

---

in: UBA, Wissenschaftliche Unterstützung des Rechtsschutzes in Umweltangelegenheiten in der 19. Legislaturperiode, 2021, p. 198 (200).

73 *Gärditz*, Kurzgutachten: Zulässigkeit und Zweckmäßigkeit der materiellen Präklusion im Umweltrechtsschutz, in: UBA, Wissenschaftliche Unterstützung des Rechtsschutzes in Umweltangelegenheiten in der 19. Legislaturperiode, 2021, p. 198 (200).

74 ECJ, Judgment of 14 January 2021, C-826/18, para. 69.

75 ECJ, Judgment of 14 January 2021, C-826/18, para. 69; also *Gärditz*, Kurzgutachten: Zulässigkeit und Zweckmäßigkeit der materiellen Präklusion im Umweltrechtsschutz, in: UBA, Wissenschaftliche Unterstützung des Rechtsschutzes in Umweltangelegenheiten in der 19. Legislaturperiode, 2021, p. 198 (206).

76 ECJ, Judgment of 15 October 2015, C-137/14, para. 81.

77 ECJ, Judgment of 14 January 2021, C-826/18, para. 69.; *Gärditz*, Kurzgutachten: Zulässigkeit und Zweckmäßigkeit der materiellen Präklusion im Umweltrechtsschutz, in: UBA, Wissenschaftliche Unterstützung des Rechtsschutzes in Umweltangelegenheiten in der 19. Legislaturperiode, 2021, p. 198 (207). See on an earlier push to already limit the right to object to the public concerned: BR-Drs. 510/20.

the legislator has already regulated this (see § 5 UmwRG)[78]. On the other hand, the determination of abusive or dishonest conduct in this context is likely to be quite difficult[79].

C. Conclusion

It has become apparent that the discussions about restrictions on environmental legal protection in Germany described above do quickly come up against legal limits. The leeway of the German legislator is at best small. Any advances would always be fraught with at least a high degree of legal uncertainty due to the sword of Damocles in the form of the higher-ranking requirements of International and European law. More legal uncertainty, however, achieves exactly the opposite of the desired aim (acceleration and simplification of procedures) and is therefore counterproductive. It is true that the provisions of International and European law are not carved out in stone; the relevant rules could of course also be changed and adapted. For one thing, however, Germany or the German government could at best work towards such changes and try to convince other Contract or Member States of corresponding projects. For another thing, such amendment procedures require quite a considerable amount of time and would therefore be an option in the medium term at best, but probably rather only in the long run. They are therefore not suitable as measures to achieve the acceleration that is urgently and, above all, promptly needed in the area of renewable energy development. Time and effort should rather be invested more sensibly. For example, the lack of legally binding concretisation of legal requirements (especially in species protection law, monument protection law or air traffic law) causes significant problems. The reduction of legal uncertainties and the creation of uniform standards would create certainty and reduce delays. In addition, the legal framework for administrative procedures still offers some options for streamlining (e.g. stricter deadline regulations, tighter

78 First assertion of the infringement in court proceedings is abusive, see e.g. ECJ, Judgment of 15 October 2015, C-137/14, para. 81.

79 Cf. OVG Koblenz, Judgment of 06 November 2019, 8 C 10240/18, para. 76; but see also *Gärditz*, Kurzgutachten: Zulässigkeit und Zweckmäßigkeit der materiellen Präklusion im Umweltrechtsschutz, in: UBA, Wissenschaftliche Unterstützung des Rechtsschutzes in Umweltangelegenheiten in der 19. Legislaturperiode, 2021, p. 198 (214).

participation procedures)[80]. Finally, restrictions on access to justice should not be part of the acceleration instruments, as the granting of comprehensive and far-reaching legal protection is a particularly high asset worth preserving. This holds especially true in a sensitive area as important to the general public as environmental protection is. The achievements based on the Aarhus Convention should not be carelessly sacrificed as a political reaction to problems in the field of renewable energy development or other infrastructure projects.

80 See in detail on reform approaches in the law with regard to wind turbines *Schmidt/ Sailer*, Reformansätze zum Genehmigungsrecht von Windenergieanlagen, Würzburger Studien zum Umweltenergierecht No. 25 of 28 January 2022; *Wegner*, Reformansätze zum Planungsrecht von Windenergieanlagen, Würzburger Studien zum Umweltenergierecht No. 26 of 11 February 2022.

International Environmental Law Enforcement Mechanisms: Ensuring Compliance with Multilateral Environmental Agreements (Meas): Non-Compliance and Dispute Settlement

*Dr. Serpil Işık**

Abstract

In International Environmental Law, a range of International mechanisms are usable to attend to the peaceble settlement of environmental disputes. This article will focus on the dispute resolution techniques and enforcement mechanisms in International Environmental Law and then ensuring compliance with Multilateral Environmental Agreements (MEAs) in the context of international environmental law.

Keywords: Dispute settlement, enforcement mechanisms, the enforcement authorities, arbitration, mediation.

I. Introduction

Recently, using the alternative ways of resolving conflicts with a neutral third party has become more popular between the parties seeking resolution of a dispute arisen among them.[1] Accordingly, various types of alternative

* Research Assistant, PhD, Istanbul University, Faculty of Law, Department of Civil Procedure and Enforcement - Bankruptcy Law, İstanbul, Türkiye. E-mail: serpil.isik@istanbul.edu.tr. ORCID: 0000-0003-4329-1138.

1 Roth, M./*Stegner*, M.: Mediation in Austria, Yearbook on International Arbitration, Vol. 3, (S. 367-3783), S. 367; *Lisnek*, P. M.: Mediation: Untangling Business Disputes through ADR, Commercial Law Bulletin, July/August 1993, (S. 12-19), S. 16; *Swinson*, S. K.: Alternative Dispute Resolution ın Bankruptcy, Tulsa Law Journal, Vol. 36, Issue 4 (Summer 2001), (S. 813-818), S. 813; *Lerman*, L. G.: The Teaching of Alternative Dispute Resolution, Journal of Legal Education, Vol. 37, Issue 1(1987), (S. 37-40), S. 38; *Goss*, J.: An Introduction to Alternative Dispute Resolution, Alberta Law Review, Vol. 34, Issue 1 (1995), (S. 1-33), S. 2; *Petillon*, L. R.: Recent Developments in Alternative Dispute Resolution, Pepperdine Law Review, Vol. 14, Issue 4 (1987), (S. 929-942), S. 929; *Scalise*, D. G./*Engels*, J. E., Alternative Dispute Resolutions: a Commercial Guide for Dispute Management, Advocates' Quarterly, Vol. 9, Issue 1(February 1988), (S. 53-76), S. 59; *Green*, E. D.: Corporate Alternative Dispute Resolution, Ohio State Journal on Dispute Resolution, Vol. 1, Issue 2 (1986), (S. 203-298), S. 205; *Glasner* Q. C., K.: Contract Disputes and Alternative Disputes Resolution: Some Observations, Advocate (Vancouver Bar Association), Vol. 59, Issue 5 (September 2001), (S. 725-732), S. 725; *Işık*, Serpil: Mediation as an Altrnative Dispute Resolution Method and Mediation Process in Turkish Law System:

dispute resolution (ADR) methods to be used to resolve disputes have been developed in the United States of America[2] (USA) in civil law systems of Continental Europe and the Middle East.[3] The number of applicable methods increased as the use alternative dispute resolution (ADR) methods became popular around the world.[4] So, there are various types of alternative dispute resolution methods used to settle disputes between parties.[5] In civil Law, the mostly preferred alternative dispute resolution methods[6] are "*arbitration*", "*mediation*", "*early neutral evaluation (ENE)*", "*fact finding*", "*private judgment (PJ) or private tribunals (PT)*", "*summary jury trial (SJT)*", "*adjudication*", "*ombudsman*", "*negotiation*", "*conciliation*", "*court-annexed arbitration (COA)*"...etc.[7]

Smilarly, in International Environmental Law, a range of International mechanisms are usable to attend to the peaceble settlement of environmental disputes.[8] (a6) Article (Art.) 33 of the United Nations (UN) Regulation states

---

An Overview, Annales de la Faculté deDroit d'Istanbul (2016), [Vol. 48, No. 65], (S. 55-87), S. 56.

2 See, *Eiholzer*, H.: Die Streitbeilegungsabrede, (Ein Beitrag zu alternativen Formen der Streitbeilegung, namentlich zur Mediation), Universitättverlag Freiburg Schweiz,1998, 1. Kapitel, Nr. 37 ff.; *Riskin*, S. 19; *Stein*, S. 284-285; Also, see, National EnvironmentalPolicy Act of 1970, 42 U.S.C. §§ 4321-4347 (1971).

3 See, *Lisnek*, S. 16 ff; *Goss*, S. 2; *Scalise/Engels*, S. 60; *Işık*, S. 57; *Bilder*, S. 471.

4 *Roth/Stegner*, S. 367; *Lisnek*, S. 13; *Petillon*, S. 929; *Abernathy*, J. M.: Alternative Dispute Resolution in Commercial Cases, Annual Survey of American Law Supplement, Vol. 1985, (S. 29-50), S. 29.

5 See, *Lisnek*, S. 16; *Berger*, Nr. 2-75, S. 51; *Goss*, p. 5; *Scalise/Engels*, p. 60; *Green*, S. 205; *Woodman*, S. 3; *Dana J.*, S. 351; *Glasner Q. C.*, S. 725; *Guidry*, S. 406; *Işık*, S. 61-62; *Bilder*, S. 471.

6 In civil law systems alternative dispute resolution (ADR) methods are effective methods to be used altogether without any exclusion (*Goss*, S. 5). According to literature, Alternative Dispute Resolution (ADR) methods, may be generally divided into tree broad catagories: "*(1) Mediation, (2) Arbitration, (3) Negotiation*" (See *Berger*, Nr. 2-75, S. 51; *Eiholzer*, 1. Kapitel, Nr. 53, S. 16; *Glasner Q. C.*, S. 729).

7 For more information about "the various forms of Alternative Dispute Resolution (ADR)" see *Scalise/Engels*, S. 60 et seq; *Green*, S. 238 et seq; *Riskin*, S. 21-24; *Dana J.*, S. 351; *Glasner Q. C.*, S. 726; *Breen*, S. 1014 et seq.; *Eiholzer*, 1. Kapitel, S. 15-29; *Işık*, S. 61 et seq.

8 See, *Sands/Peel/Fabra/Mackenzie*, S. 159; *Bilder*, S. 471. In this days, a significant number of cases on the International Courts of Justice (ICJ)'s docket have rised sunstantial environmental problems (See, *Craik*, A. Neil: Recalcitrant Reality and Chosen Ideals: The Public Function of Dispute Settlement in International Environmental Law, The Georgetown International Law Review (1998), [Vol. 10, Issue 2], (S. 551-580), S. 552).

that the central mechanisms methods, by which the peaceful settlement of disputes can be effected.[9,10]

This article will focus on the dispute resolution techniques and enforcement mechanisms in International Environmental Law and then ensuring compliance with Multilateral Environmental Agreements (MEAs) in the context of international environmental law.

II. Disputes Settlement Mechanisms in International Environmental Law[11]

A. Generally

From earliest times, third parties have played a significant role in attempting to resolve interpersonal and intergroup disputes.[12] Actually, the concept of third-party dispute settlement and roles of judge, arbitrator and mediator spread all human societies and are closely linked to the emergency of political order and law.[13]

For the International Environmental disputes, recourse to International organisations as conciliators or mediators ensure occasionally of a middle way.[14] Because, in International Environmental Law, "*diplomatic (non-legal) means*" of dispute settlement methods ("*negotiation*", "*consultation*", "*mediation*" and "*conciliation*") do not procedure legally binding decision.[15] On the other hand, some of these techniques ("*Legal means*" of dispute settlement

9 *Bilder*, S. 480; *Desai/Sidhu*, S. 102; Article (Art.) 33 of the United Nations (UN) Regulation states that the traditional methods, including arbitration, conciliation, negotiation, judical settlement...etc., or other similar to pacific means of the parties' own choise. See, Article 33 of the United Nations (UN) Charter (*Bilder*, S. 480; *Craik*, S. 551).

10 See, *Craik*, S. 551; *Bilder*, S. 480; *Hoffmeister*, S. 77; *Desai/Sidhu*, S. 102.

11 See, Dawson, Victoria C.: Environmental Dispute Resolution: Combining Settlement Mechanisms for Transnational Enforcement of International Environment Disputes, Missouri Environmental Law & Polcy Review (Fall 2006), [Vol. 14, Issue: 1], (S. 97-145); Holder, William E.: Towards Peaceful Settlement of International Disputes, The Austarlian Year Book of International Law (1968-1969), (S. 102-122); Martti, Koskenniemi: Peaceful Settlement of Environmental Disputes, Nordic Journal of International Law (1991), [Vol. 60, Issue 1], (S. 73-92); Mauseth, Mike: Resolving North America's Environmental Disputes, Denver Journal of International Law and Policy (Winter 1998), [Vol. 26, Issue: 2], (S. 871-896).

12 *Bilder*, S. 471.

13 *Bilder*, S. 471.

14 See, *Sands/Peel/Fabra/Mackenzie*, S. 159; *Stein*, S. 284.

15 See, *Craik*, S. 551; *Sands/Peel/Fabra/Mackenzie*, S. 159; *Bilder*, S. 480.

methods) ("*Arbitration*" and "*Judicial Settlement*") has legally binding decisions for the parties to the disputes.[16]

In Interntional Environmental Law, a great deal of the oldest environmental agreements didn't ensure for any dispute settlement mechanisms whether of a "*diplomatic*" or "*legal*" means. Today, modern International Environmental agreements ensure parties with a range of options for settling disputes.[17]

B. Resolving Environmental Disputes with Non-Binding and Diplomatic Means of Alernative Dispute Settlements Methods

1. Mediation

In the technique of mediation, the neutral third person is take part in like an active contributor in the replacement of offers among the parties to a controversy and may in fact tender unauthorized offer.[18] Mediation is not a mandatory method, in that the third party, unlike a judge or arbitrator, does not make the verdict. The exact conclusion can be a binding agreement between the parties.[19] There are limited reported instances of mediation being relied upon to figure out environmental controversies.[20] On the other hand, consequence of a mediation directed under the protection of the Organisation of American States (OAS), as regards to a long-standing regional controversy

16 *Craik*, S. 552-553; *Bilder*, S. 480. According to International Environmental doctrine, these dispute settlement methods can be classified into two areas (*Craik*, S. 553). (1) "*Diplomatic means*" of the dispute settlement mechanisms and (2) "*Legal means*" of the dispute settlement mechanisms. Diplomatic means of dispute settlement methods are: "*Negotiation*", "*consultation*", "*mediation*" and "*conciliation*" et seq. Legal means of of dispute settlement methods are "*arbitration*" and "*judicial settlement*" (See, *Sands/Peel/Fabra/Mackenzie*, S. 159).

17 *Sands/Peel/Fabra/Mackenzie*, S. 159; *Stein*, S. 298; *Bilder*, S. 471.

18 *Bilder*, S. 481; *Stein*, S. 286. Where the other dispute settlement mechanisms (specially: negotiation and consultation) unsuccess, somewhat environmental agreements support mediation nd conciliation (or the institution of a council of experts) to figure out controversy, all of which contain the intercession of a neutral third person (See *Sands/Peel/Fabra/Mackenzie*, S. 161).

19 *Stein*, S. 286; *Bilder*, S. 473-474; *Koskenniemi*, S. 83.

20 *Sands/Peel/Fabra/Mackenzie*, S. 161.

among Guatamala and Belize.[21] And, President Carter's mediation essential to the Egypt-Israel Peace Treaty is a last instance of victorious mediation.[22]

2. Negotiation

Negotiation, which helps to the parties to give up the most control over their dispute to a third party.[23] In the Fisheries Jurisdiction lawsuit, diplomatic means of dispute settlement technique of negotiation has been used to resolve the environmental disputes.[24] In This case, the International Law Commission (ILC) prove the fundamental objectives principal negotiation as an suitable method for the remedy of a controversy.[25] Environmental agreements deal, approximately a matter of classical implementation to the demand to provide that apply to negotiation and other diplomatic mechanisms to figure out their controversy before taking advantage of other more formal mechanisms.[26]

3. Consultation

Consultaion among states is furthermore supported by environmental agreements kind of method to prevent and figure out controversies and environmental disputes between states.[27] In Lac Lanoux[28] arbitration, the arbitral tribunal held that France had a responsibility to discuss with Spain over specific plan and project a likely to influence its expediency.[29]

---

21 In September 2002, the two facilitators appointed by the Organization of America (OAS) seth forth tenders, confirmed by the states and Honduras, for a remedy of the controversy, with the inclusion of the establishment of an ocological park and tri-state subregional fisheries committee (*Sands/Peel/Fabra/Mackenzie,* S. 161).

22 *Bilder,* S. 481.

23 *Craik,* S. 553; *Stein,* S. 286; *Bilder,* S. 477.

24 Fisheries Jurisdiction Case: United Kingdom *vs.* Ireland (Jurisdiction) ICJ Rep3 (Merits) (1974) ICJ Rep3; Germany vs. Iceland (Jurisdiction) (1973) ICJ Rep 49 (Merits) (1974) ICJ Rep 175.

25 *Sands/Peel/Fabra/Mackenzie,* S. 160.

26 Since negotiation of this type any time come about behinde covered doors, it is difficult to recognize certain instances including the accomlished remedy of arguments and controversies by negotiation (*Sands/Peel/Fabra/Mackenzie,* S. 160).

27 *Sands/Peel/Fabra/Mackenzie,* S. 160.

28 See, Lac Lanoux arbitration, 24 ILR 101 at 128 (1957).

29 *Koskenniemi,* S. 84; *Desai/Sidhu,* S. 104.

4. Conciliation

In the situation of conciliation the third person be stuck with a lot role and constantly checks up the circumstance inherent the controversy and performs official tenders for the controversy.[30] The latest example of conciliation take place in the condition of the long-standing controvery among Pakistan and Indias's architecture of the Baglihar hydroelectric barrage on the Chenab River, which pours from Kashmir into Pakistan.[31] An instance is assuming that the last Jan Mayen Island conciliation which ended in the proposition that the disputing Norway and Iceland –parties- set up a "*joint cooperation arrangement*" for the research of the facilities which were the subject of the controversy.[32]

5. Fact-Finding

Fact-Finding is method of settlement in which the parties demand to subscribe to the intervention of a third party, usually on a more formal basis, for the goal of settling specific thruths or else conducting an neutral inquiry of the controversy and, if the parties so agree attempting to suggest or define the terms of a mutually acceptable settlement.[33] Where a dispute has not been settled within six months of a demand for discussions, whichever of the parties to the controversy may put forward the controversy to neutral fact-finding committee is to put forward its report to the parties related putting forth its findings (with ground) and like this suggestions something like it considers convenient for an impartial remedy of the controversy, which the parties involved must contemplate in good faith.[34] Below the 2001 Agreement on Planet Genetic Resources[35], the 1985 Vienna Treaty[36], the 1992 Biodiversty Treaty[37] and, conciliation will be used if the parties to the controversy have not

30 *Bilder*, S. 481; *Craik*, S. 560; *Koskenniemi*, S. 83.

31 *Sands/Peel/Fabra/Mackenzie*, S. 161-162.

32 See, *Koskenniemi*, S. 83; *Bilder*, S. 481; *Craik*, S. 560.

33 *Bilder*, S. 481.

34 The 1997 Watercourses Convention issues that, where negotiation falls through to led to a accomplished consequence the parties may collectively look for the decent chambers of, or demand mediation or conciliation by, any collective Watercourse establishment that may have been founded by them (*Sands/Peel/Fabra/Mackenzie*, S. 162).

35 Art. 22, 2001 Treaty on Planet Genetic Resources.

36 Art. 11, Vienna Convention. See, *Koskenniemi*, S. 78.

37 Art. 27 Biodiversty Convention. See, *O'Connell*, S. 54.

acknowledged mandatory controversy arrangement methods by arbitration or the Interational Court of Justice (ICJ).[38]

C. Resolving Environmental Disputes with Binding Mechanisms: *"Arbitration"* and *"Judicial Settlement"*

Mediation and conciliation don't technique officially compulsory judgement.[39] If the parties to a disagreement seach for like this kind of consequence, they must choose for arbitration or appeal to an international tribunal.[40]

1. Arbitration

Arbitration contains the reference of a controversy or range of disputes, by the treaty of the sides to an *ad hoc* court of justice for binding verdict, usually on the ground of international law.[41] International arbitration has been designated something like owning for its goal the settlement of controversy among states by adjudicator of their own preference and the principle of regards for the act.[42] The Pacific Fur Seal[43] arbitration (1983), the Trail Smelter[44] lawsuit (1935/41) and the Lac Lanoux[45] arbitration (1957) externalize the historycal significance performed by arbitration in the growth of international environmental law, in bettween state lawsuits.[46] Lately, there

38 *Mauseth*, S. 872 et seq; *Tomkins*, S. 297. In 2002, a committee of the Permanent Court of Abitration accepted discretionarry regulations for the accommodation of controversies as regards the environment and/or natural facilities (*Sands/Peel/Fabra/Mackenzie*, S. 163-164)

39 *Craik*, S. 554; *Stein*, S. 286; *Bilder*, S. 473-474; *Koskenniemi*, S. 83; *Desai/Sidhu*, S. 102.

40 *Craik*, S. 554; *Koskenniemi*, S. 82; *Stein*, S. 286; *Bilder*, S. 473-474.

41 *Bilder*, S. 481-482.

42 *Craik*, S. 557; *Bilder*, S. 473-474. Application to arbitration means an commitment to surrender in good faith to the verdict. States discussing environmental agreements have costantly privileged the containment of particular judgement for the foundation of an arbitration court, with the strength to accept madatory and eventual provision (*Sands/Peel/Fabra/Mackenzie*, S. 169).

43 Pacific Bering Sea Fur Seals case (Great Britain vs. United States of America) (1893) 1 Moore 827.

44 Trail Smelter case (Canada vs. United States of America) (1983 and 1941) 3 RIAA 285. For more information about see, *Koskenniemi*, S. 77.

45 Supra note 29. Lac Lanoux case (France vs. Spain) (1957) 12 RIAA 285.

46 *Desai/Sidhu*, S. 104.

is expanding argument that states consider arbitration like an charming instrument of eliminating international conroversies.[47]

2. Judicial Settlement

International Court of Justice: The International Court of Justice (ICJ), occasionally mentioned to something like to "*World Court*" or the "*Hague Court*", is the UN's fundamental legal organism.[48] In an other saying, The United Nations' chief enforcement mechanism is ICJ.[49] The Gulf of Maine case between U.S. and Canada is a recent example of successful judicial settlement under the procedures of the ICJ.[50]

International Courts: The settlement of international controvesies may in addition to be applied to an international tribunal, which is a consistent court authorized to distribute a officially mandatory provision.[51] In the environmental area a number of international courts have accepted special significance, in an other saying, the International Law Commission (ILC), the International Tribunal for the Law of the Sea (ITLOS), the World Trade Organization (WTO) appellate Body, the European Court of Justice (ECJ), and the tribunals composed by territorial human rights agreements.[52] Morover, varied non-governmental struggle goal to found "*international tribunals*" to address international environmental problems.[53] While not constitute mandatory regulations, these ensure a beneficial direction to bring environmental problems to the caution of the communal.[54]

---

47 *Sands/Peel/Fabra/Mackenzie,* S. 170.

48 *Bilder*, S. 478; *O'Connell*, S. 51; *Wheeler*, S. 267. It was founded as a inheritor to the Permanent Court of International Justice (PCIJ) in 1945. Jurisdiction of the ICJ over a controversy depends on provided that the Court has been called for in a controversial lawsuit among two or specific international organisms (*Sands/Peel/Fabra/Mackenzie,* S. 171-172).

49 1947 I.C.J. Acts & Docs. Ch. 11, Acts. 34-38. See, *Wheeler*, S. 267; *Bilder*, S. 478; *O'Connell*, S. 51.

50 *Craik*, S. 559; *Bilder*, S. 482.

51 *Bilder*, S. 478, 482; *Craik*, S. 563.

52 *Craik*, S. 554.

53 *Sands/Peel/Fabra/Mackenzie,* S. 171.

54 *Sands/Peel/Fabra/Mackenzie,* S. 171.

D. Enforcement and International Environmental Law[55]

1. The Concept of Enforcement in International Environmental Law

Unce upon a time proof is available that a state, or a party to a treaty, has falled through to enforce an international environmental responsibility, the problem emerges as to which organisms/organisations/persons having international judicial charachter may enforce that responsibility internationally.[56] In this context, "*enforcement*" is understood like to legitimate to take surveys to provide the execution of international juristical responsibilies or to acquire a verdict by an convenient international tribunal, court or another foundation, with the inclusion of an international organism, that responsibilities are not being executed.[57]

-*International Enforcement:* At the international standard, for the non-state actors to take part an enforcement function are restricted, except that the

55 See, Brunnée, Jutta: Enforcement Mechanisms in International Environmental Law, Environmental Law Network International (Elni Review) [No. 1/2005], (S. 1-12); Bradford, Anu/Ben-Shahar, Omri: Efficient Enforcement in International Law, Ghicago Journal of International Law (Winter 2012), [Vol. 12, Issue: 2], (S. 375-431); Hagen, Paul E./Magrew, Daniel B./Wilson, Serina/McLean, Meredith: International Environmetal Law, The International Lawyer (ABA), Public International Law (Summer 1997), [vol. 31, No. 2], (S. 627-644); O'Connell, Mary Ellen: Enforcement and the Success of International Environmetal Law, (Scholarly Work, Paper 578), Global Legal Studies Journal (1995), [Vol. 3:47], (S. 47-64). Rinceanu, Joanna: Enforcement Mechanisms in International Environmental Law: Quo Vadunt, Journal of Environmental Law and Litigation (2002), [Vol. 15, Issue 2], (S. 147-177); Tomkins, Kevin: Police, Law Enforcement and the Environmen, Current Issues in Criminal Justice (March 2005), [Vol. 16, No. 3], (S. 294-306); Wheeler, Douglas P.: Enforcement of International Environmental Treaties: An Analysis, Fordham Environmental LawJournal (1994), [Vol. V, 1993], (S. 261-283); Yu, Peter K.: Enforcement, Enforcement, What Enforcement? IDEA: The Intellectual Property Law Review (IDEA 2012), [Vol. 52, Issue: 3], (S. 239-284); Zalob, David S.: Approaches to Enforcement of Environmental Law: An International Perspective, Hasting International and Comparative Law Review (Spring 1980), [Vol. 3, No. 2], (S. 299-319).

56 *Sands/Peel/Fabra/Mackenzie*, S. 144; *Tomkins*, S. 294.

57 *O'Connell*, S. 48. International enforcement may consist of at the provocation of one or a lot of states, or an international constitution, or by non-state actors. Pratically, international enforcement in general contains a compaund of the three, every moving in various abilities. The degree to which each of three actors may invite enforcement evaluates depends on the internal and judicial ground of the professed nonobservance, the issue concerned, and the international judicial responsibilities at subject matter. The perspective of enforcement is actually as regards the standing necessary to come to a place with international allegations (*Sands/Peel/Fabra/Mackenzie*, S. 144).

dicipline of human rights.[58] Under some territorial human rights, individual sacrifice, with the inclusion non-state organisms, may carry compliants through to an international organism.[59]

2. The Enforcement Authorities in International Environmental Law: An Overview

The identification of environmental law enforcement foundations is also significant in that many of the law enforcement are progressively cooperating at the international, regional, national, state and local levels.[60]

a. Enforcement by states

Like the fundamental matter of international law, states have essential importance function in enforcing regulations of international environmental law.[61] To be in a position to enforce a regulations of international environmental law, a state demonstrate that it is, in the words of the International Law Commission (ILC), an "*injured state*"[62]. The lawsuit of the former Societ Union and Chernobyl is a very significant sample of this situation[63].

---

58 *Sands/Peel/Fabra/Mackenzie,* S. 157.

59 For this reason, the European Convention on Human rights lets every individual, non-stateorganisms or group asserting to be the victim of a nonobservance of the rights in the Conventions by one of the parties to carry a lawsuit to the European Court of Human Rights (*Sands/Peel/Fabra/Mackenzie,* S. 157).

60 *Tomkins*, S. 294; *O'Connell*, S. 47.

61 *O'Connell*, S. 47; *Tomkins*, S. 301.

62 For more information about "*injured states*" see, *O'Connell*, S. 47; Article 42 of the International Law Commissions (ILC)'S 2001 Articles on State Responsibility ensures that:
"A state is entitled as an injured State to invoke the responsibility of another State if the obligation breached is owed to:
(a) that State individualy; or (b) a group od States including that State, or the international community as a whole, and the breach of the obligation:
i. Specially affects that State; or
ii. Is of such a character as radically to change the position of all other States to which the obligation is owed with respect to the further performance of the obligation."

63 *O'Connell*, S. 51; *Wheeler*, S. 262. The states wounded by the incident at Chernobyl could have taken compulsion activity when the old Societ Union rejected to ensure compensation (*O'Connell*, S. 51).

b. Enforcement by International Organisations

Latest years have seen a multiplication of international enforcement foundation working together at an international grade.[64] International organisations are Intermational judicial bodies that may search for keeping safe from their self justices and forcethe responsibilities that another have against them.[65] In spite of International organisations take part an significant legislative function in the improvement of international environmental law, their enforcement role is restricted.[66]

c. Enforcement by Non-State Actors

In accordance to traditional regulations of public International law, non-state personalities are not international judicial character anticipate inside of the resricted confines of international human rights law and its related areas.[67] Partially, non-state personalities take part a main function in the improvement and implementation of international environmental law.[68] Environmental organisations have also been related in the international application and enforcement procedure in spite of their principal function keeps going to be at the national grade, whereby political methods or by application to organizational or legal process for forcing national measures acknowledged a state in enforcing its international agreement and another responsibilities.[69]

64 *Tomkins*, S. 296.

65 *Tomkins*, S. 296. The diplomatic agencies of International institutions and territorial members in addition to act a significant role in the anlysis of controversies. This kind of diplomatic agencies may be privileged an obvious commandment to take into consideration controversies among two or a lot of parties to the pact. As another option or possibility, they may try out to satisfy controversies among parties in the non-existance of a particular procuration to do that. Eventually, the process founded below the Assembly on Reliance on Association in Europe offers an another instrument of attaining conciliation (*Sands/Peel/Fabra/Mackenzie,* S. 162-163).

66 *Tomkins*, S. 295-298. Ascendent concerns have, on the other hand canalize satates to be reluctant to carry a lot of enforcement energy to international organisations and their secretariats, in spite of there are several signals that thşs unwillingness is being come through (*Sands/Peel/Fabra/Mackenzie,* S. 151-152).

67 *Wheeler*, S. 262 ff; *Sands/Peel/Fabra/Mackenzie,* S. 155.

68 *Sands/Peel/Fabra/Mackenzie,* S. 155.

69 *Sands/Peel/Fabra/Mackenzie,* S. 155.

d. Enforcement in the Domestic Courts

Domestic courts already urge a important section of international law.[70] United Nations Conference on Environment and Development (UNCED) supported a powerful function for the non-governmental sector in forcing national environmental laws and responsibilities prior to national tribunals and courts[71], like reflected in Agenda 21[72] and the Rio Declaration[73], and at the present time implemented in the 1998 Aarhus Convention.[74] Many domestic legal systems also let the through compulsion of inernational law. Presumbly the most prominent action in the United States showing this basis is *Paquette Habana.* [75]

E. International Environmental Law Enforcement Mechanisms: Multilateral Environmental Agreements (MEAs)[76]:

One of the most considerable advancements in the range of the International Environment Law has been the emergence of non-compliance procedures underneath diversified Multilateral Environmental Treaties, taking a seat a function and conventional dispute settlement[77].

Until now the first years (in the 1990s), a considerable number of agreements have founded subsidiary bodies to overcome confirmity and dispute over non-compliance.[78] The intial was the non-compliance technique

---

70 *O'Connell*, S. 57.

71 *Hagen/Magrew/Wilson/McLean*, S. 627; *O'Connell*, S. 57 et seq.

72 Chapter 27, para. 27, 1,3, Agenda 21. For more information about this, see, *Stein*, S. 284; *Hagen/Magrew/Wilson/McLean*, S. 628.

73 Principle 10, Rio Declaration. See, *O'Connell*, S. 53.

74 *Sands/Peel/Fabra/Mackenzie*, S. 155. This consistedin the context of earlier agreements and treaties, which had got to know and supported their function, especially where individuals were the sacrifices of environmental pollution ınjury in a transboundary circumstance (*Sands/Peel/Fabra/Mackenzie*, S. 155).

75 Paquette Habana, 175 U.S. 677 (1900). For more information about Paquette Habana see, *O'Connell*, S. 58.

76 Sands/Peel/Fabra/Mackenzie, S. 163-169; Tomkins, S. 295; Brunnée, S. 2; Craik, S. 552; Hagen/Magrew/Wilson/McLean, S. 627.

77 *Mauseth*, S. 871; *Hagen/Magrew/Wilson/McLean*, S. 627; *Koskenniemi*, S. 73; *Craik*, S. 552, 555; *Desai/Sidhu*, S. 103.

78 *Hagen/Magrew/Wilson/McLean*, S. 627; *Sands/Peel/Fabra/Mackenzie*, S. 163-164; *Craik*, S. 555;

founded underneath the 1987 Montreal Protocol[79], with the inclusion of "*Implementation Commitee*" founded by the second Meeting of the Parties to the Protocol.[80] Underneath the non-compliance technique, whichever party which has booked about the other party's administration of its liabilities underneath the Protocol may put forward apprehension in writing to the secretariat, with confirming knowledge.[81] The secrateriat will after that identify, with the support of the party professed to be in nonobservance, provided that it is unable to obey with its responsibility underneath Protocol, and will deliver the unique submission, its response and another knowledge on the Implementation Committee.[82] The Committee's explanation must both include hidden knowledge and is to be made existent to whichever individual upon demand.[83] Substantially, apply to the non-compliance technique does not prejudgement the dispute settlement verdicts existent below Article (Art.) 11 of the 1985 Vienna Convention[84], which contain negotiation, good offices, mediation, arbitration, indulgence to the International Law Commission (ILC) and the foundation of a accommodation committee.[85]

After the improvements underneath the Montreal Protocol[86], non-compliance procedures have been founded underneath another Multilateral Environmental Agreements, with the inclusion of the 1973 CITES Convetion, the 1989 Basel Convention, the 1991 VOC, 1994 Sulphur, 1998 POPs and Heavy Metals and 1999 Gothenburg Protocols to the LRTAP Convention[87], the 1996 Protocol to the London Convention[88], and the 2001 Treaty on Planet Genetic Resources[89]. The two most substantial regulations, on the other hand, are reflected in the technique founded below the 1997 Kyoto Protocol and the 1998 Aarhus Convention[90].

---

79 *Tomkins*, S. 297; *Craik*, S. 552; *O'Connell*, S. 55.
80 *Craik*, S. 555; *Sands/Peel/Fabra/Mackenzie,* S. 163-164.
81 *Sands/Peel/Fabra/Mackenzie,* S. 164.
82 *Sands/Peel/Fabra/Mackenzie,* S. 164.
83 Paras. 15 and 16. For more information about *see, Sands/Peel/Fabra/Mackenzie,* S. 164.
84 *Craik*, S. 555; *Koskenniemi*, S. 78. See, Art. 11, the 1985 Vienna Convention.
85 *Tomkins*, S. 297; *Craik*, S. 555; *Sands/Peel/Fabra/Mackenzie,* S. 164.
86 *Craik*, S. 552; *Tomkins*, S. 297; *Koskenniemi*, S. 79.
87 LRTAP Convention Executive Body, Decision 1997/2.
88 Art. 11, the 1996 Protocol to the London Convention.
89 GB Resolution 2/2009, Annex. For more information about the 2001 Treaty on Planet Genetic Resources see, *Sands/Peel/Fabra/Mackenzie,* S. 164-165; *Brunnée*, S. 11.
90 *Tomkins*, S. 297; *Sands/Peel/Fabra/Mackenzie,* S. 165; *Brunnée*, S. 11.

The compliance framework take place a "*Compliance Committee*" made of two substation: a "*Facilitative Branch*" and an "*Enforcement Branch*"[91]. *The Facilitativ Branch* ensures that recommendation reliefs to parties not gathering their undertakings.[92] The Facilitative Branch in addition to ensures that "*early warning*" of lawsuits where a party is out on a limb of not obeying with its publigations goals.[93] *The Enforcement Branch*, for its side, is liable identifying necessities, or has missing its accordance to take part in the contraptions.[94] It can in addition to award provided that to regulate a party's inventory or verify the miscellany, in the form of a controversy among a party and the professional criticism crew.[95]

A prospective adherence trouble can be raised either by an professional criticism crew, or by a party about its self conformity, or by a party raising apprehensions as regards the other party.[96] The Compliance Committee lean its consultations against reports from professionals criticism crews, the subsidiary bodies, parties and another legal weldings.[97]

The non-compliance techniques underneath the Kyoto Protocol is at the time completely ready, working in according to regulations transaction acknowledged in 2006.[98]

Bibliography

Abernathy, J. M.: Alternative Dispute Resolution in Commercial Cases, Annual Survey of American Law Supplement, Vol. 1985, (pp. 29-50).

Berger, K. P.: Private Dispute Resolution in International Business: Negotiation, Mediation, Arbitration, Third, Revised Edition, Volume II: Handbook, Kluwer Law International, Netherlands, [2015].

Bilder, Richard B.: International Third Party Dispute Settlement, Denver Journal of International Law and Policy (Spring 1989), [Vol. 17, Isue: 3], (pp. 471-503).

---

91 *Brunnée*, S. 11. Both branches are composed of ten members.

92 *Sands/Peel/Fabra/Mackenzie*, S. 165; *Brunnée*, S. 11.

93 In reply to troubles, the Facilitative Branch can supply adives and impel financial and technical weldings to aid parties obey (*Sands/Peel/Fabra/Mackenzie*, S. 165).

94 *Brunnée*, S. 11.

95 Enforcement Branch will provide a folk announcement that the party is non-compliance and will in addition to folk the results to be implemented (*Sands/Peel/Fabra/Mackenzie*, S. 166).

96 *Sands/Peel/Fabra/Mackenzie*, S. 166.

97 *Sands/Peel/Fabra/Mackenzie*, S. 166.

98 *Brunnée*, S. 11-12.

Breen, J. D.: Mediation and the Magistrate Judge, University of Memphis Law Review, Vol. 26, Issue 3 (Spring 1996), (pp. 1007-1030).

Bradford, Anu/Ben-Shahar, Omri: Efficient Enforcement in International Law, Ghicago Journal of International Law (Winter 2012), [Vol. 12, Issue: 2], (pp. 375-431).

Brunnée, Jutta: Enforcement Mechanisms in International Environmental Law, Environmental Law Network International (Elni Review) [No. 1/2005], (pp. 1-12).

Craik, A. Neil: Recalcitrant Reality and Chosen Ideals: The Public Function of Dispute Settlement in International Environmental Law, The Georgetown International Law Review (1998), [Vol. 10, Issue 2], (pp. 551-580).

Connell, H. B.: International Agreements and the Australian Treaty Power, Australian Year Book of International Law [1968-1969], (pp. 73-92).

Dana J., H. H. H.: Court-Connected Alternative Dispute Resolution in Maine, Maine Law Review, Vol. 57, Issue 2 (2005), (pp. 349-448).

Dawson, Victoria C.: Environmental Dispute Resolution: Combining Settlement Mechanisms for Transnational Enforcement of International Environment Disputes, Missouri Environmental Law & Polcy Review (Fall 2006), [Vol. 14, Issue: 1], (pp. 97-145).

Desai, Bharat H./*Sidhu*, Balraj: International Environmental Dispute Settlement –Rio+20 and Beyond-, Other International Developments, Environmental Policy and Law (March 2012), [Vol. 42, Issue: 2], (pp. 102-116

Eiholzer, H.: Die Streitbeilegungsabrede, (Ein Beitrag zu alternativen Formen der Streitbeilegung, namentlich zur Mediation), Universitättverlag Freiburg Schweiz,1998.

Green, E. D.: Corporate Alternative Dispute Resolution, Ohio State Journal on Dispute Resolution, Vol. 1, Issue 2 (1986), (pp. 203-298).

Glasner Q. C., K.: Contract Disputes and Alternative Disputes Resolution: Some Observations, Advocate (Vancouver Bar Association), Vol. 59, Issue 5 (September 2001), (pp. 725-732).

Goss, J.: An Introduction to Alternative Dispute Resolution, Alberta Law Review, Vol. 34, Issue 1 (1995), (pp.1-33).

Guidry, A. M.: Alternative Dispute Resolution: Broadening The Use Through Louısıana Courts, Southern University Law Review, Vol. 19, Issue 2 (1992), (pp. 403-420).

Hagen, Paul E./Magrew, Daniel B./Wilson, Serina/McLean, Meredith: International Environmetal Law, The International Lawyer (ABA), Public International Law (Summer 1997), [vol. 31, No. 2], (pp. 627-644).

Hoffmeister, Frank: The European Union and the Peaceful Settlement of International Disputes, Chinese Journal of International Law (March 2012), [Vol. 11, No. 1], (pp. 77-105).

Holder, William E.: Towards Peaceful Settlement of International Disputes, The Austarlian Year Book of International Law (1968-1969), (pp. 102-122).

Işık, Serpil: Mediation as an Altrnative Dispute Resolution Method and Mediation Process in Turkish Law System: An Overview, Annales de la Faculté deDroit d'Istanbul (2016), [Vol. 48, No. 65], (S. 55-87).

Lisnek, P. M.: Mediation: Untangling Business Disputes through ADR, Commercial Law Bulletin, July/August 1993, (pp. 12-19).

Lerman, L. G.: The Teaching of Alternative Dispute Resolution, Journal of Legal Education, Vol.37, Issue 1(1987), (pp. 37-40).

Martti, Koskenniemi: Peaceful Settlement of Environmental Disputes, Nordic Journal of International Law (1991), [Vol. 60, Issue 1], (pp. 73-92).

Mauseth, Mike: Resolving North America's Environmental Disputes, Denver Journal of International Law and Policy (Winter 1998), [Vol. 26, Issue: 2], (pp. 871-896). O'Connell, Mary Ellen: Enforcement and the Success of International Environmetal Law, (Scholarly Work, Paper 578), Global Legal Studies Journal (1995), [Vol. 3:47], (pp. 47-64).

Petillon, L. R.: Recent Developments in Alternative Dispute Resolution, Pepperdine Law Review, Vol. 14, Issue 4 (1987).

Riskin, L. L.: The Special Place of Mediation in Altenative Dispute Processing, Universty of Florida Law Review, Vol. 37, Issue 1 (Winter 1985), (pp. 19-28).

Rinceanu, Joanna: Enforcement Mechanisms in International Environmental Law: Quo Vadunt, Journal of Environmental Law and Litigation (2002), [Vol. 15, Issue 2], (pp. 147-177).

Roth, M./Stegner, M.: Mediation in Austria, Yearbook on International Arbitration, Vol. 3, (pp. 367-3783).

Sands, Philippe/Peel, Jacqueline/Fabra, Adriana/Mackenzie, Ruth: Principles of International Environmental Law, Third Edition, Cambridge Universty Press, 2012.

Scalise, D. G./Engels, J. E., Alternative Dispute Resolutions: a Commercial Guide for Dispute Management, Advocates' Quarterly, Vol. 9, Issue 1 (February 1988), (pp. 53-76).

Stein, Robert E.: The Settlement of Environmental Disputes: Towards a System of Flexible Dispute Settlement, Syracuse Journal of International Law and Commerce (Winter 1985), [Vol. 12, Issue: 2], (pp. 283-298).

Swinson, S. K.: Alternative Dispute Resolution ın Bankruptcy, Tulsa Law Journal, Vol. 36, Issue 4 (Summer 2001), (pp. 813-818).

Tomkins, Kevin: Police, Law Enforcement and the Environmen, Current Issues in Criminal Justice (March 2005), [Vol. 16, No. 3], (pp. 294-306).

Wheeler, Douglas P.: Enforcement of International Environmental Treaties: An Analysis, Fordham Environmental LawJournal (1994), [Vol. V, 1993], (pp. 261-283).

Woodman, G. R.: The Alternative Law of Alternative Dispute Resolution, Cahiers de Droit, Vol. 32, Issue 1 (Mars 1991), pp. 3-32.

Yu, Peter K.: Enforcement, Enforcement, What Enforcement? IDEA: The Intellectual Property Law Review (IDEA 2012), [Vol. 52, Issue: 3], (pp. 239-284).

Zalob, David S.: Approaches to Enforcement of Environmental Law: An International Perspective, Hasting International and Comparative Law Review (Spring 1980), [Vol. 3, No. 2], (pp. 299-319).

An Overview of Turkish Environmental Law

Canberk Kurugöllü[1*]

Abstract

This study consists of two main parts. I n the first part, both national regulations on environmental rights in Turkish Law and international regulations adopted by Türkiye by virtue of being a party to international regulations were presented. Then in the second part, certain special procedures that could be applied in Turkish Law for the protection of environmental rights were addressed. I n the last part, considerations on the law as it should be *(de lege ferenda)* were expressed *in comparison with* the existing law *(de lege lata)*.

Keywords: environment, environmental rights, human rights, constitutional complaint, environmental protection, Turkish Law.

I. Introduction

Along with rapid technological and industrial developments, the destruction caused by world wars, world population growth, and consumption culture in the 20th century, environmental problems increased significantly and the right of 'all living beings' to live in a healthy environment was jeopardized.

Even though the extent of legal systems and laws of states that in principle are limited by country borders, environmental issues transcend these borders and concern the whole ecosystem all over the world[2]. Therefore, adopting a supra-national perspective, to ensure the maximum coordination and cooperation between countries, is of utmost importance to the determination of policies, particularly the legal policies to be applied to environmental issues directly related to countries' politics and socio-economic structures . As well as being a fundamentally judicial issue, the protection of the environment is a political and economic matter[3].

This article aims to analyze the scope of the environmental rights, along with the restrictions hampering to solve environmental problems, and to evaluate the measures to be taken for the further protection of the environment in the light of Turkish private law.

---

1 * Research Assistant, Department of Civil Law, Istanbul University Faculty of Law.

2 *M. Kloepfer*, Umweltschutzrecht, 2008, note 1 at para. 6.

3 *W. Hoppe & M. Beckmann*, Umweltrecht, 1989, p. 15 et seq..; *W. Erbguth & S. Schlacke*, Umweltrecht, 2nd ed., 2008, p. 35.; *L. Wicke*, Umweltökonomie, 4th ed., 1993, p.112 etq.

A. Development of Environmental R ights and the C urrent S ituation under Turkish Law

Before analyzing the protection of the environment and the right to live in a healthy environment in Turkish Law, it is necessary to explain how the concept of environment is defined under Turkish regulations.

There are different approaches to the concept of environment in both Turkish and German legal doctrines. [4]. To specify the scope of the right and the protection regime, the definition of the "environment" in Turkish law is addressed below. Right to environment is a basic human right directly related to all other human rights, especially to the right to life, as it pertains to the setting where human beings co-exist with all living beings [5]. Therefore, it is essential to focus on this broad definition when evaluating the protection of the environment and the right to a healthy environment.

1. Environmental Rights in Constitutional Norms

a. 1961 Constitution of Türkiye

1961 Constitution of Türkiye did not include any general provision that directly addresses environmental rights. However, Article 36 adopts the principle that the exercise of property rights shall not conflict with public welfare[6]. Article 52 states that the State shall take the necessary measures for the protection of the soil and promotion of agriculture, and Article 131 provides that the State shall have responsibilities with respect to the protection and development of forests. In Article 49 as to right to health, it is stipulated that "The State has a duty to ensure that everyone can live physically and mentally healthy and receive medical care" . Until the entry into force of 1982 Constitution, the right to environment was recognized as a constitutional right only through the interpretation within the scope of the purpose of the aforementioned articles *(ratio legis)*, but not mentioned explicitly[7].

4 *D. Güneş*, Çevre Hukuku, 2015, p. 3 et seq.; *N. Turgut,* Çevre Politikası ve Hukuku, 2009, p. 1 et seq.; *Erbguth & Schlacke, supra* note 1 at para. 1 et seq.; *Hoppe & Beckmann, supra* note 1 at para. 1 et seq.; *M. Kloepfer*, Umweltrecht, 3rd ed., 2004, p. 17 et seq.

5 For the principle of integrity of human rights, see M. *S. Gemalmaz,* Ulusalüstü İnsan Hakları Hukukunun Genel Teorisine Giriş, 2nd ed., 2012, p. 1566 et seq.

6 The Article 36 (a) of Turkish Constitution of 1961, p.10. (Available from http://www.anayasa.gen.tr/1961constitution-text.pdf)

7 *Y. Özdek,* İnsan Hakkı Olarak Çevre Hakkı, 1993, p. 123 et seq.; *Güneş, supra* at p. 160.

b. 1982 Constitution of Türkiye

As per the Article 56 of 1982 Constitution, *'Health Services and the Protection of Environment'*, which specifies for the first time that *everyone has the right to live in a healthy and balanced environment.*

This Article stipulates that the duty of the State and its citizens is to improve the natural environment, to protect the environmental health and to prevent environmental pollution. This right is granted to everyone, regardless of their legal status or citizenship. It is important to note that this article is included in the third chapter of the 1982 Constitution, which deals with social and economic rights, and is considered a second-generation human right. [8]. The importance of this fact is discerned in the framework of the Article 65, the State shall fulfill its duties within the capacity of its financial resources, considering the priorities appropriate with the aims of these duties which puts forth the State's duty in social and economic areas. The point is that, by referring to financial reasons as the excuse, the State is not supposed to derogate from the duty to protect the right to environment, especially the right of every person to live in a healthy environment.[9] The right to a healthy environment is directly related to and, in a way, a precondition for the right to life, as it is the setting in which human beings and all other living beings spend their lives and develop their material and spiritual well-being. Article 17 of the Constitution states that everyone has the right to life and the right to protect and improve their physical and spiritual existence. [10].

Besides Article 56, there also exist provisions indirectly related to the environment in 1982 Constitution.[11] Acknowledgement of the right to environment as a basic human right in the constitution is crucial because this situation does not only underline the significance of the right but also provides a constitutional control mechanism for the protection of the right. The constitutional amendment made in 2010 opened the way for applying to the Constitutional Court of Türkiye . According to Article 147(3), everyone may apply to the Constitutional Court on the grounds that one of the fundamental rights and freedoms within the scope of the European Convention on Human

8 For the theory of generation of human rights, see *Gemalmaz, supra* at 668 et seq.; see also *I. E. Koch,* Dichotomies, Trichotomies or Waves of Duties?, HRLR, Issue 1, 2005 (5), pp. 81-103.

9 *I. Kaboğlu,* Çevre Hakkı, 3rd ed., 1996, p. 45.

10 *I. Kaboğlu,* Özgürlükler Hukuku, 3rd ed., 1996, p. 296; *N. Turgut,* Çevre Hukuku, 2nd ed., 2012, p. 139 et seq.

11 e.g., Article 35(3), 44(1), 63(1), 169(1).

Rights which are guaranteed by the Constitution has been violated by public authorities. It should be noted that in order to make an application, ordinary legal remedies must be exhausted. Even though right to environment is not directly prescribed by the European Convention on Human Rights (ECHR), Constitutional Court of Türkiye takes its decisions in terms of inferences made about environmental issues on the basis of other rights in a similar vein to judicial interpretations of the ECHR, rather than referring directly to the Article 56 of 1982 Constitution in relation to the right to environment.[12] Constitutional Court of Türkiye deals with environmental issues in light of the right to the protection and development of material and spiritual well-being in Article 17, right to privacy in Article 20, right to the freedom of communication in Article 21 and 22[13], and sometimes in the framework of the right to a fair trial in Article 36[14].

c. International Legal Framework for Türkiye

Within time, Türkiye ratified several conventions regarding environmental protection. ost of the conventions adopted by Türkiye are related to coastal protection, against vessel pollution, dumping and oil pollution. The list includes treaties related to the protection of wildlife, including UN Conventions on biodiversity and against climate change, protection of Ozon layer, prevention of air pollution, and etc.

The effect of these treaties on national law is specified by Article 90 (5) of the 1982 Constitution. This article states that "international agreements duly put into effect have the force of law. No appeal to the Constitutional Court shall be made with regard to these agreements, on the grounds that they are unconstitutional. In the case of a conflict between international agreements, duly put into effect, concerning fundamental rights and freedoms and the laws due to differences in provisions on the same matter, the

12 *D. Güneş*, Çevre Hakkının Bireysel Başvuruya Konu Edilebilirliği Üzerine, TAAD, 2014(16), p. 79, 99 et seq.

13 Turkish Constitutional Court Judgment: Case C-2013/6587, *Hüseyin Tunç Karlık and Zahide Şadan Karluk* [2016], para. 41; Turkish Constitutional Court Judgment: Case C-2014/4686, *Binali Özkaradeniz and others* [2018], para. 45.

14 Turkish Constitutional Court Judgment: Case C-2013/5974, *Mehmet Bolat and others* [2016].

provisions of international agreements shall prevail[15]". Considering that the right to environment is also a basic right and freedom, it can be argued that international agreements which Türkiye was party to and was duly ratified by Türkiye on this issue are applied primarily by legislative acts of Türkiye .

d. An Essential Protection: European Convention on Human Rights[16]

Türkiye signed the ECHR on November 4, 1950 and ratified the text on March 10, 1954. Since this date, the ECHR became an integral part of the Türkiye 's domestic law successively as per the last paragraphs of the Article 65 of 1961 Constitution and Article 90 of 1982 Constitution which is still in force in Türkiye . That being the case, each provision of the Convention is of particular importance in terms of identifying the scope of rights protected, the protection of these rights, and the duties and responsibilities of the State. Nevertheless, there is no provision specifically related to the right to environment in the Convention. Right to live in a healthy environment is assessed under the *Right to Life* (Article 2)[17]. F or instance, as a result of the death caused by an explosion in a dumpsite or by a landslide, and under the *Protection of Property* (Protocol No. 1 to the Convention)[18], for instance, as a result of loss of home and property by the applicant again in the case of an explosion in a dumpsite. On the other hand, environmental rights are in general considered and protected under the *Right to Respect for Private and Family Life* (Article 8)[19]. Nevertheless, in this sense, environmental issue must have *a direct effect* on the right(s) to respect for private and family life or to protection of property of the applicant and this effect should take on *a serious dimension* and *reach a certain magnitude*[20]. Therefore, this necessitates the conduct of an evaluation to be made specifically for each specific case[21]. In

15 Constitution of Republic of Türkiye of 1982, (Available on: https://global.tbmm.gov.tr /docs/constitution_en.pdf).

16 Since the subject of the article is mainly the situation of environmental law in the sense of Turkish law, this section has been discussed in general terms.

17 ECHR Judgment: Case C-48939/99, *Oneryildiz v. Turkey* [2004]; ECHR Judgment: Case C-15339/02, *Budayeva and others v. Russia* [2008].

18 ECHR Judgment: Case C-48939/99, *Oneryildiz v. Turkey* [2004].

19 ECHR Judgment: Case C-9310/81, *Powell and Rayner v. UK,* [1990], para. 40.

20 ECHR Judgment: Case C-55723/00, *Fadeyeva v. Russia* [2005], para. 69; ECHR Judgment: Case C-4143/02, *Moreno Gomez v. Spain,* [2004] para. 58.

21 ECHR Judgment: Case C-55723/00, *Fadeyeva v. Russia* [2005], para. 96.

a nutshell, the Court does not exclusively and directly refer to the right to environment, and instead, makes an indirect contribution to the protection of environment and the right to live in a healthy environment[22]. The basis of this interpretation by the Supreme Court pertains to the obligation that the right which is brought to the court for being breached needs to be protected both under the Constitution and the ECHR, however, only personal and political rights are protected by the ECHR. That being the case, a judicial interpretation is not made on the basis of Article 56 of the Constitution which covers a right categorized under the second-generation human rights.[23]

e. Other International Treaties Which Türkiye is Party to

As noted above, international agreements on basic rights and freedoms to which Türkiye is a party and which duly enter into force in accordance with the fifth paragraph of Article 90 of the 1982 Constitution become an integral part of Türkiye 's domestic law [24]. In this respect, it is clear that Türkiye is a party to quite a few international agreements directly related to the environment . In this context, it is a remarkable development that Türkiye signed the Paris Agreement, and this agreement entered into force in October 2021 in Turkish d omestic l aw[25]. On the other hand, it is observed that international agreements that become an integral part of Türkiye's domestic law are inadequately respected by Turkish courts in their decisions.

22 *Güneş*, Çevre Hukuku, p. 168; *G. Arslan Öncü*, Özel Yaşama ve Aile Yaşamına Saygı Hakkı, in S. İnceoğlu (eds.), İnsan Hakları Avrupa Sözleşmesi ve Anayasa: Anayasa Mahkemesine Bireysel Başvuru Kapsamında Bir İnceleme, 3rd ed., 2013, p. 301, 305 et seq.

23 Turkish Constitutional Court Judgment: Case C-2013/2552, *Mehmet Kurt* [2016], para. 46.

24 *H. Pazarcı*, Uluslararası Hukuk, 12th ed., 2013, p. 20 et seq.; S. *İnceoğlu*, Anayasa ve İnsan Hakları Avrupa Sözleşmesi İlişkisi, in S. İnceoğlu (eds.), *supra* at p. 7, 8 et seq.; İnsan Hakları Uluslararası Sözleşmelerinin İç Hukukta Doğrudan Uygulanması: (Anayasa md 90/son) - Mesut Gülmez, TBB Doc. 76 (2005), p. 38, 59 et seq.; for the discussion on whether international treaty standards can be applied directly, see *R. Aybay*, Uluslararası Antlaşmaların Türk Hukukundaki Yeri, TBB, 2007 (70), p. 187, 205 et seq.

25 https://www.resmigazete.gov.tr/eskiler/2021/10/20211007-7.pdf

2. Legislative Norms

a. Code of Environment as the Basis Legislative Norm

The most basic act of legislation on the environment in Turkish Law is the Code of Environment (Law No. 2872). The relevant article is addressed to all living beings which are the shareholders of the ecosystem *(ökozentrischer Ansatz)* instead of adopting a simply human-centered approach towards the environment *(anthropozentrischer Ansatz).*[26] As per the Article 2 of the code, environment was defined as *"the biological, physical, economic and cultural setting where living beings continue to have relations and interact with each other all through their lives"* whereas the concept of the protection of environment was defined as *"the whole set of efforts to prevent the destruction, deterioration and dissolution of environmental values and ecological balance, to eliminate present deteriorations, to improve and develop the environment, to avoid environmental pollution"*. Considering this provision, it is perceived that a broad definition including cultural, social and economic settings as well as the natural environment[27] is adopted in Turkish Law.[28] The code is unclear as to what is meant by the concept of environmental values. However, it can be asserted that this concept covers soil, water, climate and even cultural and other material values besides human beings, animals, plants and all other living species.[29]

Article 3 of the code which is also comprised of principles on the protection of environment prescribes that the protection of environment is the responsibility of every person not solely the government, and the determination of environmental policies is predicated on the *right of participation.* The task of ensuring the participation of professional associations, unions, non-governmental organizations and citizens was assigned both to the Ministry of Environment and Urbanization of Türkiye and to local authorities. In the same article, it is also of particular importance to emphasize that the above-mentioned Ministry will be in charge of the coordination necessary for the fulfillment of national rights and obligations arising from international agreements on environmental issues which Türkiye is party to.

---

26 *F. Niederstadt*, Ökosystemschutz durch Regelungen des öffentlichen Umweltrechts, 1998, p. 98 et seq.; *Erbguth & Schlacke, supra* note 8 at para. 1 et seq.; *P.C. Storm*, Umweltrecht, 8th ed., 2006, note 2; *Kloepfer*, Umweltrecht, note 19 at par. 1.

27 *G. Hartkopf & E. Bohne*, Umweltpolitik, Band 1, 1983, p. 3 et seq.

28 *Güneş, supra* at p. 5; *B. Kuzu*, Sağlıklı ve Dengeli Bir Çevrede Yaşama Hakkı, 1997, p. 157.

29 UVPG para. 2 (1).

As a rule, to be entitled to a restitution in Turkish Law, four conditions shall co-exist: act or act in breach of the obligation, damage, causality between the act and damage, and fault. As per Article 28 of the Code, however, on account of the importance of the protection of environment, those polluting the environment and inflicting damage on the environment are responsible, even without the existence of the condition of fault, for the damage incurred by them on the environment and related to the pollution and deterioration they cause.[30] Moreover, in the fifth part of the Code, administrative fines and prison sentences were stipulated.

b. Turkish Penal Code and Code of Misdemeanor

Article 181 and 182 of the Turkish Penal Code (TPC) stipulate that any person who intentionally or negligently drains, discards, or wastes any substance into the ground, water, or air in violation of the technical procedures defined in the relevant laws, and thereby causes environmental pollution, shall be punished with imprisonment. The code categorizes noise and environmental pollution arising from construction works as criminal offence and intends to enhance the protection of environment.[31] [32]

Similarly, the Code of Misdemeanor (Law No. 5326) stipulates that pollution of the environment (Article 41) and making noise (Article 36) are misdemeanors and are subject to administrative fines.

c. Private Law: Turkish Civil Code and Code of Obligations

As the concept of environment concerns to the entire society, regulations on the protection of the environment are generally set forth within the scope of public law. However, on the basis of private law, the right to property is restricted to some extent in terms of certain environmental issues under the Law of Neighbors of the Turkish Civil Code (Law No. 4721). [33] Article 737 of the Turkish Civil Code stipulates that landowners are obliged to refrain from any excess that is detrimental to neighboring properties when exercising

---

30 *K. Oğuzman & T. Öz*, Borçlar Hukuku Genel Hükümler Vol. 2, 10th ed., 2013, p. 224.

31 See Article 183 and 184.

32 *E. Şen*, Çevre Ceza Hukuku – Ceza Hukuku Açısından Sağlıklı ve Düzenli Bir Çevrede Yaşama Hakkı, 1994, p. 65.

33 See also *H. Rey*, Grundlagen des Sachenrechts und das Eigentum, 2nd ed., 2000, p. 271.

their ownership rights, including the right to run a business on their land. In particular all harmful effects that are not justified by the location and character of the land or by local custom such as air pollution emissions of noxious vapors, noise, vibrations are prohibited. Essentially, the restriction is in line with the restriction imposed on the right to property in Article 35 of the Constitution and Article 683 of the Civil Code and also in parallel to the ban on the abuse of rights in Article 2 of the Civil Code.

The consequence of the violation of this restriction are set forth in Article 730, titled *Landowner's Liability*. The damage must stem from *unlawful excess detrimental to neighboring properties (übermässigen Einwirkung)*, such as dumping debris extracted from real property on neighboring real properties[34]. Thus, damages not directly related to the use of right to property are to be compensated in accordance with general provisions, provided that relevant conditions are present[35]. However, *where a landowner temporarily causes excessive and unavoidable disadvantages to a neighbor while managing his or her parcel of land lawfully (rechtmässige Bewirtschaftung), in particular by building and thus causing loss or damage, the neighbor may only claim to balance his/her sacrifice from the landowner (Aufopferungsanspruch[36]).*

A ccording to Article 715, ownerless and public goods are subject to the sovereignty of the State. No rights of private ownership apply to public waters or to land not suitable for cultivation, such as rocks and scree, firn and glaciers, or to springs rising therefrom, unless proof to the contrary is produced. The State shall enact the provisions required to govern the appropriation of ownerless land, exploitation and common use of public goods.

d. Provisions on the Environmental Liability Set Forth by Other Codes

Legal responsibility for the environment was prescribed through certain codes such as *Code of Forests, Code of National Parks, Code of Villages and Code of Ports* as well as Code of Environment, Civil Code and Code of Obligations. As put forward in the second Paragraph of Article 28 of the Code of Environment, *indemnity responsibility of the polluting party due to the damage caused is reserved also in conformity with general provisions.*

---

34 *H. Tandoğan,* Türk Mes'uliyet Hukuku: Akit Dışı ve Akdi Mes'uliyet, 2nd ed., 2010, p. 209 et seq.

35 See Article 49 and 112 TCO.

36 *K. Larenz,* Die Prinzipien der Schadenszurechnung, JuS 1965, 373.

For instance, provided that relevant conditions are present, it is likely to discern the contention between compensation responsibilities prescribed by landowner's liability in the Civil Code, responsibility of polluting party according to Article 28 of Code of Environment, by the fourth Paragraph of Article 22 of Turkish Petroleum Code (Law No. 6491), by Article 14 of Biosecurity Code (Law No. 5977) and by other laws[37] on environmental issues[38].

e. Regulations and Other Judicial Arrangements

In the framework of the process of Türkiye 's accession to the European Union, twenty seventh Chapter titled as Environment and Climate Change was opened in December 2009, and in this process, Türkiye issued several regulations[39], communiqués[40], circulars[41] and other types of judicial arrangements on environmental issues such as *air quality, waste management, water quality*[42] and *right to water*[43], *protection of nature, noise*[44].

For example, it is envisaged that critically important laws such as the Code of the Protection of Animals, Water Code, and other types of judicial arrangements will likely enter into force.[45] Through these judicial arrangements, significant steps have been taken to establish the legal basis for the protection of the environment in Turkish law. However, it is of utmost importance to overcome problems experienced in the application of the Environmental Impact Assessment Directive and the right to participate in environmental issues .[46]

37 e.g., 5312 Numbered Law on Pertaining to Principles of Emergency Response and Compensation for Damages in Pollution of Marine Environment by Oil and Other Harmful Substances Article 6.

38 *Güneş, supra* at p. 337 et seq.

39 https://cygm.csb.gov.tr/yonetmelikler-i-440

40 https://cygm.csb.gov.tr/tebligler-i-441

41 https://cygm.csb.gov.tr/genelgeler-i-442

42 Over 30% of water bodies were identified as sensitive areas. The preparation of management plans for four river basins 94 out of 25 has been completed (2019).

43 See also *Laskowski*, Das Menschenrecht auf Wasser - Die rechtlichen Vorgaben zur Sicherung der Grundversorgung mit Wasser und Sanitärleistungen im Rahmen einer ökologisch-nachhaltigen Wasserwirtschaftsordnung, 2010.

44 Türkiye 2019 Report, E.C. Doc. COM/260/final (2019), https://ec.europa.eu/neighbourhood-enlargement/sites/near/files/20190529-turkey-report.pdf.

45 https://susurasi.gov.tr/Sayfa/Detay/1497

46 See n. 44.

B. Certain Special Procedures to be Used for the Protection of the Right to Environment

1. Right of Petition, Right to Information, and Appeal to the Ombudsperson

According to Article 74 of the Constitution, citizens and foreigners resident in Türkiye, with the condition of reciprocity, have the right to submit written requests and complaints to the competent authorities and to the Grand National Assembly of Türkiye regarding matters concerning themselves or the public[47]. Additionally, everyone has the right to obtain information and appeal to the Ombudsman. The Ombudsman Institution, established under the Grand National Assembly of Türkiye, examines complaints about the functioning of the administration [48].

As a precondition of a participatory democracy, as stipulated in Article 74 of the Constitution and Article 4 of the Law on the Right to Information (Law No. 4982), everyone has the right to information [49]. With the exception of exceptional cases [50], everyone has the right to request information or documentation about environmental issues by submitting an application to public institutions or agencies [51].

All these legal procedures are essentially different manifestations of the right to participation stipulated in the Code of Environment.

2. Application to Administrative Jurisdiction

If environmental damage or the threat of environmental damage arises from the actions of the administration, the annulment of any administrative operation can be requested, and if there is also injury, the compensation for the injury can be requested by the injured party through administrative jurisdiction. Article 2 of the Administrative Procedure Law (APJA) (Law No. 2577) provides that annulment actions concerning administrative acts that are brought by a person whose interests were violated by the act, with the claim that the act is illegal due to a mistake made in one of the

47 See also Law No. 3071 on Right to Petition.

48 See also Law No. 6328 on Ombudsman Institution.

49 It should be noted that Türkiye is not a signatory to the Aarhus Convention on Access to Environmental Information.

50 Article 7, 8, 9.

51 See also *D. R. Klein,* Umweltinformation im Völker- und Europarecht: Aktive Umweltaufklärung des Staates und Informationszugangsrechte des Bürgers, 2011, p. 15 et seq.

elements of competence, form, reason, subject, and aim, and full remedy actions brought by those whose personal rights have been directly affected by the administrative acts or actions. This article expanded the condition of seeking a violation of interest, which restricted the scope of application to administrative jurisdiction, and acknowledged lawsuits to be filed to courts on environmental issues to be in the category of lawsuits that could be filed even by third parties in view of the public interest *(actio popularis)*[52]. According to this article, natural and legal persons who are suffer or incur with injury due to any activity causing environmental pollution or degradation, or who have any knowledge of such activities, can apply to the administrative bodies and demand cessation of that activity. With this provision, the right of application to administrative authorities or administrative jurisdiction was extended to those who were only informed about the incident but had no direct interest in the case of the pollution of the environment, which is a common value shared by all living beings. This article, which is a crucial provision in terms of the right of participation, serves as the basis of the administrative and judicial application. However, the fourth Paragraph of Article 125, which was added into the Constitution with the amendment made in 2010, limits judicial power to the review of the legality of administrative actions, and in no case may it be used as a review of expediency. No judicial ruling shall be passed that restricts the exercise of the executive function in accordance with the forms and principles prescribed by law, which has the quality of an administrative action, or which removes discretionary powers. This aforementioned provision restricts judges in their rulings on environmental issues in practice and in general urges them to make simple procedural assessments [53]. For instance, the assessment to be made on the location of thermal power plant is considered just as a review of expediency. This, however, restricts the scope of judicial review. Another judicial procedure that is vital in terms of applying to administrative jurisdiction pertains to the stay of execution. Demanding a motion for the stay of execution is a matter of utmost importance to environmental issues for preventing the infliction of irreparable damage. After trees are cut down, soil is poisoned, water is polluted, and living beings are killed, to what extent does the decision to be taken have any importance? Although a motion for stay of execution is granted, it is sometimes likely not to be implemented actually. Another

52 *Güneş, supra* at p. 253.
53 *Id.* at p. 257.

challenge comes to the forefront as regards the implementation of court decisions, especially on environmental issues. Article 28 of the APJA stipulates that the administration must implement the acts and take the actions required by the judgments and stay of execution orders given by the Council of State, regional administrative courts, administrative and tax courts without delay. This period, under no circumstances, can exceed thirty days from the notification of the decision to the administration. According to judicial interpretations, a court decision is supposed to be implemented in the first 30 days after its delivery. The total of 30 days is the period that can be exceeded in no way, and the implementation of court decisions immediately is supposed to be the case. Such situations mean to be the breach of the procedural aspect of the right to environment and the right to a fair trial [54].

C. Conclusion

The right to environment and its protection have gradually gained more importance in Turkish law. The issuance of judicial arrangements has gained momentum, especially with the opening of the 27th Chapter on environment in Türkiye's EU membership process. What is important is that these judicial arrangements are implemented properly and that their implementation is effectively monitored and checked. To achieve this goal, the role of education is essential. The promotion of awareness about the environment and the protection of the right to environment should be transformed into a state policy. The curriculum should be revised in this sense, cooperation with local governments and non-governmental organizations should be deepened, information on this matter should be delivered through mass media, and green transportation should be encouraged. Public awareness about the environment should be enhanced by encouraging persons and institutions that are sensitive to environmental issues. In doing so, it should be remembered that the environment is a multi-dimensional issue with scientific, sociological, economic, and political aspects that go well beyond being a matter of law alone. Therefore, it is essential to make progress in judicial processes in close contact and collaboration with other disciplines and to promote public awareness.

---

54 ECHR Judgment: Case C-46117/99, *Taşkın and others v. Turkey* [2004], para. 119.; ECHR Judgment: Case C-36220/97, *Okyay and others v. Turkey* [2005]; Diğer sorunlara ilişkin bkz. *Güneş, supra* at p. 256 et seq.

Environmental issues and the right to environment are not only matters for human beings but also a vital topic for all living beings, transcending country borders and differences between species. Therefore, instead of human-centered approaches alone, states must adopt an understanding that takes all stakeholders of the ecosystem at the center, bearing in mind that all have a function and right to a healthy environment.

Green Jobs: Meeting Point of Labour and Environmental Law

*Dr. Ayşe Ledün Akdeniz**

Abstract

The Labour Law has a dynamic and constantly changing structure. The constant development of technology creates atypical job patterns, and hence the laws have to be adapted to this new requirement. However, the legal field is not well equipped to deal with the new challenges on labour markets, employers, and workers adequately. Climate change requires expertise. A new concept, "green jobs", is making way into our everyday life. In this study, we plan to explore this new concept of green jobs and also try to evaluate Türkiye's position about creating green jobs.
Keywords: green jobs, green collar worker, green economy, green development

1. The Green New Concepts on the Market

In the 21st century, poverty, unemployment, increasing urbanization and unstoppable increase in population have led to the creation of new areas of employment, which were unheard of up to the present; while new concepts of sustainable development and renewability come to the forefront[1] and one of these new concepts is *Green Jobs.* With the surge of green jobs, concepts like green development, green collar workers have started to enter the literature.

In the classical Labour Law, blue collar workers are those that work in the industrial production lines, and white collar workers are those that work in the offices. Nowadays, we also mention green-collar workers. The green collar workers are those who work in areas such as renewable energy, productivity, organic farming, and insulation[2]. It is also noted that lawyers, engineers, advisors, teachers who work on environmental projects are also considered to be green collar workers[3]. However, these jobs must conform to decent

* Assistant Professor, Labour and Social Security Department, Istanbul University Faculty of Law.

1 *Z. Sungur*, Türkiye'de Yeşil Yakalı Mesleklerin Gelişiminde Güncel Eğilimler, in International Euroasian Economies Conference 2011, p.154.

2 *B. G. Baykan*, "Dünyada ve Türkiye'de Yeşil Yakalılar", BETAM Araştırma Notu, 09/37, 11.04.2009, p.1. Further information available at: https://betam.bahcesehir.edu.tr/wp-content/uploads/2009/06/ArastirmaNotu037.pdf (accessed on 13.01.2022).

3 *Ibid.*

working conditions[4]. Green jobs need to be decent work, i.e., good jobs which offer adequate wages, safe working conditions, job security, reasonable career prospects, and worker rights. In summary, a coordinated approach has been adopted as to green jobs, considering the components, the environment, human, and economy together[5].

2. Defining Green Jobs in ILO and EU

The green jobs help to improve energy and raw materials efficiency, to limit greenhouse gas emissions, to minimize waste and pollution, to protect and restore ecosystems and to support adaptation to the effects of climate change[6]. Therefore, the "green job" is one of the recent topics on the ILO agenda. The ILO defines green jobs as "*decent jobs that contribute to preserve or restore the environment, be they in traditional sectors such as manufacturing and construction, or in new, emerging green sectors such as renewable energy and energy efficiency*"[7]. In 2008, the United Nations Environment Program (UNEP), International Labour Organization (ILO), International Organization of Employers (IOE) and International Trade Union Confederation (ITUC) have primed a report titled as "Green Jobs: Towards decent work in a sustainable, low-carbon world"[8], which defines green jobs as works in agricultural, manufacturing, research and development (R&D), administrative, and service activities that contribute substantially to preserving or restoring environmental quality.

In 2013, the ILO launched the Green Initiative, which was considered to be a step towards to better equip the actors of the world of work to understand the challenges and opportunities of the transition[9]. The ILO has also reserved the theme 'green jobs' in its annual report, as "World

4 *O. Başol*, Dünyada ve Türkiye'de Yeşil İşlerin Gelişimine İlişkin Bir Değerlendirme, Finans Politik & Ekonomik Yorumlar, 55/636, 2018, p.80.

5 *Başol*, p.77.

6 ILO, What is a green job?, 13.04.2016. Available at: https://www.ilo.org/global/topics/green-jobs/news/WCMS_220248/lang--en/index.htm (accessed on 13.01.2022).

7 *Ibid.*

8 Green Jobs: Towards decent work in a sustainable, low-carbon world, UNEP/ILO/IOE/ITUC, September 2008, p. 3. Available at: https://www.ilo.org/wcmsp5/groups/public/---ed_emp/---emp_ent/documents/publication/wcms_158727.pdf (accessed on 13.01.2022).

9 The Green Initiative, ILO. Available at: https://www.ilo.org/global/about-the-ilo/history/centenary/WCMS_467270/lang--en/index.htm (accessed on 13.01.2022).

Employment and Social Outlook – Trends 2018 – Greening with Jobs"[10]. To this end, this report emphasizes, along with its "*Guidelines for a just transition towards environmentally sustainable economies and societies for all*"[11], that the green economy will be a major source of job growth in the future of work environment. According to ILO estimates, a shift to a greener economy could create 24 million new jobs globally by 2030 if the right policies are put in place[12].

Green jobs are also on the EU's agenda. Furthermore, with its communication dated 02.07.2014 (COM(2014) 446) the European Commission has invited the Council, the European Parliament, the European Economic and Social Committee and the Committee of the Regions to endorse green employment initiative. The Green Employment Initiative Communication supports the transition to a green, low-carbon, resource-efficient economy. In this regard, the Green Employment Initiative Communication provides an integrated framework that allows the labour market and skills policies to play an active role[13]. It is stated that the EC's Green Employment Initiative is in principal similar to the main ideas of the ILO's Jobs Programme [14].

3. *How to Approach Green Jobs?*

Generally, green jobs and green economy have been the subject of various studies to determine their effects on employment rates. It has been mentioned that the green economy will create new employment areas, but it will also

---

10 World Employment and Social Outlook 2018: Greening with jobs, International Labour Organization, 2018. Available at: https://www.ilo.org/weso-greening/documents/WESO_Greening_EN_web2.pdf (accessed on 13.01.2022).

11 Guidelines for a just transition towards environmentally sustainable economies and societies for all, International Labour Organization 2015. Available at: https://www.ilo.org/wcmsp5/groups/public/---ed_emp/---emp_ent/documents/publication/wcms_432859.pdf (accessed on 13.01.2022).

12 UN Sustainable Development Goals, Green economy could create 24 million new jobs, 03.04.2019. Available at: https://www.un.org/sustainabledevelopment/blog/2019/04/green-economy-could-create-24-million-new-jobs/ (accessed on 13.01.2022).

13 For further information about The Green Employment Initiative, see https://www.switchtogreen.eu/the-green-employment-initiative/ (accessed on 13.01.2022).

14 EU and ILO, Shaping of Future Work, Study for the Committee on Employment and Social Affairs, Policy Department for Economic, Scientific and Quality of Life Policies, European Parliament, 2019, p. 48. Available at: https://www.europarl.europa.eu/RegData/etudes/STUD/2019/638407/IPOL_STU(2019)638407_EN.pdf (accessed on 13.01.2022).

change the current employment structure[15]. Green economic development will entail the abolition of some work fields, make the current jobs green, and also create new jobs[16] . Although it is claimed that the transition to green jobs will entail the abolition of some work fields, employment problems are not only linked to green jobs. It is an undeniable fact that production methods depending on technological developments have negative effects on employment[17].

At this point, we should be aware that there are many contradictory opinions about the effects of the green economy on employment[18] . On the one hand, it has set forth that the green jobs are support for resolving several problems in the labour market, on the other hand, it has estimated that green jobs may also create new unemployment problems because of the replacing the old manufacture lines[19]. However, the idea that the protection of environment and advanced policies will have negative effects on employment has languished in the period of economic and ecological crises[20] . The research on the green economy points out the support for green jobs has increased recently[21] .

4. Position of Türkiye

The so-called "green" jobs, which aim at sustainable development by protecting environmental values and provide a decent working environment, meet the wage and career expectations of individuals, contain advanced applications on issues such as occupational health and safety started to come to the fore[22]. However, it should be noted that working in green jobs does not make any difference (for example regarding the rules of termination of the contract) in the implementation of the rules of Turkish Labour Law. In

15 *C. Özsoy*, Yeşil Ekonominin Dinamikleri: Yeşil İşler ve Beceriler, Finans Politik & Ekonomik Yorumlar, 48/562, 2011, p.21.

16 *S. Topgül*, İşsizlik için bir çözüm: Yeşil işler ve yeşil istihdam Tokat örneği, International Journal of Human Sciences, 12/2, 2015, p.1336.

17 *D. Günaydın*, "Yeşil İşler ve İşgücü Piyasasına Etkileri", Yönetim ve Ekonomi Araştırmaları Dergisi, 13/3, 2015, p.523.

18 For different opinions on this matter, see *Başol*, pp.84-85.

19 For the optimistic and pessimistic point of views on this topic, see *S. Atlama & C. Özsoy*; Possible Effects of Green Economy on Employment, in ECONAnadolu 2011: Anadolu International Conference in Economics II, p. 10.

20 *Baykan*, p.1.

21 *Başol*, p.78.

22 *Günaydın*, p.504.

other words, there is no difference in the application of Labour Law rules to green-collar workers.

The difficulties in defining the green jobs and the lack of current data regarding the employment of the green collar workers in the private sector prevent the real measurement of the green employment in Türkiye[23]. However, green development can have an impact on the countries differently depending on their peculiarities. Although careful observation of the green restructuring examples helps, Türkiye needs to produce a proper social policy which fits its peculiarities.

A research done in 2009, expressed that the number of green collar workers in Türkiye cannot be accurate documented, however, the number presumed in that period Türkiye had about 50,000 green-collar workers[24] . It has been expressed that, in 2015 the number of green collar workers was increased over 80.000[25] . Furthermore, the concept of the "green growth" took his place in the Tenth Development Plan for the first time, which was executed between 2014 and 2018. In this Plan, it has been determined that sustainable development goals to achieve the concept of "green growth" gained importance[26]. It is also stated that after the Tenth Development Plan, a more eager political will for green employment has emerged[27].

A comprehensive policy for green jobs and employment created by these jobs has not been implemented in Türkiye[28]. Türkiye is at the beginning of the transition to a green economy. However, green jobs activities have recently started to be implemented also in Türkiye. Türkiye is one of the countries where projects have been initiated and result achieved. The ILO project report "Decent Work in a Green Economy" focused on the employment aspects of national efforts of transition to a greener economy in Türkiye[29]. The results of the report show that this transformation is inevitable for companies which

---

23 *Sungur*, p.158; *A. Satır Reyhan & E. Duygu*, Çevre Politikalarında Yeni Bir Yaklaşım: Yeşil İşler Ve Yeşil İstihdam, Memleket Siyaset Yönetim, 10/23, 2015, p.36.

24 *Baykan*, p.2.

25 *Başol*, p.82.

26 See The Tenth Development Plan, p. 13. Available at: https://www.sbb.gov.tr/wp-content/uploads/2021/12/Onuncu_Kalkinma_Plani-2014-2018.pdf (accessed on 13.01.2022).

27 *Günaydın*, p.520.

28 *Günaydın*, p.519.

29 The project "Decent Jobs in the Green Economy" conducted by ILO Türkiye Office in cooperation with ILO Green Jobs Programme and with the support of the Government of Flanders and took place in Ankara on 26.03.2015 as "Conference on Green Jobs in Turkey". The Project details are available at: https://www.ilo.org/ankara/news/WCMS_372695/lang--en/index.htm (accessed on 13.01.2022).

want to reduce their negative impact on the environment and maintain their leading positions in their sectors. This study provides guidance on the steps to be taken in the upcoming period[30].

Because of the renewable energy investments and the environmental negotiations with the EU, the number of green jobs has increased substantially in the last few years[31]. Although Türkiye's green business potential is not fully known, it is considered that Türkiye has an important potential in solar energy, wind energy, hydroelectric energy and geothermal energy production[32]. Even though the number of green jobs still represents a quite low proportion of general employment figures[33] , some steps are being taken on this topic. It should also be added that, in Turkish universities and higher education institutions, there are a lot of programs which can be considered to be connected to the green economy[34].

On the other hand, economic problems created by unemployment have been on the Turkish agenda too. The ILO Convention No.102 concerning Minimum Standard of Social Security also includes the unemployment insurance. The Unemployment Insurance Code of Türkiye was accepted in 1999 by Code No. 4447[35], which came into force in 01.06.2000. This Code emerged as a separate law from Social Insurances and General Health Insurance Code[36], however it contains regulations related to Social Insurances and General Health Insurance Code in some areas[37]. The payments, according to the Unemployment Insurance Code, can only be obtained if the worker was employed, among other things, and then unemployed. Merely the ones who were once employed and then lost their jobs are within the scope of the insurance. It is not possible for a graduate, for instance, to claim unemployment benefit for the duration of job seeking[38]. Hence, the target

30 See Yeşil Ekonomide İnsana Yakışır İşler: Türkiye'den İyi Örnekler Vaka Çalışması, International Labour Organization, ILO Office for Türkiye, 2015. Available at: https://www.ilo.org/wcmsp5/groups/public/---europe/---ro-geneva/---ilo-ankara/documents/publication/wcms_368300.pdf (accessed on 13.01.2022).

31 *Sungur*, p.157.

32 *Günaydın*, p.523.

33 *Başol*, p.82.

34 *Özsoy*, p.30

35 Code No. 4447, Unemployment Insurance Code, has been published in the Official Gazette in Türkiye on 08.09.1999.

36 Code No. 5510, Social Insurances and General Health Insurance Code, has been published in the Official Gazette in Türkiye on 16.06.2006.

37 *T. Centel*, Turkish Social Law, Springer, 2021, p.219.

38 *A. C. Tuncay & Ö. Ekmekçi*, Sosyal Güvenlik Hukuku Dersleri, 21th ed., 2021, pp.709-710.

of this law is not to dissolve or diminish unemployment. It only aims to help the unemployed for a limited period of time (to cover compensation regarding the loss of income and finding a new job)[39]. To sum up, Turkish Code No. 4447 does not provide any financial compensation for those who are not employed yet. However, it should be noted that financial compensations are not the only assistance within the scope of unemployment insurance. Some services (such as finding a job, vocational training) are also provided in this Code. Therefore, it is not completely independent of policies aimed at preventing unemployment, although unemployment insurance does not aim to prevent unemployment[40]. In addition, there are various incentives for the work placement of young people in Turkish social security system. In summary, those who lost their jobs, or those who seek employment should be taken care of, one way or another. Encouragement for employment is necessary and is essential for a social state. As mentioned above, green jobs are scrutinized as part of unemployment problems. Regardless that a job is green or not, adequate employment is one of the most important problems because of the technological developments in this day and age. Hence, in this challenge, an acceptable / reasonable way should be found without ignoring ecological worries.

It should be noted that Türkiye is criticized because not having a green strategy[41]. It is suggested to encourage renewable energy investments, supporting ecological farming, having forest management systems for fighting against climate change related to aridity[42]. It is stated that the most important sector that stands out in terms of green business potential in Türkiye is the renewable energy sector[43]. To sum up, it seems necessary to observe the results of greening with jobs continuously and carefully.

5. Conclusions

The world has been facing with pollution and ecological problems caused by the capitalist production system starting from the industrial revolution to the present day, but it is evaluated that the transition to a green economy

39 *Tuncay & Ekmekçi*, p.696.
40 *S. Başterzi*, İşsizlik Sigortası, 1996, p.201.
41 *Satır Reyhan & Duygu*, p.36.
42 *Ibid.*
43 *Günaydın*, p.521.

can help to eliminate environmental concerns, causing an increase in social and economic gains[44]. In the near term, green jobs became one of the titles discussed by environmental groups. But nowadays we hear more about green jobs. If a job is green, it induces us to think of it as a specific employment type. Green jobs are not *numerus clausus*, but green jobs are supposed to fulfil some expectations such as adequate wages, safe working conditions, job security, reasonable career prospects, and worker rights. Therefore, it should be underlined that green jobs have to be decent. And without a shadow of a doubt, it is desired that any worker's job has these qualities. However, it is an important approach that in the demanding green sector, working under bad working conditions cannot comply with being a green collar worker.

There is not a sufficient database on green employment in Türkiye[45]. The Turkish legislation has not also come up with defining green jobs or green collar workers yet. However, this lack of legislation does not seem to be deficient. Specifically, this can open new horizons for green jobs. It is predicted that most of the present blue collar jobs would called green collar jobs in the future[46] . The green jobs include some brand new jobs; however existing jobs can be transformed into green jobs providing that they offer specific properties for a decent work environment.

Bibliography

S. Atlama & *C. Özsoy*, Possible Effects of Green Economy on Employment, in ECON-Anadolu 2011: Anadolu International Conference in Economics II, June 15-17, 2011, Eskişehir, Turkey.

O. Başol, Dünyada ve Türkiye'de Yeşil İşlerin Gelişimine İlişkin Bir Değerlendirme, Finans Politik & Ekonomik Yorumlar, 55/636, 2018.

S. Başterzi, İşsizlik Sigortası, Ankara Üniversitesi Hukuk Fakültesi Yayınları, 1996.

B. G. Baykan, Dünyada ve Türkiye'de Yeşil Yakalılar, BETAM Araştırma Notu 09/37, 11.04.2009. Available at: https://betam.bahcesehir.edu.tr/wp-content/uploads/2009/06/ArastirmaNotu037.pdf

T. Centel, Turkish Social Law, Springer, 2021.

Decent Jobs in the Green Economy, ILO Türkiye Office in cooperation with ILO Green Jobs Programme and with the support of the Government of Flanders. Available at: https://www.ilo.org/ankara/news/WCMS_372695/lang--en/index.htm

44 *Günaydın*, p.524.
45 *Günaydın*, p.521.
46 *Özsoy*, p.30.

Green Jobs: Towards decent work in a sustainable, low-carbon world, UNEP/ILO/IOE/ITUC, September 2008. Available at: https://www.ilo.org/wcmsp5/groups/public/---ed_emp/---emp_ent/documents/publication/wcms_158727.pdf

Guidelines for a just transition towards environmentally sustainable economies and societies for all, International Labour Organization 2015. Available at https://www.ilo.org/wcmsp5/groups/public/---ed_emp/---emp_ent/documents/publication/wcms_432859.pdf

D. Günaydın, Yeşil İşler ve İşgücü Piyasasına Etkileri, Yönetim ve Ekonomi Araştırmaları Dergisi, 13/3, 2015.

ILO, What is a green job?, 13.04.2016. Available at: https://www.ilo.org/global/topics/green-jobs/news/WCMS_220248/lang--en/index.htm

C. Özsoy, Yeşil Ekonominin Dinamikleri: Yeşil İşler ve Beceriler, Finans Politik & Ekonomik Yorumlar, 48/562, 2011.

A. Satır Reyhan & *E. Duygu*, Çevre Politikalarında Yeni Bir Yaklaşım: Yeşil İşler Ve Yeşil İstihdam, Memleket Siyaset Yönetim, 10/23, 2015.

EU and ILO, Shaping of Future Work, Study for the Committee on Employment and Social Affairs, Policy Department for Economic, Scientific and Quality of Life Policies, European Parliament, 2019. Available at: https://www.europarl.europa.eu/RegData/etudes/STUD/2019/638407/IPOL_STU(2019)638407_EN.pdf

Z. Sungur, Türkiye'de Yeşil Yakalı Mesleklerin Gelişiminde Güncel Eğilimler, in International Euroasian Economies Conference 2011.

The Green Employment Initiative, The EU Switch to Green Flagship Initiative. Available at: https://www.switchtogreen.eu/the-green-employment-initiative/

The Green Initiative, ILO. Available at: https://www.ilo.org/global/about-the-ilo/history/centenary/WCMS_467270/lang--en/index.htm

The Tenth Development Plan. Available at: https://www.sbb.gov.tr/wp-content/uploads/2021/12/Onuncu_Kalkinma_Plani-2014-2018.pdf

S. Topgül, İşsizlik için bir çözüm: Yeşil işler ve yeşil istihdam Tokat örneği, International Journal of Human Sciences, 12/2, 2015.

C. Tuncay & *Ö. Ekmekçi*, Sosyal Güvenlik Hukuku Dersleri, 21th ed., 2021.

UN Sustainable Development Goals, Green economy could create 24 million new jobs, 03.04.2019. Available at: https://www.un.org/sustainabledevelopment/blog/2019/04/green-economy-could-create-24-million-new-jobs/

Yeşil Ekonomide İnsana Yakışır İşler: Türkiye'den İyi Örnekler Vaka Çalışması, International Labour Organization, ILO Office for Türkiye, 2015. Available at: https://www.ilo.org/wcmsp5/groups/public/---europe/---ro-geneva/---ilo-ankara/documents/publication/wcms_368300.pdf

World Employment and Social Outlook 2018: Greening with jobs, International Labour Organization, 2018. Available at: https://www.ilo.org/weso-greening/documents/WESO_Greening_EN_web2.pdf